Cultured States

ANDREW IVASKA

Cultured States

YOUTH, GENDER, AND MODERN

STYLE IN 1960S DAR ES SALAAM

Duke University Press   Durham and London   2011

© 2011 Duke University Press
All rights reserved
Printed in the United States of America on acid-free paper ∞
Designed by C. H. Westmoreland
Typeset in Quadraat by Achorn International, Inc.

Library of Congress Cataloging-in-Publication Data

Ivaska, Andrew M. (Andrew Michael), 1971–
Cultured states : youth, gender, and modern style in
1960s Dar es Salaam / Andrew Ivaska.
p. cm.
Includes bibliographical references and index.
ISBN 978-0-8223-4749-1 (cloth : alk. paper)
ISBN 978-0-8223-4770-5 (pbk. : alk. paper)
1. Politics and culture—Tanzania—Dar es Salaam.
2. Clothing and dress—Tanzania—Dar es Salaam.
3. Dar es Salaam (Tanzania)—Social life and
customs. I. Title.
GT1586.5.I937 2011
306.209678'232—dc22
2010029128

For Sally and David Ivaska

Contents

Acknowledgments

This book, nearly a decade in the making, has been touched and shaped by numerous people—teachers, colleagues, friends, hosts. First and foremost, as a doctoral student at the University of Michigan I was privileged to work under the guidance of a wonderful dissertation committee. From my first week in Ann Arbor, Fred Cooper provided just the right mix of bracing critique and supportive encouragement to keep me going. Nancy Rose Hunt first inspired me to work on questions of public culture and continued throughout to nudge me in productive directions. As co-chairs, both were wise and patient mentors. David William Cohen led my first graduate course in African history and has been an extraordinarily generous and inspiring example ever since. A wealth of insight on all things Tanzanian, Kelly Askew offered invaluable advice. Juan R. Cole and Geoff Eley supported this project from early on and reminded me of the importance of making broad connections. I could not have asked for a better team of teachers.

At the University of Michigan I was fortunate to have found a vibrant and stimulating intellectual environment. Jose Amador, Shaun Lopez, Kristan McGuire, Andrew Needham, and Mario Ruiz were fantastic collaborators and supportive friends who made graduate school a little easier. In seminars, conferences, coffee shops, bars, and homes, countless other colleagues and teachers in Ann Arbor provided engaging discussion, challenging critique, encouragement, and friendship. They include Apollo Amoko, Kathleen Canning, Judy Daubenmier, Mamadou Diouf, Frieda Ekotto, Jenny Gaynor, Simon Gikandi, Rob Gray, Gabrielle Hecht, Vukile Khumalo, Anna Lawrence, Kate Luongo, Delphine Mauger, Rudolf Mrazek, Moses Ochonu, Monica Patterson, Elisha Renne, Alice Ritscherle, George Steinmetz, Ann Stoler, Penny Von Eschen, members of the Africa Workshop, the African History Reading Group, the Global Ethnic Literatures Seminar, and the Ford Seminar. Geographically farther afield, I have benefited from the comments, critique, conversation, and generous support of Jean Allman,

Felicitas Becker, Ned Bertz, Keith Breckenridge, Jim Brennan, Gary Burgess, Catherine Burns, Andrew Burton, Shani D'Cruze, Brian Edwards, Elizabeth Elbourne, Marc Epprecht, Laura Fair, Jim Giblin, Frederick Kaijage, Yusuf Lawi, Marie-Nathalie LeBlanc, Margot Lovett, Greg Maddox, Sheryl McCurdy, Claire Mercer, Jamie Monson, Eileen Moyer, Vinh-Kim Nguyen, Alex Perullo, Steven Pierce, Jeremy Prestholdt, David Richards, Heike Schmidt, Leander Schneider, Carole Turbin, Jean-Luc Vellut, Kerry Ward, Luise White, and Bob White. Lynn Thomas has been an especially generous critic. Wilson Chacko Jacob, my earliest intellectual comrade, has been a constant friend.

In Tanzania, I am grateful to all who shared with me their time, homes, knowledge, advice and support, networks and friendship. James Nindi, "Balozi" Dolasoul, Mathias Machimba, Edo Makata, Sabbi Masanja, Siasa, Rajabu, Majeshi Wanzagi, the Amijee family, and Miranda Johnson all deserve special appreciation in this regard. I thank Naomi Kaihula, Miranda Johnson, and the rest of the community and staff at the Tanzania Gender Networking Project (TGNP) for introducing me to the practice of gender activism in Tanzania. Frederick Kaijage, Yusuf Lawi, N. N. Luanda, and the rest of the history department at the University of Dar es Salaam provided crucial support, lively intellectual exchange, and helpful advice. The generous and patient efforts of the staff at the Tanzania National Archives (including, especially, Mwanahamisi Mtengula) and at the East Africana Library of the University of Dar es Salaam were invaluable and appreciated. Finally, Ned Bertz, Jim Brennan, Andrew Burton, Alex Perullo, and Leander Schneider not only shared the highs and lows of research in Dar es Salaam, but have been extraordinary colleagues and friends. To their staunch support, generous criticism, and inestimable knowledge of Dar es Salaam I owe much.

Concordia University and Montreal's wider academic community have grown from welcoming environment to intellectual home. My colleagues in the department of history have been warm, generous, and supportive from the very beginning. As department chairs, Graham Carr, Ron Rudin, and Shannon McSheffrey—joined by Fred Bode, Frank Chalk, and Norman Ingram—furnished patient and expert guidance to learning the ropes as only senior colleagues can. Rachel Berger, Omar Dewachi, Nitika Dosaj, Michelle Hartman, Caroline Herbert, Wilson Jacob, Ted McCormick, Khalid Medani, Setrag Manoukian, Laila Parsons, Najat Rahman, Elena Razlogova, Leander Schneider, Megha Sehdev, Yumna Siddiqi, Gavin Taylor, and Anya Zilberstein not only provide spirited intellectual engagement, but have made Montreal quite simply a wonderful place to live. My students at Concordia—in courses, as advisees, asresearch assistants—have enriched my years here. Particular thanks go to Kristin Biefer, Paul Hébert, Meg Leitold, Rachel Levee, Natasha Martin, Mdelwa Mehlo, George Paul Meiu, Emma Park, Anne Reigner and Adrienne Weber in this regard. In each of these contexts—Ann Arbor, Dar es Salaam, Montreal—Delphine Mauger shared these cities with me and gave life to this book. For this I will always be grateful.

At Duke University Press, I was fortunate to have this project taken on by Ken Wissoker, Courtney Berger, Mark Mastromarino, and Leigh Barnwell, who were enthusiastic about the manuscript in its earlier, unpolished form and guided it through the editing and publication process with patience and care. Special appreciation also goes to the external reviewers for Duke, whose insight and attention to both the big picture and the small details immeasurably improved the book.

This project could not have been completed without the generous support of a number of institutions. The largest period of my research abroad was funded by a Fulbright-Hays Doctoral Dissertation Research Award and a Social Science Research Council International Dissertation Research Fellowship. At the University of Michigan, a number of sources of support were crucial along the way, including the Rackham Graduate School, the Center for Afro-American and African Studies, the International Institute, the Institute for Research on Women and Gender, and the Regents' Fellowship Program. A Standard Research Grant from the Canadian Social Science and Humanities Research Council, and a Nouveaux chercheurs Fellowship from the Fonds Québécois de recherche sur la société et la culture provided support for follow-up trips to Tanzania, as did Concordia University's generous start-up research funding for new faculty.

Parts of material from chapter 2 and smaller portions of material from chapters 1 and 3 appeared in different and earlier form in the following publications: *Gender and History* 14.3 (2002): 584–607; *Africa Today* 51.3 (2005): 84–107; *Moving Worlds* 5.1 (2005): 120–31; and James R. Brennan, Andrew Burton, and Yusuf Lawi, eds., *Dar es Salaam: Histories from an Emerging African Metropolis* (Dar es Salaam and Nairobi: Mkuki na Nyota and the British Institute of Eastern Africa, 2007), 213–31.

In quiet and enduring ways my parents, Sally and David Ivaska, instilled in me and my brothers, Peter, John, and James, an early investment in border crossings. This became the ground for trajectories ever since, including my interest in African history, and I dedicate this book to them.

Demonstrators in Dar es Salaam, September 1973.
Courtesy of the Tanzania Information Service.

Introduction

POSTCOLONIAL PUBLIC CULTURE IN SIXTIES TIMES

A Sixties Moment

On September 8, 1973, an unidentified photographer working for *The Daily News* in Tanzania captured a striking image at a demonstration in the capital of Dar es Salaam supporting what would be one of the last in a series of decency campaigns stretching back to the 1960s. Examined closely, this image encapsulates a complex view of the cultural politics of a "long sixties" moment: one that both rehearses and complicates received assumptions about the way urban Africans, as national, gendered and generational subjects, city dwellers, fashioners of style and self, lived this early postcolonial era. The items of fashion condemned by the demonstrators—including miniskirts, wigs, and tight, bell-bottom trousers known locally as *pecos*—point to a landscape of transnational style marking Dar es Salaam at the time, and to Tanzanians' passionate engagement with it. The protest stood as a clear sign of this engagement, but the photo also prompts questions about its precise nature. The image, with its central "Ban the Mini" slogan, might at first glance conjure up notions of the reassertion of indigenous cultural norms against a cultural imperialism from abroad, particularly given the long prominence of such narratives in popular accounts of globalization. And indeed a vocabulary of national culture was one of the campaign's rhetorical accompaniments. But other elements in the photo complicate this reading and suggest the importance of other lines of struggle, other stories flowing into this one. If miniskirts, wigs, and pecos could be coded in part as Western, the demonstrators' own attire signals an ambivalence about Western stylistic norms at the heart of national cultural discourse. Furthermore, the demographics of the relatively young, overwhelmingly male crowd as well as the spatial specificity of the targeted offense—"half nakedness in *offices*"—hint at the gendered, generational, and material dimensions of the scene. And even pecos itself, a term tracing back to specific spaghetti Westerns of the late sixties and, even earlier, to American Pecos Bill folklore, bears the marks of a long history of Tanzanians' cosmopolitan reworking of the signs and symbols of the global mass culture industries.[1]

In recent attempts to construct global histories of the 1960s, the stories most commonly told of sub-Saharan Africa are the undeniably crucial ones of the political decolonization, national liberation, and quests for economic development that swept the continent during the critical first decade of postcolonial rule.[2] However, Africa's sixties moment, particularly in many of its cities, was also one of intense cultural ferment, ferment not divorced from the economic and political formations of this period, but rather a vehicle for a whole range of material and politically controversial social struggles. In Dar es Salaam, the demonstration captured in the photograph capped a decade that saw debate over a wide variety of concerns, including the morality of new urban youth cultures, authenticity in national cultural policy, the perceived sexual escapades of the capital's new elite, the aims and content of university education, and gendered battles over issues of marriage and women's work and movement in town.

Tanzania was not alone in this regard. From Bamako, Mali, to Lilongwe, Malawi, and several capitals in between, state efforts to clamp down on urban youth cultures plunged officials into the thick of sharp debates over the meaning of, for example, James Brown and hot pants for newly independent African nations and subjects.[3] National legislatures erupted in raucous debate over attempts to overhaul colonial-era laws dealing with marriage and child support, topics that hit at the heart of notions of women's bodies as bearers of culture as well as at the shifting political economy of urban gender relations.[4] Struggles over Eurocentric university curricula—embodied most famously in the successful effort by the Kenyan novelist and academic Ngugi wa Thiong'o and his colleagues to replace the English department at the University of Nairobi with one focused on Kenyan and African literature—resonated across the continent and beyond.[5] In Tanzania, as elsewhere, these controversies featured the prominent deployment and reworking of a domain and category of culture. But the meanings of culture and the understandings of what this field included and excluded were varied, shifting, and contested. In focusing on the cultural politics of this long sixties moment as they played out in Tanzania's capital, my book both examines the conceptual dimensions of these contests over culture

and seeks to embed them in the urban struggles around gender, generation, and wealth to which they were intimately connected.

National Culture

A number of intertwined developments, including postcolonial cultural
initiatives, changing cities, and a history of colonial debates over cultural
policy, were central in setting the stage for the cultural ferment of this
sixties moment in Tanzania as well as in contributing to the shape these
debates took. The first of these developments was a high-profile project
of national culture launched by President Julius K. Nyerere and his ruling
party, the Tanganyika (later Tanzania) African National Union (TANU),
within a year of gaining independence from Britain in 1961. Initiated
with the aim, in Nyerere's words, of "help[ing] us regain our pride in
OUR culture," this project paired a goal of recovering "tribal" traditions
and customs—in official dance troupes, oral histories, school curricula,
a so-called village museum—with a commitment to modernizing them
to fit a resulting national (and later quasi-socialist) form.[6] These twin
agendas are commonly viewed as occurring in sequence, the first giving
way to the second, with the increasingly socialist bent of official policy
from the Arusha Declaration of 1967 onward credited with the rise of
the modernizationist paradigm over a traditionalist one.[7] However, as
I argue in chapter 1, casting this pair of imperatives as coevally embedded in the national cultural project from the beginning more accurately
captures their complexity: two sides of the same coin of a cultural policy
that, notwithstanding declarations to the contrary, inherited the logic
of a similarly bifurcated colonial cultural policy.

Despite the fanfare with which it was announced, as Kelly Askew has
shown in her compelling ethnography of the cultural politics of musical
performance and the Tanzanian state, the national cultural project was
chronically underfunded and often institutionally disorganized.[8] Nevertheless, it was rhetorically powerful. Indeed, the 1960s saw an explo-
sion of public discourse around national culture (utamaduni wa kitaifa
in Kiswahili). As it was variously invoked by journalists in editorials,
lecturers at TANU's Kivukoni ideological college, officials of the Ministry of Culture and TANU Youth League (TYL) speaking at rallies, schoolteachers, regional commissioners, and cultural delegations abroad, national culture became an oft-used frame for official acts from the grand
to the mundane. It was also, as chapters 1 and 2 demonstrate, a frame

that was taken up, appropriated, endorsed, and challenged by ordinary Tanzanians as national culture became a vehicle for debate over urban cultural politics. As such, despite its sometimes uncoordinated and diffuse nature on the ground, national culture nonetheless cohered as a *project* in both official and popular imaginaries. The content of national culture was ambiguous and often seemingly contradictory.[9] But this only enhanced the ability of a wide range of state and nonstate actors to deploy it in the service of often competing agendas. What might be regarded as the official project's failure to coherently define and fill the domain of national culture in fact lay at the heart of its ubiquity and yield as a category useful to a variety of ends.

Energetic promotion of national culture was far from unique in the 1960s and 1970s. The early postcolonial period (from independence for much of Africa in the early 1960s to the widespread onset of economic crises in the midseventies) saw the rise of a host of such promotional projects across the continent. In capitals of states across the political spectrum—from Ahmed Sékou Touré's Guinea, Kwame Nkrumah's Ghana, and Léopold Senghor's Senegal to Mobutu Sese Seko's Zaire and Hastings Banda's Malawi—national theaters and dance troupes sprang up, and varieties of officially sanctioned national dress were fashioned for wear at select occasions by the political elite. Such state initiatives emerged alongside a broader proliferation of discourse on national culture. Essays by Frantz Fanon and Amilcar Cabral stressing the central importance of a cultural front in any authentic decolonization effort swiftly became iconic texts for students, intellectuals, and left-leaning political activists across the continent.[10] From East Africa came the influential epic poems *Song of Lawino* and *Song of Ocol*, in which the Ugandan writer Okot p'Bitek celebrated a "village woman" steeped in Acoli authenticity against her philandering Europhile husband and his high-heeled "modern" mistresses—a stance that was emblematic of the gendered burden of embodying national culture.[11] Vocabularies of *négritude*, an African personality, and *authenticité* peppered intellectual, artistic, and political discourse. As p'Bitek at the time described the "comprehensive cultural revolution that is sweeping post-*uhuru* [independent] Africa": "Amid the political confusion, coups and bloodshed, there are festivals of African music, dance, poetry and art exhibitions. African sculpture and paintings are found in every home in the cities and towns. Dance troupes have sprouted like mushrooms and have won applause in theatres and open-air arenas at home and abroad. The former all-white theatres, miscalled 'national theatres,' have been captured, and are staging relevant plays, mostly of African authorship and about the African situation."[12] In short, "Africa is once more becoming proud of Africa," he asserted, even while cautioning that the "revival of African culture should be for ourselves, to satisfy our own cultural interest and not to be performed at airports for tourists and important visitors."[13] Nyerere took this last sentiment further than most with his vigorous promotion of Kiswahili as a national language, particularly in the realms of primary education and government after 1967, an initiative that stands as perhaps the most successful and enduring component of the national cultural project's promotional side.[14]

To be sure, there were significant shades of difference between the various state-driven national cultural projects (to say nothing of the fundamentally different ideological positioning of many of these official initiatives, on the one hand, and the revolutionary visions of Fanon and Cabral, on the other). For some, like Mobutu's *authenticité* movement, rather more stress lay on foregrounding a vocabulary of tradition, while others were more explicit about their aim to sift tradition through a modernizationist (and in the cases of Tanzania after 1967 and Guinea, a more or less socialist) rubric.[15] And yet, as was the case in Tanzania, traditionalist and modernizationist imperatives often existed alongside one another and were mutually constitutive in formulations of national culture.[16] Moreover, the variation in emphasis in iterations of national culture across ideologically dissimilar states can also obscure other important commonalities of these projects: the centrality of tropes of colonial denigration of indigenous culture as the backdrop against which national culture was to be (re)constituted; a top-down vision of the state's role in shaping culture; strikingly similar conceptions of the specific cultural forms making up a national culture; and the disproportionate burden placed on women to hew to national cultural ideals.

But this promotional dimension, the development and staging of officially sanctioned cultural forms, was not all there was to national culture. As I will argue the Tanzanian case makes clear, national culture was constituted as much *against* a range of practices associated with alleged urban decadence as it was around the promotion of nationalized forms. Or, more precisely, the emergence of this promotional aspect of the national cultural project depended upon a foil of urban and feminized decadence.[17] In the late 1960s and early 1970s the Tanzanian state launched a series of high-profile campaigns targeting and in most cases banning miniskirts, soul music, wigs, cosmetics, trousers ranging from "drain-pipe" to bell-bottom, so-called Afro hairstyles, and beauty contests, all in the name of national culture. In each of these cases, it was the perceived association of these styles with a decadent urbanity, a dangerous cosmopolitanism, and a flouting of gendered and generational norms that made them targets. With enforcement of these campaigns concentrated overwhelmingly on Dar es Salaam and often placed in the hands of TYL patrols complete with walkie-talkies and the power to punish, national cultural operations were uniquely charged touchstones for the capital's cultural politics. A frustrated musician in Dar es Salaam lamented at the time, "If this trend of banning of one thing and another continues, the future holds prospects of: only African music, no Western clothes (at all) together with a prospect of having to apply to the Ministry of Health at six monthly intervals to get a permit for breathing!"[18] But in the controversies swirling around these initiatives, the national cultural question was only one, and often not the most salient one, of a constellation of highly charged sociopolitical issues being negotiated. Indeed, the heated and extensive debate accompanying each campaign spilled far beyond the bounds of national culture to engage some of the capital's most pressing social struggles along cleavages of gender, generation, and wealth.

A Changing Urban Landscape

The proscriptive side of national culture raises the next set of developments setting the stage for the cultural ferment of this sixties moment in Dar es Salaam: the city's changing character in the late colonial and early postcolonial periods. The targets of the Tanzanian campaigns against decadence call attention to a history of cosmopolitan styles of music, fashion, cinema, and forms of sociability in cities from Dar es Salaam to Lagos and Lumbumbashi. Celebrated by many as part of "keep[ing] up with the changes of life" and the "style[s] that [are] liked by their co-youths on earth," these practices were often regarded with alarm by architects of national cultural projects across Africa as signs that cultural "imitation" was reaching new and dangerous heights.[19] In 1967 a performance of pop bands from across East Africa was held in Kampala, hosted by a master of ceremonies calling himself Jesse James Jr. Reacting to the concert with dismay, p'Bitek wrote, "What about blond wigs on the heads of black Ugandan youths? Why the meaningless names [of the bands]: Jeabrals, Phoenix, Mods and Flames? Why the desire to sing exactly like some foreign pop star? Why should a black

Ugandan young man name himself after a white American robber, and be proud of it? There is no creativity in 'aping.' . . . How can our youths be proud of singing like some foreign poet—when they sing what, to us, is mostly irrelevant?"[20]

However, if many formulators of national cultural projects across the continent lamented that what p'Bitek called "apemanship" was reaching the proportions of a "cultural crisis," the phenomena to which they pointed had long histories.[21] Miniskirts and James Brown may have been new, but Africans' appropriation of products, images, icons, and styles originating in Euro-American mass culture industries extended as far back as those industries themselves. As scholarly work for the colonial period and earlier has shown, these appropriations stretched back to nineteenth-century Swahili coastal dwellers' complex tastes for global consumer goods, the dialogic inventions of turn-of-the-century black South African and African American choirs on tour, African mining communities' engagements with Hollywood films and cowboy imagery on the Northern Rhodesian Copperbelt beginning in the 1930s, and the "cult of elegance" developed by young Congolese *sapeurs* in conversation with Parisian high fashion in the 1950s, to name just a few of numerous examples.[22]

During the interwar period, these appropriations generated considerable unease among colonial officials wary of the sorts of claims to urban spaces and modern subjectivities they were thought to entail. As Frederick Cooper and others have established, colonial policy in the wake of the First World War was marked by a deep reluctance, even refusal, to recognize Africans as urban or modern subjects, much less as people with complicated lives and identifications that straddled and confounded dichotomies of rural/urban and traditional/modern. The kinds of self-fashioning emerging from appropriations of global culture, especially in town, were key points of friction in colonial attempts either to keep African subjects within categories of tradition and the tribe (as interwar policy was predominantly geared to) or to carefully engineer their gradual and orderly progression to a modernity that was deemed productive, not decadent (an aim increasingly reflected in urban policy from the end of the 1930s).[23]

For, despite the blueprints of interwar colonial officials, the cities *were* changing. As a wave of strikes and urban protests rolled across industrial and commercial centers throughout Africa from the mid-1930s onward, administrators from the Northern Rhodesian Copperbelt to

Mombasa and London itself were forced to begin to recognize the reality of Africans in town as more than temporary "tribal" sojourners. Beginning with halting reassessments that built upon late-1920s experiments in labor stabilization by mining companies in the Belgian Congo, by the 1940s both British and French colonial administrations were trumpeting a reorientation of policy aimed at carefully crafting modern and stable working classes in town.[24]

The realities of African life in town always exceeded such neat designs. Demographically, migration from rural to urban areas was increasing so rapidly as these policy shifts developed that most African cities saw exponential population growth beginning in the 1930s or 1940s and continuing into the postcolonial period. The growth in migration usually far outstripped that in jobs and services, resulting in large numbers of young migrants making their way through the social networks and informal opportunities for work that were crucial for survival in town.[25] Despite the fact that women developed key niches of economic activity in urban areas through beer brewing, petty trade, sex work, and property trading, until the 1960s a large majority of the new migrants were men.[26] If women's numbers in colonial towns were relatively small, however, their place in imaginaries of the city was central: the trope of the town woman embodying the moral dangers of urban landscapes was prominent in both colonial administrative circles and African communities.[27] Culturally, too, the forms and practices developed in colonial urban centers often confounded colonial expectations. For urbanization was characterized neither by "tribespeople" unable to adapt to urban life nor by the withering away of all vestiges of traditional practices that modernization was thought by some planners to entail. Instead, as even the work of many colonial anthropologists was beginning to show, Africans in town were developing hybrid cultural profiles out of the appropriation of European cultural forms to ends embedded in African lifeworlds.[28]

These patterns of urban change also appeared in Tanzania. In the late 1940s Dar es Salaam saw the beginnings of a boom in migration, one that continues to the present day. Between 1948 and 1967 the population of Dar es Salaam nearly quadrupled.[29] An observer of the time described some of the motivations of migrants: "They are drawn by success stories (not necessarily always true) of those who have gone before; the sight of goods brought home by those who have done well; and their polish; a disbelief in such stories as they hear of unemployment, and a converse belief in stories of available jobs; a mistaken confidence in an inadequate education; the discontent with country life of the boy who has been to school; a dislike of irksome duties and discipline at home and in the village and tribal society; the search for an uncontributing anonymity in town; and by the glamour of the town's reputation; all come basically because it is in the town that they can get on to a cash basis of living."[30]

Contrary to some of the hopes invested in city life, however, jobs and social services in Dar es Salaam lagged far behind population growth under colonial and postcolonial regimes alike, both of which were deeply troubled at the unproductive lifestyles many migrants were thought to lead.[31] And even as rural-urban migration continued to be overwhelmingly young, other aspects of its demographic character were changing. As in most African towns, if somewhat less drastically, in colonial Dar es Salaam the gender ratio of men to women was heavily weighted toward men, but the 1960s saw the number of women coming to Tanzania's capital (an increasing proportion of whom were unmarried) rise rapidly; by 1971 a majority of new migrants to the city were female.[32] With the 1960s new kinds of formal sector work opened to women, especially secretarial and factory jobs, a change that expanded the informal economic niches women had cultivated in Dar es Salaam in the colonial period.[33] Coinciding with continued high unemployment, official efforts to purge the city of perceived loafers, and new displays of wealth in town, the shifting patterns of women's work and movement in town became a flashpoint for expressions of young male rage—anger that, as I argue in chapter 2, was often channeled through campaigns against what was regarded as indecent dress. Together, these urban developments set the stage for some of the key social struggles, most prominently around youth, gender, and conspicuous consumption, that would be contested on the terrain of the Tanzanian state's national cultural campaigns.

Late Colonial Cultural Politics: A Vignette

Bound up with the dichotomies of traditional/modern and rural/urban that would continue to be central conceptual frames for cultural politics in the 1960s, colonial cultural policy constitutes a third set of developments setting the stage for postcolonial debates around urban culture. As would be the case after independence, cultural controversies that spilled into public debate in Dar es Salaam during the last two decades of the colonial period saw official attempts to shape culture in town seized upon by different sorts of urban residents in complicated ways. The fault lines of these late colonial debates often contained the roots of the contests marking the following, postcolonial decade.

Colonial cultural policy in Tanganyika[34] developed as part of the broader trajectories of cultural planning in British colonial Africa.[35] In the interwar period this policy was characterized by classic elements of the stances associated with the doctrine of indirect rule (a strategy of rule relying on the co-optation of African chiefs as "Native Authorities"), including a declared goal, in the words of Governor Sir Donald Cameron, "to do everything in our power to develop the native on lines which will not Westernise him and turn him into a bad imitation of a European."[36] With the tribe enthroned—or often imagined into being—as the preeminent unit of administrative discourse and practice, the cultural interventions of the Tanganyikan colonial state between the wars were generally designed to shore up tribal tradition and prevent, in the words of one official, "the immigration to the towns and the growth of the over-dressed and self-opinionated clerical type."[37] However, if in the interwar years the colonial administration was unprepared to deal head-on with Africans in town in ways that went beyond the notion of an essentially rural and tribal African subject, the 1940s saw a growing turnabout in policy. While in the 1930s *detribalization*, the colonial term for Africans acculturating to town, denoted a lamentable phenomenon to be avoided at all costs, by the 1950s it was seen as a difficult but necessary phase of the modern development of urban Africa that was now the reigning catchphrase in colonial policy circles.

Far from exhibiting a withering away of invocations of tradition, though, debates over cultural policy in the new postwar climate saw colonial officials and elite African nationalists alike working to rearticulate notions of tradition that would be at once authentic and modern. In Dar es Salaam, these efforts coexisted uneasily with rather different understandings of culture and its place in urban life, conceptions embedded in nonelite residents' enthusiasm for transnational cultural forms passing through the capital. One late colonial cultural initiative, the government's experimentation with film audience research, opens a window on this tension. As a case, it also illustrates how the fault lines of urban cultural politics in the late colonial period prefigured aspects of the struggles around national culture in the next, postcolonial decade.

As elsewhere in British colonial Africa, in Tanganyika the government established a film unit after the Second World War and charged it with producing movies to promote the administration's technocratic, modernizing projects.[38] And yet officials were increasingly uncertain about whether or not the films produced by the unit, often on such topics as modern housing and cattle dipping, were in fact entertaining to African audiences. In the officials' attempts to judge a film's entertainment value, two criteria were central to their assumptions: its popularity with audiences and its Africanness, understood as a foundation in "local African psychology." These two criteria were generally thought to be inextricable, each following logically from the other.[39] At times, however, film unit officials questioned this link, for some of them had observed that African audiences often expressed the most enthusiasm for films that challenged the dictum that a film "must not be 'foreign'" to elicit engagement. This lingering uncertainty about how to define a local African film and about whether a film's supposed foundations in "African psychology" and landscapes close to home truly fostered engagement and entertainment better than more foreign scenes led to an interest in audience research.[40]

The audience research study that circulated most prominently in administration circles focused on a South African commercial film from 1950 entitled Zonk! Produced by African Film Productions, the primary distributor of films to East Africa since the 1920s, Zonk! was a musical variety show featuring some of South Africa's most prominent black entertainers (above all, Sophiatown's Manhattan Stars) performing roles and scenes drawn from African American performances of the period. Directed by Hyman Kirstein, a white South African liberal, Zonk!'s all-black cast was reported to have had some measure of circumscribed authority in designing and choreographing the film's scenes. The show consisted of a string of fifteen musical numbers performed on a variety of sets; each scene was introduced in English and Sesotho before a drawn stage curtain by a lively master of ceremonies dressed in a tuxedo. The performances ranged from reproductions of American dance routines such as "Jumpin' Jive" to explicitly hybrid numbers like "Squeeze Me," a jitterbug scene performed to a mixed accompaniment of big band and "traditional" drums before a set of urban township dwellings representing Cape Town's District Six neighborhood. Some songs were sung in English, others in Sesotho, still others in both. Changed for each scene, the costumes mostly featured tuxedos, zoot suits, and less formal shirts and trousers for the mostly male cast and sequined dresses or plainer skirts and blouses for the few female performers. One scene, performed before a set representing a rural setting, featured a male soloist in "traditional" dress; in another the same soloist donned cowboy garb before a set of an American Western scene. In the commentary of the master of ceremonies and in some of the song lyrics, the film both reveled in Euro-American cultural references "known to many of us and unknown to the less fortunate of us" and celebrated their appropriation. As the chorus to the first song, performed in tuxedos and zoot suits, declared, "We don't need a Park Avenue, we get our talent from you and you and you and you."[41]

The screening of Zonk! in Dar es Salaam was a raucous affair. Shown at Alexandra Hall in the capital's main Welfare Center, the film was attended by an audience "composed of the illiterate and half-literate Swahili speaking urban African, with a sprinkling of English speaking people," spectators who were "used to seeing films, both at the commercial cinema and in the Alexandra Hall."[42] The audience reports from the screening gave officials plenty of food for thought, and in some ways deepened their confusion, on the question of the relationship between a film's popularity and its Africanness, for they reported a deep split on these issues between different segments of the crowd. For members of Dar es Salaam's white-collar African elite, the film was a disappointing failure. In a long letter to the head of the audience research program, Stephen Mhando, a secondary school teacher in Dar es Salaam and a prominent figure in the protonationalist Tanganyika African Association who, in the 1960s, would become ambassador to West Germany and minister for foreign affairs, explained his reaction. He began by noting, "There is no doubt . . . that the film appeals to that stratum of urban African society who have come to regard jazz, jive, swing and tap dancing (apart from Wild West films) as the last word on movies." He continued, "With 'Zonck' [sic] as a standard, I fail to see the emergence in Africa of a live theatrical art, in keeping with modern social and economic developments, for 'Zonck' is, in my opinion, a weak, second-rate derivative film without background or support in the homeland of the people who acted it." Commenting on several specific scenes in the film, Mhando expressed praise for the one or two that he thought contained "an indigenous element." But most of the scenes, the ones in which performers wore tuxedos against urban backdrops dominated by skyscrapers, received Mhando's scorn. Critiquing "The Girl on the Cover of Zonk," a musical number in which a fictional Zonk "cover girl" sang about her role, Mhando wrote, "The cover girl would have been a greater success if she had tried to act as an African girl on the cover of an African magazine 'Zonck,' instead, I think she tried to emulate

Carmen Miranda, with the result that as she sang, she portrayed on her face emotions completely foreign to the African sentiment under the circumstances; when an African songstress is carried away by the pathos etc of her song, she RARELY smiles attractively."[43]

The disappointment of Mhando, one of the "sprinkling of English speaking people" at the screening, contrasted sharply with the reactions of the wider crowd at the show. The report by a team of audience observers, including both Africans and Europeans, suggested that there was "no question that the film was a great success" and went on to describe the "delighted" and "absorbed" demeanor of viewers and some of the specificities of the "excited chatter" that went on throughout the screening. Three of the numbers "caused so much excited comment that the compère was drowned by the noise": the first featured couples dancing the jitterbug backed by a band in white tuxedos; the second, a song sung in English by Richard Majola as he tap danced in top hat and tails while twirling a cane; the third, a skit featuring a group of dock laborers in gumboots dancing in a restaurant.[44] One audience member reportedly remarked wistfully on the jitterbug scene, "We [don't know how to] dance that way in Dar es Salaam." Another, referring to the places the performers came from, exclaimed, "If you get there you can't [ever wish to] get back."[45] To the officials' surprise, the film's most poorly received scene was what officials called "the Hut Song": the number was sung by a bass soloist wrapped in a blanket and carrying a knobkerrie (the short, knobbed club popular as an accessory in parts of rural South Africa); the painted backdrop portrayed a rural setting of huts and scattered vegetation.[46] Amidst the marked lack of enthusiasm for this scene in Alexandra Hall, one man was reported to have cried out, "Stop him, take him away, we don't want him!"[47]

Opinions like Mhando's were not completely absent in the hall that night. In the only quotation noted by the report's author to have been expressed in English, one man reacted to the gumboot dancing (a widely popular scene) by declaring, "That's what we like, it's pure African." But such sentiments appear to have been overwhelmed by a keenness for the ensembles of symbols brought together in scenes of Africans displaying mastery of the latest American dancing and musical styles. "If there was an association started like that, I'd join!" one man exclaimed at the end of the show. An observer stationed at the doors of the hall summarized the conversations among departing viewers: "The general impression on the audience was that the picture was a most encouraging example of the advancement of the African. There was modern music, there was no European supervision, and it was an all African production."[48] This last statement stood in interesting contrast to the position Mhando took as he made suggestions for future film productions. On one hand, he reemphasized a need to cleave close to an African environment, something *Zonk!* failed to do in his view; on the other, he insisted that "European advice etc. will be needed in such things as scenery, make-up and stage management."[49]

As a vignette, the *Zonk!* screening reveals not only late colonial thinking on culture, but, even more important, its intersection with some of the cleavages emerging in a cosmopolitan Dar es Salaam. Colonial planners had been convinced that films needed to be culturally and thematically local in order to elicit the engagement and acceptance of the target audiences. This could take the form either of extremely technical lessons on how, say, to feed pigs or of productions rooted in a notion of "African psychology" that usually fell back on long-held colonial assumptions that the customs and traditions of a region's tribes constituted the natural repositories of local Africanness.[50] This latter conviction was one that was frequently shared by colonial officials and African elites, as Mhando's response suggests. Audience reactions to *Zonk!* were complex, for they at once confirmed officials' position that relevance to people's lives locally elicited more enthusiastic engagement *and* challenged assumptions about what really was relevant locally. If to some nationalist elites like Mhando *Zonk!* appeared derivative and far removed from indigenous experience, and to some colonial officials it seemed not very useful in promoting the kind of modernization the postwar colonial establishment desired, to a large portion of the audience that night in the capital it may indeed have captured the very dreams, concerns, and hopes of "African advancement" that loomed large in their lives in town.

Despite their interest in studying actual audience reactions, the Tanganyika administration failed to fully confront the potential lessons of experiences like the *Zonk!* study. But if the experiment with *Zonk!* did not transform colonial thinking on African spectatorship, it did foreshadow key elements of the landscape of early postcolonial debates around authenticity and cosmopolitanism, the indigenous and the foreign, that animated public debate in the 1960s and 1970s. As I show in detail in chapter 1, these postcolonial controversies often saw the nationalist political establishment promoting a vision of national culture composed of selected cultural signifiers that were at once valorized for their indigeneity as tradition *and* put through a litmus test establishing their compatibility with notions of modern decency. If this position recalls Mhando's response to Zonk!, the widespread vocal opposition to national cultural banning campaigns shared much with audiences who reveled in the African performances of cosmopolitan attachment featured in the film. In this way, the engagements with Zonk! open a window on the late colonial roots of some of the positioning on culture that would dominate Tanzania's first postcolonial decade.

Cultured States

The intersecting dynamics described above—the rise of the national cultural project, the shifts in urban demographics unfolding in relation to colonial and postcolonial anxieties about the city, and the fault lines of late colonial debates about culture—are critical contexts for the debates over cosmopolitan cultural appropriations that became so heated in early postcolonial Dar es Salaam. Against the backdrop of these developments, this book explores a number of specific debates that animated public culture in early postcolonial Dar es Salaam as a way of illuminating the urban cultural politics of Tanzania's long sixties moment. These debates, examined in the following chapters, include arguments about the canonization of select cultural forms as national; the vigorously contested campaigns to ban miniskirts, wigs, and other forms of what was considered indecent dress; controversies over iconic items of African American popular culture; university student activism on issues ranging from national service to global anti-imperialism and curricular reform; the persistently prominent, if always contested, moral panics around young women's comportment, work, relationships with men, and movement about town; the Great Marriage Debate of 1970–71 accompanying the first successful overhaul of colonial-era marriage law in the British Commonwealth; and the running commentary on rumors of scandalous liaisons between "city girls" and elite "big men" produced by Dar es Salaam's popular tabloid press.

An examination of these debates does much more than simply add to the sum of knowledge of early postcolonial Tanzania. Situated in relation to state cultural policy, urban struggles around gender, generation, and wealth, and transnational horizons of identification for young Tanzanians, these controversies are a lens through which to engage broader themes animating African and postcolonial studies. Such themes include the place of culture in relations of power, the modern as an idiom for claim making in postcolonial contexts, the trajectories of transnational cultural forms in local contexts, continuities across the colonial-postcolonial divide, and how best to approach what Achille Mbembe has called the banal vulgarity of particular forms of public political discourse in "the postcolony."[51] Like a prism that casts light differently depending on which way it is turned, the slice of cultural politics this book considers is a uniquely rich tool for illuminating seemingly disparate domains of postcolonial experience.

A number of my central arguments cluster around the complicated and often unpredictable relationship between the state and cultural production. In analyzing the Tanzanian state's banning campaigns, I suggest that official cultural interventions in early postcolonial Tanzania, as in much of the colonial period, were closely bound up with two of the state's most pressing ideological and policy problems: how to position itself in relation to the urban and to the modern. As Andrew Burton has shown, Tanzania's postcolonial political class continued, and even expanded, colonial attempts to purge urban areas of so-called undesirables deemed unproductive.[52] This continuity was more than simply the product of a colonial inheritance or legacy.[53] Rather, an abiding commitment to purging towns of the disrespectability and decadence associated with the urban was in keeping with the attitudes toward Dar es Salaam expressed by the nationalist political elite of the late colonial period—even as (or precisely because) they themselves were deeply invested in laying claim to the town as respectable urban citizens.[54]

As this group went on to form the backbone of the independent TANU government of the 1960s, the state's increasing emphasis on the rural as the ideal site for the performance of Tanzanian citizenship peaked with the Arusha Declaration of 1967 and the project of "ujamaa villagization" that it launched. (Connoting familyhood and solidarity, "ujamaa" was President Nyerere's term for his political philosophy, which after 1967 was often used to name a brand of "African socialism" and served as the banner under which TANU conducted its ultimately failed project of reorganizing the countryside into planned villages.)[55] With the national cultural project becoming increasingly visible in the form of its decency campaigns, a loose group of official and quasi-official actors—including bureaucrats in the ministry responsible for culture, ambitious TYL officials, editors and columnists at TANU's media outlets, lecturers at TANU's ideological college, and armies of youth enforcers—were mobilized in the service of cleansing Dar es Salaam of the decadence it was cast as breeding. With this context in mind, I argue that the national cultural project became a primary vehicle for coding questions of urban order in cultural terms. In an era in which civic duty was increasingly being constructed around a healthy, productive rural ideal—epitomized by scenes disseminated widely in the press of young and old, men and women, even politicians, laboring in ujamaa villages—constructions of the city as decadent, unproductive, and emasculating constituted an important foil for TANU's ujamaa ideology.[56]

If the national cultural project became a key site for the negotiation of anxieties around the urban, this process was also intimately connected to struggles over official visions of a *modern* Tanzania. Like discourse on the city, this exhibited important continuities from the late colonial period, when notions of the relationship between towns and African life, assumed to be naturally rural, were closely linked to distinguishing the appropriate paths along which traditional Africans might become modern from those paths regarded as dangerous and destructive.[57] In the postcolonial period, as modern development became the central plank of the state's raison d'être, both the promotional and proscriptive dimensions of the national cultural project enabled significant moves in relation to the modern. On the one hand, the production and authorization of a realm of national tradition, often glossed as *utamaduni* (culture), was a central element of official efforts to project an image of Tanzania on the world stage that would be simultaneously modern and marked by a difference from the West. This resonates strongly with Partha Chatterjee's now-classic account of the process by which Indian nationalists engaged colonial modernity: first, by marking out an "inner sphere" of tradition as off-limits to British colonization (in contrast to an outer, civic sphere where modern European political forms could be freely adopted) and then proceeding to attempt a vernacular modernization of that inner realm. Far from developing outside of the modern, then, tradition, in Chatterjee's argument, emerges as a crucial component of colonial and nationalist modernity, internal to modernity.[58] Similarly, in Tanzania in the 1960s, national culture became an important site for and indeed underwrote state efforts to construct and perform itself as modern-with-a-difference.

This dimension of nationalist cultural projects in the postcolonial world has generated significant scholarly attention, but considerably less notice has been paid to the second move vis-à-vis the modern enabled by Tanzania's official cultural initiatives.[59] In contrast to the first one, this move involved the proscriptive side of the national cultural project: the myriad operations targeting sundry forms of urban decadence, initiatives that, as I have suggested, were a dominant manifestation of national culture in Dar es Salaam. As residents of the capital debated bans on miniskirts and soul music, one of the arguments these contests featured was over the meaning of the modern—or, more precisely, which forms and practices qualified as modern. Faced with competing notions of being modern, officials were keen to disentangle an appropriate modern of official development discourse from cultural forms like the miniskirt and soul music. Indeed, against the claims of many urban young people, officials argued vociferously, albeit rather unsuccessfully, that these forms were in fact not modern at all. Such efforts to split a field of cultural forms associable with the modern into good and bad, productive and decadent, healthy and destructive variants, recall colonial attempts, often similarly unsuccessful, to carefully limit Africans' access to what Peter Probst, Jan-Georg Deutsch, and Heike Schmidt pithily call "modernity as contagion."[60] Amidst the attention paid to the way this bifurcation of the modern played out in colonial situations across Africa and beyond, its strong presence in post-colonial cultural policy has been surprisingly neglected.[61] In attending to this split, I argue that the Tanzanian case adds importantly to scholars' understanding of the way in which early postcolonial states in the sixties and seventies constructed and maintained modern images for themselves.

The prominence in national cultural discourse of this fraught wrestling with the city and the modern suggests that the supposed urban decadence against which the postcolonial state's most energetic cultural initiatives were launched was fundamental to the constitution of national culture, was one of its crucial "constitutive outsides."[62] In other words, short skirts, wigs, soul music, and the behavior such objects were perceived to engender were part of a key foil against which a rurally inflected national culture could emerge. In the 1960s less than 15 percent of Tanzania's population lived in urban areas. However, what was demographically marginal was ideologically central. Official portrayals of the urban in Tanzania as well as the policies surrounding it played an important part in the idealization of the rural that was so vital to state ideology in the sixties and seventies and central to the very image of Tanzania in the years since.

Yet too often projects of national culture, particularly those set in motion in the early years of independence, have been portrayed as natural or inevitable undertakings for states emerging from colonial rule, part of any proper decolonization effort.[63] This takes official proclamations of the aims of such projects—as first and foremost being about the reversal of a colonial trampling of indigenous culture and recovery of the cultural loss this entailed—too much at their word. Writing on the well-known attempt by Ngugi and others to replace the English department at the University of Nairobi in the late 1960s and early 1970s with a department of African languages and literature, Apollo Amoko demonstrates how this seemingly revolutionary move in fact reproduced intact the "ideology of English literature" it sought to transcend. He does so by situating the claims of both Ngugi's "Nairobi Revolution" and the imperial tradition of English literature that preceded it within a culture of the university that, he argues, was constitutive of both.[64] In situating the claims of overcoming colonialism made by the architects of Tanzania's national cultural project, I point to a similar process at work. Not only did the content of the tradition promoted under the national cultural rubric reproduce in some important ways colonial officials' construction of tradition.[65] Even more important, I argue, the anxious wrestling with the modern city embodied in both the decency campaigns of the long sixties and much of the colonial cultural policy they were designed to overcome makes up a principal, constitutive context for Tanzania's national cultural project.[66]

The campaigns against urban decadence highlight the fact that continuities with the colonial stretched beyond the promotional side of national culture to its proscriptive one as well. Indeed, echoes of colonial cultural policymakers' frequent condemnations of "the evils of rural Natives going to towns" and corollary concerns to "make [the Native] a good African" rather than a "bad imitation of a European" can be heard in postcolonial officials' speeches in support of the banning campaigns of the late 1960s.[67] As L. N. Sijaona, chairman of the TYL, put it in 1968 when announcing a ban on the indecent dress that his deputy had blamed for a "dilution" of Africanness among the young, "It is well known that the people whose minds have been enslaved by dehumanising practices are confined into the urban areas."[68] Noting these continuities, I suggest that Tanzania's cultural interventions of the 1960s and 1970s helped produce an effect of a postcolonial present and future distinctly marked off from a colonial past even as (or perhaps crucial precisely because) much official policy was rooted in colonial policy and continued the colonial state's interventions.[69] National culture operated as a domain in which the state could perform its own postcoloniality, its difference from its colonial predecessor, at a time when the pressure to produce tangible signs of that difference was immense. In the process, what national culture worked to efface were continuities between colonial and postcolonial cultural policy, not only in the content of national culture, but also in the abiding anxieties about urban decadence that characterized official thinking both before and after independence.

The relationship between the state and cultural production outlined thus far suggests that an attention to official culture does not simply add a piece to the puzzle of the Tanzanian state but also enables new understandings of how this state intervened in the lives of its citizens, above all those living in cities. This perspective responds to a host of recent calls to emphasize the state's importance as a cultural form, its status, in Thomas Blom Hansen and Finn Stepputat's words, as "the great enframer."[70] It also cuts against the prominent assumption that the Tanzanian—or African—state's sometime failure to politically or economically capture its citizens renders its rhetoric relatively unimportant for understanding the lives of everyday people.[71] Given the often uneven nature of state rhetoric, however, understanding the importance of official cultural policy in the lives of residents of early postcolonial Dar es Salaam is to be found much less in official blueprints than in the ways in which such plans were appropriated to diverse ends in the complex world of the city's public culture in those years. My book thus quickly moves beyond an analysis of the ideological work performed by the national cultural project for the state, one dimension of the phrase "cultured states," to the more central investigation of how official cultural discourse and interventions played out in the capital's cultural politics. These trajectories were varied and complex: national cultural campaigns were fought over, diverted, supported, opposed, reframed, and sometimes hijacked to become platforms for specific social struggles over gender, generation, and wealth. Such contests extended far beyond issues of national culture, even when conducted in the vocabulary of those issues.

This spillover effect inevitably recalls Mbembe's enormously influential insistence on the imbrication of postcolonial state and society, rulers and ruled, in an "illicit cohabitation," a shared domain of "conviviality" that "inscribe[s] the dominant and dominated within the same episteme."[72] Mbembe's proposal to approach state and society in postcolonial contexts as together inhabiting and drawing on the same world of signs is invaluable for examining the field of cultural politics in Dar es Salaam in the 1960s—a field in which many public debates blurred the lines between official and popular discourse. As multiple actors—teenage fans of soul, university student activists, young women seeking work or city girl identities in town, frustrated bachelors anxious to move up in the world, housewives troubled at their husbands' affairs—engaged and appropriated official cultural campaigns to diverse ends, these state initiatives became at once central to urban Tanzanians' lives and highly malleable in their trajectories.

But if in Mbembe's formulation the play of signs in this domain of conviviality results in a "mutual zombification of both the dominant and those whom they apparently dominate," the debates studied here call for an approach that pays careful attention to the precise ways in which such appropriations are connected to specific social struggles of the time and place.[73] Frederick Cooper's consistent stress on the ways in which official categories become "languages of claim-making and counter claim-making, whose effects [are] shaped less by grand abstractions than by complex struggles in specific contexts," is critical to this end.[74] As the following chapters illustrate, when young men appropriated official bans on indecent dress to take out their anger on city girls seen to be getting ahead in town in illicit ways, or when young women in turn used official master categories to make claims for their own patterns of urban work and mobility, these appropriations had important material effects. Rather than Mbembe's vicious circle that leaves both rulers and ruled impotent, these cases illustrate a process of leveraging, sometimes successful, sometimes not, but always to specific, if occasionally unexpected, ends.[75]

Together, the cases I examine here suggest that there were multiple notions of culture being articulated, imposed, appropriated, and contested in Dar es Salaam's cultural-political debates of the 1960s, each with its own complex genealogy. One of these, the state's notion of national culture, or *utamaduni*, saw the state simultaneously marking off a domain of authenticity in which it could stress its difference from its colonial predecessor and submitting this domain to a standard of modern decency that would underline Tanzania's status as a respectable, modern nation. As we have seen, this understanding of culture had intertwined colonial histories, rooted both in colonial constructions of African tradition and the positions taken on cultural questions by self-consciously modernizing Tanzanian nationalists of the 1950s.[76]

But in the politics of public debate in Dar es Salaam—and indeed in the struggles over dress, music, bodily comportment, student politics, and marriage playing out on the streets of the capital—this notion of culture jostled for space with other, quite different conceptions of it. In particular, national culture confronted young Tanzanians imagining a cosmopolitan field of global culture in which they saw themselves as perfectly able and entitled to participate, not uniquely or necessarily marked as Tanzanians or Africans but as modern practitioners of (or petitioners for) what James Ferguson has called "global membership."[77] Such imaginings collapsed easy distinctions between the indigenous and the foreign, instead mixing styles originating abroad, in Tanzania, and elsewhere in Africa as part of the aesthetic landscape of a desirably modern city. As one young letter writer put it in a missive on the ban on soul music attempted in 1969, "I will just give some examples of dance styles which were once popular but have now faded or are just on the point of fading away! These were Mnenguo, Rock, Samba, Twist, Rhumba, Waltz, Bollero, Monkey, Chacha, Shake, Pachanga, A Go-Go Rama, and others. . . . These are now being replaced by new ones like, Likembe, Kirikiri, Toyota, Chikuna, Soul, Tetema, Apollo and the like. Why is the 'soul' then not left alone for a while?" Like national culture, this imaginary had a colonial history, one tracing back through some of the more famous engagements with global culture of the first half of the twentieth century in African towns: beni ngoma dance troupes' incorporation of European instruments and colonial uniforms into their performances, or the "cowboy gangs" that appropriated the style and swagger of Hollywood Westerns, to take just two examples.[78]

The temptation to view these competing notions of culture as fully distinct and opposed formations, sealed off from one another, should be resisted. Official notions of national culture and the cosmopolitanism of its opponents not only bled into and influenced one another, but were also mutually constitutive in important ways. I have already suggested that the emergence and proliferation of the national cultural project depended on the field of "inauthenticity" it targeted. Conversely, young Tanzanians voicing their opposition to state cultural initiatives with very different visions of being "at home in the world" often drew upon and reworked official discourse to articulate these visions.[79] These debates served as platforms for material struggles in a Dar es Salaam full of such contests in the 1960s. Controversies over bans on dress and music, the political engagement (or lack thereof) of university youth, women's work and mobility in town, and what different sorts of women and men got out of romantic entanglements were not simply debates over meaning, but contests connected to struggles inflected by gender, generation, and access to resources.

Gendered Youth, Modern Style, and Material Inequality in a Cosmopolitan Dar es Salaam

As the culture wars of Tanzania's first postcolonial decade gathered steam on the streets of the capital, the debates and actions surrounding campaigns that had been officially cast as national cultural affairs spilled out far beyond this frame to engage a range of specific social conflicts: urban gender relations and sexual politics, women's work and mobility, struggles and crises over youth and masculinity, and competition for resources amidst a shifting political economy in which paths to power and success were increasingly dependent on the state. Indeed, the proscriptive national cultural campaigns of these years constituted one of the central vehicles and also provided an important lexicon through which these urban struggles were mediated. As case studies, they work to showcase the intersections between mutually embedded domains of state power, sexual politics, and struggles over urban space and lifestyles.[80]

Gender, generation, and wealth emerge as the three intersecting social axes most central to the debates I analyze.[81] In Tanzania, as in many other African contexts, the colonial period saw the interplay between bridewealth (or dowries) and intergenerational and gendered tensions undergoing shifts in relation to changes in the colonial economy, consumption patterns, and migrant labor. Fathers' command over the resources that went into bridewealth for their sons—cattle, in many areas—had been a crucial component of their control over the timing and prospects of young men's marriages. Beginning in the 1920s and 1930s a rapidly increasing number of young men utilized migrant labor for cash wages as a path to accumulate resources of their own that they might put toward bridewealth, marriage, and the establishment of a household.[82] In many cases, such dynamics rendered more unstable, but by no means eliminated, fathers' and elders' authority as the gatekeepers of young men's marriage prospects. At the same time, wage labor and the growing phenomenon of cash dowries in many late colonial contexts helped push up the cost of bridewealth in the mid-twentieth century, often to heights unseen for half a century or more.[83] Intergenerational tension between sons and fathers on this point continued with these shifts, even as it was reshaped in what Monica Wilson, looking back on her fieldwork of the 1930s and 1950s in Tanganyika, referred to as "zig-zag change."[84]

Young men were not the only ones traveling. As administrative centers like Dar es Salaam increasingly joined mines and sisal plantations from the 1930s onward as prominent destinations for young people in search of economic opportunities, growing numbers of young women began to make their way to town. Luise White's pathbreaking study of prostitution in colonial Nairobi is foremost among early investigations of these "town women" in East African cities.[85] As White describes, these women cobbled together livings (which were often substantial enough to allow some to send remittances home to rural families) from activities ranging from sex work to the provision of the "comforts of home" to their regular clients.[86] Although the textures and lifeways of the women of Dar es Salaam in the late colonial period have yet to be examined in the way White does for Nairobi, scattered data do exist. As I illustrate in chapter 2, this evidence suggests that women in Dar es Salaam, who composed a larger proportion of residents than in many colonial African capitals of the time, built informal economic niches in beer brewing, street hawking, domestic employment, various kinds of sex work, and, in the case of a striking number, property ownership.[87] Prostitution and its various cognates were particularly associated with the neighborhood of Kisutu, regarded as the capital's red light district through the British colonial period and into the postcolonial one before being demolished in 1974; it was a central site for the kind of landscape of female entrepreneurialism that White describes for Nairobi's River Road.[88] Kisutu was perennially derided as an area of urban blight by colonial officialdom and, perhaps even more vociferously, by the educated clerks and teachers who made up the protonationalist African Association and who were deeply invested in claiming a place for respectable Africans as town-dwelling citizens.[89]

Taken together, these trends made up a context in which the meaning of urban life for many young male migrants was often bound up with bridewealth, marriage prospects, and their relationship with senior men—and in which rising numbers of women were also working to get by in town, partly through liaisons with men who had money to spend. This situation contained great potential for gendered and generational tension and conflict. When employment for young men was relatively plentiful, as it was in the late 1940s and early 1950s, the tension was less acute.[90] In the 1960s, however, a number of concomitant shifts, as I mentioned earlier, brought about change. Exponential increases in the number of male migrants drawn to Dar es Salaam caused severe job shortages even as new sectors of formal wage labor, secretarial and factory work, in particular, were opening up to women in ways nonexistent in the colonial period.[91] Moreover, what Ferguson in another context has called the "cultural topography of wealth" was changing in the capital, captured most prominently, as I show in chapters 3 and 4, by the figure of the *naizesheni*, or "'nizer": local parlance for the beneficiaries of the Africanization of government and, to a lesser extent, of business, who were widely viewed as leveraging their new positions into wealth that they conspicuously consumed about town.[92]

Newly configured, triangular generational and gendered tensions between the capital's young bachelors, its city girls, and the new elite developing around the postcolonial state could be manifested in different ways: as, in the words of a student spokesman, the "struggle between the political and the educated elite" that erupted around student activism at the University of Dar es Salaam (see chapter 3); or as the pleading attempts by young men to steer the debate over the reform of the national marriage law toward a debate over dowries (see chapter 4); or as the powerful resentment of young men strapped for money who viewed themselves as the losers in a political economy of romantic liaisons in which they were snubbed by young city girls in favor of older, wealthier "sugar daddies" (see chapter 2). In this context, then, official national cultural campaigns and the items of fashion they targeted—already highly charged along a different axis as sites for contests over urban and modern subjectivities—were widely appropriated as platforms for the negotiation of struggles around gender, generation, and resources. As traced here, this was a triad long weighty with potential social friction. Now, in the 1960s, it was marked by the unique conjunction of the socioeconomic shifts of Dar es Salaam's first postcolonial decade. These struggles over official cultural initiatives (and indeed most of these initiatives themselves) invoked frames of varied scope, placing these Dar es Salaam–centered conflicts in wider, transnational contexts. To some degree, cosmopolitanism provides a useful heuristic in approaching this dynamic, but the notion of cosmopolitanism I work with here comes out of an attempt to broaden the way the concept is popularly understood. While a large part of the book analyzes the kinds of cultural forms that are often described as cosmopolitan (miniskirts, bell-bottoms, soul music, etc.), I seek to avoid constructing a facile, ultimately spurious opposition between forms that travel and others that are often regarded as part of a more stable local or even national domain.[93] Rather, I understand not only the forms of music, fashion, and style targeted by the Tanzanian state's national cultural campaigns, but also networks of left politics and thought and even state discourses of modernization and the national cultural project itself, as cosmopolitan forms—competing transnational vocabularies and imageries through which contests over generation, gender, and wealth were fought out in the capital. From this perspective, social struggles over culture in Dar es Salaam emerge not as local or internal practices encountering or even appropriating vocabularies, images, and practices from a "global outside."[94] These struggles, and indeed Dar es Salaam itself, are better regarded as *nodal* rather than local: the city as nodal point along competing and crisscrossing cosmopolitan networks that extend over long distances but are more bounded than the often vague concept of flows suggests.[95]

Such an approach helps capture the ambiguous and seemingly paradoxical ways in which transnational frames both enabled and complicated positions taken by various players in Dar es Salaam's debates over culture. The Tanzanian state's attempt to frame culture as national, for instance, was itself a transnational practice, part of a wave of such attempts launched by newly independent postcolonial states in the early 1960s, and it depended on and only made sense within a vision of a world stage upon which Tanzania had to distinguish itself as a distinct member of a family of nations. On the other hand, invocations of other cosmopolitan or international frames in opposition to the state's national cultural initiatives complicated such initiatives, not least in contesting the meanings of categories that were central to state legitimacy and practice, for example, youth and the modern. The tension between appeals to the national and those gesturing toward horizons of broader, global scope was a persistent one in the cultural debates of Dar es Salaam's long sixties.

Seeing Dar es Salaam in a transnational or cosmopolitan frame, particularly as part of a coastal East African zone, is neither new nor unique to the postcolonial period. Indeed, when it was founded as a site for a mainland base for the Omani Sultan of Zanzibar and soon-to-be capital of the pre–First World War German colony, it was part of an East

African coastal region that for centuries had been integrated into an Indian Ocean world.[96] Stretching from the East African coastal entrepôts of Kilwa, Zanzibar, Mombasa, and Mogadishu to the ports of Oman, the South Asian peninsula, and beyond, this was a zone that had grown up on all manner of economic, social, and cultural exchange involving Africans, Arabs, Indians, and Europeans. Following classic work on this Indian Ocean world, Jeremy Prestholdt has theorized this zone of engagement not simply as a cosmopolitan one, but as one in which East African consumption of globally circulating commodities turned the latter into "vehicles of social relation."[97] Founded too late to be integrated into this classic Indian Ocean economy in the same way the older cities on the coast were, Dar es Salaam was nonetheless shaped by the long-lasting influences of this world, including the city's large communities of South Asian traders.[98]

If this cosmopolitan frame has become a staple of histories of an earlier period on the East African coast linked to the Indian Ocean, it is much less common for the kind of later engagement with the global that this book considers.[99] And Dar es Salaam's moment of long sixties cosmopolitanism came with features that prompt insights into current debates over globalization and modernity. Two of these stand out. First, is the enabling of a contribution to the development of perspectives on a global '68. Against the backdrop of successive waves of academic and popular attention to the events, impact, and memories of 1968 in Europe and North America,[100] other strands along the leftist networks in which the events of Prague, Paris, Berkeley, and Mexico City were embedded have only just begun to be registered in academic work.[101] Dar es Salaam occupied a significant place in these networks, most directly through the left expatriate faculty members drawn in the late 1960s to the University College to teach and also to experience and play a part in Nyerere's socialist experiment. These expatriates, including such luminaries as Walter Rodney, joined an already vibrant and internationalist student left on campus that, fueled by news of Vietnam, the CIA in Africa, the writings of Mao and Fanon, and liberation movements worldwide, reached its apogee in 1968–69. But if this campus left, which I take up in chapter 3, was one manifestation of the view of 1968 from Dar es Salaam, so too, in a different way, were the struggles over the miniskirt developing on the city's streets that year.

Second, a striking aspect of the cosmopolitan debates of Dar es Salaam's sixties moment is the degree to which the modern character of objects and practices became a prominent focus of intense talk. As one secondary student explained his opposition to a 1969 ban on indecent dress that he felt hindered young Tanzanians' ability to fashion themselves along modern lines, "The current youth is well aware of the fashion revolution taking place in many countries. . . . What is widely practiced by many other peoples is also good for us."[102] In some ways these appeals to the modern, which recur again and again in the debates my book considers, conjure up the boom in recent literature on "alternative," "parallel" or "multiple modernities." [103] However, as I discuss more fully in chapter 1, in important ways these gestures were different. When young residents of the capital and official framers of national cultural policy invoked the term *modern*, an important component of these uses was the concept's singularity. To be sure, understandings of what constituted modern style or a national culture befitting a modern Tanzania were by no means uncontested or broadly shared. Indeed, arguments over what kind of cultural forms and practices might be called modern were fierce. But these quarrels were about the content of the modern, not about its singularity. The point here is more than just semantic. The supposed singularity of the modern and its fundamental pretense to being unmarked and universal—precisely, in other words, that it was not alternative—was a crucial component of its attractiveness to many in Dar es Salaam in the 1960s.[104] In thinking about the global sixties, one might speculate even that the powerful singularity of the modern as this kind of claim-making category may have been especially pronounced at the time, occurring at the high-water mark of a global confidence in modern development and progress. And yet, if this global horizon was one key aspect of the meanings of the modern in the cultural controversies of Dar es Salaam's long sixties, this was always mediated through and bound up with the gendered, generational, and material struggles marking life in the capital during that first postcolonial decade.[105]

A Methodological Point: New Sources for Postcolonial African Histories

Researched on three continents, this book is based upon a wide range of sources, including government and party archives, officially published reports and pamphlets, newspapers and magazines, letters to the editor, student journals, university records, memoirs, and interviews. One of these kinds of sources, the press, proved particularly central both to Dar es Salaam's public debates around culture in the 1960s and to my analyses of them. It is also a source base that, for all its richness, has until recently had a rather marginal career within African studies, owing in part to the authenticating status of oral history in the field. As David Cohen, Stephen Miescher, and Luise White point out, oral history and its attendant quest for the authentic "African voice" had, by the 1990s, come to assume a curious and dominant position in the field: "A transcendent status by which [oral testimonies] could stand by themselves as authoritative accounts of lived experience, unmediated and uncorrected."[106] As I hope to show here, critical use of the rich but underutilized source base that is the press can, in this context, open up some important possibilities for writing postcolonial histories of Africa.[107]

The landscape of Tanzania's press through the 1960s was dominated by four major dailies, even as it included scores of smaller weekly and monthly publications.[108] Two of the dailies were published in English, two in Kiswahili. Two were controlled by the state; the other two were privately owned and, until 1972, when newspapers were consolidated into state-run publications, enjoyed significant latitude in hosting criticism of official policy, particularly on social and cultural matters. Uhuru and its English-language sister publication, the Nationalist, were owned and operated by the ruling party, TANU, as mouthpieces for official perspectives; their print runs in the late sixties were thirty thousand and twenty-six thousand, respectively, although the Nationalist often did not sell out.[109] If the Nationalist, as the least popular of the four dailies, was read primarily by a political and business elite as a way of keeping up to date on government policy, Uhuru was much more widely distributed, not least through the party's nationwide ten-house cell system.

The Standard, with a print run of twenty-seven thousand by the end of the 1960s, served a direct readership of those with some knowledge of English, a group that in Dar es Salaam was wider than might be expected.[110] Founded in 1930 as the colonial paper of record, it was owned, successively, by the Kenyan East African Standard Ltd. and LOHNRO multinationals before undergoing partial nationalization in 1970 and a forced merger with the Nationalist in 1972.[111] The Standard's staff included Africans and Europeans and was emblematic in many ways of the slow pace of Africanization at the upper levels of management in the first decade of independence: although much of its reporting personnel was either Tanzanian or from other parts of East Africa, its managing editors through the 1960s were European. In 1970, Nyerere placed the paper under government ownership and personally appointed as editor Frene Ginwala, a South African Indian in exile for her prominent involvement in the African National Congress and in international socialist politics (in the 1990s Ginwala became the first speaker of the post-apartheid South African Parliament). Promoting a line to the left of the state and importing expatriate socialists as writers, Ginwala maintained the Standard's relative independence vis-à-vis official policy but reportedly generated a near-mutiny among the paper's Tanzanian reporters, who viewed her brief tenure as dictatorial and dogmatic.[112] After Ginwala was forced out in 1971, the paper gained its first Tanzanian managing editor in the person of her assistant, Sammy Mdee.[113]

The fourth daily in Dar es Salaam in the 1960s, the most popular of all, was Ngurumo (The thunder), which had a print run that peaked late in the decade at forty thousand.[114] Founded on the eve of independence by the South Asian businessman Randhir Thaker, the paper was sympathetic to nationalist interests—politics that earned Thaker the presence of numerous high-level government and party officials at his funeral in 1965 and the title of "a brown African" in his obituary in the TANU press.[115] By the mid-1960s Ngurumo was tremendously popular as a tabloid with a distinct flair for local news that appealed to its lower-class audience. Eschewing the international news that was a central part of the coverage of the other three dailies, Ngurumo's pages were filled with stories of people struggling to make ends meet in town as well as with sensationalist roving reporter tales featuring the sexual shenanigans of the capital's wealthy, a genre I analyze in chapter 4. If Ngurumo tended not to explicitly oppose political and economic policy as formulated at the highest levels of TANU, like the Standard it did not shy away from either initiating polite criticism of the implementation of policy or hosting opinions that were sometimes vigorously critical of official initiatives, notably those having to do with culture.

Indeed, the publishing of readers' opinions constituted a crucial dimension of the press during this period. Each of the four dailies, but particularly the Standard and Ngurumo, boasted strikingly vibrant letters to the editor pages.[116] Among TYL members charged with policing many of the cultural initiatives in Dar es Salaam, the Standard's "Readers' Forum" earned such notoriety as a site of critical comment that the league held a demonstration outside the paper's offices at the conclusion of one of its campaigns. Ngurumo and Uhuru solicited not only letters to the editor, but poetry in the long-standing Kiswahili shairi tradition. The vast majority of contributors lived in Dar es Salaam, but the wide variation of facility in Standard English and Kiswahili exhibited in the letters suggests a range in educational background among the writers. Participating as a writer or co-composer (for letters were sometimes written collectively) in these readers' fora involved not only making a point but also performing a certain kind of public self. Often writing in prose calculated to variously demonstrate rhetorical sophistication, education, social status, moral uprightness, civic responsibility, or mastery of older traditions of verbal jousting, letter writers put themselves on paper with an evident enthusiasm for the form.

This observation resonates with recent work on the importance of cultures of reading and writing in various African colonial contexts, work illustrating the kinds of status and pleasure that accompanied participation in textual worlds.[117] It also provides an illustration of Benedict Anderson's influential insights on the critical place of newspapers in the constitution of national publics (although given the realities of newspaper distribution outlined below, the scope of the public imagined in readers' letters in this case was Dar es Salaam as often as it was national).[118] Referencing and challenging other contributors' letters and thus helping constitute the critical, self-referential mass needed to constitute a named debate, letter writers often expressed the sense that their interventions on urgent issues of the day connected them to an interested community of anonymous others. As one contributor to the debate in 1969 over the reform of the marriage law put it, "As views and opinions on the proposed marriage code continue to pour into your office, I wish that mine should emerge on the surface to be read nationwide."[119]

Any use of the press as a source must take into account literacy, reach, and the broader issue, crucial in African contexts, of how newspapers were used and engaged in everyday urban life. Arguing against a view of literacy and illiteracy as all-encompassing and completely opposed states, Isabel Hofmeyr contends that Africans who are illiterate still participate in a "documentary culture" in which written texts are critically engaged.[120] As part of pathbreaking work on vampire stories in the late colonial Ugandan press, White describes how newspapers circulated in Kampala in the 1950s:

> Virtually all newspapers were read by more than one person, and many more were read aloud, translated, summarized, amended and made fun of by a variety of readers for a variety of audiences. Even newspapers written in languages that required years of schooling to read could be read out

loud in a few minutes to illiterates. The crowds . . . might not be newspaper readers, but they knew what newspapers said. Where newspapers
were sold without subscription—where all purchases of newspapers were
on the street—the need of all but the most intensely subsidized to appeal
to popular issues was great: popular stories were in demand. Newspaper
reading in Africa is a social event: not every reader was a purchaser, as
many people read newspapers on the street without buying them and
many more read newspapers handed around to friends, neighbors, and
kin.[121]

White's description resonates strongly with the case of Dar es Salaam
in the 1960s, when news, opinion, and rumor replayed in the press often became, in the words of one Tanzanian journalist of the time, "the
talk of the town."[122] The fact that each copy of a paper would circulate
among many is reflected in the rates on literacy relative to estimated
numbers of readership. A pronounced gap existed between literacy rates
nationwide (in either English or Kiswahili), which was estimated to be
29 percent in the late 1960s, and in Dar es Salaam, at 61 percent.[123]
(Perhaps underscoring the variability of such estimates, in 1975, after
major expansion of primary schooling in the 1960s and several years
of a highly successful adult literacy project, national literacy rates were
reportedly 56 percent for women and 66 percent for men.[124] In Dar es
Salaam, the rates would have been higher than in the nation at large, but
the rate for women still lower than that for men.) The literacy gap between the capital and the rest of the country, along with the related fact
that over half of the print runs of all four major dailies were sold in the
capital, combined to make regular newspaper reading overwhelmingly
a phenomenon characteristic of Dar es Salaam.[125] Working from data
collected by J. C. Condon in the late 1960s, Martin Sturmer estimates
that each paper sold in Dar es Salaam was read by at least two others
and that "40% of the 200,000 people living in the capital [in 1968] read
a daily on a regular basis."[126] In a poll conducted by Condon in 1968,
70 percent of Dar es Salaam's residents said they read a newspaper at
least two or three times a week. While such results are likely exaggerated, they are nonetheless further evidence of the positive associations
newspaper reading carried as a desirable social activity in the capital
(the self-reported rates of press consumption outside of Dar es Salaam
were considerably lower in the poll).[127] Once public readings and street-
corner discussions of newspapers are factored in, one can conclude that
newspapers and the stories, opinions, arguments, gossip, and tales of the

town they contained were a vital component of public culture in Dar es Salaam in the sixties.

Viewed as such, the press becomes a uniquely rich lens through which to analyze the public debates over culture that loomed large in Dar es Salaam during that first decade of independence—particularly since letters to the editor constituted a central vehicle and clearinghouse for these debates. The layered, fraught character of cultural politics in the 1960s that emerges so richly in the debates in the press of that era is a complexity often effaced in oral testimonies a generation later. In interviews conducted with older residents of Dar es Salaam at the beginning of the twenty-first century, I was struck by the consistency with which the early postcolonial period was cast as a "time of utamaduni," an era of authenticity free of the problems of the excessive imitation (kuiga) of the West perceived to be wracking Dar es Salaam since the 1990s.[128] As I discuss in the conclusion, the last ten years in Dar es Salaam have seen a renewed intensity of debates around global style and the crises of youth and gender that it was seen to represent. These debates exhibited both continuities and important differences from those of the 1960s but had a tendency to make tropes of an earlier era of authenticity all the more irresistible. In this context and read against a range of other sources, the public forums of the early postcolonial press open up a path to recapturing some of the period's contested vocabularies, deeply felt anxieties, and rich textures of the landscape of urban public culture in a more layered way than almost any other body of evidence.

Taken together, this evidence suggests a broader importance for the press in writing postcolonial African histories than has typically been acknowledged. Recently, both Stephen Ellis and Luise White have offered vigorous defenses of the press as a historical source. Among the most important of their respective insights is the reframing of newspapers, in Ellis's words, as "written forms of radio troittoir," referring to the much-discussed networks of rumor prominent in urban Africa and called "pavement radio."[129] Tracing vampire stories in the Ugandan press of the fifties, White elaborates a similar point. Having described the surprising breadth of newspaper circulation and the depth of public engagement with them, she goes on to theorize the press in relation to orality. "There is little point in seeking an orality that is free of the written," White writes. "Stories traveled between the two media, and speakers used elements from written and oral versions of a story to depict urban life, their own memories, and the colonial situation. . . . The lines between oral and written are not hard and fast."[130] The suggestion that newspapers and the oral commentary surrounding them were "inseparable," each bleeding into the other, is crucial for situating the public forums of Dar es Salaam's press in the sixties as access points to, as White puts it, "how people construct and construe their public culture."[131] Indeed, in the case at hand, I often found that these public forums afford richer views of the shape of the urban public cultures of the 1960s than oral testimonies forty years later, which were frequently overdetermined by the shape of cultural politics in the 1990s and by the unique power of the notion of the past as a time of cultural authenticity. As a result, my book relies much more heavily on the debates in the period's press than on interviews. As sources that embody the mutually embedded character of postcolonial political power, everyday urban life, and transnational imaginaries, the public forums of Dar es Salaam's press help further my aim here of working at the intersection of state power, urban politics of youth and gender, and global visions of modern style.

The Chapters

Chapter 1 examines the emergence of the postcolonial state's national cultural project. While this project was announced as a radical break from the colonial order, I argue that it was based upon strikingly similar assumptions about culture, tradition, and modernization and that it continued the colonial state's deeply ambiguous relationship with the city. After tracing the fortunes of the postcolonial institutions charged with developing and promoting national culture, I analyze the shifting relationship between strands of the project devoted variously to making "tribal" customs and tradition national and selecting elements of national culture based upon an explicit commitment to modernization. In the second half of the chapter, I take a different tack, exploring the constitution of national culture against a set of supposedly decadent forms and practices thought to be proliferating in urban areas, especially Dar es Salaam. Closely following the heated debates that erupted over prominent campaigns against indecent dress and soul music in the late 1960s, I highlight the emergence in these debates of struggles not only over the meaning of national culture and the status of African American culture, but also over what qualified as modern. I suggest that the national cultural project—particularly in its proscriptive form—was central to the vilification of the city that accompanied the rise of the rural as a touchstone of official ideology in the late 1960s and early 1970s. Emerging in the context of competing invocations of transnational scope, however, this was a vision that was unsettled by the competing cosmopolitan imaginaries marshaled by Dar es Salaam's youth.

In chapter 2 I explore, as a way of entering into a broader investigation of struggles over women, work, sex, and masculinity in late-sixties Dar es Salaam, the heavily gendered aspects of the serial campaigns banning allegedly indecent dress. Although these ostensibly national-cultural campaigns technically targeted both men's and women's dress, women overwhelmingly bore the brunt of enforcement, which often included physical attacks on those wearing miniskirts. Analyzing the outpouring of public discourse on the issue, I explore how, for many young men in the capital, the miniskirt came to stand in for a complex political economy of sex and accumulation in town, one in which they perceived themselves the losers. But the miniskirt was also an intensely contested sign, and as I track shifts between campaigns in 1968 and in 1970–71, I illustrate how official moves to further institutionalize the bans saw them challenged on the state's own terms.

In chapter 3 I focus on the University College, Dar es Salaam, an institution important to cultural politics in the capital in the sixties and to struggles over youth during that decade. Founded upon official hopes that it would produce servants of the nation, the University College also generated increasing fears among state officials that it was turning out graduates poised to challenge the establishment. Examining the controversies surrounding a National Service initiative of 1966 aimed at university students and the rise late in the sixties of a vibrant internationalist left on campus, I chart the struggles between anxious officials, rival groups of students and faculty, and cadres of the TYL and the National Service, who were being promoted by officials as the embodiments of a new corps of citizen-youth. I argue that struggles at and over the University College were catalysts and key sites for larger contests over the politically significant category of youth. In different ways, both the National Service crisis and the debates over the campus left showcase the ambivalence, insecurity, and unevenness marking the reproduction of an early postcolonial elite. The case of the campus left also offers a lens through which to view the ways in which imaginaries and identifications of transnational scope troubled official efforts to nationalize youth.

In chapter 4 I consider the heated debate over state attempts to overhaul Tanzania's colonial-era marriage law, a struggle that dominated public talk in Dar es Salaam at decade's end. Proposed both to mark a break with the colonial and to be a sign of a modern, progressive Tanzania on the world stage, the reforms became a site for a diverse set of struggles, pleas, and grievances. Dominating the debate early on, wives and husbands (often elite) engaged one another through appeals to different sides of official discourse in material struggles over authority and control of resources within marriages. But interrupting this axis of struggle, young bachelors attempted to steer the debate beyond the parameters of the reforms to anxieties over high bridewealth, a perceived surplus of women who were nonetheless out of reach, and the conspicuous consumption of elite men about town. In examining the various angles, agendas, and vocabularies running through the marriage debate, I use the episode to open an additional window on the nexus of tensions along lines of gender, generation, and wealth marking Dar es Salaam's long sixties. In addition, by attending to the notably jocular character of the debate in Parliament, I confront the confluence of sex and the political in public discourse, both in the marriage debate and, more briefly, in sensationalist journalism on the sexual liaisons of the capital's new elites. If this confluence had the potential for eliciting satirical critique of new forms of accumulation, it was a critique riven with ambiguity; indeed, it offers a reminder of the variable limits of different kinds of challenges to some of Dar es Salaam's emerging postcolonial hierarchies.

In its approach to this sixties moment in one postcolonial, African capital my book regards the contests over culture as central sites for the working out of some of the decade's critical urban social struggles. They also offer clues to the elaboration of and engagement with state power in urban areas. Along the way, the study uncovers a history of contest over ideas of African culture that have proved tenacious in shaping notions of the continent up to the present day. If this tenacity of particular ideas of Africa has contributed to a forgetting of the vigorously contested nature of their history, my book is aimed at recapturing a piece of that past.

National Culture and
Its Others in a Cosmopolitan Capital

Addressing Tanganyika's Parliament in December 1962, exactly one year after formal independence, President Julius K. Nyerere spoke of dance. In what would become one of his most-cited statements for decades to come, he invited his audience of fellow, largely mission-educated elites to reminisce with him:

> When we were at school, we were taught to sing the songs of the European. How many of us were taught the songs of the Wanyamwezi or of the Wahehe? Many of us have learned to dance the "rumba" or the "chacha-cha," to "rock-en-roll" and to "twist" and even to dance the "waltz" and the "foxtrot." But how many of us can dance, have even heard of, the *Gombe Sugu*, the *Mangala*, the *Konge*, *Nyang'umumi*, *Kiduo* or *Lele Mama*? Most of us can play the guitar, the piano, or other European musical instruments. How many Africans in Tanganyika, particularly among the educated, can play the African drums? How many can play the *Nanga*, or the *Marimba*, the *Kilamzi*, *Ligomgo*, or the *Imangala*? And even though we dance and play the piano, how often does that dancing—even if it is "rock-en-roll" or "twist"—how often does it really give us the sort of thrill we get from dancing the *mganda* or the *gombe sugu*, even though the music may be no more than the shaking of pebbles in a tin? It is hard for any man to get much real excitement from dances and music which are not in his own blood.[1]

In the context of this situation and because "culture is the essence and spirit of any nation," Nyerere argued, his latest proclamation was crucial: the creation of a Ministry of National Culture and Youth charged with "seek[ing] out the best of the traditions and customs of all our tribes and mak[ing] them part of our national culture." This "entirely new" ministry, said the president, represented a radical break from the colonial past and a critical part of the nation-building tasks at hand: "A country which lacks its own culture is no more than a collection of people without the spirit which makes them a nation. Of the crimes of colonialism there is none worse than the attempt to make us believe we had no indigenous culture of our own; or that what we did have was worthless."[2]

In framing the new initiative as a rupture with a colonial situation defined by wholesale deligitimation of indigenous culture, Nyerere powerfully captured twin axioms shared by the many national cultural projects springing up around the continent in the early 1960s: first, that because they were inhibited under colonial rule, efforts to articulate and promote tradition were new; and, second, that the primary scene or raison d'être of the national cultural project was indeed an overcoming of the colonial situation. Rhetorically compelling and widely shared, both assertions nonetheless entailed important occlusions. Obscured in the declaration of a radical break with the colonial past was a complex colonial history of many of the positions that would be articulated under the banner of national culture. This was a history marked, not least, by efforts on the part of elite Africans and colonial officials alike to wrestle with the questions of indigeneity and foreignness embedded in Nyerere's speech and to define and promote versions of tradition much like those that would become staples of national cultural discourse after independence. As Kelly Askew has put it in reference to Tanzania in the early-sixties, the identification and promotion of tradition was "a venture pursued in true colonial fashion."[3] The fact that these positions were being developed in a Dar es Salaam that was crisscrossed by transnational ideas, images, and cultural products made these negotiations all the more complex.

If this first founding assertion of national cultural projects has been effectively complicated (albeit in some cases implicitly) by histories of the production of tradition under colonial conditions,[4] the second is often taken for granted in much popular and academic thinking on questions of postcolonial national culture.[5] Indeed, it seems natural that national culture in the immediate wake of colonial domination should be imagined in reference to cultural loss under colonial rule. And yet a close look at the trajectories of Tanzania's national cultural project in its heyday suggests that overcoming a colonial past was only one—and perhaps not even the most primary—scene of national culture. As I begin to argue in this chapter, national culture in Tanzania in the 1960s was fundamentally as much a vehicle for negotiating anxieties about urban order, gender chaos, and undisciplined youth in a cosmopolitan capital as a tool for overcoming a colonial past.

In an additional irony, if in Nyerere's launch the national cultural project was imagined as a promotional endeavor, the activities of the various administrative units housing it (four different ministries in the 1960s alone) were notoriously thin, underfunded, and poorly organized.[6] The late 1960s and 1970s saw national culture being taken up instead as a rallying cry and a framework for social action *against* a range of cultural practices and icons deemed antithetical to it, including wigs, cosmetics, miniskirts, tight trousers, bell-bottoms, Maasai traditional dress, beauty contests, soul music, and Afro hairstyles. Particularly for Tanzania's rapidly growing urban population in this period, many of the most prominent manifestations of the presence of the state in everyday life were its proscriptive cultural initiatives. The banning campaigns were more than simply an outgrowth of a fully formed vision of national culture. Rather, the image of a decadent, feminized city that such operations helped to consolidate and maintain was a crucial foil against which national culture was constituted.

Furthermore, contrary to many popular conceptions of national cultural visions, a reference point of tradition was only one part of even the promotional side of Tanzania's national cultural project. Obvious by the late 1960s, as Askew has shown, national culture was also characterized by meanings and emphases that had little to do with the range of traditional associations outlined in Nyerere's speech and rather more to do with avowedly modernizationist visions of cultural development.[7] If existing treatments of Tanzanian national culture have explained this curious coexistence as a temporal succession from one imperative to another (contradictory) one, the promotion of tradition making way for modernizationist impulses, I suggest an alternate reading.[8] Drawing inspiration from work like Partha Chatterjee's that has attempted to imagine the colonial birth of tradition as a decidedly modern project, I argue that references to the traditional and the modern constituted an enduring two-sidedness to Tanzanian national culture—a doubling evident in nationalist constructions of culture not only after independence, but also, as I illustrated in the introduction, in the late colonial period.[9] While changes in emphasis in national cultural discourse are certainly evident and important, I interpret these trajectories less as the replacement of one reigning imperative by a contradictory successor than as shifts in the idioms through which attempts to imagine a simultaneously modern and authentic national culture were expressed.

But what exactly were the contours of the modern, of tradition, of a national culture constituted around these idioms? These parameters were always contested. In the proscriptive cultural initiatives that increasingly took national culture to the cosmopolitan streets of Dar es Salaam in the late 1960s, young Tanzanians seized upon bans on popular markers of urban style to express ideas about authenticity, tradition, and modern style that were often at odds with official ones. If debates about these campaigns showcased the extraordinary, singular power of the modern as an idiom to make certain kinds of claims about culture, the question of what exactly qualified as modern was far from settled. Indeed, in the campaigns against forms of dress and music I consider in the second half of this chapter, official attempts to distinguish the state's vision of the cultural contours of a modern Tanzania from claims upon the same from supposed decadent quarters were far from secure. Such debates unfolded in a context marked by competing transnational imaginaries, as official architects of national culture and their myriad challengers alike drew on global references that were often difficult to reconcile.

Finally, there is a generational aspect of the story to highlight here. If Nyerere launched the national cultural project with reference to the perceived cultural preferences of his own cohort of nationalists, for much of Tanzania's long sixties it was deployed against a specter of disorderly, decadent, urban youth of the next generation. The nationalists who came to power in Tanganyika in 1961 were, as in most other decolonizing contexts in Africa, a youthful, colonial-educated elite whose political victory can be partly understood as a triumph over the chiefs of the Native Authorities. If, in a context of British colonial "indirect rule," the latter men had achieved their power through control over the signs and institutions of tradition, then the young nationalists of the 1940s and 1950s had mounted their challenge by struggling to gain access to the signs, institutions, and accoutrements of European modernity as passes to new forms of wealth, status, and autonomy.[10] Nyerere himself was educated at the elite Tabora secondary school before moving on to obtain a bachelor's degree at Makerere University and a master of arts degree at Edinburgh. If Nyerere was unique in degree, his path was the norm for much of Tanzania's political class. In chiding his cohort of nationalist elites in Parliament in 1962 for their familiarity with the foxtrot and estrangement from the Gombe Sugu, Nyerere was therefore making a curious and complex statement, for it was in large part through successful appropriation of these markers of European cultural competence that this group had achieved its power.

Now in government, this first nationalist generation confronted its own youth question. Burgeoning with young migrants, a city like Dar es Salaam presented plenty of fodder for both fantasy and frustration of the efforts of its youth to move up in the world as well as competing transnational imaginaries on which both the state and its young could draw to imagine youth. Aware—and wary—of the social and discursive power of youth, officials constructed youth as both promise and threat. Writing of late twentieth-century Africa, Jean and John Comaroff have suggested that youth is marked by an "intrinsic bipolarity, a doubling." On the one hand, youth have been used as the "infantry of adult state-craft" and are often portrayed as embodying utopian hopes of better-ment. On the other hand, youth is a force that is not always easy to control, one which is "liable to seize the initiative from their elders and betters," and thus is also a dangerous category represented as embody-ing all manner of social pathology.[11] Analyzed most fully in chapter 3 with reference to struggles between state and student over the univer-sity, this is an ambiguity that also rears its head in the national cultural campaigns considered here. Indeed, the national cultural project be-came an important site of struggles surrounding efforts by the political class of the 1960s, the first generation of nationalists, to negotiate its own relationship with youth. From the initial yoking of national culture with youth in a single ministerial portfolio through the use of the TYL as the primary enforcers of so many of the banning campaigns of the late sixties, the national cultural project served as a crucial vehicle for the ar-ticulation of a vision of a healthy citizen-youth battling its decadent alter ego.[12] At the same time, the debates that erupted around the banning campaigns also served as platforms for young Tanzanians to articulate identifications with very different visions of global youth aesthetics and style that challenged any would-be official monopoly on youth.

My aim in this chapter is to examine what happened as the national cultural project was contested in a cosmopolitan Dar es Salaam. As this story unfolds, my focus moves from rehearsing shifts in the meanings of national culture within the project's positive or promotional content to what I argue was the more prominent, proscriptive face of national culture in Dar es Salaam: the banning campaigns of the late 1960s and early 1970s. The heated debates surrounding some key targeted forms and practices—particularly so-called indecent dress and soul music—showcase both the ways in which national culture was defined nega-tively against these targets and the terms upon which it was contested.

National Culture: The Promotional Project

The establishment of a Ministry of National Culture and Youth may have marked a swift and symbolically powerful shift at the commanding heights of the Tanganyikan state, but the logistics of actually developing a national culture were fraught with difficulties. The process of appointing a commissioner for culture to supervise on a daily basis what was known as the Culture Division took six months. Less than a year later, in April 1964, the Ministry of National Culture and Youth was disbanded, the Culture Division being incorporated into the new Ministry of Community Development and National Culture. Even as the division's ministerial home remained stable for three years, its appointed heads did not: between 1963 and 1965 alone, four ministers and as many principal secretaries came and went. In 1968 and 1969 the Culture Division moved ministries twice more: first, to the Ministry of Regional Administration and Rural Development, then to the Ministry of National Education and Culture. The organizational overhauls continued into the 1970s, the most extensive of them bringing the Culture Division full circle with a reestablishment of a Ministry of National Culture and Youth in 1974; this move was based, perhaps ironically, on a commissioned study by the U.S.-based consulting firm of McKinsey and Company.[13]

Organization was not the only problem. The Culture Division's share of the budget was consistently, dramatically low, even by the standards of the Tanzanian government, and this was so particularly when it was sharing a ministerial portfolio, as was the case throughout most of this period. In the five-year period from 1964 to 1969 (what would be looked back upon as the fat years for the Culture Division, if not its most effective ones), 337,900 British pounds were allocated to the division. The next five years, 1969–74, during which the division shared a ministry with Education, funding for Culture entered a gradual decline. Of the 297,136,300 Tanzanian shillings (slightly under 15 million British pounds) budgeted for the ministry as a whole for that period, the Culture Division had access to a mere 6,052,300 shillings (302,615 pounds), approximately one-fiftieth of the ministry's funds.[14]

Underfunding had a severe impact on what the Culture Division was able to accomplish. Proposed in the form of five-year plans, the division's major projects during the sixties and seventies included the expansion of the National Stadium, the building of regional museums, funding for antiquities collection, and the establishment of an art institute in Dar es Salaam. During the first five-year plan (1964–69) only one of these projects made any progress, and minimal at that, consisting of "preliminary surveys" conducted for the art institute. The next five years saw a few of the projects begun, but only the funding of the collection of antiquities and an originally unplanned project, the construction of a stadium on Zanzibar, were completed.[15] In terms of these large-scale projects, the work of the Culture Division was directed, even in the planning stages, toward institutions with long histories in the colonial period, such as museums and archaeology, and ones that were centerpieces of colonial knowledge about Africa; add to this the minimal amount of work done to reshape these institutions, and the result was that much of the Culture Division's work in this area consisted of struggling to merely maintain the institutions' essentially colonial form and content. As Askew has convincingly argued in assessing this situation, the much-touted "cultural revolution" fell far short of being revolutionary.[16]

The correspondence of Culture Division officials in the 1960s suggests that the division attempted to deal with its organizational and monetary woes by operating in as decentralized a manner as possible. This often took the form of making use of the resources of other ministries wherever possible. In August 1964, L. H. Mandara, the commissioner for culture, lamented that because of "various problems" the ministry continued to be unable to establish its own "magazine of culture"; however, he had arranged for any articles on cultural matters ("such as poetry, songs, ngoma dances, stories, riddles, traditional medicine, bridewealth, historical artifacts . . . , traditions and customs, etc.") to be published in the Ministry for Information's monthly magazine, Nchi Yetu, and he strongly encouraged officials at all levels to write.[17]

Somewhat more systematically, in 1965 the division, under the direction of Commissioner H. L. T. Chopeta and with the apparent urging of Prime Minister Rashidi Kawawa, began encouraging the formation of cultural committees at regional, district, and village levels. These committees, to be composed of area government officials and local representatives of various TANU wings (the TANU Women's League, or UWT; TYL, the youth wing; etc.), were charged with the development and promotion of art, music, and sport.[18] Though slowly at first, by the end of 1966 cultural committees in some numbers were forming, meeting regularly, and submitting minutes of their meetings to Dar es Salaam. At the ostensible center, the Culture Division's daily work consisted largely of soliciting reports from various groups at local levels—from the cultural committees and also from groups like festival organizers—and, for the higher-ups in the division, of patronizing various high-profile cultural activities around the capital.[19] Relatively powerless in terms of direct resource allocation, the Culture Division was nevertheless the source of legitimacy and symbolic patronage for groups like the cultural committees. Legitimacy flowed the other way, too, however, for the committees; although they were made up almost entirely of government or party personnel, they were regarded as a success in the fulfillment of a new imperative of "self-reliance" sweeping officialdom in the late sixties. As L. A. Mbughuni, the promoter of arts and crafts in the Culture Division, recalled, "The only means of compensating the loss [of funding for large projects] was to turn to the people themselves in a call for self-help."[20]

But whatever the ups and downs of the Culture Division, national culture, as official discourse and representation and even in the form of state-commissioned academic work, flourished in public discourse in Tanzania during this period. Even in the Culture Division's most explicit attempts to take up a vanguard position with regard to cultural policy (and these moments were few), its statements and interventions should be viewed as always already embedded in a wider, though still largely official, discursive field. For the 1960s and 1970s saw national culture (or *utamaduni wa kitaifa* in Kiswahili) as a concept and frame appearing prominently in official statements, publications, and performances at all levels of government and the party, particularly after the Arusha Declaration of 1967. Emerging from various levels of multiple institutional sites, this output was far from homogenous, instead showcasing an uneasy coexistence of sometimes strikingly different variations on national culture.

Two overlapping discourses of national culture illustrate well these different visions: first, a genre of writing, visual representation, and performance that I call the "customs and traditions" model of representing the cultures of Tanzania's "tribes"; and second, the way in which culture figured in a discourse of modern development increasingly dominant in Tanzania through the sixties and into the seventies.[21] Although the two discourses partially map on both to a shift in emphasis in national cultural development beginning in the late 1960s and to origins in different institutional spaces, they more often coexisted in tension with each other as two sides of the same coin.

As noted earlier, in his speech inaugurating the Ministry for National Culture and Youth in 1962, President Nyerere suggested how the new ministry was to carry out its mandate: "I want it to seek out the best of the traditions and customs of all our tribes and make them a part of our national culture."[22] Indeed, while each of the dances, songs, and musical instruments Nyerere recited for the parliamentarians in his speech—as opposed to the foxtrot, waltz, and rock 'n' roll—was a form associated with a tribe, the frame within which they were to be recuperated and remembered was to be unambiguously national.

Attention to "tribal traditions and customs" did indeed become a mainstay of national cultural work, especially in research sponsored and promoted by the Culture Division and in school curricula. In encouraging officials to submit articles on culture for publication, the commissioner for culture in 1964 suggested, as noted above, the following list of topics: "poetry, songs, ngoma [dances], stories, riddles, traditional medicine, bridewealth, antiquities found wherever you live, traditions and customs, etc."[23] By the end of 1974, over half of the eighty or so division-approved research projects either completed or in progress were explicitly devoted to the study of various traditions and customs of various ethnic groups. (The other half of the approved projects consisted largely of states-of-the-field reports, research connected to the promotion of Kiswahili, and the work—generally of the liberal-nationalist vein dominant in the mid- to late 1960s—of the university's history department).[24]

Consistently organized around a set of familiar tropes, this traditions and customs literature (or, as it was known in Kiswahili, mila na desturi) achieved the status of a genre during the 1960s. Mila na Desturi za Wasangu, Wasafwa na Wasagara, written by J. S. Mwakipesile, a member of the division's directorate of research on traditions and customs, illustrates the genre's defining features. In this text, the cultural practices of each of three ethnic groups—the Wasangu, Wasafwa, and the Wasagara—are narrated as discrete customs, relatively unchanging on the one hand and yet definitively confined to a temporal past on the other. The study of the Wasagara, for instance, is organized into sections entitled "Belief," "Witchcraft," "Customs of the Wasagara," "Food of the Wasagara," "The Girl," "Bridewealth," "Divorce," "Death," "The Wasagara House," "Wasagara Clothing," and so on.[25] The presentations of these components of bounded, so-called tribal societies ironically resembled nothing so much as early colonial ethnography, sometimes of the very same groups.[26] Indeed, notwithstanding the frequent declarations on the part of officials that colonialism featured, in the words of Nyerere, "the attempt to make us believe we had no indigenous culture of our own," the traditions and customs genre had a colonial history—and not only in the ethnographies of European anthropologists, but also in accounts of indigenous culture written by Africans and sponsored by the colonial government as part of postwar cultural policy.

These latter accounts were largely produced in the 1950s under the East African Literature Bureau's (EALB) Custom and Tradition in East Africa series.[27] Founded in 1948 under the guidance of the famed Kenyan settler and author Elspeth Huxley and with money that accompanied the colonial policy reforms of the 1940s, the EALB placed the promotion of "indigenous literature written by Africans and with an African background" high on its agenda.[28] By yoking its definition of indigeneity not only to African authorship (insufficient in itself, in the EALB's vision), but also to an imperative of "African background," the bureau marked out the Custom and Tradition series as the domain for which African authors would be sought and outside of which they would generally not be solicited.

Notwithstanding these strictures, a number of first-time authors responded enthusiastically to the call to submit these "stud[ies] of tribal life from within."[29] EALB administrators thought that an enthusiasm among budding African authors for writing customs and traditions texts was a natural one, although there is some evidence that the EALB received numerous submissions ("nearly every day," according to one report) that did not match the kind of African authorship the bureau was trying to cultivate.[30] African authors who did end up being published in the Custom and Tradition series tended to be mission-educated, Christian converts and budding white-collar nationalists who would not uncommonly go on to careers in the postindependent establishment. Examples from Tanganyika included Y. N. Yongolo, the author of *Maisha na Desturi za Wanyamwezi* (Life and customs of the Nyamwezi) (1953) and a trainee at the Moravian Mission's Teaching Training School in Tabora District; and Mathias E. Mnyampala, who wrote on Gogo history while serving as a Native Authority tax clerk in the late colonial period before embarking on a career as a magistrate and prominent Swahili poet in the 1960s.[31]

Circulating widely among literate Tanganyikans in the 1950s, books were generally small, often pocketbook size, and at one or two shillings, relatively inexpensive. In Nairobi, Dar es Salaam, and Kampala, EALB books were sold at commercial bookshops and lent at the libraries attached to each branch office. Outside the capitals, the bureau set up a wide borrowing system over the four territories through a network of "bookbox libraries" alongside a "postal library service" through which individuals not within reach of one of the bookboxes could register, for a one-time deposit of ten shillings, to borrow books sent and returned through the post.[32] In Tanganyika the bookboxes remained the most popular way of accessing EALB texts through the 1950s. By 1956, 100 bookbox libraries operated throughout the territory, lending 46,850 books in 1955–56 alone. By comparison, likely because of the cost of the service, only 301 Tanganyika members—generally young teachers and clerks with secondary education—were registered for the postal library service in the same year.[33] Though apparently not as popular among readers as the EALB's how-to series of instructional books, the Custom and Tradition series accounted for approximately 10 percent of all volumes printed and a similar percentage of those sold in 1952.[34]

The EALB's Custom and Tradition studies exhibited many of the features that would characterize postcolonial mila na desturi literature. Almost without exception, they were built around a pair of fundamental assumptions: that the natural repository of tradition was in the tribe and that a familiarity with tribal tradition was a crucial ingredient for, as the EALB's director put it, "building up a balanced attitude to the complexities of modern life."[35] Not all customs and traditions were deemed equally appropriate in achieving this balance. A series of tips for African authors on how to approach describing tribal practices implied the importance of this distinction as it urged authors to be aware of the difference, "found almost everywhere," between "the magic which is good" and "witchcraft (black magic or sorcery) which is bad."[36] Working through a list of bounded components of cultural practice that closely matched that of postcolonial mila na desturi texts, the EALB's African authors treated them variably, presenting some of these components as relatively ahistorical and static and others as characterized by their mutability. Customs evaluated as positive and healthy contributions compatible with the modern changes Tanganyika was living through tended to be presented in the habitual tense as stable and unchanging; others, notably so-called witchcraft and the killing of illegitimate twins, were consistently written of in the past tense, situated historically as unfortunate stumbling blocks that were susceptible to development along modern lines.[37] If these founding elements would be carried into national cultural mila na desturi texts, other key features of this precursor literature would be adjusted under the newly national imperatives of the postcolonial project. Most crucially, the habit of many of the EALB's African authors to pointedly refer to the groups about which they were writing as "nations" (nchi) was replaced by the use of the word "tribe" after independence, including in the several EALB texts that were reissued in the 1960s and 1970s.[38]

The postcolonial circulation of the traditions and customs genre was by no means confined to academic and quasi-academic research, and in the sixties and seventies the phrase mila na desturi became a mantra with a certain currency at all levels of Tanzanian society. Minutes from meetings of cultural committees at regional, district, and village levels suggest that discussion consistently centered on "traditional" medicine, music, song and dance, clothing, and arts and crafts.[39] More visibly, images of so-called traditional, tribal customs were staples of the state-run newspapers, particularly in Nchi Yetu, the Ministry of Information's news and entertainment monthly that served as a mouthpiece of the Culture Division. In January 1968, the editors of Nchi Yetu inaugurated a series on "Tanzania's tribes." Every month for several years the series offered readers a discussion of one of Tanzania's tribes firmly in the traditions and customs genre. Typically written in the habitual present tense, these articles informed readers of the particularities and often the peculiarities of the ngoma dances or marriage practices of distinct ethnic groups, with surprisingly little mention of the nation.[40]

More commonly, however, a sometimes strained attempt was made to reconcile the highlighting of tribal tradition with national culture. Such was the task of the celebrated "village museum." Established in 1966 on the outskirts of the capital, this project consisted of a permanent outdoor exhibit of over ten houses, each constructed "as authentically as possible" in a style corresponding to one of Tanzania's major tribes. A favorite for school field trips since the 1960s, the museum was an attempt to stage the nation as a collection of distinct tribes: building these markedly different houses in a single village, yet retaining their geographic and ethnic referents. Another such attempt was made with the even more highly celebrated National Dance Troupe, which, as Nchi Yetu informed its readers, "plays ngoma from every tribe in Tanzania . . . in order to preserve our Tanzanian ngoma."[41]

But the national cultural project was by no means a back-to-tradition endeavor. For if tribal custom was clearly the raw material for national culture, such custom had to meet certain standards before being celebrated as national. As early as mid-1966, commissioner for culture

The minister of community development and national culture C. Y. Mgonja tours Tanzania's newly established Village Museum in 1966. *Courtesy of the Tanzania Information Service.*

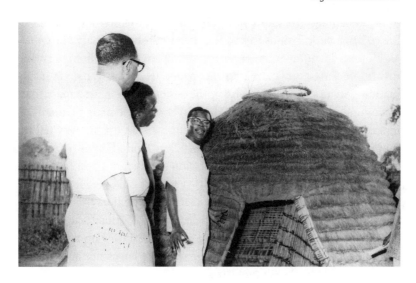

Tanzania's National Dance Troupe performs a ngoma for an audience of dignitaries at the Kilimanjaro Hotel in the mid-1960s. Regularly used for state functions, the Kilimanjaro at the time was Dar es Salaam's most upscale hotel. *Courtesy of the Tanzania Information Service.*

F. J. Mchauru, acting under the orders of the minister of community development and national culture, forwarded to division staff and cultural committees nationwide an article reprinted from *Nchi Yetu* critiquing the work of the Culture Division. The article was written by E. R. Munseri, a longtime journalist from Buhaya in western Tanzania. In the colonial period Munseri had attended Catholic seminary in Uganda and founded a number of short-lived newspapers in his home district, before securing a position after independence at the Tanzania Information Services.[42] A nationalist in the 1950s whose newspapers took a prominently antitribalist line, Munseri was emblematic of a late colonial, mission-educated intellectual with a vision for the new nation hinging on what he would call in his article a "condition of civility." In circulating Munseri's article, Commissioner Mchauru stressed that the piece expressed the author's personal views but nonetheless praised it (or passed on the minister's praise) for its potential to encourage the "development of culture."[43] The article, entitled "Enhancing and Preserving Our Culture," billed itself as a comprehensive plan for national cultural development, which, Munseri suggested, was not being properly attended to by the Culture Division.

At first glance, a number of things seemed to make Munseri's article different from the customs and traditions approach to national culture so prominent in the early 1960s. First, he began the article with a critique of an emphasis on tribal cultures as a continuation of the absence of national unity that reigned prior to independence: "There cannot be any more deception that such and such a tribe in this country is mininational and that it can develop and enhance its own culture without joining and participating in the National Culture of our Republic of Tanzania as a whole." Then Munseri went much further. In outlining "three kinds of work" involved in the national cultural task at hand, Munseri followed a one-sentence statement on collecting traditional artifacts (the first task) with a page-long exhortation of the second task: "To sift and purify [traditions] in order to remove or lessen elements that are inappropriate in that they are shameful or disgusting for a condition of civility and modern development in general." As an example of the sort of "modern development" he envisioned and a striking reminder that the national project itself was being imagined in a transnational frame, Munseri then turned to "the example of Kemal Ataturk."[44] Praising Ataturk's rule, he wrote, "Out of great desire for the development of his country, which was being strongly opposed by many, he used a sword to get rid of shameful elements disgraceful to the nation;

Sukuma snake dancers perform in Dar es Salaam during celebrations on the first anniversary of Tanganyika's independence from Britain, December 1962. *Courtesy of the Tanzania Information Service.*

he banned the turban for men and the veil for women—to straighten and widen the streets of the capital, Istanbul, he used tractors. At first, many hated it, but in the end they saw for themselves the glory of their nation and its increasing success, and they thanked him effusively and called him 'Atatürk,' meaning the Father of the Turkish Nation." Of the "contemptuous customs" Tanzanians should be rid of, Munseri included women's public wailing at deaths, the carving of "cripples" in sculpture, the use of dirty or torn clothes in comedic performances, and ngoma dances that featured snakes and simulated sex acts. In order for "the nation to be respected," these practices must go, Munseri argued, ideally in an "orderly and gradual" fashion, but if necessary, he added, "it would be appropriate to use orders, commands, or even force against those who want to delay our nation's glory."[45]

If Munseri's article seemed heterodox, however, its emphasis on purification of tradition under the sign of modern development contained distinct echoes of many EALB authors' work on customs and tradition. Consider, for instance, Anthony Mochiwa's rather representative argument not only that the few so-called undesirable aspects of (in his case Wazigua) tradition were rapidly changing with what he termed development and civilization, but also that civilization itself was essential to this process: "The degree to which civilization increasingly enters into any country is the degree to which people are able to discern much about [how to better distinguish between] good and bad things."[46] If a modernizationist logic had become enmeshed with the customs and traditions model right from that model's birth, Munseri's article saw its explicit, vigorous foregrounding in a way that was a sign of things to come. In February of 1967 the TANU Executive Council, with Nyerere at its head, unveiled the Arusha Declaration and with it a move to more explicitly socialist policies. Several economic and administrative changes followed on the heels of this announcement, including the nationalization of medium- and large-scale industrial and commercial enterprises, the establishment of a highly touted (but often evaded) "leadership code" that attempted to curb accumulation by the political elite, and an educational plan that would focus on primary school as a terminal curriculum. Also important, however, is the shift in emphasis in state discourse that accompanied the Arusha Declaration, a move that had significant consequences for the idioms in which national culture was conceived, discussed, and represented.[47]

The Arusha Declaration marked a notable shift with regard to TANU's relationship to socialism. While the party had long promoted a version of African socialism that was, in Nyerere's words, "an attitude of mind . . . and not the rigid adherence to a standard political pattern,"[48] the Arusha Declaration outlined a number of moves corresponding more or less to state practices under actually existing socialism, one of which brought the "major means of production" under state control.[49] Although the declaration said virtually nothing about culture, its emphasis on the primacy of modern socialist development had an important impact on the way national culture was articulated—what Askew has called "a new variety of selectivity" on culture.[50] Now, in addition to managing the potential dissonance between tribal and national culture, another mandate, one which had been only vaguely articulated before, became all the more explicit: assessing cultural practices in light of a criterion of whether or not they contributed to the principles and aesthetics of an ideal of development (maendeleo) that was both modern and socialist.[51]

One of the ways in which national culture was rearticulated in alignment with the ratcheting up of a developmentalist rhetoric concerned work. In a section entitled "The Conditions of Development," the Arusha Declaration emphasized that a culture of "hard work" was the first and most important condition: "Everybody wants development; but not everybody understands and accepts the basic requirements for development. The biggest requirement is hard work."[52] In the late 1960s and early 1970s, official statements about national culture increasingly identified such a culture with work. *Historia Fupi ya Utamaduni wa Mtanzania* (A short history of a Tanzanian's culture") (1974), an edited collection of essays by officials of the Culture Division, provides another example. One of the division's highest-profile publications ever, this volume was arranged, following the conventions of the traditions and customs genre, in chapters on various aspects of Tanzanian culture, including traditional education, religion, and music. But taking pride of place at the head of the list, preceded only by the introduction, was a chapter entitled "Our Work." In this chapter, A. F. Masao informed readers,

> The thing that was emphasized most by all [tribal] societies of Tanzania was doing hard work. Everyone divided themselves into groups and worked except for the very old, infants, and those who weren't fit, such as the sick. Work was given so much emphasis because the backbone of the clan and of society in general was work. A lazy person brought danger and shame upon the clan, because the welfare of the clan depended upon everyone working for the benefit of the entire clan. If people in a certain clan were lazy, then the clan was weak. In African culture, the first and foremost duty is to develop and strengthen the clan. Therefore, people exerted themselves in fulfilling this duty by working hard.[53]

Another publication of the Culture Division made explicit in its title the idea that national culture was a means to an end: *Utamaduni: Chombo cha Maendeleo* (Culture: the tool of development). It too prefaced its pieces on art, language, and games with a lead chapter entitled, "Work as the Essence and Foundation of Our Culture."[54]

With the reemergence in the late 1960s and early 1970s of an explicitness to the developmentalist imperative as the lead element in national cultural policy, the tension between this imperative and the traditions and customs base of national cultural research was brought increasingly to the fore. A report on the state of cultural research prepared in 1974 for a newly reconstituted Ministry of National Culture and Youth asserted, "The main responsibility of this research unit [the directorate of research on traditions and customs] has been defined as the investigation and documentation of Tanzanian culture, with the practical aim of determining which aspects of it should be preserved or reanimated, which should be improved, and which others—because they prove to be serious obstacles to national socialist development—must be abandoned."[55] And in a policy speech in April 1974, the new director of the Culture Division, I. K. Katoke, underlined repeatedly in language that hearkened back to that of the EALB that the first priority of cultural research was to determine "how it affects national development" and how "traditions and customs . . . may serve as a foundation on which a new and modern culture can be built."[56]

Contrary to a call for a return to or recovery of tradition, then, national culture was explicitly framed as something to be achieved. Stretching back to the colonial period as a fundamental aspect of nationalist writing on culture, this framing became especially prominent in the years following the Arusha Declaration. Indeed, while the research tasks the newly reconfigured ministry set for itself consisted of the familiar list of topics from earlier traditions and customs research, officials also explained that "it is obvious that research on these customs and traditions will only provide a partial understanding of the role of culture in modern Tanzania if they are not examined in relation to today's customs, ritual, beliefs, and the development of socialism itself."[57] More specifically, as Munseri's prescient article in Nchi Yetu had suggested in 1966, there were many tribal customs in Tanzania that simply did not match up, in the eyes of TANU officials, with the kind of modern development they were trying to achieve.[58]

The pledges made to reexamine such practices were not idle ones. Foreshadowing the proscriptive face the national cultural project would soon adopt against perceived urban decadence, late 1967 saw the launch of a campaign to outlaw Maasai traditional dress. Known variously as the Maasai Progress Plan and Operation Dress-Up, this campaign began with attempts by the regional commissioner in Arusha, a northern region with a large pastoralist Maasai population, to impose sanctions on Maasai men in the surrounding areas who wore the lubega (a robe slung over one shoulder) and used ochre as part of a body-care regimen.[59] Those who did not comply with orders to don modern shirts and trousers were subjected to various humiliations in Arusha town: transporters refused to carry them "even if they paid double the normal fare"; schoolchildren were encouraged to ridicule them; police harassed them. The campaign began to receive national attention in early February 1968 when two Kenyan Maasai ministers of Parliament, S. S. Oloitiptip and John Keen, expressed their offense. (The issue led to a brief exchange of accusations between the Tanzanian and Kenyan governments before the latter made statements supporting the Tanzanian position.)[60] Later that month, President Nyerere weighed in on the issue, meeting at State

House with a group of "reformed" Maasai from the National Service and reiterating the government's commitment "to assist the Masai to attain a level of development equal to that of the rest of the people in the country. . . . We can preserve zebras in their present state, century after century, but that cannot be done to our fellow human beings—denying them progress."[61] Formal legislative backing soon followed, with the Masai District Council (twenty-eight of whose forty councilors were themselves Maasai) passing a unanimous resolution in support of the campaign. Stated the council chairman, M. L. Ole-Konchellah, "The traditional dress which exposed the Masai's buttocks is not a shame and disgrace to the Masai, but the whole Tanzanian nation."[62]

Operation Dress-Up served as a striking example of the developmentalist or modernizationist impulse that lay within the natural cultural project. The vocabulary of shame and disgrace on an international stage used by Ole-Konchellah was closely bound up with this impulse. As Leander Schneider has suggested, Tanzanian officials employed a profoundly primitivizing rhetoric vis-à-vis the Maasai, even as they invoked Western tourists' habit of exoticizing the Maasai as creating the need for the ban.[63] Commentary on the campaign by the editor of Nchi Yetu put the issue in stark relief:

The Masai are highly praised for their bravery and their health, but, really, do their clothes merit any praise in today's world? Walking around half naked and smearing oneself with mud and ghee, carrying a club and a spear are not at all part of the development plan.

A Masai in his traditional clothes doesn't look like a member of society. Little children are afraid of him and run away as if they've seen a wild animal. When a Masai gets on a bus, most passengers scrunch up their faces and hold their noses as if they've encountered a bad-smelling insect.

When tourists come to this country to see the impressive traditional things that our country has been given by God, such as Mount Kilimanjaro and our game parks, they make every effort to take pictures of the Masai to take home as a joke. . . .

Most of those [who have opposed the campaign in letters to the editor] are people who have developed [ambao wameendelea]. I'm not sure how many of them would agree to going back to the traditional clothes of their tribe, perhaps a matetei ya kaniki, a tiny cloth that covered half their body, or even [animal] skins.[64]

This kind of exhibition of a people as being trapped in a distinctly nonmodern past, half-naked historical relics that were shocking to the senses, was not limited to the Maasai. Nchi Yetu's frequent pieces on tribal traditions and customs usually featured accompanying photos, often of ngoma dances being performed. Not infrequently, these images bore exoticizing captions that cautioned the viewer in phrases reminiscent of colonial writing for popular metropolitan audiences: "Don't be afraid!" or "Don't worry!"—this is the way this tribe does things![65] Such images were produced and read in the context of—indeed, often adjacent to—other images which required no defense and were unquestionably majestic: Nchi Yetu throughout this period was full of photos of the shiny and modern—the new oil refinery or bottle factory, Dar es Salaam's newest office building, the airport VIP lounge—offered as emblems and evidence of Tanzania's development.

It is tempting to read the increasing dominance of the modern developmentalist imperative of the national cultural project over its traditions and customs strand as a clear shift, the Arusha Declaration being the turning point.[66] However, such a temporal break is, at the very least, far from a clean one. On the one hand, invocations of tribal traditions and customs survived into the 1970s and beyond as the basic building blocks of any properly Tanzanian national cultural discourse.[67] On the other hand, even leaving aside late colonial writing like that of the EALB authors, modern development was being applied as a litmus test to tribal cultural practices years before the Arusha Declaration, as becomes especially apparent once other institutional sites of national cultural discourse are taken into account.

Kivukoni College, TANU's ideological institute, was one such site. Established in 1961 by TANU on the model of Ruskin College in the United Kingdom, Kivukoni was set up with the mission of providing training in ideology, development, and public service to adults without formal higher education but poised to make an important contribution to their communities and the nation.[68] The small student body, numbering seventy-two in 1966, was composed largely of rising cadres in party and government, trade union and cooperative workers, teachers, and a sprinkling of South African anti-apartheid activists in exile; married men, who averaged twenty-seven years of age and who often came from the regions and usually had some secondary education, made up its core. Headed by a British principal, the staff was composed of both Tanzanians and expatriate instructors who taught a curriculum centered on economics, politics, and public administration—both in theory and, more centrally, in Tanzanian state practice. While certainly not the most privileged of Tanzanian institutions of higher education,

Kivukoni became a proven way station for civil servants and party cadres rising through the ranks.[69] Its small size, English-language instruction (through most of the 1960s), and comparatively luxurious premises in a converted beach hotel overlooking Dar es Salaam's harbor contributed to its select status.[70]

Kivukoni's student journal, *Mwenge*, frequently took up cultural issues. Here, in articles often written by those poised to become an influential front line in the implementation of state policy, the modernization of tradition loomed large, while celebrations of tribal customs were almost nowhere to be found, even years before the Arusha Declaration. For instance, in 1965 a student wrote in a piece on traditional music, "In this era where 'all roads' lead to the social and economic development, it is unforgivable to overlook the role of traditional music. The question is 'How are we going to mobilise traditional music so that its role in the Plan is realised?'"[71] Another student, in a critique of polygamous marriage written in 1964, "beg[ged] all the youngsters . . . to avoid all these old ways of marrying to many wives," practices which were "useless to the government towards National Development of the country."[72] Still others wrote of the unsuitability of bridewealth in Tanzania's modern society, the exploitation wrought by traditional healers, and the ways in which mila na desturi might delay the nation's development.[73]

Rather than representing a clear-cut, temporal shift from a national culture based upon the nationalization of tribal traditions and customs to one based upon a criterion and imperative of modern development, these two discourses overlapped, coexisted, and were often even explicitly reconciled with each other. As parts of this discussion have shown, there was indeed an increasingly explicit emphasis in the late 1960s and early 1970s placed upon the necessity of evaluating tribal mila na desturi in terms of their contribution to a goal of national development that was resolutely modernizing in character; the Arusha Declaration, in establishing a new template against which policies and statements were to be judged, had much to do with this development. But this shift is nevertheless best viewed as one of emphasis and one having much to do with the varying institutional origins of differing discourses of national culture. Even before the Arusha Declaration, strong versions of modernist-developmentalist discourse emanated from TANU's ideological vanguard—Kivukoni College, for example—while the mila na desturi genre continued to frame national cultural research through the 1970s among academics seconded to the Culture Division. But rarely did either discourse appear alone. Prior to independence, as well, the negotiations of culture by rising nationalists featured not a separation of concerns with tradition and the modern as distinct and opposed elements, but rather the articulation of this pair as two sides of a coin.

Indeed, if the Arusha Declaration is viewed as a pivot point affecting the articulation of national culture, it may be just as useful to think of this shift as flowing not from its foregrounding of the modern over the traditional, but rather from its discourse on the urban. The declaration heralded a policy switch not only to more or less socialist economic strategies but also to a new prioritization of explicitly rural development. As Nyerere warned in a section of the declaration entitled, "Let Us Pay Heed to the Peasant," "There are two possible ways of dividing the people in our country. We can put the capitalists and the feudalists on one side, and the farmers and workers on the other. But we can also divide the people into urban dwellers on one side and those who live in the rural areas on the other. If we are not careful we might get to the position where the real exploitation in Tanzania is that of the town dwellers exploiting the peasants."[74]

The declaration may not have engendered a widespread transfer of actual material resources from the city to the countryside, but it did spark a marked increase in discourse and symbolic performances promoting and glorifying an ideal of healthy rural productivity. Politicians were sent to the countryside, where press photographs captured them wielding *jembes* shoulder to shoulder with the nation's ideal citizens, the peasants. Poems in the pages of *Uhuru* and *Ngurumo* extolled the virtues of farming and urged the jobless to leave city life behind them. In a telling passage of the declaration, Nyerere singled out two social categories as obstacles to the new work ethic: "village men" and "city women." Holding village women up as examples of the kind of hard workers the nation needed, Nyerere lamented "the energies of the millions of men in the villages and thousands of women in the towns which are at present wasted in gossip, dancing and drinking."[75] While such condemnation of the village men would prove to be rare (indeed, the figure of the ideal peasant-citizen ended up being quite consistently represented as male), the stigma attached to city women was an enduring and constitutive element of the vilification of the city and city dwellers in general. Within this proliferation of discourse valorizing the rural, urban space emerged as problematic, symbolizing feminized consumption versus production, decadent leisure versus healthful hard work, foreign-inspired indecency versus traditional dignity. With this consolidation of norms of Tanzanian citizenship around a rural ideal, the national cultural project took on increasing prominence as a vehicle for attacks on wayward urban others.

Operation Politics

As noted earlier in regard to the Maasai dress campaign, official positions on national culture were articulated not only through promotion of tribal mila na desturi deemed appropriate, but also through the purging (kuondoa) of practices considered antithetical to the national cultural standard of the moment. Practices perceived to be primitive were not the only targets of national cultural purge campaigns, however. Much more prominent—and much more fraught with heated debate, vocal opposition, and controversy—were campaigns launched in the late sixties and early seventies against a set of objects, icons, and practices labeled decadent and coded urban. These campaigns against urban decadence became a crucial foil against which national culture emerged.

As suggested above, the Arusha Declaration marked a racheting up of an antiurban discourse with roots in the colonial period. In their respective work on colonial and early postcolonial government efforts to "repatriate" Dar es Salaam's unemployed to the countryside, James Brennan and Andrew Burton have explored one of the key manifestations of attacks on the urban.[76] There was also a prominent cultural front to these assaults, however, one that was critical in mediating a more generalized stigmatization of the city. As a post–Arusha Declaration Dar es Salaam became the scene of successive campaigns against targets, including miniskirts, tight trousers, bell-bottoms, skin-lightening creams, wigs, Afro hairstyles, cowboy outfits, beauty contests, and soul music, these so-called cultural operations became one of the most prominent features of urban public debate. The cultural front of this operation politics was a central scene for the consolidation and contestation of meanings of the city in an age in which patriotism was increasingly pegged to symbols of rural frugality. If the TYL was frequently designated the enforcer of these campaigns, the figure of the healthy citizen-youth the league represented was challenged by other kinds of youth in the city: young men and women who fashioned themselves in relation to alternative ideas of modern style and youth not controlled by the state.

In what follows I analyze debate around two campaigns, one against specific forms of dress, the other targeting soul music. Both initiatives refined, further defined, and extended the reach of an official national culture, even as they opened up discursive terrains upon which the parameters of that national culture could be contested. The dress campaign in particular suggests that in targeting this precise set of decadent practices in a frame of modern developmentalism, backers of the bans were forced to take on challenges to the meaning of modern development itself. The modern appealed to by both the campaign's backers and detractors was at once singular, in its power as a claim-making device, and contested, in arguments over what qualified as modern. In addition, as was the case with the negotiation of positions on utamaduni examined thus far, struggles over these campaigns took place in frames extending beyond the national, with transnationally circulating images, ideas, objects, and icons serving as key platforms for debate. Prominent in the controversy over the soul ban, the tension between the national and the transnational complicated debate and troubled efforts to nationalize urban style.

"There Is Nothing Modern about Miniskirts"

The first of the wave of these initiatives was Operation Vijana (Operation youth), a campaign against various forms of indecent dress and adornment.[77] Announced in front-page newspaper headlines on October 3, 1968, the campaign consisted of a ban on "miniskirts, wigs, women's bleaches, and tight male trousers" and was aimed at "defending Tanzania's culture and furthering the aims of the Arusha Declaration."[78] Not only was the ban planned and designed by the TYL, it was to be enforced by mostly male TYL members. These cadres had been urged by top league officials—namely, Chairman Sijaona, a mission-educated civil servant who had been active in TANU since its inception and in the early 1960s had served as the first minister of national culture and youth, and Chief Commander Rajabu Diwani—to patrol urban areas and "arrest all women wearing [indecent] clothing and artificial hair."[79]

In designing and announcing Operation Vijana, TYL officials were keen to cast the campaign first and foremost as a national cultural exercise. Elaborating on the aims of the operation in a lengthy, confidential document solicited by Sijaona, Moses Nnauye, the league's second highest-ranking official and ultimately a longtime functionary in the party, began by situating the campaign in relation to Nyerere's "dance speech" of 1962 as the foundation of the ban. Young women who wore miniskirts and wigs or who used skin-lightening creams, Nnauye as-

Officials of the TANU Youth League burn a wig in the National Stadium during the National Youth Festival, February 1969. *Courtesy of the Tanzania Information Service.*

serted, "will not be able to dance African dances, nor will they be able to maintain Africanness [Uafrika], meaning it is Africanness that is being diluted."[80] The slippage from a national frame to a continental and racial one in Nnauye's "Africanness" was only the first hint in the planning document of the crucial place of a supranational frame in the imagining of national culture. For Nnauye went on to discuss a rather specific international context in which the operation's vision of national culture was being conceived: TANU-sponsored tours of "nearly every country in Europe" that high-ranking TYL leaders like Nnauye had been privileged to join as part of official delegations sent to observe European political systems. It was in Europe, Nnauye explains, that Tanzanian delegates has witnessed the "rapid developments hurling the Western world [jumuia ya Kizungu, literally, 'white world'] toward a bankruptcy of the person and human behavior." From "gangs of hooligan youths known as 'Rockers' . . . forming groups around particular styles of dress" to the "other sorts of filth . . . marriages between two men, men marrying goats or sheep, women marrying dogs" supposedly becoming topics of debate in the British Parliament, Nnauye described a landscape of moral decadence afflicting Europe under the guise of "freedom of the individual."[81] That Nnauye's vision of Europe made up the bulk of a section entitled "African Personhood"—initially curious, perhaps—only underlines the fundamental importance of an international stage in the articulation of national culture.

It was no coincidence that urban lawlessness assumed a prominent place in Nnauye's description of Europe. For alongside their justification of Operation Vijana in reference to a national cultural frame, TYL officials openly described the campaign as an intervention against a specifically urban problem. In the earliest articulations of the operation at two key meetings of TYL leaders in August and September 1968, the targeting of indecent dress was conceived as one plank in an entire platform of proposals of TYL plans to intervene in a city perceived to be in moral decay. At a press conference following the second of these meetings, Chairman Sijaona outlined the league's intentions to combat laziness, vagrancy, crime, and other exploitative practices as well as *nguo mbaya* (bad or undesirable clothing). Linking these issues in his speech, Sijaona painted a picture of an urban landscape where youths "roamed about in town without work," where "lawlessness" was on the rise, and where one encountered "half-naked" women in the streets. On the eve of the official launch of the operation, Sijaona explained that the cadres enforcing the ban would be concentrating their efforts in Dar es Salaam: "It is well known that the people whose minds have been enslaved by dehumanising practices are confined into the urban areas."[82]

As the initial announcement of the operation suggested, although the ban targeted both women's and men's dress, the enforcement of the campaign focused overwhelmingly on women as the real culprits and cast young men as the appropriate enforcers. Indeed, the vision of the city articulated through the initiative tapped into long-standing gendered logics linking urban space and feminized decadence. Examined by scholars of colonial urbanism, these logics stretched back to anxieties among European administrators and African men alike about the activities pursued by women in towns full of male migrant laborers. With some of the most significant of the limited opportunities for women's work in colonial towns having to do with providing the "comforts of home" to male workers, in Luise White's apt phrase, tales of town women tempting men sexually and diverting their earnings toward frivolous spending instead of rural savings became a widespread genre.[83] By the 1960s the anxieties linking female sexuality, consumption, and the sapping of male productivity together in a potent symbol for the city were taking on new forms and intensities for which national cultural initiatives like Operation Vijana became vehicles. Indeed, within days of the announcement of the ban—still months away from the date of its official start—violent attacks by gangs of young men on women deemed to be indecently dressed began to be reported around Dar es Salaam. These attacks and the broader politics of gender, work, mobility, and sexuality that surrounded them are taken up in chapter 2.

However, confrontation over Operation Vijana was not limited to the streets of Dar es Salaam. Within a few days of the announcement of the ban, a debate began in the local press and dominated editorial and letters-to-the-editor pages for months. By February 1, 1969, over 150 letters, dozens of poems and editorials, and over 50 news items concerning the operation were published in the capital's four main dailies and *Nchi Yetu*. In a mere sixteen days following the announcement of the campaign, the *Standard* alone published a remarkable 108 letters on the ban—only 14 of which supported it—before the editor temporarily closed the correspondence.[84] In terms of number of submissions published on any single issue, this debate was record-breaking, and it was extraordinary in its scope and intensity. Opinion on the ban was overwhelmingly critical, a fact not lost on TYL leaders, who painstakingly monitored the debate in the press, drawing up a confidential chart recording the contributors' names (or pseudonyms), addresses (if given), inferred race, and position taken on the ban.[85] Reserving the possibility of unspecified action against these epistolary opponents of the ban, TYL leaders settled in the end for a protest outside of the offices of the *Standard* in the wake of the debate it had hosted. As I have suggested, some of the ways in which the campaign was taken up placed it in the context of debates about urban gender relations, sexuality, work, and mobility (see chapter 2). Much of the debate in the press, however, did indeed engage the ban in the frame in which it was ostensibly launched—that is, as a national cultural question. A close look at the contours of this aspect of debate and at the vocabularies writers used to articulate their positions on the ban sheds light on both the underlying assumptions structuring official constructions of national culture and the specific terms upon which these constructions could and could not be contested by a literate public in Dar es Salaam.

Supporters of the ban often based their charge that fashions like miniskirts, tight trousers, and wigs were undermining Tanzania's culture on the contention that such items were foreign in origin. Opponents contested this logic, suggesting that it was futile to attempt to condemn banned fashion as imitation of foreign culture, as all mass-produced commodities, including many that were upheld by TANU itself as good and useful, were originally foreign. As one letter writer put it, "Unless they [the TYL] want to see Tanzanians going naked, they should believe me that we have no fashion in Tanzania which is acceptable as originating from this country. . . . Whatever we choose as our national dress, we shall be deceiving ourselves."[86] Several letter writers took jabs at the types of dress displayed at state spectacles, a few correspondents arguing that some traditional costumes featured in the national dancing troupes were just as revealing as miniskirts, and others suggesting that the TANU elite themselves increasingly favored a foreign-inspired sartorial style epitomized by what was popularly known as the Chou-en-Lai suit.[87] But what drew the most comment on the perceived official hypocrisy was the comparison of Operation Vijana with the campaign held earlier in the year to mandate modern dress for Maasai. As one letter writer, R. N. Okonkwu, argued, "If they want us to preserve our culture why don't we put on 'Rubega' and go half naked as our great grandfathers used to do. Because all the clothes we are putting on now is [sic] foreign culture. Moreover, if they want to preserve our culture why are they telling the Masai tribesmen to stop going half naked and put on modern dress like trousers?"[88]

But opponents of Operation Vijana were not the only ones drawing connections between the campaign against indecent dress and Operation Dress-Up, for within the logic of many supporters the two campaigns were anything but contradictory. Underpinning both was a single aesthetic standard of modern decency from which both Maasai traditional dress and miniskirts, wigs, and tight pants diverged. It was this aesthetic that one letter-writing supporter of Operation Vijana described when he stated, "What we mean and do insist upon as the African culture is decency in the way we dress; and looked at from this point of view, the ban on minis is timely."[89] Indeed, both Maasai wearing traditional dress and miniskirted women were consistently described by supporters of the campaigns as "roaming half-naked," the Maasai with their "buttocks showing," the women with their "thighs exposed."[90] And in December 1968, on the eve of the official enforcement of Operation Vijana, Nchi Yetu visually brought the two campaigns together in a single exhibition of the supposed success of Operation Dress-Up. A photograph pictured three reformed Maasai women posing in large, shapeless tops and mid-calf skirts; all were wearing shoes and all were outfitted with such accessories as a handbag, wristwatch, and glasses, in addition to their traditional beaded necklaces. The caption read, "These Maasai girls have taken off their animal skins and have completely stopped smearing themselves with mud; here's what they look like now. They are truly attractive. 'Being modern doesn't mean wearing a mini,' they said."[91]

But if both Operations Dress-Up and Vijana targeted perceived obstacles to a standard of modern decency and national development, the ways in which each was contested (or not) were radically different. For while the Maasai campaign provoked very few public statements challenging the initiative (despite being highly publicized), a flood of such statements and even legal challenges to the campaign plagued officials' attempts to enforce Operation Vijana and coalesced into a well-developed oppositional discourse. Certainly one reason for the disparity was the differential access to media experienced by the inhabitants of Dar es Salaam, where Operation Vijana was primarily carried out, and rural areas of Arusha Region, the site of Operation Dress-Up. And yet this is only one part of the story. Perhaps even more important, the meanings of the objects targeted in Operation Vijana in 1968 were considerably more unstable and contested than those accruing to Maasai dress.

The premium placed on the modern was by no means confined to the discourses of Operation Vijana's supporters. Indeed, letters by opponents of the ban were full of references to the desirability of keeping up with the "modern changes" in a world that "as time passes . . . improves and becomes sophisticated."[92] One John Nakomo voiced his complaints about the ban in terms that related to his anxieties about Tanzania's ability to keep up with such changes: "While other States are talking about improving food values, about transferring hearts, and even going to the Moon, Tanzania cannot even talk of the next constructive thing we should do! Instead, we are talking about banning mini-skirts, bleaches, beauty contests and many other minor issues."[93] Another opponent put it more pithily: "We are Tanzanians of 1968 and not Tanzanians of 8000 B.C."[94] Correspondents' satirical challenges to TYL leaders to enforce a return to "bark-cloth" if they were really serious about ridding the country of foreign influences depended upon the assumption that no one really wanted to see Tanzanians walking the streets of Dar es Salaam dressed in such clothing, which was widely viewed as a remnant of the past at odds with city life in a modern Tanzania.

But if the supreme desirability of being modern in Dar es Salaam in 1968 was common sense, quite securely in the realm of the hegemonic, the debate over Operation Vijana reveals just how unstable and contested was the notion of the modern itself. In sharp contrast to those condemning miniskirts, tight trousers, cosmetics, and wigs as affronts to modern decency, many who opposed the campaign insisted that such fashions were eminently modern. J. N. Mbussa, a TYL member disappointed with the ban commented, "Most slender men prefer slimline trousers to big and loose trousers (bombos) simply because they look smart in them. . . . Girls also prefer mini-skirts to long gowns, just because they look more modern, attractive and beautiful."[95] Another letter writer echoed this sentiment: "Nowadays almost everybody has developed the attitude of preferring tight-fitting clothes to others because we look smarter in them."[96] While TANU imagined a model citizenry committed to modern nation building along socialist lines, letter writers opposing Operation Vijana articulated a notion of being modern linked, rather differently, to an imagined network of international fashion and (differently) revolutionary youth styles associated with the events of 1968. Issac T. Ngomuo, a secondary school student, declared, "The current youth is well aware of the fashion revolution taking place in many countries. . . . What is widely practiced by many other peoples is also good for us."[97] Many letter writers explicitly extolled the virtues of "keeping up" with the latest styles, with the comings and goings of "this . . . fashion age."[98] Django, for instance, complained, "Why then has the Youth League suggested its unwanted styles of dress. Usually people prefer the latest models of everything. This is the century for minis, slack trousers, Texas costume, etc. . . . Not many people will like to put on gowns, wide trousers, etc. in this day. Such fashion has lapsed."[99]

In statements like these, a vocabulary extolling modern progress became unmoored from its associations with the national, state-centered vision of development through hard work laid out in the Arusha Declaration—and instead was attached to international cultures of self-fashioning through body adornment and consumption that the state was keen to label decadent. The responses of TYL leaders and Operation Vijana's most ardent supporters to this semantic challenge (a challenge to what was arguably the central category for the legitimacy of the developmentalist state, not to mention TANU's national cultural project), suggest that they took the challenge seriously indeed. Architects and promoters of Operation Vijana were at pains to repeatedly argue that the claims to being modern made by those displaying banned fashion were patently false. Andrew Shija, the TYL branch leader at the University of Dar es Salaam, declared that indecent dress was being paraded "under the cover of modernism," a characterization echoed by another supporter, who called banned fashion remnants of a "false imperialist modernism."[100] But the point was made most forcefully in an editorial published in TANU's *Nationalist*. Entitled "There is nothing modern about mini-skirts," it went straight to the heart of the matter: "Tanzania's goal is to create, in the least possible time, a modern African society. The problem as far as the controversy is concerned is the nature of a modern society *especially as those who wear mini skirts tend to assume that by doing so they are modern*.[101]

Reevaluating how scholars talk about modernity in postcolonial contexts has been a central concern for much scholarly work over the past two decades. Arjun Appadurai and Carol Breckenridge, among many others, have insisted upon the point that modernity is not singular, but multiple, that it is consumed in infinitely variable ways, having everything to do with the context of its consumption.[102] Taking off from this insight, scholars have argued that the wide variation in global engagements with cultural forms and social practices that can in some way be identified as modern suggests that non-Western contexts are characterized by the formation of alternative, parallel, or multiple modernities.[103] To the extent that modernity is often used to *describe* a particular social formation or condition, such conclusions are invaluable. They crucially highlight the undeniable fact that the kinds of cultural forms and practices emerging from engagements with the modern are everywhere shaped differently according to context; such forms and practices may thus be usefully thought of as alternative to a template of Western modernity which, however particular in actuality, has a history of universalizing itself in a spurious teleology of uniform progress. However, the debate around Operation Vijana suggests that some of the most fraught struggles over the modern were fueled precisely by its *singularity* as a uniquely powerful claim-making idiom (above all in the 1960s, one might even argue). When both the promoters of the campaign and its opponents called upon (quite divergent) notions of being modern to buttress their respective positions on culture, their claims resembled what James Ferguson has called appeals to "global membership": visions of a modern world to which Tanzanians were not an alternative appendage, but rather one in which they could participate as full-fledged members.[104] "What is widely practiced by many other peoples is also good for us," as Isaac Ngomuo had put it.[105] In short, from the perspective of an approach to the modern as an "indigenous category," Operation Vijana saw not the proliferation of multiple or alternative modernities, but rather an intense debate over what set of meanings a singular modern should be invested with. The larger point is one made forcefully by Ferguson: that moving too quickly to label colonial and postcolonial engagements with the modern alternative risks ruling out the possibility that in certain historical contexts part of the concept's attraction lay in its singularity.[106]

Alongside the challenge to an official modern, the identities being articulated—and indeed embodied, on the streets of Dar es Salaam—by opponents of Operation Vijana were all the more disturbing to the state because embedded within them was the performance of a young, urban style that suggested relationships between youth and both the city and the state that were at odds with those envisioned by TANU and its Youth League. Mocking TYL leaders as "old gentlemen who pretend to be youths," letter writers identified themselves with new vocabularies— "teenagers," "real youths," "unaged youth"—thereby reappropriating youth as an oppositional, not a TYL-vanguardist, category. In contrast to a model citizen-youth embodied by the TYL cadre evacuating the capital for a new calling in healthful, rural production, the new teenagers of Dar es Salaam claimed a "right" to fashion selves out of the very signs of leisure and display through which official discourse defined the city as a problematic and ideologically suspect space. In initiating proscriptive campaigns like Operation Vijana in urban areas, the reach of national culture was extended to touch peoples' lives in new, intimate ways. But by taking on cultural forms that could not be easily declared antithetical to modern development, TANU officials found themselves faced with challenges to official attempts to key political categories like modern and youth.

"Afro-Americans' Ngoma ya Taifa"?: The Short Life of a Ban on Soul

In 1970, the African Communist, the London-based journal of the South African Communist Party, published the thoughts of a Ghanaian university student named J. K. Obatala on the news that the Tanzanian government had banned soul music a few months previously.[107] "At first," wrote Obatala, who had lived most of his life in the United States but was now studying in Ghana, "Nyerere's actions appeared to me to be a deliberate slap in the face to the Afro-Americans, alas, an indication that Tanzania was relapsing into a self-induced coma of ultra-reactionary nationalism."[108] Puzzled why one of the continent's most "progressive" leaders would take such an apparently "reactionary" step, Obatala described how he discovered the answer by observing students on his dormitory floor watching a James Brown concert on television one night. Lured away from his research by "pandemonious outbursts coming from the students' lounge," the normally studious Obatala "decided to go and see what it would be like to catch 'J.B.' in Africa."[109] What he saw—James Brown "sliding over super-slick floors, flinging off one diamond studded cape after another" to the delight of the packed student lounge—convinced Obatala of the destructive influence of soul in Africa, for its "propagation of the myth of Afro-American affluence" among young Africans, who relished soul only as the latest American capitalist craze but knew little of the truth of African Americans' struggle for justice. "I felt," he recalled, "as if I had been given a one hour lecture by Julius Nyerere himself on 'Why I banned Soul Music from Tanzania.'"[110]

Soul had indeed been banned in Tanzania—on November 12, 1969, to be precise. Contrary to Obatala's account, however, the ban was not on President Nyerere's initiative, but on that of the coast regional commissioner, Mustafa Songambele, who on that day was meeting with a group of Dar es Salaam primary school teachers to discuss their students' participation in an upcoming rally. Presented with the teachers' complaints that "this type of dance . . . was a cause of bad manners in the country's youth," Commissioner Songambele agreed and promptly declared soul music "banned from being played in Dar es Salaam," effective immediately.[111]

Apparently coming as something of a surprise to his colleagues, the announcement by Songambele was met with muted official reaction. Although the government did eventually back its commissioner's initiative, official support was not made public until a week later in the rather unusual form of a letter to the editor of the Standard by the director of information services, A. A. Riyami. Citing the corruption of "our young girls, especially school children," the presence of a network of nightclubs in the capital, and the imperative to "preserv[e] our national culture" against destructive foreign influence, Riyami tried to assure the public that "the Regional Commissioner has not made a hasty decision but one which was well thought out."[112] Yet official support appears to have remained nominal, and the soul ban was not enforced on any scale approaching that of Operation Vijana (in fact, Songambele's ban was never accorded the status of an operation). Despite the lack of official action, the ban nonetheless attracted a flurry of reactions from residents of Dar es Salaam. In the week following Songambele's announcement, thirty letters were sent to the *Standard* protesting the ban, twenty-two of which were published. Chastened by official criticism of the newspaper in the wake of Operation Vijana, however, the editor decided to close the correspondence on soul after receiving and publishing Riyami's letter declaring the government's support for it, adding, though, that not one of the correspondents on soul had supported Songambele's action.[113]

It is instructive to place the ban on soul music and the discourse surrounding it in the press in the context of both Obatala's piece in the *African Communist* and Operation Vijana, which was launched less than a year earlier. Reading the soul episode alongside Obatala's intervention can serve as a starting point to tracking the transnational networks of people and knowledge implicated in the Tanzanian state's curious ambivalence with regard to African American culture and politics—an ambivalence that illuminates the management of the tensions and contradictions of national culture itself. The juxtaposition of discourses situated in Afro-American politics, those of the Tanzanian state, and the epistolary protests of the young "soul-diggers" of Dar es Salaam opens up possibilities for reading the controversy over soul as embedded in multiple agendas and rhetorics. These included competing aims of the Tanzanian state, differing positions on black transnational political solidarity, and the engagements of young residents of the capital with soul. Situated at a key point of tension between rival invocations of transnational frames of reference, the debate over soul and other forms of African American popular culture highlights how cultural debates in Dar es Salaam in the 1960s were mediated through the transnational cultural circuits running through the city. In recalling Operation Vijana I reveal both differences and similarities between the two bans and set up a comparison that is crucial to investigating the more general phenomenon of Tanzania's operation politics.

Visible signs of the people, politics, and styles of black America made a significant impact in Tanzania and particularly in Dar es Salaam in the late 1960s and early 1970s. The appearance of elements of African American culture on the Tanzanian landscape was not unprecedented. The screening of the film *Zonk!* in 1950 (see the introduction) illustrates the kinds of complicated transnational paths that black diasporic culture could take: from African American minstrelsy, through its appropriation by black performers in a South African film, to a screening of that film before an enthusiastic Dar es Salaam audience that added its own interpretations to the mix. But the earlier instances of African

American cultural influence in Tanzania were occasional and intermittent compared to the density of this traffic in the late sixties and early seventies.

Particularly after the military coup overthrowing Ghana's Nkrumah in 1966, Tanzania became the premier destination in Africa for black diasporic intellectuals and activists seeking to develop personal and political linkages between civil rights struggles in North America and liberation movements on the African continent.[114] Such visits were varied in motivation and form. Many on the left were attracted by Nyerere's commitment to African socialism and pan-African liberation; people with more cultural nationalist leanings were drawn by back-to-Africa sentiments that connected powerfully with ujamaa's declared basis in idealized African cultural norms. Between 1965 and 1975, many of the most prominent African American activists, including Angela Davis, Malcolm X, Stokely Carmichael, Eldridge Cleaver, and Amiri Baraka, spent time in Tanzania during their quasi-official tours and speaking engagements. The University of Dar es Salaam was a major center of pan-African and Marxist thought at the time and became a near-obligatory stop on the itineraries of many such activists, their speeches there often being pulled into local struggles between radical and conservative students on campus (see chapter 3).

For other high-profile African American visitors, such as the many Black Panthers for whom Nyerere provided a haven from harassment by the FBI, there were also pressing personal situations. These stays often lasted much longer than brief tours: Pete O'Neal, chairman of the Kansas City chapter of the Black Panther Party, for instance, fled prosecution in the United States with his wife in 1970 to settle in Tanzania after two years in Algeria. Having lived ever since then on a farm in Arusha, where he has lately run an exchange program for Kansas City youth, the O'Neals' stay was exceptional in length but not in form. Indeed, the late 1960s and early 1970s saw a sizeable community of African American expatriates settling in Tanzania, some of whom established themselves in rural areas as self-styled ujamaa pioneers.[115]

This expatriate community of *Wawereaji* (returnees), as the Dar es Salaam community organization called itself, was encouraged by the Tanzanian government but also encountered the ambivalence of a political establishment that was itself crisscrossed by local rivalries, struggles, and agendas. Perhaps the most prominent example of the conflicts that sometimes erupted between factions within the Tanzanian state and African American expatriates was the temporary arrest in 1974 of hundreds of black Americans following accusations that they were spying for the CIA. The Big Bust, as the event became known, began with the impounding by the Dar es Salaam port police of a shipment said to contain arms and ammunition bound for an upcountry ujamaa village and linked to two African Americans in the capital. Expanding over the next few months into a much broader surveillance of the country's "Afros," as the Tanzanian press sometimes called African Americans, the roundups ended only after vociferous personal appeals by prominent black Americans in Dar es Salaam and abroad. The timing could not have been more charged. Beginning quietly on the eve of Tanzania's hosting of the long-awaited Sixth Pan-African Congress in Dar es Salaam, an event attended by hundreds of delegates from all over the black diaspora, and picking up steam in the Congress's wake, the accusations served as a sharp reminder of the complicated position of black expatriates in Dar es Salaam. With African Americans becoming involved in domains as diverse as university student politics, policy advising in the prime minister's office, and ujamaa village pioneering, they intersected with the Tanzanian political scene in increasingly complex ways that produced moments of tension and struggle as well as new solidarities.[116]

Alongside that of the expatriate community, a different kind of diasporic cultural impact was being felt in Dar es Salaam, as the ban on soul suggests. The sounds, fashion, images, and icons of African American popular culture were making an appearance on the capital's landscape, to be consumed, engaged, and reworked alongside other transnational influences. Traced by many on the local scene to a performance by the blues star Buddy Guy in Dar es Salaam in 1968, the most popular bands in the city began incorporating soul numbers, defined broadly and often reworked with Swahili lyrics and Congolese musical influences, into their repertoires. As a local journalist described the mix in 1969, "This can be soul, blues, cha-cha, samba, the latest local crazes—'sukusu,' 'kirikiri,' 'toyota,' and for good measure, the old dances like the tango."[117] Played by bands like the Rifters, the Sparks, and Air Bantou at Dar es Salaam's small circuit of downtown bars, nightclubs, and hotels, "the hottest music in town" in 1969 generated the dance style that would be called soul and provoke the consternation of Songambele and his audience of teachers.[118] These "dancing halls," which were new additions to the social hall–dominated scene of the 1950s, did indeed feature mixed crowds of young men and women, as testimony and photos suggest.[119] Afro hairstyles and fashion associated with James Brown

Couples dance at a nightclub in Dar es Salaam in 1969. The skirt worn by the woman in the center of the photograph is of a length that would have risked being targeted in the decency campaigns of the time. *Courtesy of the Tanzania Information Service.*

The Sparks perform in Dar es Salaam, January 1969. *Courtesy of the Tanzania Information Service.*

were also popular and, like soul, met with attacks by campaigners for urban decency.

Obatala's was not the only intervention in the debate over the soul ban to assess it in relation to Afro-American politics. In the midst of the wave of letters to the press came one from Bob Eubanks, an African American expatriate writing from the campus of Dar es Salaam's University College. Addressing "those who would say that soul music is foreign music to Tanzanian Wananchi [citizens]," Eubanks discussed Afro-Americans' roots in Africa, the destruction of their original African culture under slavery, and their continuing cultural separation from white America. Cleverly appropriating vocabulary from TANU's national cultural discourse, Eubanks argued that in light of this history, "soul music, soul dancing, blues music and jazz music are . . . the Afro-Americans' Ngoma ya Taifa [national dance]. They are no more foreign to Tanzania than music from the Congo or from Zambia. We understand that each nation has to make sure that its own Ngoma ya Taifa comes first before other music. . . . But, to ban soul music and leave the music of the oppressor to be heard. . . . brothers and sisters of Tanzania do not forsake your ancestors who died in that strange and foreign land of America; and we, the Afro-Americans of today are their children. All Power to the People, A Soul Brother."[120]

Eubanks was not alone in his opinion. Many other African American expatriates in Dar es Salaam expressed distress not only at the ban, but also at the tendency (see below), of some supporters and opponents of the initiative to conflate soul with music by white (and decidedly non-soulful) American stars. Although they held opposing opinions on the worthiness of the soul ban, both Obatala and Eubanks suggested that Tanzania's position on soul music had everything to do with a correct (Obatala) or incorrect (Eubanks) assessment and appreciation of the bond that united the struggles of Tanzanians and Afro-Americans.[121] However, Tanzanian officials and opponents of the ban engaged soul— and Afro-American culture in general—rather differently.

From the moment Commissioner Songambele's remarks to the schoolteachers were made public, there was some confusion over what exactly was being targeted and why. "Can he [Songambele] give a precise definition of 'soul' anyway?" queried one letter writer.[122] The initial two-sentence report of the commissioner's statement specified that the music was banned but hinted that what Songambele and the teachers found unacceptable was the type of dance accompanying soul and its effect upon young people in Dar es Salaam. Director Riyami's letter, announcing government support for the ban, confirmed that the intended target was the public performance of soul music in nightclubs, particularly because investigations had revealed the participation of young schoolchildren in such nightlife.[123] Most letter writers seemed to interpret the ban as being directed at a specific style of dance associated with music by particular Afro-American artists, including James Brown, Wilson Pickett, and Buddy Guy (whose Dar es Salaam performance one letter writer credited with launching soul's ascendance as a "very popular dance").[124] For his part, Eubanks suggested that the city's music lovers were mistaking truly foreign music by the Beatles, the Monkees, Jim Reeves, and Elvis Presley for soul.[125]

Much as with Operation Vijana, then, the soul ban exhibited the articulation of official anxieties about perceived unruly practices among urban youth (bad manners in the paraphrased words of Commissioner Songambele), centered on particular urban spaces (in this case, the nightclub). Given this focus on urban disorder, it was not surprising that the soul ban was launched by the commissioner himself. For Songambele had, by late 1969, developed a reputation as a spearhead of the roundups of loafers and the unemployed that were becoming increasingly regular in Dar es Salaam after the Arusha Declaration. Having assumed the position of area commissioner just prior to the declaration, Songambele was at the forefront not only of rhetorical condemnations of the urban as symbol of parasitical exploitation, but also of the conversion of such rhetoric into physical (if often symbolic) operations to purge the city of undesirable elements.[126] Hailed by some and reviled by others for these actions, Songambele was a lightning rod for criticism in the wave of opposition that erupted after the ban was announced. If official reasoning behind the campaign shared much with the logic of earlier decency campaigns, so too did defenders of soul, in objecting to the initiative and invoking horizons of transnational style, rehearse many of the themes and arguments raised in the Operation Vijana controversy a year earlier.

Recalling the official reasoning that had been deployed to promote Operation Vijana, many letter writers argued that soul music was no more foreign or indecent than many officially sanctioned cultures popular in Tanzania. Responding to the logic that " 'the more our youths have been digging it, the more they have been wanting to become American,'" Mike Francis rhetorically asked, "Does it mean now here in Tanzania, the more we use or play Congo music the more we want to become Congolese? Or the more we use Chinese things say, the more we want to become Chinese?"[127] Several writers suggested that the various indigenous Tanzanian dances popular at the time were more guilty than soul of promoting bad manners. Wrote "Fairness," "He [Songambele] should attend the coming Idd and Jamhuri festivals to witness how worse Chakacha is to Soul Digging. It is a pity to see our parents including young children mouth-open clapping hands at and even giving 'tuzo' [tips] to the actor or actress who performs sexual play (buttock shaking) properly. To this, Mr. Songambele says, 'Go ahead.'"[128]

Ungando echoed this sentiment, devoting his letter to enumerating the "hooliganic" elements of the "Mkwaju ngoma" of the Zaramo; he concluded, "There is no point banning soul music which expresses the feeling of fellow Afro-Americans and does not show hooliganism or insult. We should leave out some of our local ngomas which clearly show that hooliganism is part of its elements." Still others pointed to the "Kirikiri," the "Sekuse," and the "naked . . . Kiluwa" as evidence of a perceived official double standard when it came to decency and national culture.[129]

In addition to attempting to discredit a national cultural basis for Songambele's declaration, critics of the commissioner's action also deployed arguments attempting to explain soul as a style. Situating soul as one in a long line of dance styles to achieve popularity in Dar es Salaam, many letter writers argued that banning this latest fad was both futile and unnecessary. Futile because, as the latest thing in town, it was irresistible. "Banning it will never make the youths drop it," opined Charles M. Njau.[130] As the newest "craze," noted another writer, "people went mad with [soul]."[131] And a ban would be unnecessary because soul would "like fashions die a natural death."[132] Mike P. Francis wrote, "I will just give some examples of dance styles which were once popular but have now faded or are just on the point of fading away! These were, Mnenguo, Rock, Samba, Twist, Rhumba, Waltz, Bollero, Monkey, Chacha, Shake, Pachanga, A Go-Go Rama, and others. . . . These are now being replaced by new ones like, Likembe, Kirikiri, Toyota, Chikuna, Soul, Tetema, Apollo and the like. Why is the 'soul' then not left alone for a while?"[133] Another opponent of the ban expressed a similar opinion: "There was a time when the 'Samba,' 'twist' etc. were very popular. Late in '67 Pachanga had the lead. Then came kirikiri. Now, it is sekuse and toyota. Sooner or later, soul would also suffer the same fate."[134] Such lists charting the coming and going of new dance styles appeared in over a third of the letters on the soul ban.[135] These statements resemble nothing so much as theories of modern fashion—the value of the latest, the ephemeral nature of any particular style, the premium placed upon, as one letter writer put it, "keep[ing] up with the changes of life."[136] More challenging to notions of both national culture and black culture, these interventions collapsed any easy distinction between the foreign and the indigenous, or between black and white dance, instead mixing styles originating in Congo, Tanzania, and multiple elsewheres as part of the aesthetic landscape of a desirably cosmopolitan city.

Also running through the letters describing the new dance called soul was evidence of the development of vocabularies articulating a new subcultural scene and a teenage, urban, cosmopolitan identity. Talk of downtown "soul sessions"[137] as forums for "digging" this new art form of the "protest generation"[138] abounded. Commenting that "soul . . . has doubtlessly been the most appreciated, particularly here, downtown," one enthusiast asked, "Does it mean a Saturday night out in a night club is already deprived of this one type? That we will have to go soul-less? How about our stocks of soul records at home, do they have to go in ashes? Does the law (if any) bar me from digging it within my own apartment, and is the importation of an 'I am Black and Proud' type render me possible from prosecution? Please advise and clarify."[139]

Many young writers claimed soul as their own, associating it approvingly with the teenagers, the youth, or youngsters. Ungando, for instance, complained about the ban on "soul digging" in the following words: "To me and all the teenagers this has brought a tremendous oppression which cannot be expressed. And, one unpleasant thing to note about the banning of soul is that it has reduced a great percentage of happiness to many young Tanzanians living in Dar es Salaam."[140] More than a few personalized their attack on the ban, ridiculing Commissioner Songambele as hopelessly out of touch with the times. "It appears to me that Mr. Songambele doesn't like soul music. May be because he doesn't know how to dig it," wrote Maganja-Stone Chimlo.[141] Pilly agreed: "Perhaps Mr. Songambele was annoyed when he saw one of his children 'souling' to the music from the radio. Teenagers should be allowed to go on with their soul."[142] Gai Mwashinga advised the commissioner to "keep cool," and A. J. Kanoni urged, "Those who do not know [how] to dance and who do not keep up with the changes of life in the way of music let them keep away from dancing places."[143]

Arguments about the ephemeral nature of style, derision toward "aged people"[144] like Songambele "who do not keep up with the changes," and articulation of and identification with a hip, urban identity expressed through new vocabularies and organized around a network of nightclubs came together in letters by opponents of the soul ban to make up a position on consumption and the city that, in the context of a post–Arusha Declaration Dar es Salaam, was highly charged. In the face of the declaration's intensification of an emphasis on the rural as the scene for hard work, development, and civic duty, a cosmopolitan city represented, more than ever, the foil for these attributes, and city dwellers symbols of laziness and exploitation (unyonyaji). The soul ban's focus on schoolgirls—a perennially charged problem category in the cultural politics of the time, as Lynn Thomas has shown for Kenya and as I discuss in chapter 2 for Dar es Salaam—resonated with the way in which young, unmarried women in town were frequent stand-ins for this portrayal of the city.[145]

Situated in this context, attacks on the soul ban ran counter to an official ethic and aesthetic of frugality, rural hard work, and peasant citizenship that was becoming increasingly important to the state's legitimacy at the time of the ban. Letter writers' articulation of an ethic of consumption valuing the "latest craze" and "style[s] that [are] liked by their co-youths on earth" challenged state discourse.[146] It did so not because of the strident cosmopolitanism of the celebratory statements about soul, but rather because this cosmopolitan imaginary, constructed around networks of global youth culture, was quite different from the internationalist connections invoked by the state around a network of socialist or communist countries. Furthermore, the defense by self-identifying teenagers of the nightclubs, public hall, and "dancing places" where soul was played reversed the polarities of the rural–urban dichotomies of official discourse. Indeed, in the political climate of Dar es Salaam after the Arusha Declaration, the "soul digging in clubs to which schoolgirls were reportedly lured represented a kind of conspicuous consumption by a prominent urban problem category: young people refusing the vanguard role of youth for the ideologically suspect one of teenagers.

Obatala's assessment of African young people's consumption of soul as "not [being] rooted in any genuine appreciation of the historical, political, and economic ties that bind us [Africans and African Americans] and make us a common people with one destiny" may not have been directly contradicted by the Tanzanian soul debate. But neither did this assessment capture either the personal or political meanings of soul for young Tanzanians in the context of official attacks on urban style that conformed neither to a rural aesthetic nor a respectable urban one.

And there was a similar disjuncture between Obatala's and Eubanks's concerns, on the one hand, and the motivations of Tanzanian officials in banning soul. Officials' motives were informed by anxieties over the mobility and sexuality of urban, particularly female, youth rather than by allegiance to or neglect of political affiliations and commitments to a black diaspora. Such affiliations certainly existed for the Tanzanian government, but they played out in ambiguous ways when it came to official positions on Afro-American culture.

Official ambivalence toward Afro-American culture was perhaps most apparent when noted African American personalities captured public attention during their visits to Tanzania. Coverage of Angela Davis's visit to Tanzania in August 1973, for instance, exemplifies this well. Her weeklong official visit coincided with the buildup to a new TANU campaign to ban indecent dress, the most vigorous such campaign since Operation Vijana, and both events featured prominently—indeed, competed for space—in the October issue of Nchi Yetu. Gracing the issue's cover, a space typically featuring state-sanctioned models of national femininity, was a portrait photograph of Davis sporting her large trademark Afro, dangling hoop earrings, and a stylish white pantsuit. The brief text on the cover, however, alerted readers to what was the main story of the issue and the subject of its page-one editorial: mavazi ya heshima (respectable or dignified dress). As one turned the page one encountered the two stories side by side yet again—this time with Davis's miniaturized image vacating center stage to make way for the editor's condemnation of "shameful dress." Lauded in the photo's caption as that of "a daring revolutionary and fighter for justice . . . worldwide," Davis's image competed with the editor's exhortations against "wantonly dressing up and imitating people of other nationalities."[147] Inside the magazine, full-length articles on each story followed. "Respectable Dress" attacked banned dress in national cultural terms and singled out several specific styles for special condemnation: among them the trousers (known locally as Pekosi) "worn especially by the internationally famous soul musician called James Brown"; wide belts; women's short skirts and tight pants; and the practice, popular among both men and women, of doing one's hair "to look like African Americans."[148] The biographical article on Davis—"A fighter for equal human rights"— was accompanied by photos of her visit to Arusha District. Dressed in the pantsuit featured on the cover, this time sporting large, round sunglasses, Davis was portrayed "showing clearly that she has African

Angela Davis featured on the cover of *Nchi Yetu*, October 1973. *Courtesy of the Tanzania Information Service.*

Photographers of *Nchi Yetu* capture Angela Davis on her upcountry visit to Arusha District during her visit to Tanzania in 1973. *Courtesy of the Tanzania Information Service.*

Akionyesha dhahiri kwamba ana asili ya Kiafrika hapa Bi Angela Davis anatafuna muhindi uliopikwa katika Kijiji cha Ujamaa cha Mareu katika Wilaya ya Arusha

Bi Devis anaongea na Mkuu wa Mkoa wa Arusha Bwana Mwakang'ata ofisini mwake.

roots" as she tasted some roasted maize offered by residents of an uja-maa village and chatted with the Arusha regional commissioner, A. Mwankang'ata, at his office.[149]

Although the writers and editors of Nchi Yetu at the Department of News and Information scrupulously avoided any textual mention of Da-vis's sartorial style, readers of the issue could not have helped noticing her Afro, sunglasses, pants, and jewelry—all markers of a cosmopoli-tan style that, as displayed by Tanzanians, were under attack as inde-cent, foreign, and shameful to the nation. One of the visual examples of unacceptable dress accompanying part two of the "Mavazi ya Heshima" article was striking in its affinity with the photos of Davis published the month before.[150] That Nchi Yetu made no objection to Davis's appear-ance can be attributed in part to the fact that she was not a Tanzanian but a foreign guest of honor. What the curious appearance of the two stories suggests more than anything, however, is that official cam-paigns against Afro-American culture in Tanzania were launched not in reference to the way such culture enabled or disabled a black struggle worldwide, as Eubanks and Obatala argued, respectively, but to address concerns over decency and the city. This is not to contend that Tanza-nian officialdom was blind to diasporic politics or an internationalist agenda—indeed the piece on Davis alone, not to mention the wider rec-ord of Tanzanian international alliances and commitments, strongly indicates the contrary. What I do suggest, however, is that the state con-sistently tried to frame the two issues as entirely independent, distinct, and separate, even as many of its interlocutors insisted that they were fundamentally intertwined.

This disjuncture between state and popular frames, then, allows one to see the correspondents' interventions on the issue—those of both Tanzanians and expatriates like Obatala and Eubanks—in a new light. For if state discourse featured efforts to separate and distinguish its support for a radical, black (inter)nationalism from its assault on in-decent urban others at home, many opponents of the soul ban un-dermined such distinctions. But neither did many of these opponents necessarily view soul in the terms that Obatala and Eubanks did, that is, as indexing political positions weighty with meaning in the context of black struggles worldwide. Akin to the way opponents of Operation Vijana appealed to a different kind of modern in challenging the TYL's insistence on modern decency, letter writers on the soul ban deployed a vocabulary and imagery drawn from Afro-American and international youth cultures to make claims to certain forms of urban living in Dar

Si wabaya kinadada hawa. Kuto-
kana na mavazi yao yamewapu-
nguzia heshima pamoja na uzuri
wao wa asili.

Photograph published in an *Nchi Yetu* feature entitled "Respectable Dress" portraying examples of women's dress classed as indecent. The original caption (translated from Kiswahili) read, "They aren't bad, these young sisters. Because of their dress they have lowered their respectability as well as their natural beauty." Note the affinity, in the Afro hairstyle and bell-bottom pants, with the look captured in the magazine's photographs of Angela Davis the previous month (see page 80). *Courtesy of the Tanzania Information Service.*

es Salaam. In accentuating the uneven encounters and disjunctures between these multiple positions on the soul ban, my examination responds to recent calls by scholars like Brent Hayes Edwards and Kennell Jackson to produce transnational histories of "black cultural traffic" that, to paraphrase Jackson, loosen one's views of the paths black popular culture takes.[151] Such histories, as the work of Edwards, Paula Ebron, and Catherine Cole compellingly demonstrate, must be attuned to the disjunctures, alongside the solidarities, that emerge along these routes.[152] As the negotiations around African American culture in Dar es Salaam suggest, soul music and the Afro traveled not with a fixed set of meanings but as forms that were susceptible to passionate reappropriation, reworking, and revaluing along the way.

Finally, the soul ban also shows how such cultural campaigns themselves, once launched, became subject to appropriation in sometimes unexpected ways by Tanzanians engaging official policy in public debate. The soul ban is so striking in this regard because it was, in conception and implementation, an initiative significantly different from, say, Operation Vijana. Whereas Operation Vijana was the product of deliberation by a committee of officials over the course of several days, Songambele's ban on soul began life as an apparently off-the-cuff remark in response to complaints by schoolteachers. Operation Vijana received extensive coverage and some high-profile supportive editorials in the state-controlled media, while Songambele's measure went nearly unmentioned and received only lukewarm official support. Not least, Operation Vijana was enthusiastically enforced by the TYL—indeed, it was TYL's project from start to finish. In contrast, enforcement of the ban on soul remained minimal; the TYL did not take up its cause nor was it accorded the status of an operation.

And yet it is precisely in light of these differences with Operation Vijana that what happened to the soul ban is so important. For despite its low profile (Songambele's initial announcement received a two-sentence, albeit front-page, story in the *Standard*), the soul ban generated an immediate and extensive outcry: thirty letters in a mere seven days. And opposition was not limited to the pages of the press, for, as the Dar es Salaam–bred literary critic May Joseph, remembers, the ban "created popular dissent and surreptitious circulations of soul consumption."[153] Furthermore, several opponents of the ban placed it in a context of previous cultural initiatives launched in the previous two years, expressing a frustration with an apparent trend in cultural banning campaigns. Complained Charles M. Njau, "Sometime last year the T.Y.L. came up with the banning of mini-skirts and tubular trousers. This year the Coastal Regional Commissioner has drawn our attention to the soul music. What are all these havocs for?"[154] And as another writer succinctly summed up the situation, "The story of the bans is endless in this world today."[155]

These remarks and the outcry over the soul ban in general are telling. Together, they suggest that the string of cultural initiatives launched by the government and TANU in the years following the Arusha Declaration were increasingly becoming lightning rods for urban political engagement and debate. By the end of 1969, some residents of Dar es Salaam were beginning to understand even the most ad hoc of official cultural campaigns as part of a trend, a succession of bans "endless in this world today." The proscriptive cultural initiatives of this period must be understood as more than just vehicles through which TANU attempted to impose a fully articulated national cultural project on wayward urban others; they are crucial scenes in an ongoing (re)constitution of national culture. Furthermore, in addition to aiding in an understanding of the centrality of targeted, decadent cultural forms and practices to the constitution of national culture, the campaigns illuminate the ways in which public debates over culture were becoming prime forums for engagement with a range of ongoing social struggles in Dar es Salaam. That this was true even when, as in the case of the soul ban, the measure itself had little official backing demonstrates the degree to which the social lives of national cultural campaigns stretched beyond the control of the state.

The national cultural project was hailed as a sharp, corrective break from the colonial period, but there was much about it that continued to exhibit assumptions about culture that had roots in the colonial. Among these continuities was a wrestling with the twin dichotomies of traditional versus modern and rural versus urban. In the case of the first of these pairs, postcolonial cultural policy exhibited an enduring tension between regarding tribal tradition as the fundamental building block of national culture and a deep impulse to bring that tradition in line with notions of a modern decency perceived as appropriate to a Tanzania emerging on the world stage. If the modernization imperative was increasingly prominent after the Arusha Declaration, the tensions between tradition and the modern represented less a successive shift from one set of criteria to another than two sides of a coin. Despite the continuities, the representation of the national cultural project as a sharp departure with the colonial situation was nonetheless important. Repeated in official declarations, speeches, performances, and cultural operations throughout Tanzania's first postcolonial decade, national culture emerged as a domain in which the postcoloniality of the state could be symbolically performed.

But if the national cultural project as a promotional enterprise was pivotal to the announcement of a break with the colonial, there was much more to this project than the construction of prescriptive policy. By the late 1960s, national culture was constituted as much in reference to a field of urban, feminized decadence targeted in varied operations in the capital as in relation to the promotion of nationalized forms. This anxious wrestling with urban decadence is a primary, constitutive context for the emergence of national culture. In addition, however, such operation politics did not simply impose official standards of national cultural behavior on a subject urban population. Taken to the cosmopolitan streets of Dar es Salaam, it also unleashed vigorous public contests, not least over key categories of state legitimacy. If officials were keen to disentangle authoritative notions of modern development from so-called false claims upon the modern from decadent quarters, operations' opponents laid claim to ways of being modern that challenged such efforts. Rather than constituting an alternative modernity, these claims at once affirmed a singular modern and contested its parameters. Youth too, as an official master category, was subject to challenge, as Dar es Salaam's new teenagers drew on transnational style in ways that disputed any would-be state monopoly on youth. All this jostling of competing notions of culture played out in a Dar es Salaam crisscrossed by competing transnational networks of images, icons, styles, people, and ideas. Multiple transnational imaginaries were in tension not only with national frames of reference, but sometimes also with each other. Notions of culture were far from all that was being contended for in these debates. A mutually embedded triad of social struggles around gender, generation, and wealth were becoming implicated in and reworked through the cultural contests of Dar es Salaam's long sixties.

"The Age of Minis"

SECRETARIES, CITY GIRLS, AND

MASCULINITY DOWNTOWN

Here in town clothes make the man.
—J. A. K. Leslie, *A Survey of Dar es Salaam* (1963)

In the modern world . . . men and women are in a crucial
tug-of-war in which each side is claiming for superiority.
—Peter Claver F. Temba, letter to the *Standard*,
October 16, 1970

On October 7, 1968, Tanzania's Field Force Unit (FFU), the state's riot
police, were dispatched to Kariakoo bus station in Dar es Salaam during
the morning rush hour. A major terminus for the throngs who com-
muted to work, school, and other business in the capital's downtown,
the Kariakoo station that morning was the scene of violence that would
dominate the next day's headlines and pepper discussions for months.
According to eyewitnesses, buses pulling into the station were met by
"gangs of [male] youths" who began boarding the buses and "harass-
ing all girls wearing mini-skirts or tight dresses." As a large crowd gathered, some of the attackers were witnessed pulling "indecently dressed"
young women off buses for beatings. Arriving to find the violence in
progress, the FFU fired tear gas, eventually dispersing the crowd. The
next day, the *Standard*'s reporter called the episode the "Dar riot."[1]
    This incident occurred as part of the chaotic run-up to Operation Vi-
jana, Tanzania's first major campaign against what was regarded as indecent dress (see chapter 1).[2] Theoretically targeting offending clothing
worn by both women and men, the measure focused overwhelmingly
on women's dress (most prominently the miniskirt) and was launched
and carried out in Dar es Salaam by the mostly male TYL. For nearly half

On the eve of Operation Vijana, officials of the TANU Youth
League display for the press some examples of indecent dress:
(left to right) Brigadier Rajabu Diwani (chief commander),
minister L. N. Sijaona (chairman), Joseph Nyerere (secretary-
general), and Moses Nyauye (deputy secretary-general).
Standard, December 30, 1968. *Courtesy of the Tanzania
Standard (Newspapers) Limited.*

a year—from its unveiling in October 1968 through the first few months
of its official enforcement in early 1969—Operation Vijana captured the
imagination of Dar es Salaam residents, dominating public debate in
the city and affecting everyday encounters on the street in a manner few,
if any, state interventions in the life of the capital had done previously.

The TYL billed Operation Vijana as part of the project of national
culture, and in chapter 1 I considered the debate surrounding the campaign—a significant dimension of which was focused on issues of authenticity, imitation, national identity, and being modern—in this light.
However, as physical attacks attending Operation Vijana (like the one
described above) begin to attest, there was much more to the campaign
than national culture. If the TYL was explicit that the operation was

an attack on urban decadence, it was also clear early on that a central component of this focus was a logic in which particular representations of women were potent stand-ins, in a kind of shorthand, for the ills of the city. Even if submerged in the TYL's national cultural framing of the dress campaign, statements linking women in banned fashion to an urban landscape of parasitical gain and decadent leisure were present from the beginning in the league's conception of the operation.[3] And as successive dress campaigns moved out into the streets and neighborhoods of Dar es Salaam and began to be discussed publicly, a more complicated texture of the perceptions linking women to a fallen city began to emerge—one embedded in events that surrounded the operations, a broader political economy of sex, work, and masculinity in the city, and the capital's fraught gender relations.

Operation Vijana would soon become the principal TYL activity of the year. Part of this prominence was likely owing to the massive attention garnered by the campaign from the moment it was announced—more attention, indeed, than any league initiative had ever attracted. Aside from the campaign's dominance of the press and of public talk in the city for months, it also swiftly began to be used to justify physical attacks on women in town, like the one in Kariakoo.[4] Women and girls said to be wearing miniskirts were verbally harassed at bus stations, dragged off buses, chased along downtown streets, and often stripped of their clothes by groups of young men. The TYL's response to such incidents, occurring as they did before the deadline to adopt decent dress, was ambivalent. In the wake of the Kariakoo incident, for instance, the league insisted that none of its members were involved, even as its spokesperson said he was not surprised "if the youth found the deadline too far away for them."[5] On the eve of the deadline the TYL did respond to calls for more careful planning of the enforcement of the ban, canvassing the capital with posters depicting models of decent and indecent dress and limiting the officially sanctioned enforcers to five hundred TYL cadres outfitted with walkie-talkies with which to communicate with TYL headquarters as they patrolled the streets.[6] However, despite these measures to standardize the ban's enforcement under the auspices of the TYL, complaints surfaced suggesting that some young men, TYL members and others, were attempting to take questionable liberties with young women under the guise of enforcing the operation.[7]

In this chapter I use Operation Vijana as a point of departure for a broader investigation of struggles over women, work, mobility, and sex in Dar es Salaam's long sixties. Periodic, intense debates over dress and comportment constituted a key terrain on which these contests were waged. But this terrain was a rapidly shifting one, and successive campaigns to police women's appearance and movement in the city saw changes not only in the scope and method of these disciplining efforts, but also in the emergence of new challenges to them. For many young men enthusiastically taking up Operation Vijana's call, the miniskirt had come to stand in for a complex, deeply gendered political economy of sex and accumulation in town. The miniskirt was a malleable sign, though, and if attempts to revalue it were limited in the Operation Vijana episode, later moves by Dar es Salaam's police to institutionalize the control of women's dress and movement confronted a changed situation. Perhaps ironically, the shift in the campaigns against dress from the vigilante to the more institutionalized opened the door for more robust challenges to both the dress codes and the ideological underpinning of the campaigns.

Migration, Work, and Gender in Postwar Dar es Salaam

Prior to the end of the Second World War migration in the British mandate territory of Tanganyika, while substantial in numbers, was primarily from one rural area to another. Migration was driven largely by opportunities for wage labor in agriculture, particularly on sisal plantations, and the urban population of Tanzania increased at a relatively low rate, not much faster than the population's natural growth rate. In the last decade of colonial rule, the 1950s, this pattern began to change. While rural migration continued apace throughout the decade, it began to decline steeply a couple of years before independence in 1961, slowing to a trickle by 1965. In contrast, migration to Tanganyika's urban areas shot upward in the early 1950s, beginning a boom that has lasted until the present day. Dar es Salaam received a disproportionate number of those heading for town: as noted in the introduction, in less than twenty years its population nearly quadrupled, from 69,200 in 1948 to 272,821 in 1967.[8] Jobs, housing, and social services, however, lagged far behind this exponential population growth, both under colonial and postcolonial states. Although wage employment in Dar es Salaam doubled during the 1960s, it failed to keep pace with the population boom and the expansion of primary schooling that also occurred during that decade.[9] Official efforts to construct housing and provide infrastructural support to new neighborhoods were minimal and consistently benefited the wealthy. The capital's new migrants gathered in the city's burgeoning shantytowns, which spread farther and farther out from the city center.[10]

The gender dynamics of this influx are important for understanding some of the capital's key social tensions during the long sixties. In the colonial period, those migrating to town in Tanzania, as across most of colonial Africa, were predominantly male (approximately two-thirds of migrants in the 1950s). Compared with many other African cities of the time, however, the number of women in colonial Dar es Salaam was by most accounts relatively high. Rising and falling through the colonial period, the male to female ratio in the capital ranged from 140 to 100 in 1928 and 206 to 100 in 1931, to an apparent low of 110 to 100 in 1940 and back up to 141 to 100 by 1948.[11] Despite being effectively barred from most formal wage-earning jobs, many women were able to carve out income-earning niches. Women could own property in Dar es Salaam and earn money as landlords, and a striking number did so.[12] Several kinds of informal work were dominated by women, including the selling of food to male laborers, street hawking, beer brewing, domestic employment, and sex work.[13] The city also presented opportunities for a range of relationships with men—from sex work to the provision of the "comforts of home" to regular clients, nonmarital cohabitation, and cultivating of lovers who helped pay the rent—all of which offered young women a greater degree of social and economic autonomy than could be gained through formal marriage. Such nonmarital relationships, categories of which were often blurred, were predominant in Dar es Salaam, a fact that as early as the late 1950s was thought to have "raised the bargaining position of women in the town."[14]

Despite the already relatively common presence of women in colonial Dar es Salaam, the decade following independence saw a significant rise in the proportion of women among migrants, a trend that changed the demographic character of urban areas. By 1971, women constituted a majority (54 percent) of new arrivals in Dar es Salaam, contributing to what John Campbell called the capital's "radically changing urban sex ratio."[15] Between 1948 and 1967, Dar es Salaam's male to female ratio declined from 141 to 100 to 123 to 100, the ratio for fifteen- to twenty-four-year-olds reaching near-parity at 103 to 100.[16] The demographic profile of female migrants was also changing. Regardless of gender, migrants to the capital were overwhelmingly young, continuing the pattern of the late colonial period, but the proportion of female migrants who were unmarried upon arrival grew steadily from 13 percent in 1952 to 33 percent in 1970. Many of these women had taken advantage of the growth in educational opportunities for women, which had expanded faster than those for men.[17]

Despite high unemployment in Dar es Salaam in the 1960s, the postcolonial capital did present young women migrants with growing opportunities for increased economic autonomy. Some of these built on and extended the informal income-earning niches of the colonial period.[18] Other opportunities, however, were new. While the overall percentage of town-dwelling women in formal wage employment remained very small throughout the decade (reaching 13 percent in 1970), particular kinds of formal sector work were opening up to women in ways that were nonexistent during the colonial period.[19] A male preserve prior to independence, secretarial work, for example, was one domain in which, by 1970, female employees were common (by some reports, even sought after). According to a survey conducted that year, the percentage of employees who were female in four categories of wage employment—clerical, professional/managerial/technical, public service/nursing/social work, and hotel/restaurant/bar—ranged from 24 percent to 38 percent.[20] Some of Dar es Salaam's factories, too, were hiring large numbers of women in the 1960s, the Urafiki Textile Mill and the Tanita cashew-nut processing plant (where nearly three-fourths of the employees were female) being notable examples.[21] Large majorities of women in such jobs were under the age of thirty, single or divorced, and, with the possible exclusion of barmaids, possessed some formal education.[22]

This is not to suggest that most women in Dar es Salaam were well off, earning a wage, or building futures free of social controls. On the contrary, the informal economy remained the dominant sphere of women's work throughout the early independence period, men retained a privileged position in the social and economic life of the capital, and the city's chronic shortages of jobs, housing, and social services affected women at least as severely as men. In 1970 male migrants in Dar es Salaam were over five times more likely than their female counterparts to find wage employment.[23] Indeed, one of the results of the marked increase in female job seekers migrating to Dar es Salaam in the late 1960s was a sharp rise in the female unemployment rate, which hit 20 percent in 1970.[24]

I am, however, suggesting two things. First of all, that in relation to their aims for and expectations of the move to town, urban life may have afforded relative gains for young women that did not accrue to their male counterparts. There is historical evidence, both from Tanzania and from other African contexts, that the motives, expectations, and outcomes of rural to urban migration differed considerably for women and men. Scholars have long argued that a primary motivation for migrating involved circumventing the control that elders in rural areas held over marriage options. But if for young migrant men the dream was to quickly earn a cash dowry and return, respected and admired, to the village to marry on one's own terms, for many young women "migration [was] seen as an end in itself": an attempt to take more permanent advantage of the opportunities for autonomous accumulation that the city seemed to offer.[25]

If this first suggestion remains arguable, the second one is more certain: that there was a widespread perception among young men struggling to get by in Dar es Salaam that the city was full of young women getting ahead, finding work, and gaining spending money of their own at young men's expense. As J. A. K. Leslie observed in the mid-1950s, the gap between male migrants' expectations of urban life and its reality were considerable and made harder to bear by the ready appearance of wealth and success on the city's landscape: "His aim in coming to town has been to get cash; yet he finds that he is poor (whereas in the country, with far less money, he was not): yet being poor he is surrounded by tempting things which can be had only for money; all the glamour which helped draw him to town—dances, women, drink, clothes, cinemas, taxis, require money before he can enjoy them; they are so near yet out of his reach. . . . There is always somebody to be seen enjoying the things he cannot get. . . . To get cash he needs work, yet the Government, whose duty he believes it is to provide work for all, does not give him work."[26] Moreover, many young men appear to have viewed their female counterparts not simply as disconnected others who happened to be doing well, but as engaging in social climbing through their relationships with older, wealthier "sugar daddies" and shunning relationships with young men who were unable to compete in material terms.[27]

In his observations on young male migrants, Leslie hints at the centrality of clothing to practices of self-fashioning in Dar es Salaam. Scholars have long recognized the importance of clothes as markers of social status in colonial East Africa, and a few have noted the ways in which appropriations of stylistic codes inspired by British officials and Muslim traders were key to the performance of such status.[28] Dar es Salaam in the 1950s and 1960s was a nodal point for the circulation of cosmopolitan forms of music, fashion, and film, and these forms, particularly clothes, became material for self-styling. In the case of the cowboy subculture of the fifties and early sixties, fashion fed off of the Hollywood westerns playing in the capital's several cinemas.[29] For young migrants eager to make a splash in town, observed Leslie of Dar es Salaam in the late 1950s, "how better than to buy clothes, fine clothes, bright, unusual clothes, and wear them through the streets?"[30] Indeed, in a city that to many migrants, particularly young men, seemed to promise much but deliver little, fashion was one means by which one could perform a degree of success beyond one's financial situation. Of course, as Leslie noted, "there is always scope for more display, more expensive clothes, a firmer stamp of success."[31]

In the past decade, scholars of colonial and postcolonial Africa have sought to understand, as Jean Allman puts it, "the ways in which power is represented, constituted, articulated, and contested through dress."[32] Through examinations of wide-ranging contexts from struggles over clothing on a nineteenth-century South African mission frontier through the globalized secondhand clothing industry in contemporary Zambia, this work has challenged some fundamental assumptions of a broader literature on fashion.[33] Against long-standing Eurocentric assumptions in the work on Western fashion, this Africanist scholarship has worked to displace simplistic accounts of African engagements with Western dress as being characterized by either wholesale resistance or succumbing to a hegemonic spread of Western style.[34] Instead, these accounts tell complex stories of, among other things, how "value is created in body treatments that derive from foreign sources."[35] My chapter contributes to this scholarship by examining, in part, the ways in which the meanings attached to the miniskirt and other banned fashion in Dar es Salaam in the 1960s were embedded in the local sensibilities and struggles around gendered work, mobility, sex, and resources marking the city at the time.

As I elaborated in the introduction, colonial and postcolonial states responded to the extensive changes experienced by a rapidly expanding Dar es Salaam in particular ways. Wary of what they regarded as the dangers of allowing Africans to become detribalized, British colonial officials across Africa had long discouraged so-called natives from settling in town, justifying the policy with reference to theories of the unsuitability of Africans to urban life. In the 1950s, as the extent of Dar es Salaam's population boom became clear, the government, parallel-ing British colonial policy toward urban labor across Africa, pursued a dual strategy: it tried to create a stable and "respectable" urban class of Africans, while using a variety of forceful methods in a failed attempt to "repatriate" jobless "undesirables."[36] Despite occasionally opposing such forced relocations in the late 1950s, the nationalist elite shared colonial officials' vision of developing a modern, orderly capital, and upon taking power in 1961 they continued campaigns against Dar es Salaam's unproductive *wahuni* (vagrants or undesirables, with strong connotations of immorality).[37] Such campaigns escalated after the Aru-sha Declaration of February 1967, which, aside from enacting a series of major socialist policies, upheld the rural as the appropriate sphere for development and the performance of Tanzanian citizenship.[38] The de-velopments of the 1960s regarding migration, work, and official urban policy were contemporaneous—and intersected in important ways—with TANU's national cultural project, especially in the coding of ru-ral and urban space that accompanied its campaigns against urban decadence.[39]

The historical dynamics sketched out above—booming migration, shifting job opportunities, women coming to the capital and claiming public space in new ways, an energetic state initiative to construct urban ills as cultural ones—all portray a Dar es Salaam that in the late 1960s was in the midst of considerable social change. If this was the context within which Operation Vijana was launched in October 1968, then the heated debate over the campaign showcases the way in which fashion encapsulated and became a battleground for the social struggles brew-ing in the city. The TYL sought to portray the ban as a matter of na-tional culture. But in the debate that gripped the capital, challenges to dominant notions of national culture emerged (as we saw in chapter 1) and discourse on the operation spilled out beyond TYL's framing of the campaign to engage issues of urban respectability and sexual politics. The patterns of gendered discourse and violence that erupted in the wake of the announcement of the campaign reveal that in some quarters the struggle over the ban focused much less on national culture than on questions of gender relations and sex across a charged urban land-scape. Like the debate in the *Standard*, discourse in the city's Kiswahili press—above all in the semi-independent daily *Ngurumo*—illustrates the ways in which people targeted by Operation Vijana's assault upon

certain (life)styles exploited openings in official discourse to renegoti-
ate and sustain lives in the city.

Operation Vijana and the Meanings of the Miniskirt

Reminiscing in 1984 about Operation Vijana, the veteran Tanzanian
journalist Hadji Konde recalled that while the ban had generated much
debate in the country's letters-to-the-editor pages, *Ngurumo* had published only three letters on the campaign.[40] If he was correct about one
thing—that the debate in *Ngurumo* was markedly different from that
hosted by, say, the *Standard*—Konde was overlooking the dozens of
letters, poems, editorials, and cartoons engaging the controversy over
dress that appeared in *Ngurumo* in the weeks and months following the
announcement of Operation Vijana. Few of these interventions—and of
those published in the Kiswahili press generally—featured explicit debate over national culture or foreign influence. Instead, correspondents
used Operation Vijana and the attendant focus on women's bodies and
clothing as an opportunity to air profound anxieties about women, sex,
work, and mobility in Dar es Salaam. While similar anxieties were long-
standing, they were taking on new inflections with the changing face of
Tanzania's capital in the late 1960s.

The kinds of fashion banned under the operation, particularly wom-
en's indecent dress, had long been associated with the urban. But in
the late 1960s, with the Arusha Declaration's inscription of town and
country life into a narrative of the battle between the virtuous and the
fallen, certain new elements to this association emerged. Architects of
Operation Vijana connected banned fashion to a perceived crisis of rural to urban migration. In explaining how the aims of the campaign fit
within the logic of the Arusha Declaration, TYL planners worried that
decadent fashion was threatening to spread beyond urban areas and
reach "rural areas and even *ujamaa* villages." As "mini-skirts aren't at
all complementary with *ujamaa* farming . . . and manual labor," the reasoning continued, "it's obvious that our girls will leave the rural areas
and flock to those areas [the towns] that suit their condition."[41] Several
supporters of the initiative agreed. Mohamed Jeuri, for instance, argued
that instead of "coming to the city in search of entertainment," fans of
nguo za kihuni (immoral or indecent clothing) should be back in the villages working the land:

Can a person like that really become a revolutionary? If she is told to return to the *shamba* [farm] to build the Nation, even if only for a day, will she agree? . . . Where will she put those wigs, fingernails and tight dresses? . . .

And not only that. . . . if a woman or man wears so-called modern clothing and goes home to the *shamba*, without a doubt s/he will tempt his or her friends and family greatly, make them regard the *shamba* as not a good place for life; and then they in turn will come to the city to look for that very life. Without knowing it they find themselves extremely oppressed by such a little thing: *Taiti* [tight clothing]. In this way, women sell their bodies and men find themselves with the job of ambushing people at night . . . so they can get at least one pair of tight trousers to show off to those they left back on the *shamba*.[42]

As the controversy over Operation Vijana raged, the official press began to supplement its coverage with short stories that focused on the seductive dangers of town and highlighted the role of fashion in the seduction. One such story, titled "I'll never stay in town again," told the tale of Kamili, a young country lad plagued with *tamaa ya kufika Dar* (the [very visceral] desire to reach Dar es Salaam). He ends up making the journey to the capital only to be seduced by a fashionably dressed woman who takes all his money. "What a catastrophe!" cries Kamili, as he recites the moral of the story. "I'd better head back up-country, begin farming in an ujamaa village, and start being self-reliant!"[43] The ease and economy with which a miniskirted woman could visually conjure up the relationship between a city of decadent, feminized consumption and a countryside of national productivity is made even more clear in a cartoon published in *Ngurumo* in the late 1960s or early 1970s. It portrayed a woman carrying a handbag and wearing a short dress decorated with *jembes* (hoes) smiling and declaring, "*Jembe!* I can wear it, but I won't wield it!"[44]

As Kamili's tale of his experience hints, fashions like the miniskirt stood for more than just the city. They conjured up specific female, urban types and tropes. Chief among these was the prostitute. *Ngurumo*'s main page-one story describing the first two days of Operation Vijana's official enforcement, proclaimed, "Whores and Undesirables Mind Their Manners."[45] One letter-writing supporter of the campaign asserted that the ban had been imposed by TYL "to mark their anger at the prostitution being installed by some young ladies who are also members of UWT," and that TYL cadres "must be prepared to cut out the minis not only from Kariakoo but even from the hotels where many are harbored." The letter concluded, "We cannot import culture by promoting prostitution."[46] Barmaids, generally thought to be engaged in sex work, were a common target of dress-code attacks, even before Operation Vijana was announced. In March 1968, for instance, the press reported the stoning of a barmaid on her way to work by a "mob [of] youngsters" who were "apparently incensed at the shortness and tight fit of her mini-skirt."[47]

The figure of the prostitute, with which the miniskirt was closely associated in the postcolonial 1960s, had a history in East African colonial cities. In her pioneering study of prostitution in colonial Nairobi, Luise White illustrates the variation in the category of the prostitute. From "streetwalking" to providing clients a broad array of services including meals and conversation, women in the colonial city developed a range of ways in which relationships with men entailed opportunities for material gain.[48] As suggested above, the evidence that exists for colonial Dar es Salaam, although limited, points to a picture similar to the one White paints for Nairobi.[49] The diversity of the ways in which women in colonial towns were perceived as being able to gain materially through sexual relationships with men contributed to laying the groundwork for the ways in which the female figures associated with the miniskirt extended beyond that of the prostitute to other urban types and tropes.

Indeed, in discourse around the ban and the ensuing physical attacks on women in Dar es Salaam, the miniskirt, or taiti, were also consistently tied to figures of the secretary, the schoolgirl, and the girlfriend of the sugar daddy. These were ambiguous figures, and while they would be subject to struggles to define new and viable, sometimes even respectable, urban images for women (as illustrated later in this chapter), in discourse around Operation Vijana they were overwhelmingly conflated with the prostitute. Lynn Thomas has traced anxieties in colonial and early postcolonial Kenya that schoolgirls embodied uncontrolled sexuality and "changed appearances and desires."[50] The figure of the girlfriend of the sugar daddy too has received some academic and much anecdotal and literary attention in postcolonial contexts across the continent.[51] (Sugar daddies and their girlfriends also featured prominently in fraught gender relations at the University of Dar es Salaam, as I discuss in chapter 3.) But if the association of indecent dress with the schoolgirl and the companion of a sugar daddy or "big man" was a feature of the late colonial period as well, its ties to the figure of the

Cartoon in *Ngurumo* from the late 1960s portraying an encounter between the male protagonist of the series, Bwanyenye, and a female prostitute advertising her services outside the door to her room. In response to the woman's appeals— "Bwenyenye, come on inside and wait for me . . ."—Bwanyenye admonishes her, "Go on home [to the village] to farm, don't depend on exploitation, exercise self-reliance!"

secretary were a newer addition, its emergence related to the opening up of clerical work to women in Dar es Salaam in the sixties.

The susceptibility of the figure of the secretary to conflation with illicit gain through sex was evident even in the TYL's early stages of planning for Operation Vijana. In a policy document outlining the aims and tactics of the operation, TYL Deputy Secretary-General Moses Nnauye began a section on the campaign's fulfillment of the Arusha Declaration with a theory of women and their relationship to work, fashion, and the city. "Most European women are of just two kinds," he confidently asserted. "They are either workers or prostitutes." In Nnauye's formulation the two categories were dangerously blurred, for "women working in offices or factories have time to go astray in all kinds of ways." Having framed the issue in classic national cultural style against a foil of a decadent Europe, he suggested that these patterns were beginning to affect Tanzania, for "the truth is that working girls have time to wear wigs, mini-skirts . . . and other things like that."[52]

If one maps out the numerous reports of physical attacks on and condemnation of women accused of wearing banned dress in the months between Operation Vijana's announcement and its official launch, a patterned geography becomes visible, one focused on specific spaces and sites: hotels and bars, buses and bus stations, downtown streets and offices, and the university. In an editorial on the ban, Ngurumo asserted that the problem of banned dress manifested itself "especially [among] girls who are working in offices, and a few others . . . who are in various income-earning positions."[53] For its part, the University of Dar es Salaam was a major site for confrontation over Operation Vijana, witnessing a clash between a demonstration supporting the operation staged by the campus TYL branch and a counterprotest of female students defiantly sporting banned clothing in front of their residence hall. The all-male TYL demonstration had targeted the women's dormitory, and alongside banners condemning indecent dress in national cultural terms ("Minis for decadent Europe," for example) the marchers held aloft placards apparently threatening specific women: one read, "Two devils in Hall 3, your days are numbered."[54]

But in this geography of confrontation over Operation Vijana bus routes, bus stations, and downtown streets were the most intensely and violently charged spaces. The attacks on women and girls getting off buses at Kariakoo may have been the first and biggest of the collective attacks, but several scenes of young women being pulled from buses or chased down a city center street and stripped by a group of young men and boys were reported in the press as the debate over the operation raged. Of the stories of physical attacks reported between September and February, nearly every one featured the urban workers' commute as its setting. A focus on working women's mobility about town made its way into the press debate over the campaign as well. In the midst of the controversy, one S. S. Tofiki, a resident of the city, published a poem specifying demographic statistics as the cause of his alarm over women's mobility in town. Referring to working women who "roam about" instead of "staying inside," he wrote,

> The census came around, and they increased in numbers,
> I started thinking, and crunched the numbers,
> How have you all gone wrong, failing to stay inside?
> What defect do you have, for your husbands to refuse you?[55]

The disquiet about working women commuting around town resonates with, even as it reworks, broader anxieties about mobility appearing in numerous colonial and postcolonial African contexts. Female mobility—specifically, migration from the country to the city—had long been associated with promiscuity and suspicions of illicit gain. Here this unease was being applied not simply to migration to town, but also, in an even more focused way, to movement within the city by certain categories of women. *Roaming* (*kuzurura*) was the word most frequently applied to this kind of movement. It was a term that simultaneously tapped into the long-standing unease with women's mobility and the descriptions of miniskirted women as animalistic (see chapter 1) that paired such women with traditionally dressed Maasai in national cultural discourse.

The spaces, sites, and associated types prominent in discourse and physical action during Operation Vijana all represented female accumulation, mobility, and autonomy and came together to make up a cultural topography that was the focus of a great deal of anxiety on the part of many of Dar es Salaam's young men. This interpretation occasionally surfaced explicitly in the debate over the ban. One letter writer, for instance, summed up the attack on women's dress as angst over women's work and autonomous consumption. "Inside the minis and under the wigs," the correspondent wrote, "are people with education and intelligence, able to hold down good jobs (sometimes in competition with men), with money of their own to spend, and their own ideas of how to spend it."[56]

But particular kinds of clothes were not only signs of women's accumulation and consumption, mobility, and autonomy—banned fashion was also regarded as a catalyst for these phenomena, which many young men in the capital saw as socioeconomic exploitation of men by women. As one D. Chokunegela complained in a poem published in *Uhuru*,

> You'll see Bibi Siti, with her handbag on her arm,
> Her body hugged by a *taiti*, seeking *Uzunguni* [the wealthy, formerly white area of Dar es Salaam],
> Pulling cash, from John and Damian,
> As for me, I congratulate the Resolution of the Youth.[57]

This accusation, that those who wore miniskirts were doing so in order to gain access to men and their money, was a charge that was leveled frequently and angrily by young men in the debate. As one campaign supporter put it, "I must condemn the minis from start to end. Ladies have to be guided as these young girls surely love the minis for gaining market; one dressing thus will win everybody."[58] Echoing this vocabulary, one letter to the *Nationalist* complained, "Our young girls become crazy and the happiest when putting on such kind of dress because they are gaining a market."⁵⁹

The miniskirt's role as a catalyst for "gaining market," in the views of many young men, was one inherent in the skirt's physical character itself. As Christopher Mwesiga lamented,

> We dress in order to protect our bodies from the elements and to make ourselves more beautiful. . . . But isn't it funny to put on a dress which becomes your master? You have to abide by whatever command it gives you. It forces you to walk in a certain way, it stops you from running when this is essential to your safety, it tells you "don't bend" and you cannot, dare not, do it!
>
> Thigh exposition does not only make men admire the beauty of the female sex. It also makes the observer grow sexually wild. Girls have no mercy in making people wild, and yet they do not offer satisfaction to the passions they create. . . .
>
> . . . If this trend is lucrative (I'd like someone to come out and tell me it is not), then, as an act of mercy, pity us boys who receive our minimum wage only once a month.⁶⁰

A number of notable elements of Mwesiga's plea were commonly expressed by young men in the dress debates. First, the miniskirt was often thought to be as much of an agent of the chaos perceived to be accompanying such dress as the wearer itself. As Mwesiga described it, it not only became the "master" of the girl wearing it, but, he hinted, dictated men's response to it. Furthermore, what gave the miniskirt this power to direct behavior was the "thigh exposition" it created. Whereas other items of indecent feminine fashion banned under Operation Vijana—wigs and skin-lightening creams, for example—were just as much signifiers of the fallen urban woman, the miniskirt was regarded as having unique powers of seduction precisely because of the parts of the body it revealed. Indeed, in debates ranging from the campaign for modern Maasai dress, to the costumes worn by national dance troupes, to campaigns like Operation Vijana, the exposure of thighs was more highly charged than that of other parts of the body, including breasts.⁶¹ Notions of modern decency deployed in such campaigns certainly required that breasts be covered; however, revealing tops, unlike the miniskirt, tended not to be met with the logic that they forced men to go "sexually wild." Focused speculation similar to Mwesiga's on what a woman wearing a miniskirt could and could not do without revealing her upper thighs—the example of boarding a bus came up often—was frequent

Cartoon in *Ngurumo* from the late 1960s in which the protagonist, Bwenyenye, ridicules a woman in a tight skirt as she boards a city bus. He says, "Beautiful one, are you wearing a 'taiti' or foot fetters?! If you can't get on the bus, just whisper to me—I'll jack you up with this stomach of mine."

in letters and cartoons on decency campaigns. It was in its tendency to quite literally "advertise the goods," as one male student put it, that many men situated the miniskirt's unique power to "gain market."[62]

Anxieties over young women gaining market—an idiom with connotations of capitalist accumulation and illicit gain that were charged in the wake of the Arusha Declaration's declared war on "all types of exploitation"—were especially professed by and ascribed to male TYL members and male university students. (Indeed, these two categories of people appear to have been the ban's staunchest supporters.) One opponent of the ban charged that TYL leaders and their cadres were jealous, for they "are the very ones who desire the taiti-wearers, and as soon as they fail to get them, they look for an underhanded way to take out their anger by forbidding them from wearing [these things]."[63] As for the students, we have seen that the struggle on campus over Operation Vijana featured male students making angry threats against particular women. As I illustrate further in chapter 3, this anger, and the campus politics surrounding Operation Vijana, related directly to what was perceived by male students as intense competition between themselves and wealthier, older men for sexual relationships with female students—competition in which the male students saw themselves as being at a tremendous economic disadvantage to the sugar daddies.[64]

Thus the office worker, the female undergraduate, and the girlfriend of the sugar daddy, as figures conjured up in public discourse by the sign of banned fashion, were all consistently conflated with the prostitute. All were represented as being in positions ripe with possibilities for gaining access to men and their money through sex. But in the context of changes in demography and work in Dar es Salaam, the conflation was beginning to be an unstable one. Indeed, public discourse around Operation Vijana featured attempts by some women to reclaim figures linked with banned fashion as viable urban identities.

Some of these attempts followed a UWT line that sought to celebrate women's entrance into formal wage labor as a sign of Tanzania's modern development, while condemning practices like the wearing of miniskirts in much the same terms as the TYL: as indecent assaults on respectability under the guise of modern fashion.[65] In an installment of a women's advice column called "Bibi Mapinduzi Asema" (Mrs. Revolution says) (which was tellingly inaugurated in Ngurumo during the Operation Vijana controversy and featured exhortations against banned fashion), Bibi Mapinduzi herself attempted to distinguish the office-working woman from the prostitute. Taking readers on a virtual tour of downtown Dar es Salaam in which she mapped out a geography of burgeoning women's formal sector work, Bibi Mapinduzi marveled at the "beautiful image of our . . . well-dressed girls emerging from offices with their purses" and continued, "I didn't know that we have this many women working in government and company offices." Writing pointedly that the majority of these women were "very well-dressed and moved respectably," Bibi Mapinduzi also lamented that their reputations were being tarnished by "certain women who were [recently] arrested for roaming the streets, in hotels and in bars for reasons best known to themselves." These roaming women, she said, "don't like real work" and should be forced "to leave town, to stop stealing people's husbands, and to go back to the shamba to farm."[66]

If the UWT leadership and other prominent women in high political office took a position championing public roles and work for women while attacking banned dress,[67] some young women and a few men sought to reconcile the two.[68] In October 1968, at the height of the debate over Operation Vijana, the vice president of UWT met with a group of young women who were non-UWT members at their Dar es Salaam hostel to discuss their concerns. In the "heated discussion" that ensued, the hostel residents said not only that "it was unfair that a body of men should sit down and decide what women should wear," but also explicitly justified the wearing of "shorter dresses." "Modern style dresses were cheap and suited to town living," the young women told their distinguished visitor. According to the *Standard*, "One girl said that as a secretary she had to do a lot of walking about and shorter dresses made this easier. She said that if she wore long national dress she would not be able to push her way on to crowded buses which she had to do every day."[69]

Statements like these illustrate attempts by working women to reclaim banned fashion by reinscribing it as practical, appropriate, and respectable for new patterns of work and movement in new urban spaces. More difficult to perform in a public discourse dominated by deep suspicion of female sexuality were attempts by women to celebrate banned fashion as a site of female pleasure. One woman referred, rather obliquely, to the capability of fashion to heighten "womanish feelings" that Tanzanian women, "like any other women," had.[70] Another quoted a saying she had "once read somewhere" that "'a woman's dress is like a garden-gate, which protects the property without blocking the view,'" even as she framed her enjoyment of banned fashion safely within the bounds of her marriage and her husband's gaze.[71]

But in the debate over Operation Vijana and given the way the campaign played out on the streets of Dar es Salaam, attempts to delink banned fashion from its association with female accumulation through sex and render the miniskirt respectable were few and far between. The attempts that were made in this direction faced in the operation an effort to insistently reconstruct and maintain associations between "border figures" like the secretary, on the one hand, with the image of the prostitute, the woman seeking only to gain market, on the other. For many of Dar es Salaam's young men who were failing to gain the access to resources and women that fantasies of city life promised, Operation Vijana promised to eliminate what was seen as a central tool of women who placed themselves out of their material reach. For those participating in attacks on women and even in the TYL-led enforcement of the ban, the campaign afforded an opportunity to enact sexualized performances of power over those women in the very spaces that were deemed to provide the conditions of possibility for female accumulation, mobility, and occasional autonomy. In this way, the young male rage generated around what was ostensibly a national cultural issue was intimately related to intersecting anxieties about women in urban space and the politics of sex in a post–Arusha Declaration Dar es Salaam. Such anxieties not only coincided with and reinforced the uneasy position of the city—depicted as a disturbing site of decadent consumption and femininity—within a state ideology that valorized the rural as the site of austere hard work; they also fueled the enforcement of the ban, with all its attendant rage and violence against the capital's "new women."[72]

Experiments in Institutionalization: Downtown "Swoops" and the Pauline Joseph Case

As a formal campaign, Operation Vijana did not last long; indeed, debate over the ban lasted considerably longer than its official enforcement by the TYL. Hailed by supporters as a success as early as the second week of January 1969, active enforcement by the TYL appears to have tapered off that same month, ending altogether by February. Within months, residents of Dar es Salaam were commenting on the return of banned dress to the streets.[73] Some observers later commented that young women simply took their skirts and dresses to tailors for lengthening during the campaign, returning to have them shortened as soon as the TYL patrols slackened.[74] No campaigns or measures against indecent dress were undertaken for almost two years. Then, in July 1970, letters began to appear in the press sharply criticizing the government for inaction in the face of a "frightening" proliferation of minis in the city's streets, offices, schools, buses, and bars.[75] Referencing each other and escalating to the point where Uhuru called the correspondence the "war over short dresses," many of the early calls were notable for laying a large portion of blame at the feet of the state for closing its eyes to the issue. Indeed, some openly expressed the common suspicion that political big men were encouraging the wearing of miniskirts by their potential prey.[76]

On September 28, 1970, two months after these calls began and more than eighty letters on the issue had been published, the government launched a new initiative to combat, as one TANU spokesperson put it, "the tendency of some of our girls to go about half-naked."[77] Although it shared with Operation Vijana a primary target of young women dressed indecently, the new campaign also differed from its predecessor. If Operation Vijana had at least nominally included men's styles among its targets, the new initiative focused exclusively on women and paid

Cartoon in *Ngurumo* from the late 1960s in which a young man, no model of solemn austerity himself, chides a woman for her outfit. He says, "It's just the other day that you were cleaned up and today you've come back with that very same style!" She replies, "Take off, weirdo."

considerably less attention to framing the issue in broad national cultural terms. Even more important, enforcement of the new campaign fell not to the TYL and its vigilante allies, but was placed in the hands of the police. Throughout late 1970 and into 1971 Dar es Salaam's police launched surprise evening "swoops" on the city's downtown area, arresting women deemed to be guilty of indecent dressing in a public place. Toward the beginning of the campaign, typical evening raids, often carried out twice a week, would result in the arrest of anywhere from twenty-five to one hundred women. Pressure was also brought to bear on public and private institutions like bars, clubs, restaurants, schools, and offices to bar indecently dressed women from their premises.[78] Much of the pressure seems to have gone partially unheeded, but at least one secondary school instituted a policy of sending girls with very short school uniforms home to change. The policy, which the school took seriously enough to produce mimeographed form letters to accompany offending students home, was widely publicized when a parent wrote a letter to *Uhuru*'s editor praising the administration of Zanaki Secondary School for its policy and thanking school officials for punishing his daughter. The parent included the mimeographed form, completed with his daughter's name, which *Uhuru* published prominently on its letters-to-the-editor page.[79]

As the campaign of 1970–71 progressed and was engaged in public debate, some noteworthy challenges emerged to the dress measures and the arguments being made to support them, challenges more extensive and somewhat different in kind from those voiced during Operation Vijana. The conditions within which these challenges emerged to shape a gendered struggle over work, autonomy, and urban space were complex, having to do both with the framing of the campaign itself and, perhaps even more significant, with a number of associated debates, trends, and actions occurring around the time of the dress measures.

On the evening of Saturday, October 3, 1970, Dar es Salaam police arrested thirteen women in a handful of city center bars and nightclubs on charges of indecent dressing in a public place.[80] The police raid was the second in what, over the following few months, would be a series of evening swoops on the capital's downtown in an effort to rid certain spaces of women either dressed indecently or seen to be behaving like "rogues and vagabonds."[81] Among the women taken into police custody that evening was twenty-five-year-old Pauline Joseph, an employee of a travel agency who was arrested along with several female friends as they approached the New Palace Hotel around eleven o'clock.[82] While each of her friends and indeed all of the other women caught up in the swoops pled guilty to the charges, Joseph chose to contest them. Denying the charges against her after four nights in jail—charges which carried penalties of substantial fines or months of imprisonment—Joseph was released on five-hundred-shilling bail and put on trial.[83] After three postponements her trial finally began on January 27, 1971.

Lasting four days over a period of three weeks, the timing of the trial of Joseph accentuated the public attention it received. There were several reasons why such a trial, situated as it was at the intersection of concerns over respectability, gender, and urban public space, would garner attention in late 1970 and early 1971. To begin with, the case coincided with a charged public discussion about women and work in the city, a debate that unfolded over multiple rounds and in the context of increasingly visible promotions of women's formal sector work by the state.[84] Further thickening the charged context in which the Joseph story unfolded was its overlapping, temporally and otherwise, with another kind of campaign playing out on the capital's downtown streets: the latest effort to round up the unemployed in order to "repatriate" them to the countryside. Finally, the Joseph case played out in the midst of the continuation of the swoops in which she had been caught up, raids constituting the most sustained anti-indecency campaign since Operation Vijana lapsed (or "fell into a deep pit," as one disappointed young man put it) in early 1969.[85] Like Operation Vijana, the new raids generated intense debate and a resurgence of public discourse focused on the familiar figures of prostitute, secretary, and schoolgirl that were emblematic of the shifting and contested boundary between indecency and respectability. And yet, rather unlike the Operation Vijana case two years earlier, debate over these figures in 1970–71 featured the emergence of new kinds of challenges to the ideological nexus of respectability, gender, and urban space underwriting the indecency campaigns.

The grounds upon which the wearing of a miniskirt—that is, its legality or illegality, decency or indecency—were being fought out in the Joseph case are critical. The target of the police raids in which Joseph and well over a hundred other women were arrested was not indecent dress in isolation, but its display by certain people (Tanzanian women) in particular public spaces (downtown streets, bars, restaurants, and nightclubs), often at a specific time (evening).[86] While remaining unstated in official declarations on the raids, the code here was clear. The target was being portrayed as prostitution, and indeed a majority of public interventions by Dar es Salaam residents on the issue debated the swoops in these terms. This is not to say the police were actually targeting prostitutes, as some maintained, for there is much to suggest (as several letter writers did) that the broad, elastic category of prostitute was providing cover for more general attacks on women in the city center after hours.[87] In this context, the Joseph case opened the door for challenges to the policing of dress codes on the grounds that no firm conclusions about a woman's respectability could be read off of her evening appearance in a downtown street or nightclub wearing a miniskirt, trouser suit, or wig. For Joseph, her friends, and their testimony regarding the night of October 3 all lent themselves to a narrative with a defensible claim to respectability, insofar as it fit certain popular ideals of modern development (*maendeleo ya kisasa*)—a story of modern working women of a type sanctioned by the state, participating in the life of a developing capital city alongside their male colleagues.

This narrative was indeed built up during the trial and the publicity surrounding it. References to Joseph were almost always made alongside a notation of her status as a travel consultant. At twenty-five, Joseph was unmarried. Images of female autonomy in accumulation, consumption, and enjoyment came strikingly to the fore in trial testimony by Joseph as well as by a friend present the night of her arrest, a Mrs. Mwinyipembe. In describing the events preceding the women's arrest, Mwinyipembe, who identified herself as a registered nurse, described how Joseph and a number of other female friends had attended a party hosted by Mwinyipembe on that Saturday evening. After the party the group "decided to go for a dance at the New Palace Hotel," where they witnessed Joseph and another of their friends—one who was wearing a "trouser suit"—being "shoved into a vehicle by a policeman." Deflecting aggressive prosecutorial questions about the length of Joseph's dress, Mwinyipembe provoked laughter in the court with her assertion that when Joseph arrived at her house for the party "she did not measure the length of her dress."[88] The picture painted here was one of modern women moving easily between formal sector jobs, female-hosted parties, and downtown dance clubs, all apparently without significant male supervision (that is, aside from the policemen, whose actions—including allegedly demanding at the police station that Joseph remove her underwear "for checking"—appeared to implicate them in the indecency they were charged to curtail and may only have accentuated the appearance of Joseph and her friends as comparably respectable). A telling moment in the emergence at trial of associations of Joseph with desirable emblems of a cosmopolitan modern came as defense and prosecution each marshaled authorizations for competing positions on the decency or indecency of the dress Joseph wore the night of her arrest (which was presented as an exhibit by the prosecutor). Attempting to answer testimony by UWT chair Mrs. John Mwalimu that Joseph's dress "was not Tanzanian and was a shame to the culture of the country," defense counsel Mr. R. W. Moisey argued that "wearing a dress whose length conformed with international standards such as that worn by air hostesses could not be regarded as indecent."[89]

Attempts to appropriate banned dress for respectable, modern life and work in the city had been made before. They built upon the similar claims made in the context of Operation Vijana by the young working women at the UWT hostel, albeit perhaps even more powerfully and certainly more visibly with the public attention garnered by the Joseph trial. And yet the grounds on which the charges against Joseph were fought out in and around the trial were not exclusively or even primarily focused on the question of whether or not the miniskirt was a respectable or appropriate outfit. Rather, much of the trial centered on the question of whether or not women had a legal right to wear what they wanted.

With the exception of his brief attempt to defend the length of Joseph's dress as lying within the bounds of international standards of decency, Joseph's lawyer tried to sidestep the respectability issue by underlining the absence of a Tanzanian law regulating the length of dresses and arguing that it would be the duty of the national legislature, not of the court or the police, to enact such regulations.[90] And in the end, it was a criterion of legality, not decency, on which the decision in the trial hinged. In his final judgment the presiding magistrate acquitted Joseph of all charges, including that of indecency, even as he lamented that she was, in fact, indecent. Saying that the dress Joseph wore the night of her arrest was found to rest six inches above her knee, Resident Magistrate C. U. Osakwe judged that "any . . . decent girl will think twice before putting it on." He then went on in his official judgment to wonder why Joseph, "obviously not endowed with good looks and shapely legs, and whose thighs are more of an eyesore than a pleasant sight . . . should be desirous to engage in the latest craze of mini-dresses." Nonetheless, ruled Osakwe, her indecency aside, Joseph's arrest constituted a "flagrant encroachment on the powers of the legislature and no doubt interference with individual liberty and freedom."[91]

In a lengthy post-trial interview with the *Sunday News*, published along with a photo of her posing in a minidress as a full-page feature on the paper's Women's Page, Joseph stressed both strands of challenge present during the trial: that the miniskirt was not indecent and that women in Tanzania had a legal right to dress as they chose. The queries of the unnamed interviewer focused repeatedly on questions of respectability and decency. In response to this line of questioning Joseph on the one hand insisted that "this dress [the mini] is like any other." Asserting that she was a working woman who had "been putting on minis for years" but was now the center of public attention in a manner that was embarrassing not only for her but also for her parents upcountry and her employers in town, Joseph attempted at length to disentangle the miniskirt from prostitution:

> Q [Interviewer]: But have you considered the charge that minis and such dresses are at the root of immorality and decadence in society?
>
> A [Joseph]: What do you mean? Do you mean prostitution? You should not forget that prostitution started from time immemorial when minis were unknown. The cause of prostitution in our countries is the suppression of women and their lack of material wealth. That is partly why Parliament has passed the marriage Bill recently stressing equality

of husband and wife. One has to remember that the traditional dress of the Wamasai does not by any means suggest that these people are prostitutes. In Uganda, the West Nile women go about naked but there are less prostitutes there than in the nightclubs of Kampala. The half-dressed Giriama women of Kenya are surely less prostitute than the "sophisticated" Kikuyu women of Nairobi.[92]

Furthermore, Joseph pointed out, images of the miniskirt in Dar es Salaam's media landscape were far from universally disapproving. "The dress is even advertised in newspapers and in cinemas. They say, 'This is what a modern girl should look like,'" she was quoted as saying.

At several points in the interview, however, Joseph countered the reporter's attempts at getting her to comment on the decency or indecency of the miniskirt by turning the discussion to the legality of policing dress. Answering a question as to whether she thought decency was "part and parcel of a good and disciplined socialist society Tanzania is aiming at," Joseph replied, "This must depend strictly on the law of the country." Her victory in court was a "victory for justice," she asserted, one which had "helped prove the worth of the Tanzanian law." Asked at the end of the interview for a "general word of comment on the whole episode," Joseph chose to reiterate the focus on the law and a discourse of "women's rights": "At this juncture in the country's development, women should stand firm in defense of their rights. They should not allow their rights to be swept away by the political current."[93]

As a moment in an ongoing gendered struggle over downtown space, the Pauline Joseph episode showcases the charged and contested character of the female office worker as a border figure between a respectable downtown presence for women on the one hand and prostitution on the other. The case was not alone in this regard in 1970–71, for it unfolded alongside other debates about working women in town and their relationships with men, debates that echoed some of the themes being played out in the street, police station, and court in the Joseph saga. Taking account of this larger discursive context allows one to begin to track some of the shifts taking place in the time between Operation Vijana and the Joseph case in the contest over the meaning of the female office worker.

Representations of the secretary appeared in many ways in the late 1960s and early 1970s, but the competing ways of valuing or devaluing this figure throughout the period gathered under two kinds of signification that were profoundly at odds yet almost always appeared in close proximity to one another. On the one hand, the secretary oper-ated as a sign of a modernizing Tanzania, confirming or, perhaps more accurately, standing in for the nation's progress in developing toward international standards of urban business and life. In the mid-1960s, secretaries frequently appeared in advertisements in Dar es Salaam's press as fetish "equipment" of the modern Tanzanian office, often rep-resented as more machine than human. Despite (or perhaps in an effort to counteract) the deep suspicion with which secretaries were regarded in some quarters, notably by young men with few career prospects and businessmen's wives anxious about their husbands' potential for office affairs, the Tanzanian state took an approving line for women in office work throughout the 1960s and 1970s. Women working in office jobs in Dar es Salaam were favorite subjects for relatively frequent features in the state-run press in which they were depicted in glowing terms as the progressive face of a nation with a bright future.

However, such approving depictions of the secretary were far from stable, for they were often confronted by a discourse that represented female office workers downtown not primarily as signs of desirable modern development, but as linchpins of an illicit system bordering on prostitution in which secretaries sought material rewards in exchange for sex with their male superiors. One example of this view, albeit one which regarded its subjects more as passive victims than diabolical agents, was a submission to the *Standard* by one Dixon Mubeya. Titling his letter "Working Girls," Mubeya situated the phenomenon against a backdrop of "African traditional customs [that] want a woman to be a wife, mother and home maker." "Why then," he continued, "should young girls nowadays be employed in private enterprises, parastatal bodies and even in Government offices? Ostensibly the primary purpose is to provide employment for women who enjoy the equal rights with men in Tanzania; but on the other hand they provide good adornment and ornamentation in the offices. . . . But contrawise, these girls come as some of them do usually from needy families unwillingly agree quite frequently to be exploited and turned into temporary mistresses of their departmental bosses; and others would spend most of their time in the offices talking about men."[94] Others conflated secretaries and illicit gain through sex even more explicitly, like the man who, in arguing for a tax on prostitution, said that many women in formal sector work were simply "part-time prostitutes": "i.e., during daytime they are busy in of-fices, factories, hospitals, 'maendeleo' [development], etc. and during night time are again busy in 'selling their bodies.'"[95]

No man
can resist
her...

What's her secret?
New Rexona toilet soap. No other soap
has the rich cadyl oils that make your skin
smoother and softer. Rexona, with its
silky lather, its seductive, expensive perfume
and its rich, nourishing cadyl oils, is
the secret of so many beautiful women.
No man can resist the girl with...

...smoother, softer skin

and that's the
promise of
New REXONA

REXONA
with Cadyl | for smooth skin

An advertise-
ment from
1969 for
Rexona soap
featuring
a modern
secretary
and her gift-
giving boss.
*Courtesy of
the Tanzania
Standard
(Newspapers)
Limited.*

The debates surrounding Operation Vijana had seen the relatively delicate attempts to reclaim secretarial work as a respectable occupation
overwhelmed by the much more prevalent and insistent conflation of the
secretary with the prostitute out to gain market. Yet the relative power
of the two competing views of the secretary was shifting. By the time
of the Pauline Joseph case the enforcement of dress codes had moved
out of the hands of a semivigilante TYL and into those of the police and
reluctant magistrates; the number of women, an unprecedented number of them unmarried, migrating to the capital had surpassed that of
men; and state promotion of women's formal sector work had steadily
increased. The material and ideological fields had shifted.[96]

As Joseph stood trial for public indecency, heated discussions about
women and work were taking place in Dar es Salaam. Concerns over

increasing employment of women in wage-labor jobs in Dar es Salaam had been present throughout the sixties but became more charged in late 1970 and early 1971 owing to a confluence of forces: on one hand, the launch of a massive effort to round up the armies of unemployed young for repatriation upcountry; on the other, an energetic and visible campaign by governmental and party institutions to legitimize and promote women's entry into blue- and white-collar jobs. This promotion campaign included pitches by the UWT at well-publicized speeches but extended far beyond the UWT's efforts to regular, full-page features in the Kiswahili press of the party. Among such features were reports on women's progress that explicitly and repeatedly highlighted women's emancipation and equality with men as urgent and necessary parts of the building of a modern, socialist Tanzania. Some of these reports exemplified an older, essentially conservative line (prevalent in UWT statements through the 1960s), but a majority of features took more radical positions decrying the existence of gendered occupational norms and urging women's entrance into male-dominated spheres of employment "if [the] nation wants to be capable in any way of developing."[97] For instance, a full-page layout in Uhuru entitled "Education and Women's Progress" criticized the overwhelming prevalence of schoolgirls pursuing home economics and declared, "These subjects [like home economics] are certainly important for all, boys and girls, but usually these courses that are known as girls' subjects don't lead them [girls] to wage employment. If education for women can be thought of as one way to develop the country's economy, then it is necessary for more education in technical subjects to be made available for women so they have greater choice of work after their education. . . . The time for saying that a certain job is for men only has passed."[98]

The photo chosen to accompany this feature, complete with approving caption, was of a young woman working as a downtown gas station attendant, filling the tank of a car, and it joined numerous other visual and narrative portraits in the press of women in a range of urban formal sector jobs. These portraits included detailed profiles of women in professions out of reach for all but the tiniest minority of Dar es Salaam's women (like Julie Manning, Tanzania's first female lawyer, her younger colleague Augusta Madere, and member of Parliament Bernadette N. Kunambi, all profiled in Uhuru as "women of today's Tanzania"),[99] but they also included features of women in less elite careers: electricians, nurses, and secretaries were all glowingly profiled in the state-run press

around this time, and even barmaids were stridently defended by Uhuru's T. N. Mshuza, one of working women's most vigorous champions
in the press.[100]

The proliferation of official representations of working women did
not necessarily signal a commitment on the part of the government to
provide the structural conditions necessary for a large increase in opportunities for women to gain employment in the formal sector. Some
degree of such commitment did exist and was steadily increasing after
the Arusha Declaration, for instance in the shape of efforts to increase
rates of female enrollment in school—both in the primary-secondary-
college track and in the massive adult education campaign launched in
the late 1960s—and encouraging government offices and parastatals to
hire women. But such efforts relied heavily on repeated exhortations,
and the proportion of women in the formal workforce remained low.
And yet, despite the fact that female wage laborers represented but a
small segment of women in the city, particular kinds of formal sector work, secretarial work, for instance, were opening up to women in
ways that were nonexistent during the colonial period. These positions
tended to be highly visible and emerged, in conjunction with the miniskirt, as convenient targets for the articulation of the anxieties of young
men as they assessed their own prospects for achieving goals of work
and family that the city held out so tantalizingly.

Appearing in tandem with the launch of the most recent wave of
roundups of unemployed men, this profusion of officially sanctioned,
positive images of female workers—combined with the sight of young
women spending their days downtown searching for office jobs (all too
successfully, and with preferential treatment, some men believed)—
provided an important context for men's anxieties.[101] One area of concern was the supposed negative effects of women's wage labor on the
relationship of the working couple. In August 1970, amidst the widespread calls for government action on indecent dress that resulted in
the raids in which Joseph was arrested, Uhuru published the results of
a study of workers at two Dar es Salaam factories, Tanganyika Textiles
and Tanganyika Tegry Plastics. Featuring interviews with male and female workers at the plant, as well as with a local Catholic priest, the
study sought "to investigate why so many of those [couples] that split
up in town are working couples."[102] In answering this question, workers of both sexes painted a picture of relationships beset by male jealousy, a mutual lack of trust, and a fragility attributed to the self-reliance

One of the many women who worked in the Urafiki Textile Mill in Dar es
Salaam, pictured here with a male supervisor in the late 1960s.
Courtesy of the Tanzania Information Service.

women gained through wage labor. As Alli Abdallah, one of the textile
factory workers, put it, "There are men who have intense jealousy, and
this is one of the problems in married life. Since the wife is earning
her own money she's free to not be cautious in life, because whatever
happens she'll be able to be self-reliant [*kujitegemea*] even if she is left
[by her husband]." He continued, "Some working women have the bad
habit of coming home late, and they're always using work as an excuse,
which many times isn't true."[103] Female workers agreed that "working
gives women more freedom [*uhuru*]" and added that such freedom included a reluctance to tolerate an abusive husband: "Girls these days
are progressing in a major way [*wako kwenye maendeleo makubwa*], and
that condition of being beaten by their husbands . . . it makes a girl feel
ashamed and she can decide to leave him."[104]

Some female workers seemed to confirm men's fears, asserting that
the flexibility afforded women by work applied not only to money, but
to sexual liaisons as well. Mariamu Omari described how "if a woman
finds someone to please her outside [her marriage], she loses desire
for her husband and disagreements erupt," and opined, "Sometimes
women become scornful because they have work."[105] For their part,
some of the men interviewed complained of the material difficulties of

getting married and keeping a wife satisfied. With one worker noting the burden of accumulating enough to pay bridewealth, another asserted, "Sometimes a woman gets so accustomed to entertainment, but when the husband changes this situation suddenly, perhaps because of his means, the woman . . . becomes dissatisfied with these changes and disagreements result."[106]

These expressions of a crisis of masculinity arising out of a nexus of women's work and mobility in the city, high rates of unemployment for both men and women, and perceptions of these phenomena, were not new, although the contours of the crisis were growing clearer. What was more unprecedented, however, was the vocabulary being used to describe the consequences of women's autonomous accumulation and increased mobility. "Freedom" (uhuru, the term for Tanzania's independence from colonial rule), "development" or "progress" (maendeleo, the single most important goal, indeed the expressed raison d'être, of the state), and "self-reliance" (ujitegemeo, a keyword of the post–Arusha Declaration, socialist project) were words endowed with a nearly unassailable value difficult to match in Tanzania in 1970.[107] Conveying not only official approval, but also popular desirability, the use of these terms to describe the effects of increasing female autonomy, even by those disapproving of these effects, is remarkable and is evidence of a major shift in the terms of the debate about women, work, and respectability. If a close association between women's formal sector work and gaining market through sex was still eminently present, it existed alongside assumptions that women's work was a politically positive goal, an element of the progress, development, and self-reliance of an independent Tanzania.

Not that men in Dar es Salaam were growing more comfortable and secure with the idea of women earning their own wages in town. Indeed, as another round of debate developed in the press in early 1971 over the perceived high numbers of women being hired in offices and factories, interventions by men on the issue strongly indicate the contrary.[108] One young man, a student at the Modern Commercial College in Dar es Salaam, wrote a letter enumerating the pressures on even relatively educated, unmarried men in town. Pleading with the government to instate a policy of hiring men first and paying them more than women, Thade S. Pella cited the difficulties of marrying as constituting a unique burden on the unemployed young man, a burden, he argued, that current practices of hiring young women in large numbers was exacerbating:

When a man wants to marry he has to furnish a house and pay a bride-wealth to the woman's parents, and women don't have these kinds of problems.

Now, if a woman has a job and the man doesn't, what will that be like? I think it will be a problem. As if it's not enough that the woman has a job, she takes on a swagger and scorn for men. You'll find many women, those with work, without husbands; but you'll find some of them with children, maybe two or three. If you ask her who fathered these children she has nothing to say. How will these children who have no father live?

If you ask that same woman why she doesn't want to marry she answers because husbands are scarce. This is not true. It's because of the haughty and scornful attitude that they get from having work. . . . So many problems result from men not being able to find work.[109]

Others, like J. T. Mnali, extended complaints about the burdens shouldered by men in town to the case of married men. Adding his support to those calling for a state- and private-sector policy to hire men first, Mnali argued that "a husband is someone with many more problems than women, for he has to first provide for his family." He intimated that jobs were wasted on women, who, "once they are educated . . . don't concentrate on their jobs but are always thinking of men, and many of them end up . . . pregnant."[110] This last complaint was part of a chorus of accusations about the behavior of young women hired to work in offices downtown, accusations that accompanied most calls for a reduction in hiring women in such jobs. Such allegations deployed the familiar trope of the secretary out to advance herself materially through sex. Suggesting that offices were being used as brothels, one civil servant wrote, "Go into some of the various Government offices and factories that hire girls. The girl knows she's at work, but you'll see her taking her mirror out of her little handbag. Here you see her looking at her lips, there you see her putting powder on her face; here you see her combing her hair, there she is doing this and that all in order to attract the young men she works with. Can work really be respected like this?"[111] Another man likened the hiring of women to sex work, claimed that eight out of ten girls in every office or factory were pregnant, and lamented the "big heads" that he suggested secretaries' liaisons with higher-ups gave these "office girls."[112]

Even so, the expressions of frustration and victimhood on the part of men contained repeated nods to the equality of women and men, to women's right and freedom to work. "All people are equal, I agree,"

wrote one man, issuing a disclaimer that appeared in many of the letters critical of the practice of hiring "so many" female office workers:
"Men and women are equal, even in the right to be hired."[113] Even the
attempts by some to question the kind of freedom that would result in
the presence of large numbers of women in formal sector jobs are indicative of the degree to which concepts like freedom, equality, and rights
had gained a foothold as terms in which women's formal sector work,
urban mobility, and accumulation were being debated. Many acknowledged that state policy, correctly in their view, insisted on equality and
nondiscrimination.[114] Even Pella, near the end of his letter, evidently
felt the need to preempt expected criticism of his call for advantages for
men in hiring and pay, dismissing those who would call this discrimination.[115] And indeed, many women were charging just that, answering
men's letters by suggesting that calls for restricting the hiring of women
were "pushing our development as women backwards," that harassment of women on city streets was indicative of men's, not women's,
indecency and lack of respect, and even that "what Europeans thought
of Africans is what you African men are thinking of women."[116] "I urge
our Government," one young woman wrote, "to consider women as human beings, as capable and free people—to give them the rights they
deserve and the freedom, and the equality they hunger for."[117]

If defenses of appearing and moving about downtown in a miniskirt
were most often made by attempting to ascribe to such women the respectability of the well-behaved (by either appropriating discourses of
modern development and equality or deploying a standard of legality),
late 1970 also saw signs of rebellious interventions that eschewed such
gestures. In a fierce debate on the miniskirt that directly preceded and
quite likely occasioned the launch of police raids on downtown streets
and establishments in October 1970, a young woman named L. I. Minja
entered the fray in a way that made her intervention a lightning rod of
heated argument for months and turned her into an emblem of opposition to dress code campaigns.[118] Minja's first letter to the editor of *Uhuru*, appearing near the very beginning of this round of letters on dress
codes, briefly but sharply challenged the first two submissions on the
issue which *Uhuru* had just published. Both written by men, these first
two letters had picked up on a brief statement by a member of Parliament criticizing "'minis' and other shameful dress." (That an MP would
raise the issue in parliamentary discussion is yet another indication of
the remarkable breadth of controversies over women's dress, cropping

up in domains of high politics and popular networks of rumor alike.) Seizing upon the MP's comment, the two male letter writers used it as an occasion to excoriate the government for failing to use its institutional power to eradicate the miniskirt.[119] For her part, Minja wrote that neither Bw. Ng'amba nor Bw. Nere had said anything meaningful on this matter that was troubling "our hearts as girls," and she countered that the government was properly attending to more important tasks than "intruding on someone walking in the street or at home saying, hey, why are you wearing a short dress." She ended her letter by asking whether either of her interlocutors had visited neighboring cities like Nairobi or Kampala.[120]

Minja's letter, despite its brevity, provoked a flurry of responses. Ranging from the furious to the patronizing in tone, all deployed gendered and generational metaphors to rebuke Minja for challenging her fathers and elders so impudently.[121] All ridiculed her invocation of Nairobi and Kampala, which hinted that Dar es Salaam was nothing compared to these neighboring founts of cosmopolitan style; two respondents likened Minja "and her crowd" to "wild animals"; one man, in a lengthy rant, vowed to destroy her miniskirt "school":

> You are hereby informed that if you venture to establish that school of yours in this Tanzania, teaching lessons of wearing short dresses, [we'll] grab sticks, axes and machetes, and if that doesn't work, we swear [we'll] get the 'City' [in English] to give us Caterpillars [bulldozers] to destroy that school. And if there are any students in that school, believe me, I'll take them to a school that teaches respect and appropriate dress for a Nation that doesn't tolerate disgrace.[122]

But this vitriol paled in comparison to that occasioned by Minja's response to her critics. Entitling her second letter "Talk 'til you tire, we're not listening," Minja engaged one critic in particular, Pembe A. Ng'amba, or Mzee wa Shamba (countryside elder), as he pointedly signed his letters despite living in Dar es Salaam. Turning Ng'amba's performance of righteous antiurbanism on its head, Minja ridiculed him as being hopelessly out of touch with a desirable ethos of cosmopolitan urbanity:

> Considering that he [Ng'amba] says that he's a *mzee wa shamba*, it'd be better for him to go live out there on the farm. The countryside and the city are not a bit alike. You elders [*wazee*], your time has passed, and this is our time as youth. . . . You might as well go live on the farm, plant your

vegetables, and don't get hot and bothered for nothing by lovely city girls [*visura vya mjini*; literally "city faces"]. . . .

Another thing you said to me was that I should visit Congo, Sudan, Ghana; what do you mean? Every country has its own style. If I go there I certainly won't change my outfits, in fact, I'll sew them even shorter. . . .

Dear old man, I'm telling you that as for this opportunity to berate girls for their dress, you may as well grab a hoe and go to the *shamba* to farm vegetables—they'll give you good health and life, or some cents to post a letter like this.[123]

Such flagrant denigration of the rural ideal that was a central plank of the assault on urban youth culture and of post–Arusha Declaration official rhetoric more generally, such refusals to respect generational hierarchies of authority, combined with Minja's explicit celebration of the urban and self-conscious identification as a "city girl"—these gestures went beyond attempts to assert the *decency* of the miniskirt. And if Minja's intervention was extraordinary for its explicit articulation by a woman in print, it paralleled other challenges to the sort of moral authority that underlay not only the dress campaigns but broader concerns over the behavior, pose, and self-expression of some of Dar es Salaam's city girls. These concerns often surfaced as complaints about schoolgirls, often portrayed as an unapologetically pleasure-seeking group that refused to observe public decorum and gendered or generational hierarchies of authority. In a vociferous discussion occurring on the eve of the police swoops on downtown in 1970, outraged men exchanged personal tales of witnessing groups of abusive and disorderly schoolgirls on buses, hurling "hot words" at male passengers who tried to scold them for failing "to behave like true schoolgirls."[124] One concluded, "Schoolgirls persist in wearing mini-dresses, indulge themselves in all sort of sophisticated culture, and apart from this, misbehave toward the public. This is so grave that the public can justifiably question the kind of game they are up to."[125]

However, the challenges by young women and girls that went beyond trying to claim the miniskirt for respectability tended to be met with ferocious volleys of verbal assault and dismissal and were unable to gain the kind of foothold achieved by the assertions of decency and legality. Minja's powerful rebellious interventions provoked an astounding thirty-five letters responding specifically to her statements, all but a handful heaping vitriolic scorn upon her. The debate saw nearly one hundred letters and poems published over three months.[126] By contrast,

Joseph won her case, and those arguing in favor of women in offices and factories achieved success in reframing these positions in the eminently respectable terms of equality, freedom, modern development, and self-reliance, even as such work remained closely associated in many quarters with the miniskirt and gaining market.[127] Success in this struggle owed much to the protagonists' ability to take advantage of both the form of the new dress campaign and available discourses surrounding it to exploit the ambivalence that lay at the heart of the figure of the working woman in banned fashion. Energetic official promotions of women in formal sector work provided a vocabulary and set of associations that were seized upon to strengthen claims for normalizing new patterns of women's mobility and "freedom of dress" in the city. Likewise, while the move to enforce the new dress campaign through the institutions of the police, schools, public- and private-sector business represented an expansion of the scope of the policing of dress codes, this very institutionalization lent itself to Joseph's combating of the measures on legal grounds in court. Successful reframing was by no means equally accessible to women in Dar es Salaam regardless of levels of material and social capital. Indeed, for women working as bargirls, for instance, who were generally less educated and less well off than those in formal sector positions, both the nature of their labor and the way it was perceived tied them much more stubbornly to the bundle of deep-rooted associations between men, urban women, and accumulation through varying shades of sex work that were a feature of colonial and postcolonial urban landscapes.

By the early 1970s, the female office worker had emerged as a border figure that could be struggled over with considerable success, in a way that figures of rebellious city girls, eschewing claims to respectability, had not. Rooted in a history stretching back to the late colonial period of migration, work, accumulation, and sex in Dar es Salaam in which many young men perceived women to be pitted against them, this struggle over women's work and movement intensified and assumed new forms as a result of socioeconomic, ideological, and discursive shifts in the 1960s. Many of these shifts were contested: if the opening up to women of areas of formal sector work exacerbated perceptions among some young men of women's advancement at their expense (through exploiting sexual liaisons, many suggested), it also allowed women to contest certain stigmatizations of their presence, dress, and comportment in downtown public space. Likewise, if the introduction in the 1960s of campaigns for national culture afforded young men new avenues for acting out their grievances against certain kinds of women, an increasing promotion by the state of women's participation in the public sphere provided a new discursive weapon to contest these attacks. The struggle over the boundaries and signs of respectability thus offers a reminder of the inextricability of the material and discursive dimensions of the contests.

The notion of the border figure can be useful in engaging and refining elements of Mbembe's arguments concerning postcolonial and urban popular politics. His theorization of an "illicit cohabitation" characterizing these politics critically illuminates some dimensions of the contests examined in this chapter. The "logic of conviviality" that unites Mbembe's rulers and ruled under a single episteme offers a compelling framing device for the appropriations of official idioms, categories, and ideological forms by nonofficial actors that periodically marked the struggles over the dress campaigns in Dar es Salaam. And in some cases, as Mbembe would argue, this logic does indeed seem to render ineffective the very opportunities for critique it opens up (something illustrated even more clearly in chapter 4 with reference to the debate over relations between elites—"'nizers"—and city girls). However, as this chapter has suggested, arguments directed at points on the edges of the hegemonic could also exploit the ambivalence with which border figures like the secretary were invested to gain footholds toward revaluing these personas. Mbembe's formulation, which leaves one with a closed circle of "disempowerment" and "zombification," is too flattening, tells only half of the story. Indeed, the gender struggles and urban politics that run through this chapter offer evidence of the sheer unevenness of these contests. For even as some tropes and types of public discourse around women's behavior—the city girl, for instance—proved resilient in the face of challenges launched by women seeking to revalue them; others, like the secretary embodied by Pauline Joseph, lying ambivalently on the border between respectability and indecency, were more susceptible to traction-gaining claims. These contests were fought out in part on the terrains of both transnationally circulating products like the miniskirt and the urban initiatives of the national cultural project. But they are also reminders that each of these terrains was appropriated to ends that went beyond a national–transnational axis to the urban gender struggles that marked early postcolonial Dar es Salaam.

Of Students, 'Nizers, and Comrades

YOUTH, INTERNATIONALISM, AND THE UNIVERSITY

COLLEGE, DAR ES SALAAM

> The pride, the status of being the group upon which the future of
> this young nation of Tanzania largely and exclusively depends! It is not
> an individual person, place, town or region that will depend on us, but
> the whole nation at large. Fellow youths, we are the cream, the echelons
> of this society.—D. Philly, "Future of Tanzania lies with her youth,"
> letter to the *Nationalist*, November 9, 1970

> The nation says to its youth, "We want your service." And the youth
> does not then turn to the nation and say, "For how much?"
> —President Julius K. Nyerere, speaking to University College students
> demonstrating in opposition to the new National Service proposal
> of 1966, October 22, 1966

The decade of the 1960s in Tanzania, as in many other parts of the world,
saw the increasing salience of youth as a celebrated and contested political category. As I described in chapter 1, youth emerged as a category
closely associated with the national cultural project in important ways:
the initial yoking of national culture and youth in a single ministerial
portfolio and the position of youth as both the targets and the enforcers
of campaigns against indecency, for instance. But some of the most intense generational conflicts over youth playing out in Dar es Salaam in
the sixties developed at yet another site, one that would become central
in the cultural debates of the decade: the brand-new national university
constructed as a showpiece of Tanzania's new, postcolonial era.

The nationalist movement in Tanganyika in the late colonial period,
like many such movements across Africa, was in many ways a youth
movement. As I have noted previously, the rise of the young nationalists
of the late 1940s and 1950s and their eclipsing of the elders of the Native
Authorities were enabled in large part through the new generation's ac-

cess to formal education and wage labor jobs that put them in a position to gain some autonomy from older generational hierarchies. Youth had long been a politically charged category in societies across Tanzania as elsewhere on the continent, one linked less to age than to social status, particularly for men.[1] Now, in the 1960s, the first generation of young nationalist leaders was in power, holding state bureaucratic posts, and they were faced with the task of renegotiating their own relationship with youth. A persistent ambiguity characterized this renegotiation. On the one hand, the state explicitly raised the visibility of youth as a political category, establishing a cabinet portfolio for youth, mobilizing institutions like the National Service and the TYL, and, in the late 1960s, holding high-profile, annual national youth festivals.[2] Political leaders frequently praised youth in grandiose terms as the key to Tanzania's bright future. But if officials saw in youth a potent political category with great potential for being mobilized in the service of the state, they also moved to marginalize young people who posed potential challenges to that vision, as I began to illustrate in chapter 1. Dar es Salaam's growing population of unemployed young and its new teenagers, perceived to be identifying with decadent trends in cosmopolitan style at odds with a national ethic of frugality and hard work, were two categories of youth the state regarded with suspicion. University students constituted a third.

Established on the eve of independence as a nationalist triumph, the University College, Dar es Salaam, was an institution in which high hopes were placed. As was the case with universities across Africa and the recently decolonized world, this university was justified by the political elite with the argument that it would be a training ground for a loyal cadre of high-level manpower serving national goals as propounded by national leaders. In its very nature, though, the university complicated the youth question. Not only did it widen the category of youth by extending the age of nonautonomy, it also brought together some of Tanzania's most highly educated young people in a privileged cohort with shared cultural sensibilities and high career expectations. Tanzania's ruling nationalist elite was still relatively young in the 1960s, many of its members being in their thirties, and although they held the reins of political power, graduates of the university would possess unprecedented educational qualifications surpassing those held by all but a tiny minority of the first generation of bureaucrats. For their part, many students would come to see this generation as stubbornly ensconced in privileged positions that had come too easily and that they were too slow to share; the figure of the "'nizer," or *naizesheni*—the slang term for the quintessential elite of the 1960s, seen as leveraging positions through the Africanization of government and business into undue accumulation—became a principal target of these sentiments.[3] As I show in this chapter, the university had the potential to produce rivalry between these two groups as much as loyalty of one to the other.

Further complicating the hopes of officials, Tanzania's university through the 1960s and early 1970s became a place where students were exposed to connections with cosmopolitan networks, cultures, discourses, and movements that were often nonnational in scope and impact. Of major importance in this regard was the left internationalism that flourished at the University College beginning in the late 1960s. From its founding, the University College faculty was composed almost entirely of expatriate Britons and North Americans whose politics, in the institution's early years, tended to be liberal and laudatory of the new nationalist governments across Africa. But while non-Tanzanians continued to dominate the teaching staff into the 1970s, 1967 saw the beginnings of an influx of a sizeable number of expatriate faculty members who were decidedly on the left (and mostly Marxist), including figures like Walter Rodney, Giovanni Arrighi, and John Saul.[4] Located in a city that was increasingly a haven for exiles from the left liberation movements of southern Africa, the University College for a decade after 1967 was a significant nodal point for the internationalist left. And faculty were certainly not the only, or even the main, agents in this development, for even as the first of the leftist teachers were arriving, a multinational group of students, well informed on developments in Vietnam, African liberation struggles, and the activities of the CIA, were building a fledgling campus movement that was broaching some early critiques of the postcolonial state.

In this chapter I focus on some of the notable struggles that centered on the university in the 1960s, conflicts that illuminate the fraught renegotiation of youth in Tanzania's first postcolonial decade. If the University College was established to produce servants of the nation, by the mid-1960s state officials were worried that the institution was just as capable of fostering careerist rivals or an undesirable kind of vanguard capable of challenging state practices from the left. I examine here two struggles that marked the relationship between and among the political elite, diverse university students and faculty, and the TYL and the National Service as vehicles of the state's new hopes for mobilizing loyal youth. The first of these developed around an attempt to include univer-

sity graduates in a National Service program, the second around the rise
of the left on campus.

The National Service Debate: Social Anatomy of a Crisis,
or, the Disciplining of an Educated Elite

On October 22, 1966, a Saturday, residents of Dar es Salaam who lived
near Morogoro Road, the thoroughfare bisecting the city from west to
east, encountered an unprecedented sight. Identifiable in the red academic gowns they had chosen to don for the protest, over four hundred
Tanzanian university students marched down the middle of the road
on a ten-kilometer trek from the campus of the University College to
the city center.[5] For those bystanders who had not been following the
dispute between the government and the students in the newspapers of
the past week, the placards and banners the demonstrators held aloft
carried oblique clues as to its nature: "Kawawa Must Quit," "Terms
Harsh—Colonialism Was Better," "Remember Indonesia."[6] For the
many people who had been following the dispute in the press and its
renderings in networks of gossip and rumor, the context of the march
was perhaps more clear: for weeks debate had been building in the
letters-to-the-editor pages of Tanzania's press over a government proposal to make the voluntary National Service program mandatory for
graduating university students. Vice President Rashidi Kawawa, who
conveniently announced the proposal and guided it through the Parliament to become law while students were on vacation, sparked outrage over the move with a majority of Tanzanian students at University
College, who decided to signal their people power in a public march
against the new service requirements.

What was not yet apparent, either to those observing the march or to
the marchers, was the central place the march and the events surrounding it would assume in historical accounts and memories of Tanzania's
early postcolonial period. The National Service crisis of October 1966
would come to represent the marker of a shift in the history of the university and its relationship with the state: the moment that heralded the
end of a stridently elitist university that was failing in its role to produce servants of the nation and the beginning of a radical campus, a
"people's University" at the service of the state's drive for modern, socialist development.[7] While evidence of the kind of shift hailed in these
accounts is not entirely lacking (albeit considerably more ambiguous

than these narratives suggest), I argue instead that the National Service crisis is best viewed as one of a series of episodes that illustrate the complexities of a generational struggle over resources. The University College was central to many of these episodes, including the National Service crisis of 1966; the struggles over curricular reform that followed in its wake; the disruption of Rag Day by a group of leftist students in 1968; controversy over a well-publicized speech by Walter Rodney in 1969; and the banning of the University Students' African Revolutionary Front and its magazine, *Cheche* (Spark), in 1970.

Opened eight weeks before independence, in October 1961, the University College was Tanganyika's first university and an outgrowth of demands voiced by both TANU nationalists and visiting UN mandate missions to Tanganyika since the Second World War.[8] One context out of which such demands arose was the territory's segregated educational system, which consisted of separate and far from equally funded schools for Europeans, Asians, and Africans. Another was the increasingly energetic attempt by the colonial administration to link primary schooling for Africans to a rural and agrarian livelihood.[9] Initially paying little heed to African anger at these discriminatory policies, the British colonial administration was increasingly forced to take such opposition into account after TANU's landslide electoral victories in 1954 and 1958 and the opening of the Legislative Council to African delegates. In its brief to the UN visiting mission in 1954, TANU included in its recommendations for educational reform a demand for a separate university college in Tanganyika. (At this point the few Tanganyikan students who entered university generally attended either Makerere in Kampala or other foreign institutions.) The colonial administration eventually acted on this demand, joining Kenya, Tanzania, Uganda, and Zanzibar in 1958 in a commitment to support a federal University of East Africa with constituent colleges in Nairobi, Kampala, and Dar es Salaam. University College, Dar es Salaam, was originally slated to open in 1965, but shortly after taking the reins of "responsible government" in late 1960, TANU shortened the timetable, announcing that the college would open in 1961.[10]

No separate campus for the university having been built, the University College was opened in what had been TANU's headquarters on Lumumba Street, on the edges of downtown. This location was seen from the beginning as a temporary one, and in 1964 the university moved to its present location, a lavish campus built largely with British, Scandinavian, and American grants on a hill nearly six miles from downtown.

With the move came an expansion of the university's curriculum. The Lumumba Street location featured only one faculty, law, which was to be Dar es Salaam's specialty by agreement with the other colleges of the University of East Africa. The larger campus, however, familiarly called the Hill, facilitated the gradual addition of faculties of arts and science, medicine, agriculture, and, in 1973, engineering. The university's student body grew rapidly, from a first class of only fourteen law students in 1961 to more than two thousand resident students by 1970, when the University of East Africa split into three independent entities and Tanzania's constituent institution was renamed the University of Dar es Salaam.[11] Throughout the 1960s and 1970s a significant proportion of students (approximately 25 percent in 1967) were drawn from outside Tanzania, largely from Kenya and Uganda.[12] Until 1967, admission to the University College was determined by sixth-formers' performance on the Cambridge Examination.[13] While throughout the 1960s, as noted, a majority of university faculty were expatriates, many of whom were visiting or on short-term stints in the capital, the administration was taken over by Tanzanian staff somewhat earlier, the first principal, Cranford Pratt, being succeeded by Wilbert Chagula in 1965.

In its very design, the new campus set the university apart as an elite institution. Its physical placement on a rise overlooking the city at a distance lent it, quite literally, an aspect of an ivory tower. Even by the standards of European and North American universities, the campus was well appointed; by Tanzanian standards it was luxurious. Students were housed on campus in individual rooms in four tower blocks and relied on university-hired workers to clean their rooms, wash their clothes, and cook.[14] Even elite Tanzanian visitors to the university in the early 1960s reportedly expressed shock at the high quality of the campus facilities.[15] As President Nyerere revealed in his address at the opening of the new university campus, the annual cost to the Tanzanian government of housing and teaching each student at the university was "about 1000 [British] pounds," approximately fifty times the country's average per capita income at the time.[16]

Although pointedly drawing attention to the yawning gap between the resources being expended on the university and the general material condition of the country at large, Nyerere was not suggesting, in the early 1960s at least, that the high costs were problematic. As he would later reflect, "When the University College of Dar es Salaam was first planned, the concern of everyone . . . was the comparability of the new institution with its sister College at Makerere. We were concerned to

The University College pictured shortly after its construction in 1964, with the city of Dar es Salaam in the distance. *Courtesy of the Tanzania Information Service.*

build an attractive permanent campus, with housing and facilities to attract high-powered expatriate staff, and we were determined to demonstrate from the beginning our commitment to high standards of scholarship. We rejected the idea of a University which was physically akin to the economic level of the country, or to the living standards the students would be coming from."[17]

If the president did not place the extravagant sums spent on the university in a negative light, however, he and other TANU leaders repeatedly articulated a condition upon which such spending rested. As Nyerere declared in his address opening the new campus, "This sort of expenditure is only justified in the circumstances of our country if one condition is fulfilled. The expenditure must lead to an increase in the wealth of this United Republic, and it must contribute to the raising of the standard of living of the mass of the people."[18] Various analogies were deployed to illustrate the desired relationship between the students supported by the state at the university and the people. Appearing in the government's first Five-Year Plan, of 1963, one likened the students to a man given all the remaining food in a starving village in order to sustain him on a journey to fetch help.[19] Another, included in Nyerere's address opening the new campus, described a large group of travelers pushing a stalled bus up a hill with one of their number at the wheel: "The brute force of our people's strength alone will not be sufficient to reach the top. That strength has to be combined with the scientific use of every atom of skill in steering, in coaxing the engine, in changing gear and in applying the brakes and the accelerator at the right moment. If the effort relaxes or if the thought about the best way round the obstacles is not applied, then the bus will roll back—crushing under it not just the driver and those who claimed to know the way forward but, worse still, masses of those who have humbly applied such knowledge and such power as they have to the overall purpose."[20]

Expressing more than just a general hope that the establishment and maintenance of a national university would contribute to development efforts, such illustrations were linked to specific tasks faced by the Tanganyikan state in the early 1960s. Chief among these was the Africanization of the civil service and the professions, which in 1964 remained staffed almost entirely by expatriates. Having campaigned on a rapid program of Africanization, the TANU government was under considerable pressure to carry this out, and yet with fewer than 150 Tanganyikan university graduates at independence, carrying this out for the higher levels of employment was easier said than done.[21] The University College was thus regarded as indispensable to the government's oft-advertised need for "high-level manpower."

The elite that the University College was producing was largely male—manpower indeed. In the late 1960s and early 1970s women made up approximately 15 to 18 percent of the student body, mostly in the humanities; one female political science graduate recalled that male students often condescendingly referred to the humanities with a feminine acronym, SHE, for Swahili, history, and English.[22] There is considerable evidence that gender relations on campus were often intensely fraught. "The campus Rift Valley," as one student characterized the gender divide, was perhaps one of the two or three most widely discussed matters in public debate on the Hill, the conflict often revolving around male students' access, or lack thereof, to sexual relationships with their female colleagues.[23] Campus slang frequently cast the divide in geopolitical terms such as the "cold war."[24] The women's dormitory, officially named Wolfson Hall or Hall III, was portrayed by male students as a Republic requiring passports and visas; those visiting or leaving campus on dates were known as imports and exports; female students were frequently referred to publicly as "local goods."[25]

Student newspapers and journals in the late sixties and early seventies brimmed with battles between women and men on the issue. Male students frequently complained bitterly that their female colleagues were socially apathetic, "social failures" who were reluctant to attend the dances, film screenings, and concerts organized for entertainment on campus.[26] Instead, went a common refrain, female students preferred the company of older, wealthy, off-campus sugar daddies.[27] As one male student grumbled in a mock astrology column addressed to campus women, "That boyfriend of yours likes to feel that he really matters to you. You are heading for trouble if you don't express your love to him more fully in various ways, while you do it to your sugar daddy. . . . After all, you're his girlfriend, and he has some claim on you."[28] Male students were said to keep close watch on the comings and goings of off-campus men being "imported" to Wolfson Hall, writing poems ridiculing sugar daddies and their "prey," spreading rumors about numbers of pregnancies and abortions, and holding "import of the year" competitions[29]:

> This year's import definitely rolled to Wolfson. To say the least, the enormous balloon fell out of a Volks Wagen car with a beautiful tennis-ball head. In fact it was difficult even to the importer to figure exactly where his mouth was, put away the fact that this man can't of course scratch an inch on his own back. While 'Punch trainees' were kept excitedly busy screening 'Sugardads' on one week's wall painting the rest of the students laid an ambush for two weeks for a sort of being that trespasses the campus, to "put asunder our joined relationship."[30]

As the last sentence of the quotation hints, public "outing" of relationships between female students and off-campus men extended beyond the pages of the student newspaper. Most notoriously, a genre of public graffiti known on campus as wall literature or Punch, after the British satirical magazine, specialized in graphic accusations against individual women for their rumored sexual escapades. Some recollections made at the beginning of the twenty-first century frequently suggested that Punch was a form of critique that in its early years had focused on political topics, degenerating only in the 1980s to attacks on women. Conditioned by the high-profile case in 1990 of Levina Mukasa, a university student who committed suicide after she was "Punched," this narrative is at odds with evidence from student papers of the early 1970s that discuss Punch as first and foremost a means of controlling female students' sexual behavior.[31]

Some women on campus fought back publicly against the charges being leveled at them in the rumor mills on campus. In addition to the frequent complaints lodged by women against constant attacks featured in the "oppressive" wall literature, some residents of Wolfson Hall tried to publicly articulate the dilemmas of their own positions as a minority among "frustrated men."[32] Some described a campus where they were continually subjected to unwanted advances: "It is the opposite sex—the males against which I have a point to raise. . . . I go to the Cafeteria, a cool eye lands upon my thigh. I go to the movie, a whistle rings in my ears. I go to the library, I stretch myself to fetch 'language' by Bloomfield, I suddenly feel a manly hip against mine."[33] Others directly confronted the accusation of "social apathy," one woman explaining that she and her friends avoided the dances because "we do not enjoy the rough handling that the drunkards accord us" and that "you [men] will appreciate our fears of rape, or even beating after the dances as relevant. Such things have happened here."[34] Still others tried to describe the delicate balancing act some women faced in searching for the kind of relationship they desired—often one resulting in marriage to an economically eligible bachelor—amidst the threat of exposure in the wall literature.[35] Fear of the embarrassment of such exposure kept many women away from social functions, one female student suggested.[36]

If for many male students the "crisis of the sex ratio" on campus pointed frustratingly, in a domain central to dominant conceptions of masculinity, to their status as yet-to-arrive, elites still-in-waiting, for many university women the situation highlighted the potential dangers threatening their own efforts at building upwardly mobile lives.[37] Many men's perception of losing out to older, wealthier, more established (but perhaps less educated) sugar daddies was made more poignant for those male students who regarded themselves as a rising elite. Such sentiments may well have sharpened the generational tensions playing out through the events examined in this chapter. And yet, despite being inflected through the uniquely privileged situation of life on the Hill, the sexual politics on campus nonetheless shared much with the wider dynamics of gender relations in Dar es Salaam examined in chapter 2.

The centrality of the university to the national project, both as prestige object and highly touted key to the country's economic future, was not lost on students at the Hill. Furthermore, the frequent reminders that higher education was an unearned privilege accompanied by an obligation to serve the nation worked as a double-edged sword. On the one hand, such exhortations were designed to serve as a check on

The student cafeteria at University College in the late 1960s.
Courtesy of the Tanzania Information Service.

Students at University College in the mid-1960s. *Courtesy of the Tanzania Information Service.*

university student elitism and did indeed convey, in theory at least, the idea that the highly educated were indebted to the country's peasants and workers for enabling their education. Perhaps more powerfully, however, such calls to service highlighted, often explicitly, the indispensable nature of university students' knowledge and skills to the future of the country—and in so doing reinforced what Saul, a prominent member of the expatriate socialist faculty at the university, described as "the *generalized elitist mentality* of successful students" who were quite conscious of their place at the top of a narrow apex of educational achievement.[38] Saul, who taught in the political science department and was a keen participant observer in campus politics during his seven years in Tanzania, related this attitude to what he called the mystique of high-level manpower among government officials and students alike: "Small wonder that the students, reminded at intervals of the 'precious' nature of their potential contribution, become persuaded of their likely indispensability. The logic of the market and the rhetoric of manpower planning thus combine into a heady brew of nascent elitism."[39] Concerns over student elitism at the University College were at the center of the National Service crisis of 1966.

The student protesters' long march from the Hill to the State House that Saturday in October was a pivotal point in a trail of shifting debate, negotiation, correspondence, and spectacle in the weeks before and after the event itself. Rumblings over the proposed measure the students were protesting—compulsory National Service for graduates of Form VI and above—had begun a full year prior. The National Service program had been developed, with Israeli assistance, in 1963 as a voluntary corps of young men and women who would undergo political, military, and agricultural or vocational training as a prelude to nearly two years spent working on "nation-building" projects.[40] Competition for places in the service was intense, mainly among primary school dropouts, for whom the program offered a path to a potential position in the military or the party.[41] By 1965, however, officials of the TYL (who had originally proposed the service program), National Service leaders, and high-level government officials, including President Nyerere and Vice President Kawawa, all had begun to speak out against the lack of interest in joining the National Service shown by the country's most highly educated youth. Officials charged that a perception had grown up that the program was, as an official National Service report remembered it, "a dumping pit for those unlucky ones who failed in other spheres of life, notably those who for one reason or another could not go beyond primary school level."[42]

In the context of such concerns, Vice President Kawawa announced in November 1965 a plan put forth by the government to make National Service compulsory for graduates of the university and professional schools and for students finishing Form VI as a terminal degree. Under the proposal, a two-year period of service would be divided into various components for these ex-students: an initial three months of basic training at a National Service camp; two months in rural nation-building work such as road construction or farm work; eighteen months in a job for which one was well suited, often in teaching or civil service, during which time he or she would be paid 40 percent of the job's regular salary and be required to wear National Service uniforms during working hours; and a final month in the camp concluding with a "passing-out" ceremony.[43]

It was not long before the government's proposal began to draw public comment, much of it disapproving, from students at the University College. The opening salvo was a letter from Boniface M. Kimulson, president of the University Students' Union (USUD), criticizing the terms of the government's plan and recommending alternate terms.[44] Kimulson highlighted two aspects of the plan that were especially galling to students: first and foremost, the salary reduction; and second, various conditions of daily life and work under National Service that might not "march with some of [the university graduates'] basic educational and social standards." Citing what would become a principal element of student opposition to the National Service plan in the months to come, Kimulson described the responsibilities faced by university students under pressure to send money to their parents, "most of whom regard us as ''nization' (a big officer)": "No wonder most of them serve us with monthly circulars to remind us of our moral and financial obligations to them." If Kimulson was counting on eliciting public support for the students' case, this reference to familial obligations may have been more effective than his suggestion that 40 percent of a university graduate's salary was impossible to live on, or his concern that university students should enjoy easier access to loans for cars and lower taxes "to cater for our social requirements." Incorporating his criticisms of the plan, Kimulson suggested that the government shorten the service requirement to three months of military training followed by employment "without any financial or uniform obligations."

Together, Kawawa's statement and Kimulson's letter generated a flurry of comment, and before long a full-fledged debate was in swing. Over the course of the year from the announcement of the proposal through the aftermath of the demonstration in October 1966, the debate highlighted fault lines between and within various elites and the central place of different kinds of youth, both sociological and rhetorical, in these turf wars. More specifically, the National Service proposal became a site upon which a generational struggle was played out between the first generation of nationalist political leaders and an up-and-coming group of youth poised to enter top jobs and positions. If this conflict had been simmering during the first few years of independence, the National Service crisis of 1966 brought it out into the realm of public, national debate and illustrated the ambivalence, insecurity, and unevenness marking the reproduction of an early postcolonial elite.

Within days of the appearance of Kimulson's letter, critiques of his grievances began to appear in the *Standard*. Above all, these letter writers attacked Kimulson and students at the University College in general for what was regarded as an unjustifiable unwillingness to sacrifice by the already privileged. Wrote Elton and Daniel, "Mr. Kimulson . . . seems unwilling to serve the nation because of his wrong idea—that he is superior to others who volunteer to serve."[45] Adopting a pseudonym from a slang term for a poor person, Baba Kabwella criticized Kimulson's suggestion that students be granted loans for cars, objecting that "education should not be regarded as a stepping stone for loans, big salaries or cars. We should only be proud of education if it wipes out our ignorance and not because we expect big salaries after completion of our academic years or because we want 'Nizations.'"[46]

Notably, however, some of the first public criticisms of Kimulson were made by individuals who were evidently among Dar es Salaam's most well heeled. One Elice Leo, who castigated university students for regarding National Service as beneath them, listed an address in Oyster Bay, the capital's most upscale neighborhood.[47] And the first published reaction to Kimulson's letter came from a Tanzanian student recently returned from studies in the United States who "inform[ed] Mr. Kimulson that a National Service training camp is not a luxurious picnic hideaway" and offered up Peace Corps volunteers in Tanzania as true examples of sacrifice.[48]

Students' responses to such critiques, including from Kimulson himself, were not long in coming. In his first published response to critics,

Kimulson focused on Leo's letter: "I am not at all surprised to note that most of those who have attacked me on this issue are residents of Oyster Bay who I gather are 'naizations' *and are already out of the wood*. . . . [T]hese naizations, like Elice Leo, should sacrifice one third of their monthly incomes to the National Service in view of the fact that they cannot join the National Service because of their present official commitments. . . . I question the logic in forcing graduates to sacrifice . . . while the big officers are left intact."[49] Similarly suggesting that critics of "students' attitude" were among the rich and powerful who would not be negatively affected by compulsory national service, another student speculated that "they are motivated by fear of active graduate competition in business and social circles."[50]

But if responses such as these featured attempts to redeploy a vocabulary of 'nizations and situate critics of student complaints as, in fact, the true elite, they also extended and deepened perceptions of university students as a selfish, privileged, and arrogant group.[51] Self-identifying as the "cream" of society and an "intelligentsia class . . . [who] constitute a special category of reasoning and approaches to social problems," several student letter writers expressed concern that the National Service program as it was designed could not accommodate youth of differing "standards."[52] As Damien Lubuva, a member of USUD, put it, "Social amenities e.g. houses and food etc., available at the National Service camps [should] be improved to the extent that they will be generally acceptable to the various classes of Servicemen, some of whom will be professionals whose fields demand certain standards of social etiquettes."[53]

Such statements, several of which were couched in highly academic prose and speculated on opponents' educational levels, drew angry responses from letter writers. Some pointed to student letters as evidence that youth at the university considered themselves a class apart, out of touch with the material hardship of the vast majority of Tanzanians. Simmy Massawa from Singida, referring to students at the University College, charged that "the people who are supposed to save Tanzania from exploitation of the few . . . the so-called 'privileged class' . . . are among those who have great desire to develop or perpetuate it."[54] Other letters showcased attempts to mimic, if not parody, the academic jargon of several university students' protests. Such was the case in a long response to Kimulson by A. B. Mkelle, a Form IV leaver. Peppering his letter with references to Hume, Kant, and the "great theory of Mendelian inheritance," Mkelle contested Kimulson's characterization of an "intelligentsia class" and argued for a definition of the intellectual not limited to the university: "I would personally define the intelligentsia as consisting of all those whose decision in the process of living would not wholly be influenced by blind or untutored experience but having been endowed with the capacity to summon further advice from the pool of general education that they have received."[55] Emerging quite early in the debate, the contest over the meaning of terms and social categories like "'nizer" and "intellectual" would only get increasingly heated as the controversy over National Service continued to fester throughout 1966.

Actions and statements shaping the National Service controversy were not confined to the press. Throughout 1966 politicians at all levels of government and the party began to speak out on the issue. In January, R. S. Wambura, junior minister in the office of the vice president, opened a University College TANU Club (which would later take a stand opposing the government's National Service plan) on behalf of Vice President Kawawa. In his speech Wambura chided university students, saying, "One has no right to call himself a true citizen of the nation which he has not built and is not prepared to build."[56] A month later Finance Minister A. H. Jamal publicized a rumor that university students were petitioning for reduced vacation residency rates to allow them to avoid returning to their upcountry homes for the holidays; he warned students that they were in danger of becoming outcasts.[57] And in June President Nyerere publicly entered the fray for the first time in a speech he delivered at the University College to an international assembly of the World University Service. The speech was reproduced in full in the Tanzanian press the next day. Charting back and forth between affirming the university as a site for the production of "objectivity in the search for truth" and its role in fulfilling nation-building goals, Nyerere spent much of the speech decrying student arrogance and suggesting that the university's physical environment might be to blame: "Every time I myself come to this campus . . . I think again about our decision to build here and our decision about the types of buildings. . . . We do not build skyscrapers here so that a few very fortunate individuals can develop their own minds and then live in comfort, with intellectual stimulus making their work and their leisure interesting to themselves. We tax the people to build these places only so that young men and women may become efficient servants to them. There is no other justification for this heavy call being made on poor peasants."[58]

Three weeks after Nyerere's speech, Vice President Kawawa announced that a bill on National Service would soon be submitted to Parliament.[59] The announcement came one day after Kimulson was forced out of office in murky, highly contested circumstances. Although the removal was the immediate result of a USUD referendum that Kimulson lost by a one-third margin, the referendum itself was made possible only by the suspension of the union's constitution by the University College principal, Dr. Wilbert Chagula. Announced on very short notice and held on a Sunday, the referendum saw a strikingly low participation rate and was called despite Kimulson having received a vote of confidence from the *baraza*, a student assembly.[60]

With Kimulson deposed and University College students away from campus on vacation, the government made its move, releasing in late September a white paper containing the final National Service proposal that would promptly go to the Parliament for debate and ratification. Government officials had previously stressed that the views of affected students would be considered in the drafting of the final bill (and indeed the National Union of Tanzania Students (NAUTS) had met with Kawawa and Nyerere to discuss the measure).[61] However, while it clarified that the 40 percent salary would be paid in addition to the standard monthly National Service allowance of 180 shillings (making the actual salary reduction for a university graduate 23 percent after taxes), the white paper maintained the terms of the original proposal.[62]

Having died down between February and September, public debate over National Service was revived with unprecedented intensity after the release of the white paper. Public discourse on the issue in the first three weeks of October replayed many of the same elements, arguments, positions, and vocabularies that had characterized the debate at the beginning of the year: the focus of opposition to the plan on its salary component, the length of service proposed, and the pressure felt by university students to satisfy their parents' impatience for a payoff from their investment in education; suggestions by opponents to the plan that National Service, in the absence of a more hierarchical structure, was unsuitable for the very highly educated; and condemnations of university students as being overprivileged and out of touch with the nation's needs.[63]

Two aspects of the new spike in discourse were striking, however. The first was an intensification of a vocabulary of generational tension and confrontation. Speaking to the National Assembly at the conclusion of the debate on the bill, which was approved by all but one dissenting MP,[64] Kawawa was paraphrased on the front page of the TANU daily as follows: "[Kawawa] said that the Government had no intentions of oppressing and exploiting the youths. He explained that they will join the National Service just as parents send their children to maturing camps. . . . 'Should it be their habit to say these old men are unwise, I would laugh at them because a youth hasn't got as much wisdom as an old man who has a lot of experience,' he said."[65] Or, as the *Standard*'s reporter paraphrased part of the same speech, "The scheme had been decided by elderly men, and in Africa no old man was unintelligent. A youth might have wisdom, but this would not surpass the wisdom of old men. If old men were unintelligent, would the youths be where they were today?"[66]

Some student opponents of the bill responded sharply to Kawawa's invocation of an African habitus to lend authority to what was seen by many as an attempt to put youth in their place. W. Mufumya argued,

> It is a misconception to think that M.P.'s can act as or like parents and elders to the students. . . .
>
> It is true that Africans are, in their culture, different from some other races but they are human like all others. To say that old people in our community never go wrong is to deny the existence of it.
>
> Why do married sons often separate to establish homes of their own? Why must an elder son be present at discussions in which a father is expected to pronounce a final word?
>
> No! M.P.'s are the equals of the electorate and they cannot claim superhuman wisdom.[67]

The University College TANU Club, in taking a stand against the bill's passage, cleverly—and perhaps a little mockingly—turned Kawawa's metaphor against the government's position. The club's statement on the issue read in part, "It is felt that this crucial issue was not given its due share of time during the debates, in accordance with the belief that 'the elders sit under the big tree and talk until they agree,' which means that MPs should have been given enough time to exhaust the issue rather than rushing it through."[68] Not all students were critical of the bill's passage and Kawawa's words on elders and youth. G. D. T. Lusinde, a student at Kivukoni College, TANU's institute for training high-level party cadres, submitted a letter to the *Nationalist* that expanded the vice president's metaphor into a full-fledged analogy equating Tanzanian governmental institutions with structures of authority "in the far off days of our ancestors." In those traditional times, Lusinde asserted, "governments were maintained by the elders and there was no opposition to the customary laws imposed by the needs of the society of the time. . . . And the youths of those days accepted and carried out the laws passed to them by the elders." Relating Nyerere and Kawawa to traditional leaders and the National Assembly to the *baraza*, Lusinde dismissed the grumbling of students opposing National Service as "rather bogus . . . as far as these people originate from African ancestors (and not European ancestors)."[69]

Alongside the articulation of the issue in terms of fraught norms of generational relations, the new flurry of public discourse surrounding the bill's passage was accompanied by a new focus on consumption in the struggle over the referents of the label "elite." In the wake of swift condemnations of the white paper by prominent university student groups, a renewed chorus of voices arose attacking the perceived privilege of students at the Hill, for whom, a letter in the *Nationalist* charged, even two years was too long to start *kula nchi* (literally, to eat the nation, an expression commonly used to describe political corruption).[70] In response to these now-familiar condemnations, some university students tried to shift public attention to the material wealth of high-level government and party leaders ("those already long in civil and public service").[71] The TANU Club's statement on the white paper centered on juxtaposing the ethic of frugality which the National Service plan was billed as generating with "the luxurious lives led by many of the nation's leaders in huge houses and cars."[72] Two days later C. L. K. Chawe, a member of USUD, expanded on this comparison in a letter which the *Standard*'s editor announced, prematurely, it turned out, would be the final one published on the issue. Using a geography of wealth in the capital to concretize his accusations, Chawe wrote,

> In the past and up to now there has been a vertical but unnecessary rivalry between our political leaders and students. Students have been accused of living in an "ivory tower," being arrogant and demanding too much from the public. One wonders whether a student at the University College which is next door to Manzese, a student at the Teachers' College in the center of Chang'ombe, a student at the Medical School at the periphery of Kariakoo are actually living in an ivory tower?
>
> Is it the tall buildings which are referred to as ivory tower? Who is nearer to the people, a Benz-driven individual living in Oyster Bay and working in Azania Front or a pedestrian student living in the centre of Chang'ombe at the periphery of Kariakoo area?[73]

Published just one day before the university students' dramatic protest march on State House, this supposedly final letter made explicit an important area of conflict between university students and the incumbent political elite, the "vertical rivalry" which had been simmering over the course of the previous year. If university students were being asked to sacrifice time, salary, and status to, in effect, delay their entry into the high-level posts nearly guaranteed to them at this point, they were being asked to do so by those whom many students regarded as "already out of the wood" and bent on making it more difficult for the next generation to follow the same 'nization path.

The decision of the university students to demonstrate that October was made in the context of reports of powerful student demonstrations, protests, and uprisings occurring across the formerly colonized world. In November 1965, the same month Vice President Kawawa announced the government's original National Service plan, student protests erupted in a number of capitals—Delhi, Cairo, Tel Aviv, and, not least, Dar es Salaam—over Britain's refusal to use force against Ian Smith's breakaway settler regime in Rhodesia. In downtown Dar es Salaam, students from the University College demonstrated outside the British High Commission and destroyed the high commissioner's car before being dispersed with tear gas and rebuked by Nyerere for their violence (although he implied that their outrage was justified).[74] In January 1966, as the early debate over National Service raged in the Tanzanian press, Moroccan students in Algiers took their ambassador hostage in his own embassy to protest the murder of a prominent Moroccan opposition leader in Paris.[75] The next month saw Ugandan students in Britain threatening to strike and occupy the Ugandan High Commission in protest over their government's refusal to raise their bursary allowances to keep up with inflation in the United Kingdom—an act which prompted the editor of Tanzania's *Sunday News* to lament, "Scarcely a day goes past without university students somewhere expressing discontent with their lot."[76] On the eve of the National Service march, front-page stories in the Tanzanian press reported the revolt of students in northern Indian cities.[77] And throughout 1966 demonstrations by thousands of students in Indonesia against Sukarno's rule garnered attention, leaving a physical mark upon the University College students' protest in Dar es Salaam, which featured placards warning the Tanzanian government to "Remember Indonesia."[78]

These reports of student protests worldwide were given prominent, if often negative, coverage in the Dar es Salaam press, where they consistently appeared on the front page. Constituting a vital international context within which the debate over National Service and indeed the struggle over youth in Dar es Salaam generally were taking place, the mounting wave of student action cannot but have emboldened the students of University College, Dar es Salaam as they returned from vacation and contemplated marching.

The student protest march, a ten-kilometer walk in which the participants, clad in their academic gowns, chanted and displayed slogans critiquing the National Service plan, its architects ("Kawawa Must Quit"), and even the overall performance of the postcolonial state ("Colonialism Was Better"), attracted much attention. But what pushed the march to the fore of public debate, talk, and rumor nationwide for several weeks was Nyerere's response to it. Once downtown, the demonstrators had planned to end the procession at the vice president's office by presenting him with a petition. Upon approaching Kawawa's office, however, the protesters were diverted by riot police toward State House, further down the road. Awaiting the marchers as they were shepherded into the State House grounds, Nyerere ordered the students to gather before the terrace where he sat flanked by Kawawa and fourteen ministers. Once all had gathered, a student spokesman arose and read a petition aloud. Featuring arguments that had been rehearsed in the long-running public debate on the issue, including the implication that highly paid political leaders were getting off scot-free, the petition concluded with the following words: "Unless these terms of reference and the attitude of our leaders towards students change we shall not accept the National Service in spirit; let our bodies go, but our souls will remain outside the scheme. And the battle between the political elite and the educated elite will perpetually continue."[79]

Nyerere responded at length in an impromptu speech that, by all accounts, began softly but gradually grew angrier.[80] Shifting back and forth between defending the logic of the government's National Service plan and expressing outrage at the students' demands, the speech wound toward the following conclusion:

> You are right when you talk about salaries. Our salaries are too high. You want me to cut them? . . . I'm willing to slash salaries. Do you want me to start with my salary? Yes! I'll slash mine. I'll slash the damned salaries in this country. Mine, I slash by twenty per cent, as from this hour. . . . The damned salaries! These are the salaries which build this kind of attitude in the educated people, all of them! All of them! Me and you! We belong to a class of exploiters! I belong to your class! . . . I have accepted what you said. And I am going to revise salaries permanently. And as for you, I am

asking you to go home. I'm asking all of you to go home. Rashid [Vice President Kawawa]! You are responsible to see that they go home.[81]

The 412 students taking part in the demonstration, 338 of whom were from the University College and constituted about two-thirds of the Tanzanians at the university and 80 percent of Tanzanians in the faculties of arts and social sciences and law, had been indefinitely expelled. For these students and their families this outcome was a severe blow. With the vast majority of the expelled being the first in their families to attend not only university but secondary school as well, they were the bearers of tremendous hopes for a future of high-level positions that would benefit entire networks of kin, expectations to which students' letters in the run-up to the protest alluded. As for the proposed salary cuts, they were indeed put into effect soon after the demonstration: Nyerere's salary and those of cabinet ministers were reduced. In publicly confirming the cuts, the government went to some length to suggest that they were part of "an objective long contemplated" rather than a spur-of-the-moment measure.[82]

The matter did not end there. As the expelled students were taken from State House to be fingerprinted and sent home, TANU headquarters instructed party and TYL branches, the UWT, and the National Service to organize counterdemonstrations in Dar es Salaam the following day to show support for Nyerere's action.[83] Among those rallied were hundreds of cadres from the National Service who performed a highly symbolic rebuttal of the student protesters' demonstration—a reenactment-in-reverse of the students' march, beginning at State House with the delivery of a resolution in support of the president and ending at the University College with a protest march around the campus. Downtown, thousands participated in the TANU-organized demonstration, which culminated with a rally and a two-hour speech by Nyerere broadcast nationally on the radio.[84] Beginning on the Monday following the demonstration and continuing for weeks, messages of loyalty and support for Nyerere pouring in from provincial officials, secondary students and administrators, and parents began to be reported as front-page news in the press—a phenomenon which was to last for weeks.[85]

As state officials were strategically maneuvering the cadres of the TYL and the National Service into position as embodiments of ideal citizen-youth, the party press was publishing one editorial after another condemning the "unpatriotic students" of the University College. The erstwhile, much-touted role of university students as critical to the nation's development was not so subtly challenged in much official discourse in the aftermath of the demonstration. Paraphrasing Nyerere's speech of the previous day, the Nationalist declared in a masthead editorial that "this country . . . will be built by steeled youths, vigilant and dedicated to hard work, nursed in the problems of their country." The students could decide, through "a searching self-inquiry," whether they would meet the "challenge to youth."[86]

Official statements also featured repeated reference to supposed norms of respect for generational hierarchy. The actions of the students, the Nationalist asserted, constituted "conduct utterly foreign to African traditional respect for authority."[87] And on November 4 NAUTS issued an apology that cast the conflict in much the same terms. The statement read in part, "What happened recently between the students and our government was [a] misunderstanding between father and son. It is clear that the son was wrong and so the son today apologises to his father. Kind father, pardon us your children. . . . Our co-operation of father and son should continue."[88]

Several dimensions of the National Service crisis made it a critical pivot point in the renegotiation of youth. Crucial in the way the debate over the service plan played out was the frequent charge by student opponents that the plan was being promoted and welcomed by a generation of political leaders who, as Kimulson had put it, were "out of the wood." This first nationalist generation had ridden to the forefront of the anticolonial movement of the 1950s and acquired prominent positions in an independent TANU state as part of a generational challenge to the elders of the Native Authorities aided by this new generation's possession of formal education and other accoutrements of European modernity. But by the mid-1960s, as the struggle over National Service makes clear, many up-and-coming university students regarded themselves as being in a "vertical rivalry" with this political elite. It was with both a sense of entitlement to top posts by virtue of their postsecondary education that often exceeded that of high-level officials and a conviction that the incumbent elite was attempting to hold them back that student protesters declared, "And the battle between the political elite and the educated elite will perpetually continue."

The debate on the National Service plan, then, involved a struggle between an older generation of nationalist politicians and civil servants and a new generation of the very highly educated poised to enter top jobs. In the aftermath of the demonstration, the state made moves to raise the profile of a politically favorable category of youth, elevate the TYL and the National Service to fill that category, and threaten the demonstrators with effective exile from the youth who would build the nation. Of course, the state desperately needed the skills and qualifications of university graduates if Africanization was to proceed apace, but the threat of political marginalization was sufficient to bring the demonstrators back to the conflicted "co-operation of father and son" on which depended the reproduction of the postcolonial ruling elite.

The Rise and Fall of the University Left

The renegotiation of youth that developed in the aftermath of the National Service demonstration was soon complicated by the emergence of new voices in this struggle. If the students' protest was a catalyst for the state's vigorous promotion of a new cadre of model citizen-youth in the form of the TYL and the National Service, the crisis also helped enable the emergence of a new potential challenge to an official monopoly on youth—this time in the form not of elitist students perceived as reluctant to sacrifice for the nation, but of a vocal, international leftist presence at the University College. While constituting only a small minority of students and faculty on campus, this left contingent was essential in establishing the university's reputation across Africa and the world as an important nodal point of socialist thought and activism. Indeed, the radicals, as they were often called in Dar es Salaam, managed to achieve a visibility far beyond their numbers. What has been far less noted, however, is the importance of the university left to local politics in Dar es Salaam, and more specifically to the struggle over the category of youth in the late 1960s and early 1970s.

In the wake of the wave of public and often highly performative denunciations of university students following the demonstration against the National Service plan, Nyerere issued the Arusha Declaration nationalizing all medium- and large-scale industry and committing Tanzania to more or less explicitly socialist policies. Within weeks of the issuance of the declaration, another major policy paper, entitled "Education for Self-Reliance" (hereafter ESR), emerged from the president's office. ESR took off from the vociferous calls to reform education that had been building in response not only to the National Service demonstration, but also to public debate over a crisis of an ever-increasing number of primary school leavers that far outstripped both secondary school places and opportunities for wage labor. ESR proposed a number of measures designed, on the one hand, to restructure primary school as a potentially terminal course of study preparing students for rural, agricultural labor; and on the other, to bring secondary and higher education more in line with an ethic of self-reliance and service to the nation. A central keyword of the decade or so after 1967, "self-reliance" in the context of a secondary school or university could theoretically encompass a variety of measures to correct elitist attitudes: from the establishment of a school farm on which the students would depend to revision of the curriculum to make it more supposedly relevant to Tanzanian realities.[89]

As a general policy document, ESR did not include many details on what the plan would mean for the University College. But even before ESR was released, university administrators, in cooperation with the government and party officials, were planning a major conference to address how the University College might be reformed in the wake of the so-called tragedy of the National Service crisis. The "Conference on the Role of the University College Dar es Salaam in a Socialist Tanzania" was held in March 1967, just two days after the announcement of ESR. The public speeches at the conference, delivered by high-level government officials (including the vice president) and university administrators, presented a more or less united front: declaring the need for reform but tempering such urgings with calls for measured deliberation.

Behind the scenes, however, the conference proceedings were deeply divided. A group of faculty members who came to be known as the Committee of Nine had submitted to the conference beforehand a lengthy, detailed proposal for a radical restructuring of curriculum, faculty appointments, administrative structure, and staff–student relations.[90] The committee, which was composed entirely of expatriates, only one of whom, a Kenyan, was East African, included scholars who would go on to become household names in international leftist circles; the nine were Giovanni Arrighi, Catherine Hoskyns, Grant Kamenju, Frances Livingstone, James Mellen, Sol Picciotto, Walter Rodney, John Saul, and Herbert Shore. All young Marxist scholars who had arrived in Tanzania in the mid-1960s (Shore was by far the oldest at forty-five), the group showcased multiple nationalities, disciplinary backgrounds, and career trajectories, not to mention being a microcosm of the kind of cosmopolitan left scene to which Dar es Salaam played host at the time. Arrighi, an Italian political scientist who had arrived at the University

College after being deported from Smith's Rhodesian white-settler regime, eventually joined Immanuel Wallerstein and Rodney in developing the world systems analysis tradition of global economic critique. Mellen, having come to Tanzania after being fired from his political science teaching post at Drew University in New Jersey in a high-profile case involving his public expression of support for the Viet Cong at a teach-in, would go on after his return to the United States to help found the radical leftist group, the Weathermen. Kamenju was a rising star in Kenyan literary criticism, a colleague of Ngugi wa Thiong'o in graduate school at Leeds, who had reportedly introduced Ngugi to Fanon; he went on to head the department of literature at the university for many years. Shore, while teaching drama at the University College, became a close confidant of Eduardo Mondlane, the founder of the Liberation Front of Mozambique (FRELIMO), who was in exile in the Tanzanian capital, and would go on to be active in multiple southern African liberation movements after Mondlane was assassinated in Dar es Salaam in 1969. Hoskyns, Livingstone, Picciotto, and Saul would all move on to long academic careers in the United Kingdom, Israel, and Canada; although Saul was the only one of the four to remain focused on Africa in his research and writing, all maintained activist profiles that their years in Dar es Salaam no doubt played no small part in shaping. Rodney, the Guyanese Marxist scholar who would become perhaps the most widely known of the nine, remained in Tanzania until 1974, completing How Europe Underdeveloped Africa there, before returning to Guyana and a political career that ended in his assassination in 1980.

If the committee's proposal professed the same general goals as that of the government and university officials who had spoken on the issue (the transformation of a University College based upon hierarchy and privilege), it proposed changes considerably more far-reaching and more explicitly socialist than those anyone had suggested. Seizing upon the new commitment to socialism and self-reliance proclaimed by the state, the Committee of Nine had produced a proposal that made many high-level officials, both in and out of the university, highly uncomfortable. The centerpiece of the committee's intervention was a proposal to reorganize the curriculum of the University College around an interdisciplinary (or, more accurately, an antidisciplinary) Common Course in social analysis. Conceived as an assault on the fragmentation of knowledge produced by the university's organization along Western disciplinary lines, the Common Course was aimed at enabling students to develop a "comprehensive understanding or questioning of capitalist economy, society, and culture as a system"—an understanding which, the committee hoped, would produce students "equipped to confront the theoretical, practical, and strategic problems of Tanzanian socialism . . . as socialist intellectuals" rather than as elitist technocrats.[91] Not simply a minimal requirement, the course would stretch over the full three years of a student's tenure at the University College and occupy "not less than 1/3 of the student's time" each year. Coursework in the first and third years would focus on social change in Africa, and more specifically Tanzania, while the second year would examine "the international system" focusing on the development of capitalism on a global scale and the emergence of a socialist alternative.[92]

In addition to the Common Course, the Committee of Nine made a number of other recommendations: the recruitment of a larger percentage of faculty from socialist countries and from East Africa (the latter preferably having done their study abroad in the Eastern bloc) to counter the predominance of expatriate teaching staff drawn from capitalist Britain and the United States; increased representation of government and TANU officials on the university's key decision-making bodies, the deliberations of which would be made more accessible to the university community; and, finally, a bundle of detailed suggestions on making the relationships among staff, students, and faculty more egalitarian and enhancing students' service to surrounding communities and to the nation.[93]

The committee's recommendations were not wholly unprecedented. Indeed, most of the proposal's suggestions were taking off from wider calls for related measures, like ideas for some kind of core course requirement and the widespread calls in the Nationalist's letters-to-the-editor page for overhaul of a reactionary faculty suspected of instigating the National Service protests.[94] However, the committee's intervention was by far the most detailed and far-reaching of proposals coming from within either the university or state apparatus in the run-up to the conference.

During and after the conference itself, opinion among the university faculty broke down into three main factions.[95] A modest number of mostly British faculty members had backed the student demonstrators wholeheartedly during the National Service crisis, and in its wake they apparently found it difficult to offer suggestions for a revamping of a university system with which they saw little wrong. Given the overwhelming consensus in public discourse at large for the need for university reform of one sort or another, this position was considerably enfeebled. Between the other two factions, however, a battle was brewing. On the one hand was the Committee of Nine's proposal, backed by its authors and a handful of additional allies, for an overhaul of the university in the directions of socialist instruction and radical interdisciplinarity. On the other hand was a much larger, if originally less vocal, group—including a wide majority of the African teaching staff and a sizeable proportion of the expatriates—that occupied a middle ground, articulating a need for modest reform but wary of the platform put forward by the Committee of Nine. In the course of deliberations in the committee and panel meetings at the conference, it was this third group whose position carried the day.

Whereas the final recommendations that emerged at the end of the conference included, at a glance, some of the key elements of the Committee of Nine's proposal, these were considerably watered down in substance. For instance, while the idea of a common course was endorsed, the recommendation that it go a long way in supplanting disciplinary curricula was sidelined, and the matter of the content and length of the course was "left to the College for further consideration."[96] And that was in the heat of the moment. As the National Service crisis grew more distant and the competing proposals for reform wound their way through the university administration, those wary of the consequences of adopting the Committee of Nine's proposals succeeded in keeping curricular overhaul to a minimum. Among the factors in play for the moderates were fears of the potential loss of some of what had been gained through the slow progress of the Tanzanianization of the faculty through the 1960s—and many of those who stood to lose most from a weakening of individual departments were Tanzanian department chairs who, in most cases, were the first nonexpatriates to hold their positions. Support for the Committee of Nine's position remained concentrated among expatriate socialist faculty members; and when Rodney changed sides as the final decision on the Common Course proposals approached in 1972, the committee's proposal lost out to a much more modest plan for core instruction, placed under the control of existing departments.[97]

But the presence on campus of a vocal contingent of international, socialist faculty members in the late 1960s and early 1970s is only one part of the story of the University College left. Even as scholars such as Rodney, Saul, and Arrighi were arriving on campus, the reputation of the University College, Dar es Salaam was attracting students with leftist inclinations from across East Africa. And if the faculty left was the chief contributor to the international image the university would soon acquire as an important center of Third World socialist thought, the student left was arguably more embedded in the fault-lines of local politics and struggle in Dar es Salaam. It was largely through student initiative, inspired, aided, and encouraged by alliances with members of the faculty left, that the institutions, events, and daily practices that contributed to the building of a left presence on campus were developed.

The student left was a small minority on campus in the late 1960s and early 1970s—numbering fewer than one hundred in a student body of approximately sixteen hundred by 1970.[98] Its beginnings, in 1967, were even smaller. In a recollection written in 1970, Yoweri Museveni, later president of Uganda and a founding member of Dar es Salaam's student left, described his first days as a student at the University College in mid-1967:

> Before I came to Tanzania, I expected a lot, probably too much, of the Tanzanian Revolution. At a distance, one gets an exaggerated image of Tanzania's anti-imperialist stance. You get the image of clearheadeness regarding socialism, anti-imperialism, Pan-Africanism etc. You get the impression that most of the government leaders, ministers, top Civil Servants etc., are devoted cadres with a high level of political consciousness. . . . All such impressions, I have since discovered, are exaggerated. . . .
>
> It was mainly because of this over-evaluation of Tanzania's achievements that while at home in Uganda, I was determined to come to Tanzania at any cost. . . . In fact, if for any reason, I had failed to gain admission to University College, Dar es Salaam, I would not have gone to University at all. . . .
>
> Thus, expecting all this from Tanzania, I arrived at the College in July 1967. I was, almost immediately, disappointed on arrival at the College. I found that the students were lacking in militancy and were even hostile, not only to socialism, but even, at least some of them, to the whole question of African Liberation. At any rate there was no clear, militant commitment on the part of the broad sections of the student body. Instead, most of our extra-curricular time was taken up by frivolous activities: drinking, dancing and watching decadent Western films. . . .
>
> Against such a background, a group of us decided to form a revolutionary students' organisation.[99]

The organization Museveni referred to was the Socialist Club, started by an international group of students from Tanzania, Kenya, Uganda, Malawi, Sudan, Southern Rhodesia, and Ethiopia and a few faculty members, including Rodney.[100] Remembered as "just a study group rather than being an action front as well," members of the Socialist Club rather quickly founded a new group, the University Students' African Revolutionary Front (USARF).[101] Inaugurated in November 1967, USARF would be the focal point of the university's student left over the next three years, until its highly publicized banning in late 1970.

The student left on campus may have been small in numbers, but under the banner of USARF it was visible and vocal beyond its size. The movement's success in achieving a certain prominence on campus and in national political debate was due not only to the high level of commitment of its participants, but also to the coalescing of an energetic, collective scene around USARF-organized lectures and discussions, teach-ins, provocative actions, and its lively journal, *Cheche*. Liberation, revolution, and worldwide socialist struggle were in the air, and USARF members voraciously read, exchanged, and debated texts connecting them to international networks of left theory and praxis, networks whose representatives would frequently appear at the University College, as if confirming Dar es Salaam's connectedness to the most vital movement of the time, the drive for progressive global change.

Museveni traced the rise of the student left on campus to the catalyzing impact of a visit in 1967 by Stokely Carmichael, one of an impressive roster of left intellectuals and activists to visit the University College in the late 1960s and early 1970s.[102] In addition to those, like Rodney, Arrighi, and Horace Campbell, who stayed to teach at the college, this roster included C. L. R. James, Cheddi Jagan, Gora Ebrahim, Angela Davis, and Samir Amin.[103] Cultivating in the university's radical minority a sense of connectedness to internationalist struggle, these visits also underlined the distance between USARF's exceptionally engaged members and the rest of the student body. Issa Shivji, a Tanzanian law student of South Asian origin who would go on to have a career as a local scholar and activist, nostalgically recalled in 1992 the mood surrounding USARF's well-attended guest lectures:

> I believe it was some time in 1968 or 1969 that the University Students' African Revolutionary Front (USARF) organised a public lecture by that grand old man, a great historian, C. L. R. James, the author of *The Black Jacobins*. He gave a series of fascinating lectures on this campus. He was giving one of his lectures in ATB [a hall at the university] on a night like this. (At that time, there was never a night when we did not have some activity going on.) C. L. R. was talking about his own participation in

various revolutionary movements and writings. There, with his long fingers, he would be leafing through the selected works of Lenin quoting one passage after another. It was a great lecture. After he had finished, one gentleman, I presume a science student, stood up and asked, "What do you mean when you say 'bourgeoisie'?" It caused a stir and then there was total silence: silence of embarrassment. We were all embarrassed and James was visibly furious and irritated. He pointed his long finger to the front line where the lecturers were sitting and asked "what are you teaching these fellows?" The student who had asked the question felt like saying "I am sorry." That was in 1969.[104]

In addition to bringing guest speakers to campus, USARF engaged in a range of other activities. In accordance with its stated commitment to an engagement of the broadest scope—"within the University, Tanzania, Africa, and the world in general"—the group routinely issued statements and distributed leaflets and pamphlets analyzing and taking positions on major events ranging from the Soviet invasion of Czechoslovakia to Kenya's banning of the opposition Kenya People's Union to the Tanzanian government's karadha scheme granting state-supported loans for the purchase of private cars; each of these moves was condemned.[105] The group's most active members launched public campaigns against several faculty members whose politics were deemed suspect, accusing at least one American visiting professor of having connections to the CIA.[106] Perhaps continuing in the short-lived tradition of their institutional predecessor, the Socialist Club, the members of USARF organized "ideological classes" with the participation of sympathetic faculty members such as Rodney. If USARF's guest lectures drew overflow crowds, the ideological classes, which met on Sunday mornings, seem to have been popular only with the group's members.[107]

Perhaps most enduringly, USARF launched a journal, produced by students in mimeographed form. Named Cheche—the Kiswahili word for "spark," an invocation of journals of the same name launched by Nkrumah and Lenin—the journal featured in-depth articles by students and faculty, for example, "Mathematics and Ideology" and "How Socialist is Sweden?," reprinted articles by people like Amilcar Cabral and review essays on the classic texts of Fanon, Mao, and Lenin, and published lists of suspected CIA agents operating in Tanzania, cartoons, and dispatches from members visiting other capitals. USARF's chairman declared in Cheche's inaugural issue that it would be a journal unafraid to take on "the so-called 'African Socialism[s]' that have sprouted up everywhere in Africa";[108] and indeed the magazine did not shy away from publishing what endures as one of the most trenchant critiques of the Tanzanian state: Shivji's "Tanzania: The Silent Class Struggle," a piece that analyzed the Arusha Declaration as the "triumph of a bureaucratic bourgeoisie," written while the author was in his third year of law school.

But it was USARF's targeting of some campus events that brought to a head the deepening mutual antagonism between students on the left and their more conservative classmates. The most prominent of these incidents—one that would go on to occupy a celebrated place in members' memories of USARF's career—was the group's disruption of Rag Day in November 1968. Modeled after an institution pioneered at British universities and sponsored by the World University Service, Rag Day was an annual event in which students from the University College would "dress in rags of every colour and description"[109] and walk the streets of the capital's wealthy districts soliciting money for the poor. On the eve of the event in 1968, USARF held a meeting at which, according to Shivji, "the whole question of the role of charity and philanthropy in a bourgeois society was analysed" and was determined to be merely a "euphemism for those who plunder by the ton and give by the ounce."[110] Condemning Rag Day as a mockery of the poor, the front resolved to sabotage it. The next morning Rag Day participants emerged from the cafeteria to find that the tires of the lorries and tractors that were to take them to town had been slashed and the university gates blocked with makeshift barricades manned by USARF members. A shouting match ensued, campus guards and the police were summoned, and, with the USARF students claiming to have convinced these authorities of the justice of their cause, the event was canceled, never to be revived.[111]

The press gave prominent space to the cancellation, the Standard devoting an editorial to lamenting the event's disruption, while university students on either side of the issue launched into an acrimonious public debate. The organizers and supporters of Rag Day argued that the nature of the event had been misconstrued by USARF members, insisting that students intended not to mock the poor by dressing in rags, but simply to draw attention to the charity effort by "put[ting] on their traditional dresses and other make-ups which make them look funny."[112] Several students angrily suggested that members of the "so-called 'vanguard of revolutionary youth'" were simply naysayers who "interpret[ed] melodrama as revolution" and objected to "bourgeois" charity while contributing nothing to the poor themselves.[113] Others suggested that the government should be worried about what kind of subversive act USARF adherents might attempt next,[114] as one letter writer focused on the group's international membership to question why it included so few Tanzanians.[115] One student, E. R. Byarushengo, concluded his letter with a mocking reference to a nickname for student radicals circulating on campus: "We want an alternative from the 'Ches.'"[116]

Several USARF members and supporters returned the incriminations. Situating Rag Day in a tradition developed in elite universities in the capitalist West, these students argued at length that the event amounted to "bourgeoisie hypocrisy."[117] As Museveni, the chairman of USARF, wrote in a letter to the editor of the *Standard*, "Charity is a product of a vicious system of exploitation lubricated by small handouts to the 'less fortunate' and other toiling sections of the population."[118] This analysis was echoed in most letters written by USARF supporters, including one submitted by an ally in the expatriate faculty left at the college who characterized the declared intention of the Rag Day solicitors to contribute their would-be proceeds to a local orphanage as "serv[ing] only to indulge the hypocritical emotions and deepen the complacency of those whose concern for the plight of orphans goes so far as the small change in their pockets, but stops short of any policy that would make a real impact on their standard of living."[119]

Meanwhile, in vocabulary that resembled and doubtless was conditioned by dominant representations of university students in the wake of the National Service crisis, several USARF members lambasted the supporters of Rag Day as privileged and ungrateful consumers. In a comment rooted in the fraught sexual politics on campus discussed early in this chapter, Wasilwa Barasa accused Rag Day participants of "emptying countless bottles of beer at the women's Halls of Residence" as "the revolutionaries were busy putting the vehicles out of action." More extensively, B. G. Choka declared, "The university student in this country is one of the smartly dressed and privileged citizen [*sic*]. It is not by chance he belongs to that group. The poor people have paid taxes to remain with nothing for his family and it is this money that pays for the students' education. . . . With this money, the student buys a suit, a record player or an expensive radio. How come, then, that the same student and an 'intellectual' chooses to mock the same people who have paid for his education and all the luxurious privileges he gets? By celebrating Rag Day, we are being ungrateful to those who have suffered for us."[120]

Although USARF students' criticism centered, at least in part, on the figure of the same "privileged" and "ungrateful" university student so roundly condemned by the government in the National Service crisis two years earlier, state officials were reluctant to see the university left as an unambiguous ally. On the contrary, as leftist students and faculty at the university grew increasingly vocal throughout 1969 and 1970, high-level officials began to make moves to clip their wings.

The catalyst for the first of these moves was a speech given by Rodney at the East and Central African Youth Seminar, organized by the TYL and held in Dar es Salaam in December 1969. Gathering representatives from thirteen national and liberation youth movements, including delegations from Kenya, Uganda, Zambia, FRELIMO, and the Popular Movement for the Liberation of Angola, the seminar focused on the role of youth in the "African revolution" and was opened with great fanfare by Vice President Kawawa. While the speeches by Tanzanian state officials like Kawawa presented a back-to-the-land challenge to youth, declaring that young people's primary task at hand was the "transformation of the . . . countryside" (a call that dovetailed with the increasing push to accelerate villagization), Rodney's speech took a somewhat different interpretive tack on the question of youth and revolution. Reproduced in full the next day in the party newspaper, the speech presented a sweeping critique of the general condition of postcolonial governments across the continent, insisting on the class basis of such governments (petty bourgeois) and calling them the beneficiaries, at the expense of Africa's toiling masses, of the "Briefcase Revolution" that negotiated an end to colonial rule. Singling out Zanzibar as the only African territory in which "the neo-colonial exploiters were removed by revolutionary violence," Rodney called for the "recognition of armed struggle as the inescapable and logical means of obtaining freedom" from African governments for whom the label "socialism" functioned simply as "a bush behind which to hide their exploitative tendencies."[121] Zanzibar, a semiautonomous domain within Tanzania's Union, had seen its main socialist-nationalist party achieve its final victory over colonial power in 1964 in an overthrow of the Arab sultan, who had long been a puppet ruler under the British; the revolution ended in a violent purge of the island's Arab and South Asian population in which some three thousand people were killed. Given that the island nation lay less than fifty miles off the coast of Tanganyika, the reference to Zanzibar was a highly challenging one for the TANU government.

Two days after the *Nationalist* reproduced Rodney's speech in a feature, the paper published a scathing response in the form of a masthead editorial. The consensus among the University College community at the time was that the editorial originated from State House.[122] Entitled "Revolutionary Hot Air," the editorial distanced the newspaper and the Tanzanian state from the speech and attacked Rodney's "intolerable" call for "'Revolutionary Violence' to overthrow the governments of independent African states." It also professed shock that Rodney's target "presumably includ[ed] the Tanzanian government!" and concluded with a warning: "Those who insist upon indulging in such practices will have to accept the consequences of their indulgence."[123] Two days later a long letter from Rodney appeared in the *Nationalist* largely backing down from the more radical positions of his speech. In it he "clarified" that he did not mean to place "Tanzania in the same bag with those petty-bourgeois governments who have no intention of emancipating their people" and declared that if calling for revolutionary violence in other African countries went against Tanzanian policy, then his "indulgence will certainly cease."[124] Although the rebuke of Rodney appears to have been prompted above all by a desire to preempt any charges by neighboring states that Tanzania was inciting uprisings against more conservative governments, it also contained more than a hint of an increasing wariness within TANU of pressures from the left. In terms of the atmosphere at the University College, this official rebuke was seized upon by portions of the student body as a blow to the campus left and a vindication of their own frustration with the USARF crowd for whom Rodney was perhaps the chief faculty ally.[125]

Not two months later the student left on campus suffered another defeat in the eyes of the wider student body. In February 1970 President Nyerere visited the Hill for a question-and-answer session with the students and faculty. The visit coming amidst what the USARF chairman claimed was a whispering campaign warning of a communist threat to TANU, the atmosphere surrounding this charged event appears to have been one of great expectations on both sides of the vocally divided student body.[126] On the one hand, the USARF left was hoping to hear the president validate or take on board their positions and perspectives; on the other, the conservative majority of students were watching closely to gauge Nyerere's response to the so-called radicals, whom many students regarded as an increasingly shrill presence on campus. Many of the questions addressed to the president at the session were put forward by student leftists addressing such concerns as the government's karadha scheme, its commitment to socialism, and the continued hiring of "non-socialist foreign experts" in the country. According to Saul, who attended the meeting, "the tone and tenor of the [president's] answers were such as to make the radicals look foolish."[127] Museveni, who quite possibly was among Nyerere's questioners that day, put it more strongly, in words that implied a conspiracy: "The ground had been prepared. The questions from among us were arranged in such a way, that the President had no alternative but to regard us as spoilt children who did not understand elementary facts about life. The President supported the Karadha scheme which we had opposed; the reactionaries were elated—we had been, according to them, crushed. But only one thing saved us—the President had not specifically denounced us which was the only thing the reactionaries wanted."[128]

Such a denunciation was not long in coming, however. USARF's activities continued throughout 1970, several of their interventions making headlines and contributing to the charged mood on campus.[129] It was an election year for student government at the college, and over the course of campaigning it became clear that, with some success, students on the left were energetically attempting to gain key positions, including the presidency of the Dar es Salaam University Student Organization. In October USARF targeted a much-anticipated performance given at the University College by Up with People, an American musical youth group on a worldwide tour billed as exhibiting the "unlimited optimism of youth."[130] Charging (accurately) that the ensemble was an institution associated with the right-wing Moral Rearmament Movement, USARF members attending the show showered the band with packets of milk and later issued a statement condemning Up with People as a "Yankee propaganda group."[131] But USARF's most provocative act of the year was to publish, in a special issue of *Cheche*, Shivji's essay "Tanzania: The Silent Class Struggle." The piece was a lengthy, detailed, explicitly Marxist analysis of what Shivji characterized as the neocolonial character of Tanzanian social structures. As noted above, Shivji charged that the reforms of the Arusha Declaration, much touted as a substantive step toward socialism, in fact marked "the triumph of a bureaucratic bourgeoisie"; the essay concluded, "Building socialism is the workers' and not the bureaucrats' business."[132] Such an explicit centering of class struggle was at powerful odds with the Tanzanian state's preferred narrative of the national story since independence, and the Shivji issue was to be the journal's last. On November 12, 1970, both *Cheche* and USARF were declared banned.

In announcing the order, the authorities were at pains to explain why they would ban a group so apparently committed to the stated goal of building socialism in Tanzania and so demonstrative of Nyerere's call in 1966 for careerist university students to become committed activists. The initial reason for the ban, according to the authorities, was that *Cheche*'s name, inspired by a Leninist journal, "tended to give the impression that Tanzania was building 'Russian socialism.'"[133] A day after the ban was made public, however, the *Nationalist*'s masthead editorial provided another explanation:

> To enable the youth to play their rightful role in the political life of the country, the Party has its own youth organisation—the TANU Youth League. . . . Looked at from this standpoint there was really no need of having another political youth organisation at the University whereas TANU Youth League has already a branch there. . . .
>
> How much more relevant will this [discussion on the party] be now that all such discussions and debates will be channeled through the T.Y.L., the proper political organ of the youth? . . .
>
> It should be emphasised that the action . . . should not be taken as an attempt to stiffle [sic] revolutionary activity of the youth, either at the Hill or elsewhere. Let it be understood that as far as TANU is concerned, the youth of Tanzania can be as radical and as revolutionary as they wish, provided they do this through the institutionalised organs of the people.[134]

Indeed, the dissolution of USARF was followed immediately by the promotion by university officials of the TYL campus branch as possessing a "monopoly of political activities on the Hill."[135] In attempting to justify the ban on USARF, TANU officials had argued that the front and TYL shared political goals and some members, and to a limited extent this was true.[136] During USARF's tenure, some of the group's Tanzanian members had infiltrated the TYL campus branch, which had previously been, in the words of Shivji, "a typical student leadership involved in little beyond the usual mundane campus concerns"; USARF's attempts to create a more activist and leftist TYL reportedly caused consternation at TYL headquarters.[137] However, despite the limited cooperation between the two groups, the USARF left generally considered TYL to be an insufficiently radical organization, both in goals and in tactics.

More important, TYL, as an exclusively Tanzanian organization, lacked by definition one of USARF's great strengths: a broadly international membership. Many, if not a majority, of USARF members,

Led by Chairman Sijaona, officials from TANU Youth League headquarters present members of the University College league with a new van for the organization in 1968. *Courtesy of the Tanzania Information Service.*

including some of its most active adherents and its chairman, Yoweri Museveni, hailed from other African countries. USARF members prided themselves on this internationalist sensibility, not least because it mirrored their commitment to a political vision of a global movement of socialist liberation sustained by its own border crossings. And if the group's radicalism had been fueled by its internationalist character, all but a minuscule left fringe of TANU officialdom viewed it as a threat. The soothing official reassurances of USARF–TANU affinity—that members of the front could simply continue their activities in TYL— painted over the fact that people like Museveni (who, incidentally, had just graduated) would be excluded. Moreover, even for those like Shivji, who as Tanzanian nationals could join the TYL, the intent of the state's attempt was perhaps clear: No longer would a group for which international socialism formed the horizon of goals be allowed to exist independently.[138]

The dissolution of USARF did not lead to a complete halt in the activities of the campus radicals, which continued to some extent into the 1970s under the TYL. But things were not the same. Shivji would later comment, for instance, that *MajiMaji*, the campus TYL journal that replaced *Cheche* had neither the spirit of student militancy nor the ideological consistency of its predecessor.[139] With the TYL, the anxieties of the TANU elite trumped the socialism it was ostensibly dedicated to building.

Conclusion: Struggling over Youth in Dar es Salaam

The late 1960s were crucial years in the struggle over youth in Tanzania, and more particularly in Dar es Salaam. These years had seen the intensification of the Janus-faced nature of official constructions of youth as both key to the nation's health and development, and the potential core of its rot. The tension between these two constructions lay at the heart not only of the campus struggles, but also in the rising profile of the TYL in national cultural operations against Dar es Salaam's so-called decadent teenagers, the introduction of annual National Youth Festivals held to coincide with the anniversaries of the Arusha Declaration, and the more general trend in official rhetoric of foregrounding a vanguard role of youth in the state's most grand projects, such as the consolidation of the countryside into *ujamaa* villages.[140]

The struggles and controversies surrounding the University College throughout this period occupy a unique and important place in illuminating the state's attempt to manage youth in the 1960s. Invested with the hope that its graduates would have a catalyzing and accelerating effect upon national development, constituting a loyal cadre embodying the best skills and energy of a youthful nation, the University College instead developed as a source of anxiety for and challenge to officialdom. On the one hand, it was feared that rather than molding students in ways that conformed to the ideal citizen-youth, the university was turning out ambitious careerists who were making uncomfortable demands on the political elite that challenged this first generation of ruling nationalists. On the other hand, when a cadre of committed activists did emerge, it was, for most in the TANU establishment, the wrong kind of vanguard, one that also posed uncomfortable questions pointing to the "hidden class struggles" (to use Shivji's phrase) of Tanzania's limited experiment with socialism. Fueled by the transnational networks of people and ideas that ran through the university, USARF's internationalist vision existed in tension with official goals for youth. If, in these contexts, the National Service for the University College was devised as a way to rein in those perceived as having their eyes on 'nizations, the promotion of the TYL to steadily increasing prominence was, from the

As part of the National Youth Festival in 1969, TANU Youth League cadres perform against the backdrop of a North Korean–inspired audience card show at the National Stadium in Dar es Salaam. *Courtesy of the Tanzania Information Service.*

point of view of state officials seeking to mold a national relationship with youth in which they held the reins, a way to develop the right kind of vanguard.

If official rhetoric alternately portrayed youth as heroes and saboteurs, the TYL was meant to deal with both: provide a model of austere, rurally oriented, hard-working nation builders and serve as the main agent for policing perceived decadent, lazy, and corrupt manifestations of youth in the capital. As I noted in chapter 2, however, Youth Leaguers' actions were never quite so clean-cut, and their campaigns against decadence were shot through with a vigilante masculinity rooted in a political economy of frustration arising in the midst of shifting patterns of gendered work, movement, and sex in Dar es Salaam.

The story of campus politics told here helps illuminate some critical dimensions of the long-running struggle over generational hierarchies that has been such a prominent feature not only of Tanzanian, but also of broader African power politics.[141] As Jean-François Bayart, among others, has pointed out, many of the grand shifts of twentieth-century African history—according to which eras are marked out and periods assigned—also constituted the terrain upon which deeper sociopolitical dramas were played out, generational struggle being a primary example. As he put it in referring to the colonial period, "The era of the Whites became the era of insolence, when 'children,' 'their mouths on fire,' came out of their silence and, adding insult to injury, appropriated the sartorial art, the art of '*la sape*' [the practice of dressing in European designer clothing]. School, new media, and salaried employment all procured for them an empire of extroversion that each day further escaped the comprehension of the elders."[142] But this generational rivalry, as Bayart himself acknowledges, did not begin with the colonial conquests, and it did not end with the birth of the new, independent nations of the 1960s. Indeed, like so many other sociopolitical dramas playing out beneath and through these grand shifts, it crossed the colonial–postcolonial divide under the sign of national politics. As the story of the University College exemplifies, national politics *as a vehicle* was often powerfully shaped by the generational tensions and struggles playing out beneath and through it, policy debates over National Service impossible to understand apart from generational tensions over 'nizations. That the generational contests unfolding at the University College were bound up with, riven by, and worked out through the politics of transnational networks of activists and gender relations on campus serves as yet another indication of the inextricability of these cleavages, categories, and lines of struggle.

Perhaps even more important, though, this history of the University College serves as a reminder that sharp challenges to generational hierarchies can come—indeed not uncommonly have come—from those closest to the top of these hierarchies as much as from those excluded from advancement within them; from youth within close reach of their elders as much as from youth as a lumpen group of the disenfranchised. Some of the most influential recent arguments about youth in Africa— ones that insightfully situate youth as a potentially powerful force to either be harnessed by elder political elites or threaten them—have focused on youth as a marginalized social category, one that gains its volatile power from its disenfranchisement.[143] This marginalization is a crucial factor in African generational politics, as analyses of the contemporary phenomenon of child soldiers or Nicholas Argenti's examination of the embodied memories of a centuries-long history of youth exclusion in the Cameroonian Grassfields, to cite just two examples, demonstrate so well.[144] Indeed, as I discuss in chapter 4, exclusion from the fruits of adulthood could be a powerful driver behind disenfranchised young men's critique of a generation of postcolonial male elites in Tanzania too, even as the ambivalence of that critique all too often ended in its projection onto young women. But as Dar es Salaam's history of campus politics suggests, important generational challenges have also come from more privileged categories of youth, those potentially poised to inherit their elders' positions but frustrated at the perceived efforts of the elders to delay or place that inheritance in doubt. University youth were a highly advantaged lot, and their challenge to the 'nizations of the male political elite, elders who were "out of the wood," was an attempt to secure claims to a path up the ladder of generational hierarchy that was viewed as more uncertain than it should have been.

And yet neither is this a simple story of generational hierarchy contested, for USARF's challenge showcased less the anxious wrestling over advancement along vertical paths of status highlighted by the National Service crisis than the ways in which transnational alliances, identifications, appropriations, and solidarities could complicate these contests. If the construction of a pliant category of political youth with national boundaries was an important part of official efforts to maintain control over generational hierarchies, the USARF left called into question this vision with one based on international socialism and transnational mobilization that drew its sustenance from networks that stretched beyond the borders of Tanzania. That they did so while developing a critique of the TANU state as a "bureaucratic bourgeoisie" made it all the more challenging. The transnational networks of people, philosophies, symbols, and causes that helped create the extraordinary scene of the University College left is yet another example—alongside, yet quite different from, the stylistic appropriations highlighted in chapters 1 and 2—of Dar es Salaam's status as a node along these networks. Nodes like these—Dar es Salaam, like so many other African capitals of the time—provided the raw material for its young to construct alternative notions of youth with which the state had to grapple to manage within a national frame.

"Marriage Goes Metric"

NEGOTIATING GENDER, GENERATION, AND

WEALTH IN A CHANGING CAPITAL

On Wednesday, March 25, 1970, the *Nationalist* devoted a full page to an imagined telephone conversation between two well-off Tanzanian men under the title "Marriage Goes Metric." Cast as a giddy celebration of the initial approval by Parliament of the Tanzanian government's controversial reform of the country's marriage laws, this conversation between Kisikosi and Sembo began with the following declaration:

> IT HAS PASSED! It has passed! Long Live Adam! Never, in our glorious struggle for equality, justice and human dignity, have such a minority of our population—the men—asserted so vehemently its feudal prerogative, patriarchy, to lord it over the majority of the population—the women. . . . Never, in the long history of the emancipation of women have such a fabulous and flamboyant army of the amazons of "the United Women of Today," armed to the teeth and possessing the deadly weapons—jealousy and gossip—scattered, apolitically, in disarray and conceded defeat without even firing a single anti-feudalism shot at the men!
>
> Sembo, Sembo, is that you, old boy, is that you! So it has passed! I am delighted, old boy, yes I am. It is high time we went metric in the rites of marriage in this country.[1]

Gradually revealed to be well-off residents of Dar es Salaam, Kisikosi and Sembo focused the rest of their lengthy conversation on the ongoing battles each of them had been waging with their respective wives, Mariam and Angela, over this stage in the proposed marriage law reforms, battles which both men saw themselves as having won. In mocking tones, the men rejoiced at the parliamentary defeat of the "kitchen nonsense" of their wives, who could now be told to "stop [their] prattling about one man, one wife, equality and dignity!" And a good thing too, the men thought, for their wives had begun to make headway in pegging equality between spouses in marriage to the state's official commitment to socialist equality enshrined in the Arusha Declaration—"read[ing] the Arusha Declaration upside-down," as Kisikosi complained of Mariam. Turning to commiseration, the friends told tales of the lengths to which they had to go to maintain multiple mistresses around town, all the while avoiding their wives' "network of informers." "What more do they want from us?" Sembo lamented. He continued, "Angela is now expecting our tenth child; your Mariam has her eighth. We have bought them cars, they have chicken farms, they have servants, they eat what they like, when they want—and still they want us to be cooped in the house, listening to their nagging while life ebbs away just like that! No, Kisikosi, no. I don't want ever to come and regret . . . this is the zenith of our lives and it comes only once. I am going to tell Angela that I want a fresh young wife to help her to care for me . . . legally . . . especially now that the White Paper has been passed."

Though imagined, this conversation referred to the very real controversy surrounding the year-and-a-half-long battle over official proposals to overhaul Tanzania's colonial-era system of laws governing marriage. From September 1969, when the government unveiled its proposals in an official white paper, through March 1971, when the final version of the bill was voted into law by Parliament, the controversy swirling around the proposed United Law of Marriage came to dominate public talk in Dar es Salaam at multiple social levels. Formal parliamentary arguments, while raucous, lengthy, and closely watched, were merely the capstone on several months of intense public debate in bars, offices, homes, and street corners across the city. Like similar cultural controversies in the years preceding it, this one played out on the platform of the daily press, drawing letters from hundreds of correspondents and generating such intensity as to prompt President Nyerere to personally call for an extension of public debate on the matter.[2]

Like many other cultural contests that gained the public's attention in Dar es Salaam in the 1960s, the debate over the United Law of Marriage proved to be an umbrella under which a broad range of struggles around gender, generation, and new forms of accumulation gathered. Officials like Nyerere, Attorney General Mark Bomani, and Vice President Rashidi Kawawa, who shepherded the bill through passage, saw the reforms as part of a project of shaping a modern, progressive Tanzania in the spirit of the Arusha Declaration. And yet as public conversations over the measures gained momentum and became increasingly fraught, the proposed law became a site for the airing of a diverse set of anxieties over issues ranging from perceived demographic gender imbalances, to women's consumption patterns, to sharpening distinctions of wealth and status among men. Some of these issues are signaled in the staged dialogue between Kisikosi and Sembo: for instance, the oft-cited official justification for the law in terms of standardization ("going metric"), even amidst widespread recognition that debate over the bill was a vehicle for an intense battle of the sexes. As imagined by the columnist of the *Nationalist*, the core of whose reading public was the political and civil servant class of the capital, the conversation between Kisikosi and Sembo highlighted one of the axes along which the gendered struggles at work in the debate played out. Centering as it did so heavily on questions such as polygamy, which only a wealthy minority could afford, struggles along this axis pitted well-off men of the rising sixties elite against women either of some education or closely associated with the TANU UWT, satirized by Sembo as the "United Women of Today." Though sometimes cast by participants in cultural terms as an argument over African culture, women's rights, and international norms, this debate was also a heavily material one indexing the gendered fault lines of new patterns of accumulation in Dar es Salaam.

However, this axis of struggle satirized in the "Marriage Goes Metric" dialogue represents only one dimension of the multifaceted debate over the proposed law. For even as heated arguments developed over polygamy, adultery, inheritance, and the parameters of husbands' and wives' authority in marriage, other voices emerged at angles in the debate to place different sets of questions on the table. While often of less pressing concern to elite men and the UWT, such issues, including a chorus of distress at the high cost of bridewealth and widespread anxiety over a perceived demographic "surplus" of women, grew to occupy prominent places in the debate. Equally notable was a drumbeat of accusations, often from young men, that the Law of Marriage was simply a bid by male political elites to eliminate barriers to enhancing their status through the acquisition of women. Put forward by the multiple publics engaged in the debate over the law, these claims and counterclaims, rumors and anxieties intersected in complicated ways.

The struggles between husbands and wives over resources and authority within marriage and the generational tensions between bachelors and senior men over access to women and marriage reflected long-standing but shifting dynamics in colonial Tanzania and across Africa. As I outlined in the introduction, there was an ebb and flow to tensions between sons and fathers over the provision of bridewealth and the timing of marriage.[3] Beginning in the 1920s and 1930s and accelerating through the late colonial period, young men's use of wages from migrant labor as a potential route to greater control over the timing of marriage and the establishment of a household served to weaken, but by no means eliminate, fathers' regulation of these milestones. The meanings urban life had for young male migrants were also, as a result of this increasing control, often bound up with hopes and anxieties about marriage prospects and relations with senior men. As for relations between urban, often elite husbands and wives, scholars' work in contexts spanning the continent has illustrated the centrality of negotiation over resources to conjugality, whether monogamous, polygynous, or combinations of or movement between the two.[4] With the 1960s new developments intersected with these patterns, developments that played out in the debate over the marriage reforms. In particular, accumulation by new elites, many of whom were connected to the state, became a critical issue in the discussion, as it had in the related debates in neighboring Kenya that Lynn Thomas has examined.[5] This was the case both for women whose husbands were men of some means and for young bachelors. Married women who often possessed significant formal education but whose material and social status nonetheless depended on their husbands' incomes were anxious to maintain their material security against the threat of outside wives or mistresses; the bachelors condemned elite men for monopolizing women through their economic power, embodying a model of masculinity regarded as being out of reach for the vast majority of young men in town.

In the bulk of this chapter I track the debate over the Law of Marriage as offering insights into the nexus of struggles over gender, generation, and wealth marking Dar es Salaam in the late 1960s. One axis of contest dominated the debate early on: that between husbands and wives over important aspects of the law itself. Later on, young men attempted to steer the debate beyond the law's parameters toward grievances related to the generational, gendered, and class politics of life in town. Three specific themes of these pleas became prominent: concern over high bridewealth; frustration over a supposed surplus of women of marriageable age, women who were nonetheless out of reach; and an undercurrent of suspicion that the marriage reforms were being selfishly promoted by and for male political elites as a vehicle for their own material interests.

This third dimension of the debate brings into relief a key feature not only of the marriage law debate, but also of a number of other cultural controversies of the late 1960s, that is a proliferation of discourse on the leisure and sexual practices of Dar es Salaam's new male elite. By turns condemnatory, breathless, boastful, and envious, public attention on the shenanigans, real or invented, of "big men" points to both the potential for political critique embedded in such sensational debates and the ambiguity of that critique. This dynamic was at work in the marriage law debate, but it also proliferated at other levels of public discourse in the late sixties. At the end of the chapter, I briefly examine this proliferation through a reading of a long-running, tremendously popular sensationalist tabloid column. Entitled "Janja Yake" (his or her cunning), the column featured ribald tales of "city girls" and big men in compromising situations across Dar es Salaam's urban landscape and won both acclaim and opprobrium for *Ngurumo*, the Kiswahili daily in which it appeared. Juxtaposing readings of the place of elite lifestyles in the marriage law debate and "Janja Yake" draws attention to the multiple arenas in which sex and politics intersected in charged ways in the cultural debates of the late 1960s as well as opens up the crucial question of resistance in these domains of what Achille Mbembe has called conviviality—an issue which Mbembe and others have productively placed at the center of investigations of postcolonial African cultural politics.[6]

Reforming Matrimony as Postcolonial Cultural Project

Prior to the passage of the reformed Law of Marriage by Parliament in March 1971, marriages in Tanzania had continued to be legally governed by the nexus of marriage laws laid down by the British during the colonial period. Such carry-over of colonial legal norms in the realm of marriage, as in many other domains, was not unusual in the 1960s. Indeed, Tanzania was the first former British colony to successfully replace its colonial marriage laws; a handful of other countries, notably its East African neighbors, Kenya and Uganda, had contemplated doing so.[7] Kenya's long-debated and ultimately stalled attempt at reform of its marriage law not only preceded but also provided a foundation for Tanzania's proposals.[8] Many of the TANU government's proposals for reform (described in detail below) would be drawn directly from those laid out by the Kenyan Commission on the Law of Marriage and Divorce a year earlier.[9] Adding to this example of transnational, regional exchange of legal expertise between sometimes quite ideologically divergent East African states, the Kenyan commission's efforts were reportedly inspired by the African Conference on Local Courts and Customary Law, held in Dar es Salaam in 1963.[10]

The British in Tanganyika had set up not a single regime but a system recognizing multiple categories of marriage laws: civil or Christian, contracted either before a state official or in a church but falling under the same rules; Islamic, with variations according to sect; Hindu; and customary, involving a large number of community codes. The laws governing each type of marriage often varied radically, for instance, in Christian and civil marriages prohibiting polygamy and in customary and Islamic marriages allowing it. In addition to incorporating conflicting rules according to recognized membership in a particular community, the colonial system implicitly ranked these forms of marriage in a hierarchy, with the civil and Christian marriages at the top. Polygamous marriages could be converted into monogamous ones, but not the other way around. While rules of evidence stipulated that spouses in monogamous unions could not be compelled to testify in court against their partners, the rule did not extend to spouses in polygamous ones on the assumption that the mutual trust presumed to characterize monogamy was impossible in marriages with multiple wives. Perhaps most blatantly, while so-called primary or native courts had jurisdiction over Africans married according to customary or Islamic laws, Hindus, non-African Muslims, and anyone, including Africans, married in a civil or Christian ceremony had access to the state court system.[11]

In proposing the marriage law reforms, the TANU government included high among its reasons the untidy multiplicity that marked the colonial code and the inequality it entailed. Indeed, the white paper laying out the proposed reforms devoted its first paragraph to painting a picture of the unwieldy nature of the reigning order.[12] In official discourse on the reforms, though, there was much more to the impetus for reform than simply logistical standardization. Paired with and eventually overshadowing a rationale of standardization was a presentation of the law as being an important part of building a modern, progressive Tanzania marked by a commitment to women's rights and religious and racial equality that sharply distinguished it from a colonial history of discrimination that had gone before.[13] As Vice President Kawawa asserted when introducing the white paper before Parliament, "The first matter that Government places before anything else in these proposals is to eliminate the existing discrimination between various types of marriage in the country. Another fundamental element in these proposals is to try to get rid of various points [in the existing laws] that oppress women and prevent them from having equal rights with men."[14]

In numerous official statements on the government proposals, these goals were linked to vocabularies of both modern progress and a break from the colonial. In his presentation of the white paper to Parliament, Kawawa made a point in his opening speech of casting the reforms as a departure from the indignities of colonial practice:

> Until now Government law on marriage was a law that was at base Christian; that is, civil marriages were the same as Christian marriages. In truth, this is an historical issue. When the colonialists came to rule this country they came with their various laws, including the law of marriage. In their own country the government law of marriage was the same as Christian marriage, so here too they brought those very practices. That's why the law on civil marriage here looked exactly the same as the law on Christian marriage. Anyone who contracted a civil marriage was regarded in such a way that his type of marriage was the same as the Christian type, even if he himself wasn't a Christian! . . . The Government has seen that it cannot have a state law that makes a certain thing wrong for one kind of person while it isn't wrong for another kind of person.[15]

Rather than framing this departure from the colonial in terms of a recovery or return to tradition, however, official discourse on the law portrayed it as an essential step for a modern Tanzania to take, especially as it concerned the equal rights of women. In attempting to preempt expected criticisms that certain elements of the proposed reforms would "make serious incursion on the rights of the husband," the white paper stressed, "It is essential that the law should protect the rights of the wife so that she may bring up her children to be good citizens." It concluded by asserting this as part of the task of "ensur[ing] that the country does not deviate from the path of progress."[16] In a masthead editorial supporting the final version of the law, TANU's *Nationalist* even more pointedly positioned the bill as a vehicle for demonstrating national progress on the terrain of women's rights. It asserted, "The question that we must ask ourselves in 1971 is whether these institutions [taking additional wives without a previous wife's permission, for example] should be maintained. Indeed the question that must be asked seriously is: If we continue to maintain such institutions are we not in effect saying that we are at exactly the same level of understanding and development as our great grandfathers who indulged them hundreds of years ago?"[17]

The dual emphasis on the law's capacity to mark a break from the colonial while furthering Tanzania's modern progress through its stated commitment to equality for women resonates with arguments Partha Chatterjee has made. With reference to Indian nationalism, Chatterjee argues that colonial nationalism marked off an inner sphere of tradition and the feminine as off-limits to the colonizer and then proceeded to attempt a vernacular modernization of that realm.[18] This observation helps shed light on why, in defending the government's proposals, officials often appealed to vocabularies of both what was "common in a village" for women and what "human rights" entailed for them.[19] In this debate in which issues of gender and culture intersected so intimately postcolonial developmentalist nationalism, in Tanzania as elsewhere, involved a double move: one that cast women's affairs as a realm simultaneously to be protected as tradition, and to be carefully and selectively reformed into a modern amalgam of the best of old and new.

Proposing and Debating the Reforms: Gendered Struggles over Marriage

On Tuesday, September 9, 1969, the TANU government published its proposals for the reform of the country's marriage laws in a white paper. Coming less than three years after the Arusha Declaration of February 1967, which established a widely referenced blueprint for orienting Tanzania toward a socialist development, the white paper was one of a handful of high-profile moves to bring successive socioeconomic domains into line with the spirit of Arusha (including the Education for Self-Reliance plan discussed in chapter 3). More immediately, the spark credited by observers with igniting the marriage reforms was a High Court ruling several weeks prior that had acquitted a Christian man who had taken a second wife of the crime of bigamy. The judge in this case granted the man, who had pleaded guilty, an absolute discharge on the grounds that the law discriminated against a group of people (Christians) on the basis of their religious beliefs.[20] In doing so, the ruling had drawn attention to the unevenness of the existing marriage laws not only on the question of polygamy, recognizing it as legal for some but not for others, but more broadly.

Aiming in this context at a broad overhaul of the law that would address this unevenness, the white paper laid out a host of measures touching on nearly every dimension of marriage. Its major proposals were as follows: First, it suggested a legal stipulation that marriage be a voluntary union, allowing for either party to withhold consent, and that the standardized minimum ages for marriage be set at fifteen for girls and eighteen for boys. Second, in what would become perhaps its most controversial point, it proposed that polygamy be legalized by the state and that men be allowed to convert their marriages from monogamous to polygamous ones conditional upon the freely given consent of the first wife. Third, on the payment of bridewealth, it proposed a system in which dowries could be paid to the bride's family in installments and marriages would be legal in the eyes of the state even in the absence of a dowry.[21] Fourth, it maintained that a wife should have the right to pursue damages against a woman with whom her husband had committed adultery, bringing the rights of women on this point in line with those of men. Fifth, in an effort to "provide for the protection of the woman who lives with a man for a long time without being legally married to him," the white paper proposed that a cohabitation of two years or more be legally considered marriage, assuming each partner was legally capable of being married. Final among the major proposals, addressing the conviction that "divorces should not be treated lightly," was a call for the creation of a nationwide system of Conciliation Boards. Couples would not be able to divorce legally without first going before one of these boards, in which a committee would permit dissolution of the marriage "only if it is satisfied that the marriage had completely broken down."[22]

In each of these items the government aimed to strike a balance between its ostensible goals of achieving equal treatment under the law for all types of marriage, on the one hand, and equality between women and men on the other. In many cases this balancing act proved delicate. For example, while the law, as many would point out, was fundamentally unequal in permitting polygyny but not polyandry, the architects of the white paper attempted to cast the clause legalizing polygyny in terms of a concern for granting women a choice they had lacked: the choice to continue to be married to and materially provided for by a husband bent on marrying a second wife. Throughout the white paper and government statements promoting the reforms different strands of official discourse were stitched together in a sometimes uneasy coexistence. As Kawawa's statements insisted variously, the government had a commitment to respect "good traditional customs" as well as an expectation that "as the country progressed, people would find it impossible to look after more than one wife."[23] This kind of articulation of a realm combining "good tradition" with a "good modern" was not unique to discourse on the marriage law; indeed, it recalls the discursive maneuvers involved in the construction of national culture analyzed in chapter 1. As the white paper went out into the realm of public debate, however, its delicate compromises would be vigorously called into question by Tanzanians on various sides.

In issuing its proposals in the form of a white paper and calling for public debate on it, the government was taking a unique path. Its typical practice was to introduce proposed legislation to the legislature before opening up any public debate on it; in such cases debate in Parliament served as a surrogate for wider dialogue. And yet while significant public discussion on the marriage reforms was expected (particularly after the Kenyan experience, which saw vigorous debate follow the commission charged with traveling the country to solicit opinion),[24] the government appears to have underestimated the degree to which its proposals would come to dominate public conversations in the months to come. The government's initial plans were to solicit Tanzanians' views for four weeks and then submit the proposals to Parliament.[25] In light of the outpouring of opinion that followed the white paper's publication, President Nyerere announced to TANU's National Executive Committee that discussion would be extended for another three months.[26]

In fact, it continued well beyond that. In the midst of the flurry of debate in the press, the hundreds of letters to the editor published on the issue, the radio programs, UWT seminars, and countless informal conversations revolving around it, the government announced a second extension of discussion.[27] Parliament did not have its turn at debating the white paper until March 1970; the final bill, revised in response to some of the criticisms of the original proposals, took another year to pass. During the last four months of 1969, the so-called Great Debate would grow to such prominence that it began to be used as a reference point for other, often unrelated news: In late September, a previously planned comedy about marriage suitors to be performed at the Aga Khan secondary school was covered by the *Standard* under the headline "Marriage Scuffle Goes on Stage"; three months later, a front-page headline on a debate in Italy over the divorce law read, "'Marriage Debate'—Italian Style."[28] Like previous debates in the press, this one demonstrated the passion and excitement accompanying a culture of letter writing that, by the end of the decade, was at its peak. One young man wrote, "As the views and opinions on the proposed marriage code continue to pour into your office, I wish that mine should emerge on the surface to be read nationwide."[29] And the controversy resonated beyond Tanzania's borders: in May 1970, the *Standard* published a letter on the marriage law from a Tanzanian student studying in Quebec.[30]

Within days of the public release of the white paper, it became clear that the government's proposals were drawing considerable opposition from a number of different, even dramatically opposed, directions. In the first letter on the matter, a woman living in Dar es Salaam pointedly drew attention to the contradictions embedded in the state's efforts to eliminate multiple inequalities with the proposals. "I appreciate that changes in the Marriage Ordinance will, in the eyes of the law, eliminate discrimination against a section of society, the Christians," the woman wrote, using the pseudonym "Feeling Cheated." "But, how about eliminating discrimination against approximately half of the population instead of just a section, namely we women! How can a law be considered fair if half of the population could have up to four wives yet the other half could be entitled to only one fourth of a husband?"[31] Nor was this a lone voice. Over the next several weeks, many women echoed these sentiments. "A Wife" writing from the capital asserted that such a bill would be against "human rights," arguing, "Certainly, one cannot talk about the equality of the sexes if a man can have 1 to 2 wives but a woman can only have ½ to 1 husband." Responding directly to a man who had suggested a husband should be permitted to take a second wife if the first "suffers a permanent malady and is not fit for sexual intercourse," she wrote, "So what, if the husband suffers a malady, is impotent or sterile? Certainly the poor wife should have a right to take another husband who can perform his duties!"[32]

As these letters illustrate, some women opposed to allowing the conversion of monogamous unions to polygamous ones complained that the proposals were unfair in not allowing polyandry. Other women took a different tack, portraying that clause as a salvo in a broader battle over the material fortunes of wives and their power to regulate husbands' taking multiple women. In a letter in which she also called for the strengthening of the Affiliation Act's provisions for fathers' maintenance of children born out of wedlock "to make sure that some clever men are not evading their responsibilities," a Mrs. T. S. Karumuna hinted at wives' anxieties about material security in situations in which "her power of stopping him [from taking another wife] is limited." "The problems of marrying many wives are really many and sometimes disastrous," she wrote. "It is debatable whether a husband in his present economic and social circumstances will be able to share his love among his wives equally. The last wife who is normally comparatively younger and may be more modern, is usually the beloved one and she thus gets extra of everything love-wise and material-wise. This is bound to put the whole household in chaos."[33] Peppering their letters with references to costs of living, the inability of the vast majority of men to support more than a single wife, and the limited power in the hands of wives to press for changes in their husbands' behavior, many women joining the debate concurred.[34]

Officials like Attorney General Bomani repeatedly stressed in response to the criticism that conversions of monogamous marriages to polygamous ones would be entirely conditional on the consent of the first wife.[35] But many women questioned whether such consent could really be freely given and expressed deep suspicion that this clause would instead provide cover for husbands seeking younger wives. For instance, in a passionate letter that cited "Feeling Cheated"'s letter as inspiration to write and tell her that "she's not alone in her fear," one woman called the consent clause a "mockery and unrealistic." She asked, "Do you think such husbands will humble themselves to discuss and ask genuinely for their wives' consent whenever they decide to marry? . . . The majority of husbands will make the situation so tough that the wife will have no other alternative but to say 'Yes' or sign the consent form. Will this be fair to wives? Under the present marriage the husbands can be sued and the wives can demand compensation etc. But, under the proposed law, the husband will be covered by the so-called 'consent forms.'"[36]

In their arguments against polygamy, women letter writers drew on a number of discourses, perhaps chief among them one of modern progress. In letter after letter, writers attempted to situate polygamy in an allegedly traditional past, a past that a progressive Tanzania should be committed to moving beyond. One woman simultaneously challenged the generalization that in the past Tanzanian society was polygamous and argued that even its existence as a luxury of a minority in those days was no justification for its continuance in the present: "Now, gone are the days for [sic] with the constant developments our society has changed religiously, educationally, politically, economically, and culturally. It is thus impracticable to go back to the original speculative life of our fore parents. Politically we are now in the era of Arusha Declaration which in one of its aims stresses equality of all human beings regardless of sex hence the full emancipation of women. Polygamy (unless it is a religious vow such as Islamic law) and equality are incompatible."[37]

Another woman, in responding to a male correspondent who had defended polygamy as a key part of African tradition, suggested that "our forefathers'" reasons for taking several wives no longer applied. "Probably, [he] is not aware that he does not need all these wives in the 20th century. Where are all the fierce tribes, where are the big shambas to be cultivated by the hand and not by the machine? . . . And what about sales tax with such a band of wives?"[38] Another woman put it more bluntly: "This is 1969, gentlemen, not the Pleistocene era."[39]

In their insistence on the malleability of traditional practice and deployment of an ethic celebrating keeping up with the times, these statements recall rhetorical elements of the debates over Operation Vijana and the ban on soul music. Some of the arguments put forward by many of the women expressing opposition to the white paper's proposals on polygamy exhibited the kind of appropriation of official discourse seen in the debates over women and work (see chapter 2). Linking their arguments to the nearly unassailable keywords of official political rhetoric post-Arusha, equality among them, these women shared with the white paper a discourse yoking modern progress for the nation to equality for its women. Yet they deployed this vocabulary in somewhat different ways. If, as I argued above, official rhetoric on the reforms combined invocations of tradition and modern progress, arguments made by many women on the law were cast in a more unabashedly modernizationist vocabulary.

The debate in the press was not the only terrain on which women were raising such challenges. On the day the white paper was released, the UWT was holding its biennial conference in Mwanza, on the shores of Lake Victoria. Although the meeting was originally intended to focus on choosing a new leadership, the white paper ended up dominating the agenda. In a raucous discussion on the proposals, vigorous opposition to clause 10, the one proposing to permit conversion of marriage types, was voiced. Prefiguring and perhaps even helping to shape one of the sentiments that would be voiced so strongly in women's letters on the issue, the conference was reported as resolving, "If men are allowed to marry more than one wife then women should as well be allowed to have more than one husband. Let us make it a 'Reciprocal Policy.'"[40] As a rhetorical strategy, one likely intended to be a comic dig at men, given that the delegates would almost certainly have seen polyandry as an impossible goal, this resolution nonetheless pointedly called attention to the inequality of the white paper's submissions on polygamy. In addition, the delegates proposed that the government's suggestion that

Delegates vigorously applauding a speaker at the TANU Women's League biennial conference in Mwanza in September 1969. *Courtesy of the Tanzania Information Service.*

a wife be granted the ability to sue a woman with whom her husband commits adultery be amended to allow for husbands, too, to be sued in such cases. Finally, the conference resolved that dowries, as the "life-blood" of marriage, should not be curbed by legislation, something the white paper had not fully stipulated, but which Lucy Lameck, parliamentary secretary for health and social welfare and a prominent UWT leader, had called for at the meeting. Despite strenuous opposition to points in the government's position, the conference's opposition to the white paper was not total. In the end, the delegates voted to support the proposals if they were amended along the lines of UWT concerns, perhaps in an effort to avoid having the association appear to be out of step with the government.[41]

The women writing letters to the press to express their opinions on the white paper were largely part of what Marjorie Mbilinyi called the new women of Tanzania's first postcolonial decade—a literate minority of urban-dwelling women of some formal education—but the same was not necessarily true of UWT delegates.[42] As Susan Geiger has shown, the organization in the late 1960s was far from homogenous and had to manage tensions along lines of generation and education that bubbled beneath its surface. The UWT membership, rank and file and leaders alike, included a founding cohort of older, often illiterate activists from the organization's pre-independence days as the TANU Women's Section. In the 1960s, as the organization was steered away from the direct political mobilization of the TANU Women's Section toward a more technocratic focus on "developing women," the early cohort was joined by younger women with formal educations, sometimes, though rarely, acquired abroad, and professional training. These younger women steadily gained influence within the organization through the decade but did not displace the founding cohort. Although generation and level of education divided them, the two groups each possessed considerable socioeconomic status. This status, often connected to their husbands or to male relatives in politics, was enhanced through the benefits that active membership in the UWT, particularly in Dar es Salaam, could bring, chief among them the sought-after trips to England, East Germany, China, and other allies on which UWT delegations were sent.[43]

Although the early cohort in 1970 was still predominant and formally educated women were still a minority within the organization, the leadership at the time of the Mwanza conference was a mixture of women of both groups, who appear to have coalesced along with women letter writers around the critiques offered of the white paper. These critiques point to widespread struggles on the part of women of varying economic and educational backgrounds, struggles to maintain and expand leverage over material resources within marriages in a context of anxiety around the perceived ease with which husbands might divert such resources toward younger mistresses or additional wives. As Sarah Nyirenda, a UWT official, was paraphrased as explaining, it was "felt that if the law was enacted on the present provisions in the paper it would only safeguard the rights of husbands' mistresses and not the wives."[44] In this regard, the arguments against making polygamous marriages easier for husbands to contract and calls for any new law to allow wives to sue adulterous husbands (and not just the other woman) can both be seen as arising out of the very material concerns underscored in the debate.

The Mwanza conference turned out to be a notable early moment in the public debate over the marriage proposals, less because of any authoritative weight its resolutions may have carried than because of the sizeable backlash it triggered. Indeed, as the debate gathered momentum, the fact that the early moments of public comment on the proposals had been marked by women forcefully voicing opposition to polygamy prompted male anger. Even if it had likely been proposed as a rhetorical strategy to point to the inequality of privileges granted to women and men, the Mwanza delegates' call for a "reciprocal strategy" allowing polyandry became a lightning rod for scornful condemnations of women's interventions in the debate. One M. K. Kazwika, for instance, prefaced his defense of the white paper by lambasting at length the "sheer nonsense" of UWT delegates "unanimously clapping hands" at the suggestion of a reciprocal policy. Kazwika wrote,

> Would the (UWT) women stop being funny please, and get on to something worth talking about, bearing in mind they are using people's money to transport them and accommodate them and feed them. . . . Let us see the possibility of a woman marry [sic] a number of men. To my feeling I suppose this capable woman will establish a roster for the three or four husbands she has. Let us suppose she has two husbands and she has a weekly shift. This woman will have to satisfy sexually both Mr. A and B. This means she will have a continuous sexual affair for a minimum of 20 days a month, and a minimum of 240 days a year because each man will make sure he gets her maximum service because he knows the following week she would be at Mr. A's. I think these women are asking for trouble because for sure they won't be able to sexually satisfy more than one man.[45]

Such notions of women's natural inability to match male sexual prowess constituted a recurring motif in the outpouring of ridicule directed at women who put polyandry on the table for discussion.[46] Some men combined this logic with the additional claim (one that would also become prominent more generally in the debate) that since women outnumbered men, polygyny made natural sense, while polyandry would only exacerbate a female surplus and lead to homosexuality among the leftover women. "Let us face a few facts," urged one man:

> Sexual force or urge is stronger in males than in females. . . . Just watch and observe the Nature. Among various species, you find one male having several females for sex purpose. There are times when females are completely debarred from enjoying the sex act for weeks or months (you know, due to pregnancy, periods, suckling, etc). This again applies to animals and birds as well. Now, during such times, the males, whose sexual force is so strong, must either impose upon themselves "self discipline and control" or try to find a second partner, whichever is the less strenuous. . . . Numerically, females exceed males. Apply the principle of one

male for one female. There will be females left over. . . . Could the Creator have made extra sexes just for no purpose? . . . From the enumerated facts, polyandry is both illogical and absurd.[47]

Declarations of the absurdity of polyandry were not limited to men. In a letter combining highly scientific vocabulary with an appeal to "the genetics of our culture," a woman at the University College's Faculty of Agriculture mocked the "women [who] 'logicise' by equality to marry more than one man."[48] It was another female university student and UWT member, however, who provided one of the few direct responses to the wave of derision directed at the Mwanza conference, challenging claims that men could uniquely satisfy multiple partners and suggesting Tanzanians should "try and see if you men can be as tolerant as women are."[49] Centered on a frank description of women as sexual beings, this challenge was met with an irate scolding by a male correspondent—one that was illustrative of the anger generated among some men by the un-abashedly oppositional and public nature of women's participation in the debate: "It is a pity to hear from a woman writing such unpardon-able fallacies in public; that a woman can marry two or several men! I have never heard of such views since my childbirth that a woman can serve two or several masters for the whole of her life."[50]

If some of the most vehement commentary by men focused on scorn-ing the notion of polyandry, male correspondents also articulated po-sitions on the white paper itself. Men's opinions of the proposals on marriage were far from monolithic. For many young men, the primary concern was neither polygamy nor the balance of power within mar-riages, but dowries (see below). Rather different from and in some ways opposed to most young men's positions on the proposals, though, an-other prominent strand of male opinion developed around qualified support for the white paper, a defense of polygamy, and a question-ing of the need for women's consent. A letter from E. K. Buberwa is a case in point. Generally welcoming the white paper as a masterpiece, Buberwa nonetheless urged that it be amended to allow husbands to marry a second woman without the first wife's consent. Referencing a familiar trope, he explained, "There are some jealous wives who would not tolerate sharing a husband with a fellow wife, especially the more sophisticated women of the present decade."[51] Many others agreed, ar-guing that requiring wives' consent would undermine male authority and decision-making power in the marriage. As one male correspon-dent asserted, "When a man wants to marry the second wife it means that he wants her and it is a must that he should have her. He has grave reasons in doing so."[52]

If women who argued against clause 10 of the white paper often cast their appeals as ones for modern progress and attempted to paint polygamy as a remnant of a bygone past, many men defended the institution by invoking this very notion of polygamy's rootedness in a deep past as proof that the practice was an essential tradition to be protected. Writing as "an African man" in support of the government's attempt to legalize polygamy, K. K. John argued, "The code is more African in nature, history and in all its set-up. It demonstrates to the world, how an African society is; not how it should be, it brings back that African dignity which was robbed away by colonialist missionaries who saw evil in whatever Africa stood for."[53] Many others agreed that the proposals, if implemented, would mark a salutary return to what were "natural phenomena in African society."[54] Some went further, associating a litany of evils, including adultery, prostitution, and homosexuality, with the importation of monogamy and positing polygamy as a solution to these ills. As "Nuptus" charged, "Those who shout against legalizing polygamy do also connive with 'legalised homosexuality' practised in some civilised countries. Facts, mind you."[55]

While there may be something stereotypical in the way idioms of traditional and modern were invoked on either side of the debate over polygamy, situating each side in relation to an official Tanzanian discourse on culture that in the late 1960s melded a modernizationist ethic with a hearkening back to tradition is important. As I suggested in chapter 1, this national cultural discourse entailed a self-professed modernization of tradition even as this process was cast as an effort of cultural recovery. The bifurcated quality to official discourse on culture—one that often extended beyond cultural matters to become almost a default move in official rhetoric in the late 1960s—made it possible for both pro- and antipolygamy voices to draw legitimating parallels between their respective positions and foundational elements of official discourse. As Lynn Thomas has argued in the context of the debates in Kenya in 1969 over that country's Affiliation Act and its would-be marriage law reforms, "The oppositions of 'traditional' and 'modern,' 'African' and 'Western' operated less as accurate descriptions of discrete political realms than as popular idioms through which to contest the nation's future."[56]

I have provided examples of women who appealed to a socialist modernization embodied in the Arusha Declaration to buttress their arguments against clause 10 of the white paper. To opposing ends, arguments by men in defense of polygamy often contained similar invocations of key elements of official discourse and practice. One apparently rather wealthy man writing in response to the UWT Mwanza meeting's critique of polygamy cited his disgust with it and described at length the productivity of his four wives, two of whom were "peasant farmers in the village," and connected it to a future in which "polygamy will accelerate Ujamaa villages."[57] Another wrote to urge women to accept the white paper over the objections of their "apparently enlightened and thus misguided" sisters, concluding more pithily, "Good ujamaa is the product of polygamy."[58] The politically potent charge of exploitation that became widespread after the Arusha Declaration was used by one man to argue against any restrictions on husbands' authority in matters of marriage.[59] Employing metaphors drawn from the worlds of work and politics, he wrote, "For every African the criteria of marriage is two-fold. A young man has two objectives in mind when he decides to marry. First and foremost he wants children and secondly, he wants more food and a helper in economic life. If a wife fails to fulfill these objectives then she is not worth retaining. . . . In terms of our Tanzanian socialism, she will be a typical 'mrija' [exploiter] for she has failed to give a quid pro quo—something in turn. . . . A husband is like an employer who has the right, under the law, to retain or dispense with his employee."[60]

Invocations of tradition and official policy were not the only familiar motifs woven through defenses of polygamy. As perhaps could be expected in a debate involving concerns over gendered authority, autonomy, and the material implications of marriage, the elastic bundle of tropes around women, prostitution, consumption, and "gaining market" also appeared, particularly in some of the most virulent of these defenses. Several letters presented the policy options as a choice between polygamy and the prostitution that would surely increase with a surplus of single women. A letter from one man arguing that "attaching strings to marriage codes would be creating problems for our menfolk" raised the specter of uncontrolled town girls through the figure of the materialistic, romantically fickle young woman: "Our girls of today are still very raw to understand what a civilised marriage is. It is evident that they are very giddy in this matter. Today, they want to 'taste' a scholar, tomorrow they cry for Benz-owners and another day they feel deeply fallen for well-to-do boys. Do you think the new marriage law will cool down such sex-hungry girls?"[61] Replying angrily to "A Wife" who had written a letter challenging men's capacity to sexually satisfy multiple wives, "A Husband" expressed the widespread opinion that women's lust was at base material rather than sexual. "A woman of unsatisfied sex-hunger, unlike a man, is mentally abnormal . . . and is therefore graded to be a prostitute," he wrote, before launching into an explanation of the opportunistic character of women that could lead to single wives turning their homes "into a prostitution camp":

> She [referring to his interlocutor] wants us to send women abroad for further education, and thereafter? These women will still be maneuvering in towns on their return home, making it a hell out of men by twisting their waists here and there, showing what it takes inside, and moving their eyes like chameleons in signaling the words 'I love you.' They would do this purposely, just to attract men as this is very natural since women are human magnetism flowers. The single-wifed men will certainly fall and very heavily too. And the polygamous husbands will also fall, but slightly. . . . If polygamous marriages cannot be accepted by women in our society it is evident that the women are shamelessly voting for prostitution, a thing which they have failed to stop, mainly because of increasing number of free women who tempt free men and married one-wifed husbands as well to take advantage of tasting the challenging free beauty of their modern world.[62]

As I demonstrated in chapter 2, one could associate sentiments such as these with the frustration of unmarried, urban young men who viewed many single city girls as gold diggers determined to use romantic liaisons as a vehicle for gaining market. But these tropes had wide circulation and usage, a fact which their appearance in letters defending polygamy reflects. For such letters tended to be written not by young men, but by their seniors, men who were more established, relatively well-off, and usually somewhat older in social terms. As I discuss in the next section, young men's interventions in the marriage debate, which were numerous and substantial, were overwhelmingly focused not on defending polygamy or on the battle over the relative power of husbands and wives within marriage, but on the question of dowries. These young men's positions on the controversy, analyzed below, bring into sharp relief issues of generational contest and tensions between and among men that were played out on the terrain of the marriage debate. Here I simply want to stress that it was largely the views of men who were somewhat older, more established, relatively well-off, and married that made up the strand of male opinion I have considered thus far:

one coalescing around support for the white paper's proposed legitimation and defense of polygamy and some opposition to the requirement of women's consent.

This axis of debate—one pitting women who were either highly involved in the UWT or part of a literate minority against established, married men of some means—opens a window into some of the gendered tensions that accompanied the rise of a postcolonial elite in the 1960s. If most women's interventions in the debate encompassed bids for shoring up their material security within marriages, the vehemence with which many married men responded indicates that they perceived such claims as threats to their decision-making power and control over household resources. The ease with which men conflated women's calls for stronger limits on husbands' ability to channel resources to multiple women with the well-worn yet powerful trope of the grasping, jealous, greedy housewife was emblematic of this.

This element of the controversy hints at the complex negotiations and abiding anxieties about control over resources and paths to accumulation that were bound up in relations between husbands and wives in the marriages of the new urban elite. The debate in the press was not the only forum in which such anxieties and negotiations became visible. They were also a prominent feature of the long-awaited formal debate on the white paper that took place in March 1970 in Parliament, a body whose members were emblematic of Tanzania's new postcolonial political class. At the time of the marriage debate, only 7 of Parliament's 179 members were women. As nearly every one of these women took to the floor to forcefully voice reservations about the proposals and in terms which largely matched those of women in the wider debate, statement after statement by their male counterparts responded to these challenges as material threats to husbands' preeminence within couples. In an impassioned statement MP Violet M. Baraka of Njombe South expressed the material stakes of the proposals on polygamy for senior wives' material well-being:

> One sees that that first wife, and the second, and the third, all of them become *second-hand* [English in the Kiswahili original]; and then it's the youngest one who continues to enjoy [*kupata raha*] in all kinds of ways, whether it's food, the good life, or clothes. So here one sees that in economic terms and in terms of money inside [the household] it becomes a problem. It forces that first wife to become a beggar, she can't live well,

she and her children, food becomes a problem. Therefore, a situation like this from a perspective of funds [kwa upande wa mapato]—I'm not even criticizing things on the grounds of the marriage [of multiple women] in and of itself because I know men, whether they are given permission or not, they can go ahead and just marry. . . . But I'm standing up for the issue of money [mapato].

. . . Money from the husband's salary should be immediately divided to allow that first wife and her children to get food and other essential things. . . . This is my request on Clause 10; I ask this particularly in terms of funds because we've already seen, Honorable Speaker, that even if some people haven't married multiple wives . . . when a husband loves another girl, that wife at home finds herself in serious trouble in terms of food, while the children are suffering in every way and are becoming complete beggars. I therefore ask the Government to protect us women by instituting this matter of a right to funds—especially in terms of [a husband's] salary because I see this issue as extremely important.

I'm not even getting into the issue of marrying [multiple wives] because some people like to marry [this way] and others don't; but what I am taking a stand on is the matter of money and food because the issue of the salary is becoming a real problem in households—especially in the households of various officials, it's becoming a major problem to provide for their wives, Mr. Speaker. They [the wives] really have a problem, as some of them can drink nothing but porridge—without even sugar—for as long as three days without seeing their husbands.[63]

For their part, most male MPs who spoke on the marriage reforms tended to respond to interventions like Baraka's with jocular yet uncompromising reassertions of husbands' preeminence in the "rule of the house" and the disposal of material resources within it. C. M. Mzindakaya, a prominent and popular speaker in the debate, put it this way:

In the ruling of a couple's household the husband is the boss. (Applause.) We can't duck that. (Applause.) And if a single Honorable Member rises to oppose that I'll be shocked. . . . Even children know that the father is the Chairman. (Laughter.) So I don't want women to come duping themselves into thinking that the equality the Government is talking about is of that level. (Laughter.) . . .

In reality, my expenses are not divided equally at home. Because if we wanted to split them equally—to say truly this is equality between me and my wife—we would have to plan this week-end [English in the original], if I decide to leave her and go off on my own, I'd have to turn around and give her a car for her to go off on her own too, give her money, for her to come home when she likes when she's finished her visits with her friends, her fellow women. This we can't do, we can't.[64]

Neither Mzindakaya's invocation of his personal life nor the laughter his statements provoked was unique. Indeed, much of the parliamentary debate over the marriage reforms took on a tone of ribald jocularity that often hinged on the perceived humor of male MPs' stake in the law and their imbrication in the drama of urban sexual relationships, gendered power, wealth, and status that the controversy foregrounded. Part of this can be tracked in the timing of the many outbursts of laughter that punctuated the debate and were recorded in its official transcript. Against a backdrop of public accusations and rumors that male MPs had considerable self-interest bound up with the outcome of the marriage reforms, some of these moments of laughter hinted strongly not just at MPs' acknowledgment of this self-interest, but at a reveling in it as well. Vice President Kawawa's introduction of the white paper's proposed mechanism to allow for the conversion of monogamous marriages to polygamous ones was met with laughter and cheers.[65] And his attempt to stress the government's seriousness in requiring husbands to acquire the truly genuine consent of the first wife before taking of an additional wife without frightening or torturing her was greeted by more laughs from MPs.[66] One of the most unrestrained moments of mirth during the debate came as some male MPs connected problems with wives at home to the widespread perception that male politicians used their offices (in both meanings of the word) to pursue adulterous relationships with women. A good example is the speech by S. B. Msonde, which moved quickly from a defense of a husband's "right to beat his wife," a practice the white paper would prohibit, to a description of the ease with which politicians might be accused of sexual impropriety by jealous wives:

> Mr. Msonde: Another issue, Honorable Mr. Speaker, has to do with Clause 18 [of the white paper] that says . . . a husband won't have the right to beat his wife. Now—(laughter)—there are some women, quite a number as I understand—(laughter)—who aren't satisfied until they're beaten by their husband—(laughter and applause)—that's when she says that this husband really loves me. (Laughter.) Now in terms of this section, Honorable Mr. Speaker, I would ask that this clause be removed.

Other MPs: Absolutely! Hear, Hear!

Mr. Msonde: So that it reads that if any wife creates a problem, she can be beaten two or three slaps. (*Laughter.*) So that that wife can be fulfilled in her goal of saying that she's loved by her husband. And another thing, Honorable Mr. Speaker, [the white paper] says: ' . . . The Law proposes that a wife have the right to sue another woman who has illicit sex with her husband.' This isn't right. In truth, for the most part, although we on both sides, women and men, can be jealous, the woman is more jealous [*ana wivu zaidi*].

A Member: Yes! (*Sawa!*)

Mr. Msonde: And it will be a real problem even for us leaders, because we're always meeting with various people; and there are those wives of ours who are jealous (*wenye wivu*). She'll find you sometimes [meeting with] a woman who has come with a problem she has and here you've locked her up in your office, you've welcomed her into your office and closed the door, you're talking with her. (*Laughter.*) Well, maybe one time your wife can come and find you busy attending to that one with her problem. That can create some serious malice on the part of jealous women.[67]

Considerations of wife-beating, potentially philandering politicians, and jealous wives would arise many more times in the debate, each time to much laughter.[68] In this they joined a number of other topics—greedy mistresses, homosexuality, cuckolded husbands, taiti-wearing temptresses, visions of ujamaa villages torn apart by adultery accusations—that contributed to the jocular tone so prominent in the debate. As MPs joked about women's market value,[69] the marriage reforms' alleged potential for enabling an economy of gold digging on the part of serial mistresses,[70] and the special susceptibility of elites to these schemes,[71] it indeed seemed, as Kawawa observed, that "on this subject . . . each of us in this Parliament is an expert."[72]

It would be a mistake to read the jocular and personalized nature of the debate simply as a superficial or unremarkable aspect of the deliberations. In part, as Thomas has noted of the debate in Kenya's Parliament over the Affiliation Act, the jocular character of the discussions resonates with Achille Mbembe's elaboration of a "phallocratic system" of postcolonial politics underwritten by "the unconditional subordination of women to the principle of male pleasure."[73] In addition, the intersection of the jocular and the personalized that marked the Tanzanian debate points to the central and particularly charged place of elite lives and leisure in public discourse on sex, gender relations, money, and the city.

Writing of struggles over women's political representation in Kenya in the 1960s, Audrey Wipper argued in 1971 that the use of often sexualized humor was one of several tactics used by male politicians to "deflect women's demands." The jocular tone of the Tanzanian parliamentary debates on marriage could certainly be said to have created the sort of "air of levity" that Wipper suggests made women's demands more easily defused or dismissed.[74] In the Tanzanian case, however, women's demands on the marriage bill were not so easily dismissed.

Indeed, female MPs' vocal opposition to aspects of the white paper, particularly clause 10, was so forceful that when the government brought the final bill before the Parliament in January 1971, it was revised in ways that would partly meet their key demands. First, it involved a partial concession to the opposition to legalizing the conversion of monogamous marriages into polygamous ones with the consent of both husband and wife. Whereas the white paper had proposed allowing any marriage to be "potentially polygamous," the final bill specified that monogamous marriages conducted in Christian ceremonies could not be converted to polygamous ones; on the other hand, it reiterated that marriages conducted under Islamic, customary, or civil ceremonies could legally become polygamous ones with consent of husband and wife, and that any Tanzanian couple was free to choose whether to marry in a religious, customary, or state ceremony.[75] Second, the final bill was more explicit than the white paper in declaring property accumulated during the marriage to be the joint property of both husband and wife. A number of stipulations followed from this, including that in cases of divorce property would be jointly shared, and in cases of a husband's death such property as required by the wife to support herself and her children would pass in the first instance to her and only after that to the husband's family.[76]

While the first of these revisions to the reforms was as much a bow to religious officials' wariness about the law's potential to interfere in religion as to female MPs' position on clause 10, the parliamentary debate over the final bill, like that over the white paper a year earlier, was dominated by issues of gendered power within marriages. This time, however, the sides of the contest were reversed. The debate, as lengthy, intense, and clamorous as the first, saw female MPs broadly supportive of the bill now that clause 10 was adjusted. In contrast, the vast majority of male delegates who spoke went to great lengths to cast the law as a foreign imposition that would "turn men into women" and, with the inheritance and alimony provisions, grant even more opportunities for exploitation of men by serial wives.[77] While Kawawa and Bomani firmly made the government's case that the reforms were necessary for modern progress and socialist equality, while stressing that the final bill was a compromise that would violate neither religion nor good traditional customs, many male MPs, rather than rejecting the bill outright, resorted to calling for the law to be delayed for more discussion.[78] The government stood its ground, however, Kawawa intervening at female MPs' request to quash a last-minute amendment to allow for husbands married in Christian ceremonies to renounce the Christian faith and thereby render their marriages "potentially polygamous."[79]

After this defeat, the final bill passed with most male MPs' support—but not with the unrestrained celebration portrayed in the imaginary conversation of Kisikosi and Sembo.[80] For the government, it seems, the desirability of passing a law coded as modern and progressive trumped the resistance to the final version expressed by so many male MPs. Furthermore, when viewed against the repeated defeats of the Kenyan bill, as analyzed by Thomas, the form of its final passage in Tanzania—accompanied by small but significant concessions to demands of female MPs on polygamy and property—showcases the relative success achieved by a certain class of Tanzanian female activists in carving out political space for particular kinds of gendered critique. Even if often a target of male ridicule, the fact that polyandry achieved such prominence in the Tanzanian debate, in contrast to the Kenyan case, further highlights this relative success.[81] Indeed, despite the often powerful tendency of certain aspects of the debate, like the ribald jocularity of much male elite commentary, to blunt such efforts to expand rhetorical space, one should not lose sight of what many of the Tanzanian women involved in the debate considered real gains in their negotiation of urban gender relations.

"But What of the Young Bachelor?": On Bridewealth, Demographics, and 'Nizer Lifestyles

Thus far I have been primarily concerned with recounting and analyzing those aspects of the controversy over the marriage law that involved debate over the terms of the law itself.[82] But as the controversy continued, it expanded beyond the parameters of the bill itself and became a platform for the airing of a wider field of grievances, anxieties, and arguments around the intersection of gender, generation, status, and consumption in Dar es Salaam. This talk produced themes that began as subtexts but quickly assumed prominence in the debate. Raising such issues as dowries, urban gender demographics, and elite consumption and leisure, these themes bring to light new layers, questions, social constituencies, and axes of debate that entered the marriage controversy at angles to the ones considered above. They also complicate a view of the marriage controversy that would see it simply as a battle of the sexes. For one of the key struggles playing out in each of these "spillover themes" was a generational one between young men and their more established elders.

Although far from dominant at the beginning of the debate, one of the concerns that began to be invoked in the margins of the marriage controversy only to swell to become one of its most prominent themes was an argument about dowries. Articulated primarily by young men, whose overrepresentation in the social demographic of letter writers helps explain its rise to prominence, comments on dowries began as calls on the government to rework the white paper so as to "make it easier for us bachelors to get married."[83] These first pleas often came from self-identified young migrants to Dar es Salaam who cast their arguments in the form of personal tales of their difficulties in amassing high dowries. As A. S. Magooge wrote from the capital in the first letter to comment on the matter,

> Myself I am from Musoma [a large town on the shores of Lake Victoria]. I was intending to go on leave to marry. I proposed to a certain girl and she agreed, so I wrote to her father discussing the marriage dowry. I was surprised to hear that he wanted 45 cows and 25 goats. Without wastage of time I told him I could not afford to produce said dowry. When I ask why the dowry is so high, the answer comes that it is our traditional custom. I beg our Government to look carefully into this sort of exploitation, and to put a limit on the payment of a bride price, especially in the Mara Region. Of course, this is not marriage but selling a girl.[84]

Others of these early pleas were even more specific in tallying the high cost of marriage and the kind of bargaining system that young men endured. "I wrote to my parents in Tarime," recounted a young man based in Dar es Salaam, "and the reply I got was that I should first pay 50 head of cattle or 7,000/- [shillings] including other charges incidental to marriage. It costs 7,854/- to marry!"[85] Citing similar figures as "an attempt at conspicuous consumption" by "our parents," Venance F. Ngula decried the "'round-table' bargaining" that attended the process of fixing a dowry. To the authors of such pleas, the white paper's recommendation that dowries be payable in installments would not solve the problem and only put husbands in a state of indentured servitude.[86] For most, only a strict legal limit on dowries or the abolishing of the payments altogether would "alleviate the situation."[87]

As entreaties from bachelors steadily increased, three pivotal interlocking dimensions to their appeals emerged. Most fundamental was a strong sense of generational tension. In letter after letter young men cast themselves as "we bachelors" "struggling as hard as [we] can to have a better standard of living" and achieve the modest aim of marrying "his only one loving girl"—a goal being blocked by the "old ones" bent on preserving an "archaic" and "prehistoric" institution.[88] Rather than appearing in isolation, however, this generational strain was often inflected through two other axes of social tension shaping urban young men's anxieties and their commentary on dowries. Rotating around fraught urban gender relations, the first of these surfaced as frustration over the plight of the young male migrant of modest means in the face of the supposed twin exploitations of high dowries and the economic demands of city girls seeking market. In the words of one young man, "Why should the male pay for the female for whom he is going to toil day and night to make happy all round? . . . These housewives spend most, if not all, of their [husbands'] earnings on cosmetics and new fashions. . . . If anything women should pay dowry."[89] Second and relatedly, generational tension was also inflected through anxieties around the visible signs of unequal accumulation and consumption through which city life was often interpreted. Many young men writing on dowries contrasted their own plight with the situation of more established men, who, because they were "married or have a big potato [an idiom for wealth associated with a state sinecure] can give a deaf ear to this cry."[90]

Nowhere did the intertwined character of these three elements—tensions over generation, gender, and accumulation—appear more clearly than in a virulent, drawn-out exchange triggered by a letter from a S. Nyakire, an established married woman of Dar es Salaam who was critical of bachelors' complaints on dowries. Coming relatively early in the marriage debate, when letters raising the issue of dowries had only begun to trouble the margins of the discussion, Nyakire's intervention was a response to the letter by Magooge, who had objected in relatively mild terms about his experience with high dowries in Musoma. Taking a mocking tone and deploying notions of Tanzania's regional and ethnic material inequities, Nyakire wrote, "I do not understand how Mr. Magooge, who is claiming to come from Musoma, is surprised at a dowry of 45 cows and 25 goats. This amount of dowry is purely our traditional custom. We have plenty of cows, goats and sheep and if he does not have, it is himself to blame. You cannot expect a Zaramo [the dominant ethnicity of those with coastal origins] to pay 45 cows and 25 goats if he does not have them nor can afford them."[91]

Responses to Nyakire's jab from offended young bachelors were swift and sharp. Calling her a member of "an older generation" whose time had passed, some of these young men portrayed Nyakire's notion of Musoma dowries as part of a prehistoric past that should "be remembered by those who want to write some books regarding the old customs of Musoma people."[92] Others were more specific in challenging the justice of Nyakire's position by describing twin, twentieth-century dynamics of dowry inflation in Mara Region (in which Musoma was situated) and a gradually decreasing local economic base from which dowries might be paid. Suggesting that it was "difficult for a married woman to understand . . . how a man sacrifices to marry a wife," one young man claimed that "fantastically high bride prices" in Mara were a relatively recent phenomenon, one that went along with a decrease in access to cattle herds as more and more land was devoted to agriculture and increasing numbers of young men "remain[ed] in towns."[93] Magooge, the original object of Nyakire's derision, concurred, describing a whittling down of family wealth from one generation to the next.[94] And in a passionate letter one Peter Mwitta Jr. emphasized both the generational struggle underpinning the Nyakire exchange and young men's attachment, particularly in contexts of intersecting generational and gendered tensions over issues such as dowries, to romantic love as a marker of the modern. Wrote Mwitta,

> Mrs. Nyakire is quite wrong. Although it [a dowry of 45 cows and 25 goats] is our traditional custom, our parents could by now sit down and discuss the possibility of the old system for paying high dowry so that their modern children can marry more easily—like other Tanzanians. This could also add love between the husband and the wife. . . .
>
> We present Mara youths will not tolerate such exploitations—especially those working in various towns and the cities. Furthermore, there are not

plenty of cows nor sumptious [sic] goats at Mara these days as stated in Mrs. Nyakire's letter—but there were many during the years 1900–54.[95]

Intertwined with these signs of generational tension were moments of gendered anger and anxiety in which Nyakire's young male interlocutors expressed frustration at their perceived vulnerability to the schemes of potential mates. Magooge included in his response to Nyakire's letter worries about the type of girl who, once married, "becomes so brutal and rude . . . and sometimes becomes a prostitute," while another of her respondents linked his anxieties concerning dowries to city girls out of reach, arguing that a lowering of the dowry would lessen the number of women roaming the city.[96] Indeed, concerns about the economic difficulties facing young migrant men were not infrequently directed, in the marriage debate more broadly as well, at the supposed place of young urban women in these struggles, as exploiters out to squeeze men financially. As Thomas found in the case of debates over the Affiliation Act, notions of women's consumption patterns became a focus of criticism here.[97] Complaining that under the white paper proposals "women would be encouraged to change husbands like underwear and prostitution would be stepped up," a Mr. Shayo asked, "In any case, why should a man be required to defray the cost of cosmetics and furnishings for a woman who runs away from him to establish an unlicensed brothel elsewhere? Is this an approved type of mrija [exploitation]?"[98] On one hand, the centrality to the dowry commentary of the Nyakire exchange was somewhat curious in that it pitted young bachelors against an older woman rather than the older men who were arguably the main focus of young men's dowry grievances. From another angle, however, that this exchange was with a woman may well account for its vehemence, as it provided a highly charged opportunity for young men to combine their generational *and* gendered sense of victimhood. As one of Nyakire's critics ended his letter, "The question of brideprice has to be solved, for men have been exploited for [too] long."[99]

Although they grew to become a significant theme in the marriage debate, young men's concerns about dowries gained little traction at the parliamentary level or in the government's redrafting of the law. Unlike some of the UWT demands, dowry regulations beyond the installments option proposed in the white paper were not included in the final bill. Neither did the issue gain much support outside of its young, male constituency. Such disinterest appeared to be a source of frustration for some young men in the debate, including a few who explicitly lamented the lack of greater support for abolishing dowries among the white paper's female opponents. Attacking the calls for polyandry made at the UWT Mwanza conference and querying why delegates "still insist on dowry paying," one such man rather patronizingly advised women, "I assure you of this, for your sake: if you want to claim to be men's equals and have a better say get rid of the dowry."[100] The general lack of encouragement for such appeals among women engaged in the debate and the defense of dowries by most of the few women engaging the issue illustrate the rift between young men and women in their respective criticisms of the government marriage proposals.[101]

Generational tensions between young men and elders of the sort exhibited in the interventions on dowries were not a new phenomenon. Indeed, as Margot Lovett has shown, control over marriage options was a perennial point of struggle between young men and their elders in Tanzania, above all in the colonial period, when young men's increasing access to wage-labor threatened to loosen the control male elders held over the timing of marriage.[102] By the late 1960s, though, in the context of several of the shifts I discussed in chapter 2—namely, the increasing visibility of young women in town, the rise of concerns about consumption patterns and lifestyles of a new, male postcolonial urban elite, continued difficulties for young men in finding urban employment, and a resulting crisis of masculinity—newly charged dimensions to these tensions had begun to be expressed by young migrant men. One of these was visible in a second theme that began quietly in the margins of the marriage debate only to become one of its conventional wisdoms: deep anxieties around a perceived, often exaggerated demographic surplus of marriageable young women.

Claims of a severe demographic imbalance afflicting Tanzania, including gender ratios as high as six women to each man, were widely at odds with census figures, which put the countrywide male-female ratio at 95 to 100 (118 to 100 for urban areas).[103] Made with such frequency that by late in the marriage controversy it began to be referred to as simply "the surplus," this illusionary imbalance was marshaled by participants taking opposing positions in the debate.

The claim was popular among men but took on quite different meanings in the arguments of young men and of established men. For established men the "pressing" issue of "females greatly outnumber[ing] the males" was repeatedly cited to back up arguments defending polygamy and supporting the white paper.[104] Polygamy, it was argued, would provide husbands for surplus women and thereby prevent "the problems of prostitutes, mistresses, unmarried, lonely mothers and their illegitimate children."[105] In contrast, for young, unmarried critics of the white paper the surplus seen as an opportunity by their established, would-be-polygamous elders was instead a source of profound frustration: marriageable young women were deemed to be plentiful but out of reach. As a letter from one bachelor based in Dar es Salaam argued, "The protagonists of polygamy argue that in order to give security to women in our society, men must embark on a marital spree and have more than one wife. All right for the married, for the over 30s, the middle-aged. But what of the young bachelor? It seems that using the same statistics [those suggesting a female surplus], if polygamy is legalized in this country, only about five percent of the male population of this country might benefit."[106] If young men's frustration was directed primarily at city girls gaining market in the debates over urban young women's dress, comportment, and employability (see chapter 2), here it was aimed instead at an older male elite. Bernadette Kunambi, a female MP, captured this well when referencing the issue of a female surplus in parliamentary debate, warning that if an imbalance continued the country might begin to witness "coups" directed at polygamous households.[107]

A third and final spillover theme marking the debate over the United Law of Marriage revolved around suspicions about the place of political elites in the proposed reforms. Early on in the controversy, a handful of the white paper's opponents began to speculate about the timing and content of the proposals by suggesting that interested "big shots" had engineered the proposed reforms to allow themselves to "pursue the fashion of taking on a number of wives" with greater ease.[108] Accusations linking male elite self-interest with the white paper took two main forms. Some making this charge argued that elite investment in the new law had a decidedly material aspect to it. As the first letter writer to raise the issue in the debate put it, "Frankly speaking, this will benefit those holding big posts in Government, to claim more allowances when traveling or proceeding on leave, etc."[109] Another explained, "Take the example of a civil servant who is married to more than one wife. . . . Will the Government give fares for all or will he choose only one (the Government also) of them to accompany him to Paris, Moscow or Peking?"[110] Most of those raising the question of elite self-interest assumed the answer to be that the state would extend the perks, benefits, and allowances for matters like travel and health care to the additional dependents that the well-to-do would gain under the white paper's proposals and that this was a strong incentive lurking behind the reforms.[111] For the debate's participants and observers, these suspicions appeared to be confirmed early on by a civil servant's own intervention, one that expressed enthusiastic support of the white paper's proposals on polygamy and urged the government to make sure that multiple wives and their offspring would qualify for all of the perks accruing to a single wife: "For example, medical care, traveling facilities for them, as well as allowing more children to be given consideration on taxation allowances."[112]

Others charging elite self-interest cast their accusations more broadly, linking government positions, the accumulation of wealth and women, elite leisure, and the performance of power. In his contribution to the marriage debate, C. J. Mtenga situated these elements in relation to the Africanization of officialdom that was such a fundamental element in the emergence of the political elite of the 1960s. He wrote, "Obviously, the section of the code, that a marriage can be converted from monogamous to polygamous with the consent of the wife, was put there to suit the interests of the big potatoes. Now that they have regretted for marrying early before Africanisation, they would prefer young girls to appear with them in the public. Of course, their deprived wives would be silenced by their excessive incomes. In doing this, it was forgotten that the majority of our people are leading a hand-to-mouth life.[113] Mtenga's words were joined by those of others who included in their letters references to the everyday material pleasures and accoutrements of elite lives, like the bachelor who intimated that the reforms were designed by and for "an upper class of polygamous 'wabenzi' or 'wa-404'" (common appellations for the political elite named for the Mercedes Benz and Peugeot 404 cars they drove).[114]

Such interventions call attention to the importance of visions of leisure and consumption in critiques of elite self-interest. Criticism directed at government perks and allowances also focused largely on the elements of these perks, especially travel, that loomed large in the idea of the good life that came with a government post. Alongside all of the other elements considered thus far, then, the debate over the marriage law afforded a platform for the airing of anxieties over a nexus of accumulation, leisure, and conspicuous consumption by a rising political elite—a nexus in which the possession of women assumed a central place in the representation and performance of power by these "town-lords."[115] These connections resonate with Jean-Francois Bayart's influential theorization of a postcolonial "politics of the belly"—a phrase that captures not only the widespread use of eating as a metaphor for achieving high status and domination over others, but also a dynamic historical relationship in many African contexts between political power, the consumption and display of scarce resources (from luxury goods to women), and the ability to control the redistribution of wealth as a means to maintain a following.[116]

However, if this dimension of the marriage debate opened up elite accumulation to critical scrutiny, this was a critique fraught with ambivalence. The focus on leisure and conspicuous consumption provided an important entry point and target for frustration with the unequal distribution of the rewards of independence, but it also revealed envy of elite lifestyles as much as sustained critique of the inequalities. While some participants in the debate were unequivocal in their criticisms of the white paper's proposals as unfairly augmenting elite men's already luxury-filled lives,[117] others conveyed the sense that what was objectionable about the excess of elite male lifestyles was less the inequality, per se, to which it pointed, than their exclusion from enjoying similar luxuries as young bachelors.[118] For instance, the Dar es Salaam bachelor, cited above, opposed the white paper's proposals on polygamy not with a critique of the practice, but with the suggestion that the law would be "all right for the married, for the over 30s, the middle-aged." "But what of the young bachelor?" he continued. Counting himself among those unable to benefit under the reforms "because the wealthy 'wabenzi' [will] have availed themselves of the privilege of possessing many wives," he concluded his letter with a plea to MPs to "please . . . spare some thought for the peasant, the common man and bachelor. They too matter."[119]

This ambiguity of critique recalls Mbembe's argument that public commentary on postcolonial power often simultaneously engages in potent critique of spectacles of elite excess and is drawn into an "illicit cohabitation" with those in power under a shared symbolic order erected by state power and deployed by the dominating and dominated alike.[120] If the spotlighting of the grotesque and vulgar has been the most remarked upon aspect of Mbembe's landmark article "Provisional Notes on the Postcolony" (1992), the arguably more crucial part of his analysis in this piece is his focus on how discourses of cultural politics in the postcolony can simultaneously be bitingly satirical as political critique and have their oppositional potential blunted by trafficking in the very symbols and motifs shared by and working in favor of the powerful. This is a significant dynamic, one that is important to examine and ground in a historical specificity that Mbembe's article largely eschews in favor of pursuing more generalized insights. The ambiguity of young bachelors' critiques of elite lifestyles in the marriage debate gives a glimpse of this dynamic at work, but in order to examine it further I conclude with a discussion of a wider genre of popular narrative concerning male political elites, their rumored liaisons with young, urban women, and conspicuous consumption.

"Janja Yake": Ribald Comedy, 'Nizer Wealth, and the Ambivalence of Critique

One of the key sites on which this narrative genre was popularized was in sensationalist stories of the sexual shenanigans of big men about town that were a staple of *Ngurumo*, Dar es Salaam's most popular daily in the 1960s. *Ngurumo*'s pages in the 1960s brimmed with tales of scandalous encounters between 'nizers (*naizesheni*) and city girls (*visura wa mjini*). Cast as "street stories" supposedly observed voyeuristically by *Ngurumo*'s band of roving reporters, the tales were generally fantastic, satirical, and characterized by formulaic plotlines: A city girl seduces a 'nizer in a bar, the two go to his house together and are caught having sex by the 'nizer's wife, whose sudden appearance forces the city girl to escape out a window and run naked down the street. A city girl lives like a queen for six months by tricking her 'nizer boyfriend into believing she is pregnant with his child. Driven by their desire for clothes, multiple mistresses fight publicly over a single 'nizer in front of his mansion. A 'nizer grows rich by prostituting his wife. A fourteen-year-old schoolgirl lies about her age and spends a weekend having sex with a 'nizer at his beach house. A city girl tries to cement her relationship with her 'nizer by using skin-lightening cream only to have him reject her after she suffers burns on her face. Faced with her endless appetite for clothes, a 'nizer tricks his mistress into sleeping with his friend in order to leave her. A 'nizer is embarrassingly accosted in his government office by his city girl mistress.[121]

Far from being a marginal presence in *Ngurumo*, these kinds of stories were consistently placed on the front page of the paper, often under the heading "Janja Yake" (His or her cunning), and for months at a time would appear nearly every day. Presented in a vocabulary and form of oral storytelling, Janja Yake items constituted a genre that appears to have been *Ngurumo*'s most popular feature among readers prior to the advent of the Bwanyenye comics in mid-1967.[122] While they indexed intersecting anxieties over wealth and gender in Dar es Salaam's changing urban landscape, the tales also point to an ambivalence about 'nizers and to ways in which the intense gendering of these kinds of narratives placed limits on their potency as political critique.

To begin with a story that reveals in more detail some of the generic elements of these tales, on September 6, 1966, *Ngurumo* published a Janja Yake piece relating the escapades of a group of Dar es Salaam 'nizers' weekend trip to Tanga. In the story, titled "City-girl beaten 'til her miniskirt falls off," the roving reporter breathlessly tells of how he follows the party of four 'nizers taking a pleasure trip to Tanga in their cars, "as 'nizers are used to enjoying the cool Tanga breeze on the weekend." As soon as they arrive they are spotted by a city girl who grabs two of her friends and follows them into a bar. Seeing the girls with their straightened hair, "the orders start to fall like rain," and the group begins a long session of drinking and dancing on the 'nizers' tab. After two of her friends leave to return to their regular boyfriends, the remaining city girl decides to leave the dance floor to follow them, at which point one of the 'nizers angrily follows her out to the parking lot to recoup his losses. A tremendous fight between the 'nizer and his hoped-for date for the night ensues in the muddy parking lot—a fight which ends, hilariously for the onlookers in the story, in the girl's skirt being torn and coming loose, and her being left in her underwear covered in mud.[123]

Tamer than most in that it portrayed no actual sex, this story nevertheless contains elements which appeared over and over again in *Ngurumo*'s tales of these kinds of compromising encounters. The figure of the city girl in these stories is nearly universally portrayed as scheming in her pursuit of material pleasures through these liaisons (indeed the Janja Yake of the title usually, though not always, refers to the city girl in the story). As a tale of a wild 'nizer outing at Dar es Salaam's Sinbad nightclub put it in its opening line, "These days certain city girls in Dar es Salaam have launched their 'master plan' to suck men dry before running away."[124] Outwardly identified by her miniskirts, skin-lightening creams, straightened hair and wigs, the figure of the city girl is also one closely paired with offices (wherein she is often portrayed as finding work on the basis of her good looks) and a shirking of motherly duty (such as abandoning her baby in favor of dancing the night away).[125] Contemptuous of ordinary men who lack the means to support their lifestyles, the city girls are unrelenting in their pursuit of 'nizers. Among the stock features of Janja Yake stories were their endings, in which haughty city girls are placed in a variety of humiliating poses often involving involuntary public nudity or urination, fates which their 'nizers usually, though not always, escape.[126] These endings disturbingly mirrored or perhaps even prepared the ground for the gendered violence on the streets of Dar es Salaam at the time, which not infrequently saw gangs of young men chasing down women deemed to be dressed provocatively and stripping them of their clothes. Considering the context of fraught gender relations in town and the young male working-class audience to which much of Ngurumo's copy was pitched, there is much in these textual humiliations of city girls that reads like fantasies of enacting sexualized displays of power over young women who were perceived as being frustratingly out of ordinary young men's reach.

The figure of the city girl and these stories' consistent condemnation and degradation of her were familiar elements in the discursive landscape of Dar es Salaam in the 1960s. What is less clear-cut are the ways in which the figure of the 'nizer was constructed in the stories, for they divulge an ambivalence about this character and his power, wealth, and masculinity. On the one hand, there is a critical edge to the ways in which these stories read as comments upon growing distinctions in wealth in the early postcolonial period. As one reader protested in a poem,

> Everywhere he goes, walking in the city,
> The 'nizer is peeked at, even with a telescope!
> If he makes a little mistake, all his secrets are out
> You harass the 'nizer, for everything he does.[127]

Indeed, numerous tales describe in exquisite detail the wealth and resources to which 'nizers had access: automobiles, beachfront houses, weekend getaways, evenings at the club. The description of the Saturday night out at the Sinbad nightclub, for example, goes so far as to enumerate details of the cover charge and the prices of each brand of beer consumed. Rarely is the 'nizer portrayed as a good steward of his bounty and privilege. Rather, he is consistently cast as a libertine spending his days and nights in pursuit of drink, food, and, above all, women. The office is less a scene of productive work than one of decadent consumption: another means through which 'nizers could acquire mistresses through the selective hiring of secretaries. One Janja Yake tale, in which a 'nizer supports his lavish lifestyle by prostituting his wife every night, turned prostitution into a metaphor for 'nizers' accumulation in a critique that dovetailed with the way in which some political cartoons of the period, particularly in the weeks after the Arusha Declaration, used the figure of the female prostitute as a symbol of economic exploitation.[128] (See, for instance, the image on page 98.)

These portrayals of the 'nizer intersected with real-world accusations being launched in this period of the run-up to the Arusha Declaration of naizesheni abusing their privileges by, for example, using their official cars to pick up women—accusations which in June 1966 led to a discussion in Parliament about whether lifts in official cars should be offered to young women.[129] Indeed, among its readers, Ngurumo's sensationalist journalism may have played a part in laying ideological groundwork for the Leadership Code enacted in tandem with the Arusha Declaration, which attempted to place limits on politicians' accumulation. In Ngurumo's pages, at least, the code appeared as the culmination of apprehensions about a presumed rise in conspicuous consumption in the capital in the late sixties.

And yet if satirical portraits of 'nizers as slothful and decadent contained elements of a critique of the sources, distribution, display, and uses of wealth in postcolonial Dar es Salaam, the critique was blunted, if not entirely undermined, by the gendering of these tales of sexual escapades. Nothing in Janja Yake's stories sets the city girl up as a model of respectable femininity; she is consistently cast as a predator. By contrast, the 'nizer in these tales is imbued with a number of characteristics that set him up as a compelling masculine model, despite his flaws: first, he has the power to command material resources and a lifestyle that places him in Dar es Salaam's most desirable locations, spaces which were often named in Janja Yake stories as if to add another sheen of realism to the tales. Second, unlike the stories' city girls, these textual 'nizers are overwhelmingly cast as innocent, if comic, participants in their escapades; indeed, in contrast to the predatory nature of the city girl characters, 'nizers are rarely presented as scheming tricksters and quite often cast as victims. The instances in which 'nizers are portrayed as tricking their city girl counterparts are exclusively ones in which the 'nizer either is an imposter or resorts to trickery in a desperate attempt to rid himself of the predations of a greedy mistress.[130] Such deceptions, while provoking laughter at the 'nizer's expense, are never cast as blameworthy actions and instead would have confirmed for many young male readers their suspicions of city girls' attempts, as the Janja Yake column put it, to "suck men dry." Third, the 'nizer in these stories is virile, if nothing else, a man with unfettered access to and power over the very women who, in many young men's opinion, held themselves aloof from them.

For *Ngurumo*'s young underclass male audience, each of these elements was compelling. They offered variations on the power and resources many of them could fantasize about commanding someday as successful men (or attaching themselves to as lucky clients of established men). In setting 'nizers up as powerful, if compromised, models of masculinity, Janja Yake stories softened the potential critique of conspicuously consumed wealth embedded in their texts. Indeed, if these tales indexed intersecting anxieties about wealth and gender prominent among young men in Dar es Salaam, ultimately the gendering of the stories acted to overwhelm and undermine the antagonism toward the 'nizer figure in favor of one directed at the city girl. The disparity in hostility directed at these two figures suggests that gender and generation may have been somewhat different kinds of fault lines in this context. While both were important in the context of young male anxiety about rising inequality in Dar es Salaam in the sixties, hostility against the city girl was much more openly, directly, and loudly proclaimed. Young men's frustration with their 'nizer elders, on the other hand, a vertical relationship that presented high stakes for young men in maintaining because their futures often depended on remaining in successful men's good graces, was much more likely to be blunted or even sublimated, often through displacement onto the image of city girls as agents of urban exploitation and ruin.

In embarking on a reform of the United Law of Marriage, the state sought at once to mark a break from the colonial by eliminating the hierarchy that privileged Christian marriage under the British code and to cast that break as one befitting Tanzania's status as a modern, progressive nation on the world stage. As was so often the case in these public debates of the long sixties, the controversy over the marriage law spilled beyond the parameters of the official initiative. In examining the Great Marriage Debate, I have used it to shed light on struggles over gender, generation, and wealth in Dar es Salaam—struggles that were taking place at a somewhat different level from the ones explored in the last chapter. Some of the contests that arose in the debate were between married men and women, often rather elite, over the terms of marriage. At issue here was the question of control over resources within a marriage; these struggles revealed concerns by elite men and women alike to either maintain or secure control over the resources of the household. If successful men, including many politicians, seemed eager to use a legal loosening of the strictures on converting monogamous marriages to polygamous ones as a path to enhancing the prestige of their households, wives worried about the diversion of household resources to younger potential wives in such scenarios. In these contests, the double-sided nature of official discourse on matters of culture became a resource, with husbands' appeals to notions of African tradition being countered by wives' appropriation of a discourse of modern progress to make arguments for "women's rights" in monogamous unions.

But if this axis of conflict dominated the public debate in its early stages, it was soon complicated by other concerns, particularly those of young bachelors, entering the fray. Implying that the reforms were tailored to the interests of wealthier, senior men, many young men used the debate as a platform to air their anxieties about unaffordable dowries, a demographic imbalance imagined to be afflicting Tanzania, and 'nizers' conspicuous consumption. For young men these frustrations were connected. Amidst a seeming surplus of young, marriageable women, bachelors viewed the paths to their own marriage prospects as being blocked by the combined effect of dowries inflated by senior men and the perceived mutual preference of young women and older sugar daddies for one another. Embedded in these sentiments was considerable fodder for sharp tension along both generational and gendered lines. If the national cultural decency campaigns, as explored in chapter 2, became platforms for young male rage against women of their own generational cohort, it was critique of their generational seniors that emerged most strongly in the marriage debate. As the discourse on these elite men in both the marriage debate and the Janja Yake tales reveals, however, this was an ambivalent critique. For although a focus on 'nizers' scandalous liaisons about town rendered their conspicuous consumption open to criticism, it failed to undermine their status as powerful, if flawed, models of masculinity. Indeed, if this chapter pinpoints the possibilities for certain critiques of the changes wracking early postcolonial Dar es Salaam to gain footholds and traction on the terrain of public debate, it also offers reminders of the tentative and unstable nature of some of them.

Conclusion

A study in urban cultural politics, this book has been about a particular sixties moment in the history of Tanzania's capital. This was a moment in which debates over culture constituted a critical terrain upon which several of the decade's key social struggles were negotiated and fought out. The remarkable prominence of these debates—over dress, music, hairstyles, student activism, secretaries and city girls, marriage, and elite lifestyles—as well as the shape they took developed out of the confluence of a number of dynamics marking the era. The rise of the national cultural project, the changing shape of urban tensions around gender, generation, and wealth, the availability of transnational images, vocabularies, and styles for self-fashioning, the extraordinary stakes attached to youth as a political category, and the emergence of enthusiastic engagement with the press as a forum for public debate all intersected to help sculpt the debates of the decade.

Some of these struggles were fought out on the platform of the national cultural project. Launched with great fanfare a year after independence, Tanzania's national cultural project was cast as a recovery effort, an exercise in rescuing tradition from its trampling during the colonial period. A focus on nationalizing tribal tradition was only one strand of the project, however, for it coexisted alongside an increasingly hailed commitment to filtering such tradition through criteria defined as modern before being welcomed as national culture. Rather than representing a succession of contradictory or even distinctly separate agendas, these two strands were mutually constitutive, two sides of a coin. With an eye on Tanzania's place on the international stage, architects of national culture were keen to promote a national tradition that would represent Tanzania as simultaneously modern and distinctly non-Western. Furthermore, despite being born out of declarations of a break with the colonial, the national cultural project shared much with positions taken on cultural policy by both colonial officials and nationalist elites in the decades leading up to independence.

Such continuities—in the construction of tradition in relation to the modern and in the anxieties over urbanization that cultural policy channeled—did not, however, negate the importance of the declarations of a break with the past. Invoked repeatedly in the proliferation of national cultural discourse through the 1960s, this rhetoric of rupture worked to help create an effect of a postcolonial present, an era marked off from the humiliations of the colonial period. That the national cultural project itself—alongside other realms of socioeconomic policy—exhibited continuities with the colonial only heightened the irony of this postcolonial effect. For even if the representations of national culture displayed at sites ranging from official functions to school curricula bore the marks of a long history of colonial-era inventions of tradition, they also stood as condensed testament to the nation's postcoloniality, its overcoming of the colonial. To borrow Andrew Apter's insights on the postcolonial Nigerian state, here was continuity with the colonial at the very site of its erasure.[1] As implied by the pithy yet ambivalent Kiswahili phrase, uhuru wa bendera, or "flag independence," shedding the colonial did not automatically accompany the achievement of nation-state status; postcoloniality had to be produced and maintained. Tanzania's national cultural project was part of this, even as its unevenness (and, indeed, the very circulation of a phrase like "uhuru wa bendera") points to limits of its success in maintaining a postcolonial effect.

That the national cultural project fell far short of its stated goals as a promotional endeavor did not prevent a discourse of national culture from proliferating in public talk in Dar es Salaam. Such proliferation, though, was accomplished above all through the banning campaigns that became a primary, if generally unrecognized, part of the national cultural project in the second half of the 1960s and into the 1970s. Indeed, for residents of Dar es Salaam, it was the campaigns against a perceived urban decadence that constituted the face of national culture, its presence in their everyday lives. Entwined with official declarations framing the national cultural project against a colonial foil, these banning campaigns revealed a quite different but ultimately just as fundamental and more immediate scene of national culture: its constitution against a range of wayward urban others. Against this field of urban, feminized decadence, national culture could emerge as a vehicle for the projection of a healthy, rural ideal of frugality, authenticity, and masculine productivity that dominated official notions of civic duty, particularly after the Arusha Declaration.

Taken to the streets of Dar es Salaam and its forums of public talk, campaigns against urban decadence were contested, appropriated, and redirected in myriad ways. In some of these engagements the contest over national culture was joined, with young people in Dar es Salaam directly challenging official parameters of authenticity and foreignness, decency, youth, and the modern. Drawing on transnational cultural icons, images, ideas, and items of style crisscrossing Dar es Salaam, opponents of bans on indecent dress and soul music articulated notions of modern style and teenage identities at odds with official categories of modern decency and TANU party youth. In these contests, an official construction of the city as an ugly, decadent foil of post–Arusha Declaration nation building was confronted by other imaginings of the city and its possibilities, ones viewing it as part of transnational networks of modern style that marked the era.

Others redirected these debates, eschewing the national cultural frame to turn the campaigns into vehicles for struggles over the fraught field of gendered, generational, and class tensions in town. In the context of the confluence of rising unemployment, the opening up to women of particular niches of secretarial and factory work, the intensification of official roundups of the urban jobless, and the visibility of 'nizer wealth and consumption in the capital, young men used the decency campaigns to air grievances against young women and, to a lesser degree, older men. Perceiving a constriction of their opportunities for upward mobility *as men*, many young men in Dar es Salaam conflated women's work and mobility with "gaining market": illicit gain through sex with wealthier men. In some cases, this frustration took on violent forms, as decency campaigns were marked by physical attacks on young women deemed to be dressed indecently. For their part, some young women fought back against these charges, seeking to disentangle targeted fashions and office work, on the one hand, from gaining market on the other. If these efforts to assert the respectability of fashion and work achieved some success, other attempts to validate a more defiant city girl identity were much more difficult to pull off in the face of the persistent conflation of the markers of such an identity with wayward femininity.

These social struggles around gender, generation, and wealth led in other directions too. Developed as an institution of national pride, the University College of Dar es Salaam was a highly charged site of generational tensions of a somewhat different sort from the ones erupting in the battles around urban popular culture. Invested with official hopes of producing a loyal, if potent, cohort of youth serving the nation, the university also had the capacity to produce rivalry between the first, incumbent generation of nationalist leaders and its student body of rising elites, as illustrated in the dramatic debate surrounding the student protest against National Service in 1966. Moreover, the university was an important node for circuits of transnational ideas, ideologies, and iconic personas of a global left, circuits that served as vehicles for challenging the state from another direction: that of a youth vanguard whose political horizon stretched beyond the nation and was not as pliant as the youth envisioned by officials.

In the reform of the United Law of Marriage, too, the contest over an institution ripe with social tension saw multiple publics attempting to steer the debate in differing directions. Here, the triad of gender, generation, and wealth intersected yet again. On one level, the debate reflected long-standing tensions between married women and men—and itself became a battleground for such struggles—over the control of material resources within marriage. For elite wives in particular, fears of wealthy husbands using a new legal validation of polygamy to squander the household's resources on multiple wives drove an ultimately successful effort to defeat this aspect of the reforms, an effort that played on the sometime importance the state placed upon women's rights as a sign of a modern Tanzania on the world stage. For many of Dar es Salaam's young bachelors, on the other hand, the reforms were yet another sign of their perceived exclusion from paths to marriage as an important component of successful masculinity. Attempting to steer the debate toward issues of the high cost of bridewealth, a supposed inaccessible surplus of marriageable women, and the conspicuous consumption of senior male elites, the bachelors cast their interventions as generational grievances. These critiques, in both the marriage debate and other, more sensationalist domains of public discourse, were ambiguous, however. For if they opened up 'nizer lifestyles to criticism, they also reinforced the status of such elite men as models of virile masculinity to which many young bachelors aspired.

Focusing on these critical moments of debate that marked Dar es Salaam's long sixties opens a window into the fault lines of many of the decade's social struggles, the kinds of things being fought over, and the vocabularies—often stretching beyond the nation—through which they were negotiated. Such a focus also contributes to new understandings, both in Africa and beyond, of urban cultural politics; national political culture; social struggles around gender, generation, and wealth;

and transnational dimensions of postcolonial histories that have too often been conceived in a national frame. First, approaching the early postcolonial period through the lens of its debates over culture helps recast notions of urban state-society relations, indeed of urban politics, in this period in important ways. One of these involves new understandings of how the state manifested itself in the everyday lives of urban residents. The case of Dar es Salaam in the sixties suggests that a cultural domain was a vital front in these efforts. Coding alleged problems of urban society in expressly cultural terms, the decency campaigns that were such a critical component of the national cultural project extended the state into intimate realms of the lives of people in the capital. In Thomas Blom Hansen's and Finn Stepputat's terms, cultural banning campaigns constituted one of the ways "the state appear[ed] in everyday and localized forms."[2]

A focus on the proscriptive side of official cultural policy brings this dynamic sharply into view in a way that a simple consideration of national culture's promotional dimensions largely misses. The proscriptive dimension of the national cultural project best reveals the ways in which official notions not only of national culture, but also of the kind of modern image the early postcolonial state was so invested in were constituted negatively against a gendered field of urban decadence. This foil of urban decadence was crucial for official efforts to split the modern and distinguish its own association with a decent, productive modernity from a decadent one. For the ideological task of consolidating national culture as a symbol of a modern postcolonial state on the world stage involved distinguishing official culture not only from a so-called primitive tradition left behind, but also from unsavory aspects of Western modernity. That the forms and practices labeled decadent in official discourse had their own claims upon the modern made this split all the more fraught and difficult to achieve. These claims at once shared with their official rivals a vision of a *singular* modern and fiercely contested the content of this modern. This dynamic has important implications for the way one views engagements and contestations with the modern in postcolonial contexts. Indeed, it would be a mistake to view the competing claims to the modern articulated by Dar es Salaam's young denizens of soul music or drain-pipe trousers as the making of an alternative or parallel modernity. Rather, a fundamental component of these claims for those making them was precisely the singularity of the global modern being envisioned—one that positioned Tanzanians not as authors of alternatives distinguished by their difference from an imagined global norm but as full-fledged participants.

If a cultural domain enabled the extension of the state into urban people's lives in new ways, however, this was a process the state could little control. The cultural initiatives aimed at Dar es Salaam were enthusiastically engaged, seized upon, and appropriated in ways that often led away from and beyond the field of national culture. Official vocabularies and discursive frames were crucial to these efforts, even as they were used to lend weight to claims that often challenged the stigmatization of specific urban, gendered ways of being in town. As was the case in Pauline Joseph's challenge to the dress ban, such moves sometimes involved people appropriating state discourse to point to gaps between official ideology and its unequal application. Other instances saw Tanzanians reworking concepts and categories dear to the state in ways that both reaffirmed the importance and challenged the content of these categories. Such was the case, for example, in the debate over Operation Vijana, as participants articulated ways of being modern and youthful that were at odds with official versions of modern development and youth vanguardism.

Examining both sides of this process—the extension of the state in urban areas through its proscriptive cultural campaigns, on the one hand, and the appropriation of these initiatives by urban dwellers in multiple, often unforeseen directions, on the other—yields insights relevant to specific, ongoing questions over the nature of state-society relations and urban politics in postcolonial Africa. One of these debates has a prominent pedigree in Tanzanian studies: it revolves around the degree to which postcolonial states in Africa have been able to capture their citizenry, to exert control over citizens' lives, or to fill a discursive field by exercising what Achille Mbembe has called the *commandement*.[3] Because the state in the present case was central in providing vocabularies and frames key to urban public debate but never able to control the directions of public engagement with these frames, this book helps explain the seeming paradox of early postcolonial states' simultaneous prominence and weakness. On one hand, the book challenges assumptions that the state's sometime failure to capture its citizens renders its rhetoric relatively unimportant for understanding the lives of everyday people; on the other, it suggests that the kind of prominence official rhetoric achieved on the urban landscape was often testament less to the power of the state than to its limits.

This formulation resonates with Mbembe's call to approach the state and its subjects as bound up in a domain of "conviviality" in which rulers and ruled are enmeshed in shared categories and discourses.[4] Indeed, the present case points to the vital nature of this insight for studies of urban, postcolonial cultural politics. And yet, several of the debates examined here also query Mbembe's vision of state-society relations in an important manner. Rather than the "mutual zombification" and "impotence" that Mbembe contends turns this shared domain into a vicious circle with little hope for progressive change, the debates considered here suggest a much more complicated picture. Not only did some of the appropriations of official discourse that marked Dar es Salaam's public debates have important material effects, they also were characterized by a leveraging of such discourse toward precise and explicitly articulated ends and sometimes real gains. For historians of postcolonial cultural politics, this points to the importance of simultaneously being attuned to the discursive traffic between rulers and ruled and to the ways in which this discursive cohabitation often blunts the oppositional power of resistance (both insights following Mbembe) and avoiding a static version of the notion of conviviality that can mask rather than reveal historical change.

These implications of this book for Mbembe's argument also point to ways in which these stories of cultural debate during Dar es Salaam's long sixties help illuminate the politics of gender, generation, and class in urban postcolonial Africa. The stories I have told here certainly contain many moments that reveal the double-sided ambiguity of "conviviality" that Mbembe's articulation of this notion illustrates so well. And yet, close attention to the social struggles with which these instances of "cohabitation" are bound up also suggests that the outcomes of these discursive negotiations are not uniform—that they often vary according to the kind of social cleavage involved. For generational struggles—as exhibited, for instance, in young bachelors' critiques of their 'nizer elders in the National Service crisis and marriage debate—Mbembe's conviviality captures both the ease with which such critiques gained traction and their susceptibility to cooptation back into the vertical hierarchies of status and patronage of which they were a part. In this way, university students' protests against National Service requirements drew on notions of what elders' behavior toward the youth who would succeed them should be, even as these complaints of a failure of responsibility on the part of a 'nizer elite were ultimately cast as a misunderstanding by chastened protestors pleading to be readmitted to the co-operation of father and son on which their futures depended.

On the other hand, struggles around horizontal social cleavages like gender and, to some degree, class appear to have been less likely to be marked by the kind of ambivalent cohabitation that so often blunted the gains of generational critique.[5] This did not mean, however, that these struggles were necessarily more successful, for, as was the case with assertions of city girl identities, they also had a much more difficult time gaining political traction in urban public discourse. When critiques of gender relations did gain significant toeholds, as in the victories of urban, married women in the marriage debate or the success at redefining the parameters of working women's dress and mobility in forums like the Joseph case, it often flowed from the protagonists' appropriation of powerful vocabularies that carried official endorsement to cast their claims. While such appropriations underline the importance of Mbembe's emphasis on viewing rulers and ruled as embedded in shared discourse, they also highlight the real shifts that can attend these claims, their place as part of a dynamic historical landscape.

This book's examination of the cultural debates of Dar es Salaam's sixties moment also helps bring into view a transnational frame for postcolonial African histories. Crisscrossed by images, icons, ideas, and items of style originating in multiple elsewheres, Dar es Salaam's urban landscape provided much material with which invocations and identifications of transnational scope, alongside the national and subnational, could be fashioned. Of course, even in the context of the dominance of national (if not nationalist) history that has accompanied much of the period of independence, the framing of postcolonial societies transnationally is not unprecedented or merely recently developed. Reacting to the blind spots of the nationalist historiography of the 1960s, scholars working in the tradition of dependency or world systems theory in the 1970s, for instance, insisted on situating postcolonial, or neocolonial, societies in a global economic system. Nor has the national reigned supreme in the more recent work by scholars (mostly nonhistorians) performing social and cultural analyses of postcolonial African contexts: nuanced attention to subnational social cleavages has long interrogated the national frame. My book's contribution to East African postcolonial histories in this regard lies in the way it situates local invocations of a transnational frame in conversation with national (the national cultural project, for example) and subnational ones (social struggles around gender, generation, and wealth). Highlighting the ways in which such frames of varied scope both enabled and existed in considerable tension with one another suggests the importance of keeping them all in view.

In his book *Routes* James Clifford offers stimulating thoughts on such tensions between the national and the transnational, or translocal, as he calls it. This is a tension in which "nationalisms articulate their purportedly homogenous times and spaces selectively, in relation to new transnational flows and cultural forms, both dominant and subaltern."[6] It is a useful insight for many of the stories this book tells, for official notions of culture and the transnational influences crisscrossing Dar es Salaam were not hermetically sealed, a priori separate entities from one another. Indeed, the national cultural project itself was constituted in relation to both an international horizon of nation-states and the more challenging cosmopolitanisms of Dar es Salaam. This drama of the national being constituted through all manner of transnational crisscrossing, only to repress the latter as subversive, is an important one (and indeed it is a dominant narrative in both Clifford and much literature on transnational culture). And yet, my book has also worked to situate tensions between the national and the transnational in relation to other axes of struggle in Dar es Salaam—along cleavages of gender, generation, and wealth—that do not always fit such a narrative. Sometimes glossed over in work on transnational culture, one of Clifford's conclusions has been crucial here: "What matters . . . is who deploys nationality or transnationality, authenticity or hybridity, against whom, with what relative power and ability to sustain a hegemony."[7]

At century's end, when the fieldwork research for this book was beginning, intense public controversies of striking surface similarity to those of the early postcolonial period provided frequent echoes of those earlier debates. The shape of these latter-day cultural politics, however, emerged against the impact that world-historic shifts of the last twenty years had had on everyday life in Dar es Salaam. As happened in much of the former third world, Tanzania's economy was dealt a crushing blow by the oil shocks, plunging crop prices, and generalized global recession of the 1970s. In Tanzania's case, the catastrophe was compounded by the disruption of rural production under Nyerere's enforced "villagization" of the countryside in the 1970s and by the nation's praised but costly invasion of Uganda in 1979 to oust the dictatorial regime of Idi Amin.[8] The country's increasing impoverishment through the end of the 1970s and the 1980s increased the state's dependence on loan deals with the World Bank and the International Monetary Fund. As was the case across Africa and beyond, these agreements mandated a set of structural adjustment measures that effectively downsized the state. Budgets for education, health, and other social services were slashed, civil service and parastatal jobs were shed, price controls were relaxed. On a level of everyday life, the 1980s remains defined in the minds of many Tanzanians, even the better-off residents of Dar es Salaam, as a time of sometimes drastic shortages of even the most basic goods.[9]

With these economic troubles came hard times for the national cultural project as well. In both its prescriptive and proscriptive dimensions, funding and support fell off for both the Culture Division and the kinds of TYL campaigns that had been so prominent through the early 1970s. Kelly Askew observed that by the early 1990s official support for the remaining staff of the Cultural Division had shrunk to the point where salaries were no longer paid with regularity, and many staff were scouting about for paths into the world of nongovernmental organization work.[10] If what had been a key platform for the debates of the 1960s and early 1970s was shrinking, an important forum for these debates, the press, had changed too. With the *Standard* having been nationalized and folded into the TANU-run *Nationalist* in 1972 (to form a new state publication, the *Daily News*) and *Ngurumo* having died out by the mid-1970s after two years of financial pressures and intermittent publication, an independent press had all but disappeared by the late 1970s. The kind of public engagement with the press witnessed in Dar es Salaam's long sixties—in both the density and dynamism of letters-to-the-editor pages and the tendency for papers to become host to critical debates of the time—was not a feature of the state-run press after the mid-1970s. These trends by no means, however, signaled a disappearance of the issues that had undergirded the public controversies of the long sixties. Indeed, several of the dynamics attending the social struggles being fought out on the terrain of the debates of the sixties, notably the increasing numbers of working women in Dar es Salaam coinciding with generally high rates of joblessness, continued through the late 1970s and 1980s. Nor did the presence of material for the development of transnational identifications and imaginaries disappear. Indeed, the late 1970s and 1980s were a high point for a booming Congolese music scene in Dar es Salaam, fueled by its status as a center for exiles from Mobutu's Zaire, and local martial arts scenes driven by the kung fu films of Bruce Lee, to take just two examples.[11]

In a move nearly unprecedented among his cohort of leaders of one-party states, President Nyerere agreed to step down in 1985, resigning as head of the party five years later. His presidential successor, Ali Hassan Mwinyi, rapidly accelerated the liberalization of the economy and, under pressure, began more cautious moves to legalize opposition political parties and—for the first time since 1972—newspapers not controlled by the state. By the 1990s, the extreme shortages of even the most basic goods that had plagued Dar es Salaam throughout the 1980s had disappeared, but this was accompanied by a rapidly widening gap between rich and poor.

The landscape of Dar es Salaam by the late 1990s was marked by the juxtaposition of extremes of wealth and poverty characteristic of African capitals in an age of neoliberal, multinational capitalism. Some Tanzanians, often those with connections to the state or international business, benefited immensely from this reorientation, able now to accumulate assets and consume conspicuously in an unprecedented way. However, for a vast majority of the population, namely, Tanzania's working poor, liberalization brought little improvement and often a decline in living standards, one accompanied by the withering of whatever safety net had existed before. In relative terms, former lower- and mid-level public employees were often hardest hit. Those in this group who did not have the connections or the capital to compete in the economy of the 1990s often exhibited a nostalgia for the state as it had existed in the seventies, with its job security, structured grades, and guaranteed perks like rent subsidies, scooters, and cars.[12]

The cultural politics of the 1990s both reflected these immense changes and were sites upon which they were being negotiated. Cultural forms remarkably similar to those debated in the late 1960s continued to be charged, but the politics around these forms had shifted considerably, not least with the relative retreat of an activist state in cultural matters. The traditional Maasai dress under attack in the 1960s as a primitive embarrassment to the nation was, in the year 2000, being touted not only by the local tourist industry, but also by private security firms catering to Dar es Salaam's newly rich as a symbol of formidable and noble guards. Featured prominently in television and on billboard advertisements for these companies, young Maasai men wearing lubega and plaited hair were much sought after for this work; so much so that rumors circulated of men from other ethnic groups dressing up in stereotypically Maasai dress in order to get work.[13]

As in the 1960s, when the campaign against Maasai dress received widespread comment in the press only in reference to debates over Operation Vijana or soul music, the changed valuing of the Maasai generated little debate. Controversy over many popular cultural forms, however, swirled as intensely as in the 1960s, in many cases fueled by a competitive tabloid newspaper industry that exploded in the late 1990s. Echoing the influence of African American culture in the Dar es Salaam of the 1960s and 1970s, rap music and performance is one example.

Dar es Salaam's rap music scene began in the late 1980s and early 1990s as a genre performed largely in English by well-off young people who in many cases were the offspring of prominent figures and had been abroad as children.[14] But by the late 1990s the genre had undergone a massive shift: it was now performed nearly entirely in Kiswahili by mostly male youth of all social classes, including many of very little means. Adopting and adapting styles of dress, speech, and comportment from the U.S. hip-hop scene and individual stars like the late Tupac Shakur, rappers, club-goers, and fans developed a pose-about-town that many Tanzanians regarded as the embodiment of *uhuni*, the concept connoting vagrancy, immorality, and gangsterism that had since colonial times been part of the vilification of the city.[15] Against the backdrop of this critique and the continuing severe shortage of jobs for young adults in town, some youth subcultures were developing and performing celebratory claims to urban space that did not rely on, and even sometimes explicitly opposed, appeals to conventional notions of respectability.

In the public debates over contentious popular cultural forms in Dar es Salaam in the late 1990s, including hip-hop music and style, beauty contests, comic books, and miniskirts, both the controversies and the practices they focused on were generally regarded as unprecedented, decidedly phenomena of the nineties. With the emergence of transnational images, products, and styles often dated in popular memory to President Mwinyi's rule, the cultural landscape of the Nyerere decades tended to be portrayed, by young people especially, as a time of an unproblematized or pure *utamaduni* (culture).[16] In this regard, one of the aims of this book has been to track a longer history of cultural appropriations that often confounded notions of the authentic, a history that stretches back far beyond a postmodern, neoliberal moment. Always about far more than utamaduni, these appropriations were embedded in social struggles that have helped shape not just the texture of everyday life in twentieth-century Dar es Salaam, but also the shifting possibilities of defining what it meant to live in town.

Notes

Introduction

1 In his article on dress campaigns in Zanzibar, Thomas Burgess cites one of his informants as tracing his enthusiasm for the new bell-bottom style to having seen the Italian Western film "My Name is Pecos" (dir. Maurizio Lucidi, 1966). Burgess, "Cinema, Bell-Bottoms, and Miniskirts," 309. The film drew on an early twentieth-century genre of American Pecos Bill folklore. See, for instance, Bowman, *Pecos Bill: The Greatest Cowboy of All Time*.

2 See, for instance, Katsiaficas, *The Imagination of the New Left*; Fink et al., 1968; Daniels, *Year of the Heroic Guerilla*; Caute, *The Year of the Barricades*.

3 For a personal look back at the Bamako scene, see Diawara, "The Sixties in Bamako"; for references to attacks on clothing deemed indecent and inauthentic in East Africa, including Malawi, see Wipper, "African Women, Fashion and Scapegoating"; Mazrui, "Miniskirts and Political Puritanism," and "The Robes of Rebellion."

4 See, for instance, Thomas's compelling analysis of the Kenyan debate over the Affiliation Act in her book, *The Politics of the Womb*, chapter 5; for an early analysis of the debate over the Marriage, Divorce and Inheritance bill in Ghana, see Vellenga, "Who Is a Wife?"

5 Ngugi, "On the Abolition of the English Department"; for an analysis of Ngugi's "Nairobi Revolution," see Amoko, "The Problem with English Literature."

6 Speech by Nyerere delivered to Parliament, December 10, 1962, quoted in Ministry of National Culture and Youth, *Cultural Revolution in Tanzania*. For a pioneering and insightful account of Tanzanian national culture, see Askew, *Performing the Nation*, esp. chapter 5. See also Lihamba, "Politics and Theatre in Tanzania after the Arusha Declaration, 1967–1984."

7 This view characterizes even Askew's account, which describes the initial phase as a "turn toward traditionalism [that] entailed a sudden rejection of modernization." Askew, *Performing the Nation*, 171, 178–79.

8 Ibid., chap. 5.

9 Ibid., 14.

10 Fanon, "On National Culture," in his *The Wretched of the Earth*, 165–200; Cabral, "National Liberation and Culture."

11 p'Bitek, *Song of Lawino and Song of Ocol*.

12 p'Bitek, "What Is Literature?" in p'Bitek, *Africa's Cultural Revolution*, 15.

13 p'Bitek, "The Future of Vernacular Literature," in p'Bitek, *Africa's Cultural Revolution*, 33–34.

14 Topan, "Tanzania: The Development of Swahili as a National and Official Language."

15 For Mobutu's *authenticité* policy, seen through the lens of its impact on the Zairean music scene, see White, *Rumba Rules*, esp. chapter 3; on the Guinean case, see McGovern, "Unmasking the State."

16 For an argument on tradition as a product of modernism, see Gikandi, "Reason, Modernity, and the African Crisis."

17 For varying formulations of the mutual constitution of high and low, see Bakhtin, *Rabelais and His World*; Stallybrass and White, *The Politics and Poetics of Transgression*; Mbembe, "Provisional Notes on the Postcolony."

18 "Musician," letter to *Standard*, Nov. 19, 1969.

19 Mynah, letter to *Standard*, Nov. 20, 1969; Charles M. Njau, letter to *Standard*, Nov. 20, 1969.

20 p'Bitek, "Pop Music, Bishops and Judges," in p'Bitek, *Africa's Cultural Revolution*, 3.

21 Ngugi, introduction to p'Bitek, *Africa's Cultural Revolution*, ix. I should reiterate here that my aim is neither to collapse the important and sometimes large differences between different intellectuals involved in various projects of national culture nor to suggest that those I mention were equally involved in these projects; rather, my aim is simply to point out the shared sense of a cultural landscape in crisis among a broad range of intellectuals and policymakers involved in some way in articulating national culture.

22 Prestholdt, *Domesticating the World*; Erlmann, *Music, Modernity, and the Global Imagination*; Ambler, "Popular Films and Colonial Audiences"; Burns, *Flickering Shadows*; Burton, "Urchins, Loafers and the Cult of the Cowboy"; Gondola, "Dream and Drama:"; Gandalou, *Dandies à Bakongo*. Other important examples include Burke, *Lifebuoy Men, Lux Women*, and Hunt, *A Colonial Lexicon*.

23 Cooper, *Decolonization and African Society*; Cooper, *On the African Waterfront*; Burton, "Urchins, Loafers and the Cult of the Cowboy"; Mamdani, *Citizen and Subject*.

24 On early efforts at stabilization on the Copperbelt (and their reversal during the Depression), see Cooper, *Decolonization and African Society*, 45–47; Chauncey Jr., "The Locus of Reproduction"; Higginson, *A Working Class in the Making*. On the broader British and French policies through the postwar period, see Cooper, *Decolonization and African Society*.

25 Epstein, *Politics in an Urban African Community*; Leslie, *A Survey of Dar es Salaam*; Southall and Gutkind, *Townsmen in the Making*; White, *The Comforts of Home*; Burton, *African Underclass*.

26 The classic East African study of women in town remains Luise White's examination of prostitution in colonial Nairobi, *The Comforts of Home*. Also see Little, *African Women in Town*.

27 See, for instance, Parpart, "'Wicked Women' and 'Respectable Ladies'"; McCurdy, "Urban Threats"; Chanock, *Law, Custom, and Social Order*.

28 The conventional wisdom surrounding "detribalization" was being challenged in the 1950s by some of the social scientists attached to the famous Rhodes-Livingstone Institute for Social Research in Lusaka and the East African Institute for Social Research in Kampala. The best of the work produced by anthropologists and sociologists at these institutions was arguing in the 1950s that new African migrants in town "situationally" emphasized or deemphasized a range of identi-

fications, both tribal and otherwise, in the course of lives in town. This approach, associated largely with the long underappreciated anthropologists of the Manchester School, had the great strength of neither ignoring nor fetishizing tribal identification, but of regarding it as both powerful and mutable. Good examples of this brand of work include Mitchell, *The Kalela Dance*; Epstein, *Politics in an Urban African Community*; and Southall and Gutkind, *Townsmen in the Making*. In the 1970s and 1980s the work of the Manchester School was harshly—and to a great extent unfairly—condemned by critiques such as Bernard Magubane's "A Critical Look at Indices Used in the Study of Social Change in Colonial Africa." More recently, a few historians and anthropologists have insightfully reevaluated the school's contributions. Most notably, see Cooper, *Decolonization and African Society*, 369–72, and Ferguson, *Expectations of Modernity*, chapter 1. For a groundbreaking examination of work at the Rhodes-Livingstone Institute highlighting the crucial ways in which African research assistants shaped the scholarship of the institute's anthropologists, see Schumaker, *Africanizing Anthropology*.

29 Sabot, *Economic Development and Urban Migration*, 43–50.

30 Leslie, *A Survey of Dar es Salaam*, 1–2.

31 For excellent analyses of continuity between colonial and postcolonial regimes in official urban policy and rhetoric, see Burton and Jennings, "The Emperor's New Clothes?"; and Burton, "The 'Haven of Peace' Purged." On colonial constructions of city and countryside, also see Mbilinyi, "'City' and 'Countryside' in Colonial Tanganyika."

32 Sabot, *Economic Development and Urban Migration*, 90.

33 For the openings of new categories of formal employment to women, see Swantz and Bryceson, "Women Workers in Dar es Salaam"; Bryceson, "A Review of Maternity Protection Legislation in Tanzania," 175–78; Bryceson, "A Review of Statistical Information on Women in the Work Force Seeking Employment in Dar es Salaam and Their Families' Economic Welfare." On the early informal niches of the colonial period, see Geiger, *TANU Women*, 31–38; Leslie, *A Survey of Dar es Salaam*, 168–69; Burton, *African Underclass*, 56; Brennan, "Nation, Race and Urbanization in Dar es Salaam, Tanzania, 1916–1976," 56.

34 Tanganyika was the name for the colonial territory which became Tanzania after independence.

35 These broader trajectories have been most authoritatively and comprehensively set out in Cooper, *Decolonization and African Society*. For examinations of this process in more specific contexts, see Cooper, *On the African Waterfront*; Lindsay, *Working With Gender*; White, *The Comforts of Home*; Burton, *African Underclass*; Iliffe, *A Modern History of Tanganyika*. On the colonial construction of tradition in Tanganyika, see Askew, *Performing the Nation*, chapter 5; Iliffe, *The Making of Modern Tanganyika*, chapter 10. For elsewhere on the continent, see Ranger, "The Invention of Tradition in Colonial Africa"; Apter, "The Subvention of Tradition"; Chanock, *Law, Custom, and Social Order*; Mudimbe, *The Invention of Africa*.

36 Cameron, "Native Administration," July 16, 1925, Tanzania National Archives (hereafter TNA) 7777/20, quoted in Iliffe, *A Modern History of Tanganyika*, 321.

37 Mumford, "Malangali School," quoted in Iliffe, *A Modern History of Tanganyika*, 339.

38 On colonial film policy elsewhere in British colonial Africa, see Burns, *Flickering Shadows*.

39 Norman Spurr to Member for Social Service, Aug. 29, 1950, TNA 41128, 9.

40 Norman Spurr to Member for Social Service, Aug. 2, 1950, TNA 41128, 9.

41 Zonk! (dir. Hyman Kirstein., African Film Productions, 1950). For more on Zonk! in the South African context, see Davis, In Darkest Hollywood.

42 Norman Spurr, CFU—Dar es Salaam, "A Report on the Reactions of an African Urban and Rural Audience to the Entertainment Film 'Zonk,'" August 1950, TNA 41128, 12A.

43 Stephen Mhando to Mr. Whitlam-Smith, Aug. 23, 1950, TNA 41128, 10.

44 Introducing gumboot dancing (a dance style popular with South Africa's migrant laborers), the master of ceremonies in the film joked that the "delightful" restaurant in which the scene was set was "the Ritz-Carlton, to be precise" and proclaimed that it was the "first time in the world's history that this dance has been presented to a motion picture audience." Zonk! (1950).

45 Both of these statements were evidently made in Kiswahili. The second quotation appears to have entered the report as a somewhat awkward translation of Ukifika pale huwezi kurudi (If you get there, you'll never want to return). Norman Spurr, CFU—Dar es Salaam, "A Report on the Reactions of an African Urban and Rural Audience to the Entertainment Film 'Zonk,'" Aug. 26, 1950, TNA 41128, 12A.

46 Zonk! (1950).

47 Spurr, CFU—DSM, "A Report" (1950).

48 Ibid.

49 Mhando to Whitlam-Smith, Aug. 23, 1950.

50 Spurr to Member for Social Service, Aug. 2, 1950, TNA 41128, 9.

51 Mbembe, "Provisional Notes on the Postcolony."

52 Burton, African Underclass.

53 For a cogent critique, with reference to Mahmood Mamdani's Citizen and Subject, of the reliance on a notion of a colonial legacy to explain colonial-postcolonial continuities, see Cooper, Colonialism in Question, introduction.

54 Burton, African Underclass, 73–76, 235–38.

55 See Nyerere, Ujamaa: Essays on Socialism. For insightful rereadings of ujamaa and the villagization project, respectively, see Hunter, "Revisiting Ujamaa," and Schneider, "Developmentalism and Its Failings."

56 On state policy and rhetoric vis-à-vis an "unproductive" city, see Burton, "The 'Haven of Peace' Purged."

57 Burton, African Underclass; for a broader, continent-wide context, see Cooper, Decolonization and African Society.

58 Chatterjee, The Nation and Its Fragments; also see the essays in Mitchell, ed., Questions of Modernity.

59 Alongside Chatterjee's work, see, for instance, Pemberton, On the Subject of "Java," and Apter, The Pan-African Nation.

60 Probst, Deutsch, and Schmidt, eds., African Modernities, 4–7.

61 For attention (sometimes implicit) to this bifurcation of the modern in colonial contexts, see, for example, Comaroff and Comaroff, Of Revelation and Revolution, vol. 2; Hunt, A Colonial Lexicon; and Probst, Deutsch, and Schmidt, African Modernities. For a broad discussion of postcolonial negotiations of the modern, see Mitchell, ed., Questions of Modernity.

62 I borrow the term "constitutive outside" from ibid., introduction.

63 See, for instance, Kaba, "The Cultural Revolution, Artistic Creativity, and Freedom of Expression in Guinea"; Arnoldi, "Youth Festivals and Museums," 55; Askew, *Performing the Nation*, 169.

64 Amoko, "The Problem with English Literature."

65 See also Askew, *Performing the Nation*, 168–69, for attention to this dynamic.

66 This argument draws inspiration from Amoko's in the sense that it represents an attempt not simply to interrogate the content of national cultural discourse, but also to situate the claims of this discourse in what are alternate and sometimes overlooked contexts: in Amoko's case, the culture of the university; in my case, anxieties over the urban and the modern.

67 The first quotation is by E. C. Baker, district officer at Tanga, quoted in Nottcutt and Latham, *The African and the Cinema* (1937), 42; the second is by Sir Donald Cameron, governor of Tanganyika (1925–31), quoted in Iliffe, *A Modern History of Tanganyika*, 321.

68 *Standard*, Dec. 30, 1968. For the deputy's quotation, see Moses Nnauye to Katibu Mkuu, Umoja wa Vijana wa TANU, "Taarifa ya Operation Vijana," Dec. 20, 1968, in TNA TYL/OV/40/C/46, p. 1.

69 For the notion of a "culture effect," see John Pemberton, *On the Subject of "Java,"* 9. Examining the construction of an authentic Java underlying cultural discourse in Soeharto's regime, Pemberton writes, "The power of an indigenous discourse so self-consciously concerned with what constitutes 'authentic' (*asli*) Javanese culture, with a 'tradition' (*tradisi*) that must be preserved at all costs, operates to recuperate the past within a framework of recovered origins that would efface, for the sake of cultural continuity, a history of social activism from the late 1940s to the mid-1960s. In doing so, it discloses not so much the effects of culture per se, but the force of what might be called, refashioning Foucault, the culture effect: the production of a knowledge, that called 'culture,' as certain of its own assumptions as it is devoted to recovering the horizons of its power by containing that which would appear otherwise." For work that examines the continuities in policy between the colonial and postcolonial periods in Tanzania, see Burton and Jennings, "The Emperor's New Clothes?" and Burton, "The 'Haven of Peace' Purged."

70 Hansen and Stepputat, eds., *States of Imagination*, 36–37. See also Steinmetz, ed., *State/Culture*; Mitchell, "Society, Economy, and the State Effect"; Mbembe, "Provisional Notes on the Postcolony"; Bayart, *The State in Africa*.

71 Hyden, *Beyond Ujamaa*.

72 Mbembe, "Provisional Notes on the Postcolony," 4, 10.

73 Ibid., 4.

74 Cooper, *Colonialism in Question*, 24.

75 Mbembe, "Provisional Notes on the Postcolony," 4.

76 On the colonial construction of tradition in Tanganyika, see Askew, *Performing the Nation*, chapter 5; Iliffe, *The Making of Modern Tanganyika*, chapter 10. For elsewhere on the continent, see Ranger, "The Invention of Tradition in Colonial Africa"; Apter, "The Subvention of Tradition"; Chanock, *Law, Custom, and Social Order*; Mudimbe, *The Invention of Africa*.

77 Ferguson, *Global Shadows*, chapter 6.

78 Mike P. Francis, letter to *Standard*, Nov. 20, 1969; Ranger, *Dance and Society in Eastern Africa*; Burton, "Urchins, Loafers and the Cult of the Cowboy"; Ambler, "Popular Films and Colonial Audiences"; Powdermaker, *Copper Town*.

79 The phrase "at home in the world" is borrowed from Brennan, *At Home in the World*. Among the work theorizing official and popular discourses as drawing on one another within a shared realm, see Mbembe, "Provisional Notes on the Postcolony," and Yurchak, *Everything Was Forever Until It Was No More*.

80 Among the Africanist work that has pioneered the consideration of these domains as being mutually embedded is literature on reproduction and sexuality in colonial urban contexts. Examples of the most innovative of this work include White, *The Comforts of Home*; Thomas, *The Politics of the Womb*; and Hunt, "Noise over Camouflaged Polygamy."

81 The intertwined character of these cleavages has been a classic theme in Africanist work stretching back at least as far as the work of Claude Meillassoux, stressing the importance of viewing gender, generation, and resources in a single frame. More recently, a range of scholars, often investigating struggles over marriage and reproduction, have extended examinations of this triad into new domains. To take but two East African examples, Lynn Thomas and Brett Shadle have built on the pioneering work of Luise White and Nancy Rose Hunt to show how issues of marriage, bridewealth, female circumcision, and sexual relationships became sites upon which multidimensional struggles between elders, young women and men, and colonial officials were negotiated. Thomas convincingly makes the case for the centrality of a "politics of the womb" to African colonial history; she sees this politics also as a lens through which continuities and transformations in gendered and generational struggles across the colonial-postcolonial divide can be tracked. See Meillassoux, "From Production to Reproduction"; Wilson, "Zig-Zag Change"; Chanock, *Law, Custom, and Social Order*; Thomas, *The Politics of the Womb*, esp. chapters 4, 5; Shadle, *"Girl Cases"*; White, *The Comforts of Home*; Hunt, *A Colonial Lexicon*.

82 Lovett, "'She Thinks She's Like a Man,'" 49; Wilson, "Zig-Zag Change." Accounts of similar dynamics in other parts of colonial Africa are numerous. See, for instance, Guyer, "The Value of Beti Bridewealth"; Lindsay, "Money, Marriage and Masculinity on the Colonial Nigerian Railway," 140; Peel, *Ijeshas and Nigerians*, 118–19; Chanock, *Law, Custom, and Social Order*.

83 Guyer, "The Value of Beti Bridewealth"; Shadle, *"Girl Cases,"* xii; Mutongi, "'Worries of the Heart,'" 74.

84 Wilson, "Zig-Zag Change," 404. Wilson was referring specifically to intergenerational tension over bridewealth among the Nyakyusa of Tanganyika, as plotted over the course of the twentieth century.

85 White, *The Comforts of Home*; for other early work on women in colonial and early postcolonial towns (work that was usually more impressionistic than White's monograph), see, for instance, Kenneth Little, *African Women in Town*; Gugler, "The Second Sex in Town"; Wipper, "African Women, Fashion, and Scapegoating."

86 White, *The Comforts of Home*.

87 Geiger, *TANU Women*, 31–38; Leslie, *A Survey of Dar es Salaam*, 168–69; Burton, *African Underclass*, 56; Brennan, "Nation, Race and Urbanization in Dar es Salaam, Tanzania, 1916–1976," 56.

88 White, *The Comforts of Home*; Burton, *African Underclass*, 125, 145; Burton, "The 'Haven of Peace' Purged," 146–49. Perhaps tellingly, official plans for the area that was Kisutu in the wake of its demolition in 1974 centered around a musical conservatory to be constructed for the Ministry of National Culture and Youth. The

conservatory was never built, and today the area is occupied in part by the Dar es Salaam Institute of Technology, a vocational college.

89 Burton, *African Underclass*, 125, 145; Ivaska, "Wholesome Cinema, Censorship, and the Urban/Rural Divide in 1930s Tanganyika." For a portrait of the men of the African Association in Dar es Salaam, see Iliffe, *A Modern History of Tanganyika*, chaps. 12, 13.

90 Burton, *African Underclass*, 214–17.

91 On job shortages in the 1960s, see Bujra, *Serving Class*. For the openings of new categories of formal employment to women, see Swantz and Bryceson, "Women Workers in Dar es Salaam"; Bryceson, "A Review of Maternity Protection Legislation in Tanzania," 175–78; Bryceson, "A Review of Statistical Information on Women in the Work Force Seeking Employment in Dar es Salaam and their Families' Economic Welfare."

92 For the first and one of the only references in academic work to the "'nizer" as a category, see von Freyhold, "The Workers and the Nizers." For Ferguson's phrase, see Ferguson, "The Cultural Topography of Wealth."

93 This follows a similar argument made recently in an article by Harry Englund in "Cosmopolitanism and the Devil in Malawi."

94 Examples of work that relies upon this kind of local/global dichotomy include Miller, ed., *Worlds Apart*; Hannerz, *Transnational Connections*; Pollack, Bhabha, Brekenridge, Appadurai, "Cosmopolitanisms."

95 For the concept of global cultural flows, see Appadurai, *Modernity at Large* (1996). For a compelling critique of the indeterminacy of Appadurai's framework, see Cooper, *Colonialism in Question*, chapter 5.

96 For one of the best historical examinations of this coastal region, see Glassman, *Feasts and Riot*.

97 Prestholdt, "East African Consumerism and the Genealogies of Globalization," 1. For classic work on the economic formation of this Indian Ocean zone of exchange, see Sherriff, *Slaves, Spices, and Ivory in Zanzibar*; Chaudhury, *Asia Before Europe*.

98 On South Asians in twentieth-century Tanzania, see Brennan, "Nation, Race and Urbanization in Dar es Salaam, Tanzania, 1916–1976."

99 Exceptions to this include Moyer, "Street-Corner Justice in the Name of Jah"; Perullo, "Hooligans and Heroes"; and, on Zanzibar, Burgess, "Cinema, Bell-Bottoms, and Miniskirts."

100 For instance, see Ross, *May '68 and Its Afterlives*; Rowbotham, *Promise of a Dream*.

101 Katsiaficas, *The Imagination of the New Left*. The recent, two-part *American Historical Review* forum (February and April 2009) on "The International 1968" is testament to the new prominence of a "global '68" frame. However, despite its gestures toward a global scope, this forum makes only tentative moves outside of the geographic sites within which 1968 is generally remembered. See especially Suri, "The Rise and Fall of an International Counterculture," and Marotti, "Japan 1968."

102 Ngomuo, letter to *Standard*, Oct. 16, 1968.

103 Gaonkar, *Alternative Modernities*; Appadurai and Breckenridge, *Consuming Modernity*; Larkin, "Indian Films and Nigerian Lovers"; Lau, ed., *Multiple Modernities*; Schoss, "Dressed to Shine"; Appadurai, *Modernity at Large*.

104 Two recent critiques of the literature have been particularly valuable for the formulation of this argument: Ferguson, *Global Shadows*, introduction and chapters 6, 7; and Cooper, *Colonialism in Question*, chapter 5.

105 The recent collection by the Modern Girl Around the World collective of scholars is an example of scholarship that succeeds in holding this global horizon and the situated struggles through which it gained meaning in productive tension. See Weinbaum, Thomas, Ramamurthy, Poiger, Dong, and Barlow, eds., *The Modern Girl Around the World*.

106 Cohen, Miescher, and White, *African Words, African Voices*, 2–3.

107 In the past several years a handful of pathbreaking uses and defenses of the press as a source for colonial and postcolonial African history have appeared, many of which I discuss below. They include Ellis, "Writing Histories of Contemporary Africa"; White, *Speaking with Vampires*, chap. 8; Glassman, "Sorting Out the Tribes"; Cohen and Atieno-Odhiambo, *The Risks of Knowledge*; Thomas, *The Politics of the Womb*, esp. chap. 5; and (for an ethnography of the press in contemporary Ghana), Hasty, *The Press and Political Culture in Ghana*.

108 For an exhaustive list of publications as well as perhaps the only comprehensive survey of Tanzania's colonial and postcolonial press, see Sturmer, *The Media History of Tanzania*.

109 Konde, *Press Freedom in Tanzania*, 55, 65.

110 Ibid., 55.

111 Sturmer, *Media History of Tanzania*, 100.

112 For more on the fascinating story of Ginwala in Tanzania, see Konde, *Press Freedom in Tanzania*, 59–63; Sturmer, *Media History of Tanzania*, 120–26.

113 Konde, *Press Freedom in Tanzania*, 61–63; Sturmer, *Media History of Tanzania*, 126.

114 Konde, *Press Freedom*, 43; Sturmer, *Media History of Tanzania*, 69.

115 Konde, *Press Freedom*, 42.

116 While cases have occasionally been noted in African newspapers of letters to the editor having been written by reporters and editors themselves, all available evidence—including journalists' oral and published memories and the volume, style, and generic variation among letters—indicates that this was very rarely the case in Tanzania's four main dailies in the 1960s: Konde, *Press Freedom in Tanzania*; interviews with James Nindi (Dar es Salaam, October 9, 2000) and Generali Ulimwengu (Dar es Salaam, April 20, 2001). For cases of internally produced letters, see Rob Nixon's discussion of South Africa's *Drum* magazine in his *Homelands, Harlem and Hollywood*.

117 See, for instance, Newell, *Literary Culture in Colonial Ghana*; Barber, ed., *Africa's Hidden Histories*; Peterson, *Creative Writing*; White, *Speaking With Vampires*, chapter 8; and Powdermaker, *Copper Town*.

118 Anderson, *Imagined Communities*, 61–63.

119 John Z. Nzwala, letter to *Standard*, October 14, 1969, 4.

120 Hofmeyr, "'Waiting for Purity,'" 22. Derek Peterson has made a similar argument in his fascinating history of Gikuyu engagement with the written word in colonial Kenya, *Creative Writing*, 5.

121 White, *Speaking With Vampires*, 252–53.

122 Konde, *Press Freedom in Tanzania*, 43. Glassman similarly suggests that in colonial Zanzibar "political journalism of the time carries traces of many street-corner arguments." Glassman, "Sorting Out the Tribes," 400.

123 Sturmer, *Media History of Tanzania*, 117–19.

124 United Republic of Tanzania, *Analysis of African Women and Men*, 85.

125 Sturmer, *Media History of Tanzania*, 117–19.

126 Ibid., 110.

127 Ibid., 119.

128 Interviews with Mathias Machimba (Dar es Salaam, Nov. 4, 2000 and Jan. 30, 2001), Limi Ally (Dar es Salaam, July 18, 2004), Majeshi Wanzagi (Dar es Salaam, Feb. 28, 2001), Sabbi Masanja (Dar es Salaam, April 27, 2001), Miriam Zialor (Dar es Salaam, May 3, 2001), Esther Ngomba (Dar es Salaam, July 20, 2004).

129 Ellis, "Writing Histories of Contemporary Africa," 20.

130 White, *Speaking With Vampires*, 260–61.

131 Ibid., 264.

Chapter 1. National Culture and Its Others

1 President Nyerere to Parliament, December 10, 1962. Reprinted in Ministry of National Culture and Youth, *Cultural Revolution in Tanzania*, 3, 4. This famous quote often appears (as it does on the cover of the pamphlet from which I drew it) in close proximity to an equally famous photograph of Nyerere enthusiastically playing a large traditional drum as a young boy watches him; indeed, the quote and the photo appear so often together that each has the effect of conjuring the other.

2 Ibid.

3 Askew, *Performing the Nation*, 171.

4 For Tanganyika, see ibid., chapter 5; Iliffe, *A Modern History of Tanganyika*, chapter 10. For elsewhere on the continent, see Ranger, "The Invention of Tradition in Colonial Africa"; Apter, "The Subvention of Tradition"; Chanock, *Law, Custom, and Social Control*; Mudimbe, *The Invention of Africa*.

5 See, for instance, Kaba, "The Cultural Revolution, Artistic Creativity, and Freedom of Expression in Guinea"; Arnoldi, "Youth Festivals and Museums," 55; Askew, *Performing the Nation*, 169.

6 Askew, *Performing the Nation*, chapter 5.

7 Ibid., 178–80.

8 For an example of an account of temporal succession from traditionalist to socialist and modernizationist imperatives, see Askew, *Performing the Nation*, 171, 178–80.

9 Chatterjee, *The Nation and Its Fragments*.

10 Iliffe, *A Modern History of Tanganyika*.

11 Comaroff and Comaroff, "Reflections on Youth," 20, 24, 29. For Tanzania, see Burgess, "Introduction to Youth and Citizenship in East Africa"; Burgess, "Remembering Youth"; Burgess, "The Young Pioneers and the Ritual of Citizenship in Revolutionary Zanzibar"; Brennan, "Youth, the TANU Youth League and Managed Vigilantism in Dar es Salaam, Tanzania, 1925–73."

12 James Brennan has captured the relationship between TANU and its Youth League with the phrase "managed vigilantism." Brennan, "Youth, the TANU Youth League and Managed Vigilantism in Dar es Salaam, Tanzania, 1925–73."

13 McKinsey and Company, *Coordinating the Development of Culture and Youth*. For details on what Kelly Askew has aptly called the Culture Division's institutional "wanderings," see Askew, *Performing the Nation*, 184–86, and the review by the

Culture Division's promoter of arts and crafts, L. A. Mbughuni, *The Cultural Policy of the United Republic of Tanzania*.

14 Mbughuni, *Cultural Policy*, 26, 29. See Coulson, *Tanzania: A Political Economy*, for a broad picture of the finances of the Tanzanian state in this period. In 1967, one British pound equaled twenty Tanzanian shillings.

15 Mbughuni, *Cultural Policy*, 26–29.

16 Askew, *Performing the Nation*, chapter 5.

17 Commissioner for Culture to the Regional Community Development Officer, Aug. 28, 1964, TNA 540/CD/CR/46. About two weeks later the commissioner's letter was forwarded to community development officers and assistants in all coastal districts. See Regional Community Development Officer to Community Development Officers et al., Sept. 14, 1964, TNA 540/CD/CR/46.

18 Minutes of the Meeting to Discuss the Question of the Promotion of National Culture, Aug. 5, 1965, TNA 540/CD/CR/46. Secretary, District Cultural Committee, Utete, Rufiji to "Wananchi," May 28, 1966, TNA 540/CD/CR/46. Report of the Cultural Committee Meeting, Feb. 10, 1966, TNA 540/CD/CR/46.

19 As example of the latter, see the letter from Starehe Youth Club to the Regional Development Officer, DSM, July 14, 1966, TNA 540/CD/CR/46.

20 Mbughuni, *Cultural Policy*, 27. For a striking account of the confusion and frustration at the lack of official direction that often reigned in cultural committees at the local level, see Askew, *Performing the Nation*, 172–76.

21 For a foundational account of the traditionalist and modernizationist dimensions of Tanzanian national culture, one that situates them less as overlapping or mutually constitutive than as temporally successive, see Askew, *Performing the Nation*, chapter 5.

22 Ministry of National Culture and Youth, *Cultural Revolution*, 4.

23 L. H. Mandara, Commissioner for Culture, to Regional Community Development Officer, Aug. 28, 1964, TNA 540/CD/CR/46.

24 A majority of Culture Division projects were in fact conducted by academics at the University of Dar es Salaam and appropriated by the division.

25 Mwakipesile, *Mila na Desturi za Wasangu, Wasafwa na Wasagara*.

26 See also Askew, *Performing the Nation*, 171, on this point.

27 For a detailed study of this series as part of a genealogy of national cultural discourse in the 1960s, see Ivaska, "Custom and Tradition for the Modern African."

28 Elspeth Huxley, "Literature for Africans: Report" (1945), 1, in TNA 32525, vol. 1, 127A; East African High Commission, *East Africa Literature Bureau Annual Report, 1955–6*, front matter.

29 C. G. Richards, foreword to the series Custom and Tradition in East Africa, in Mochiwa, *Habari za Wazigua*, iii–iv.

30 C. G. Richards to Norman Spurr, TNA Ref. C/2/7, Aug. 1, 1950; East African High Commission, *East Africa Literature Bureau Annual Report, 1960–61*, 12.

31 Yongolo, *Maisha na Desturi za Wanyamwezi*; Mnyampala, *Historia, mila na desturi za Wagogo*. For a fascinating discussion of Mnyampala's biography and account of the Gogo, see Gregory Maddox's introduction to an annotated reissue of Mnyampala's text: Mnyampala and Maddox, *The Gogo*.

32 People across East Africa borrowed EALB books far more than they purchased them. In 1952, the ratio of books lent to volumes sold was slightly less

than 4:1. East African High Commission, *East Africa Literature Bureau Annual Report*, 1952, 5.

33 East African High Commission, *East Africa Literature Bureau Annual Report*, 1955–6, 7; East African High Commission, *East Africa Literature Bureau Annual Report*, 1956–7, 6.

34 East African High Commission, *East Africa Literature Bureau Annual Report*, 1952, 4.

35 C. G. Richards, foreword to the series Custom and Tradition in East Africa, in Cory, *The Ntemi*, v–vi.

36 "Helps and Explanations for African Authors, No. 3—Notes on Recording the Social and Political Organisation of African Tribes" (Nairobi: EALB, 1961. mimeograph), 3.

37 For examples, see Yongolo, *Maisha na Desturi za Wanyamwezi*, and Mochiwa, *Habari za Wazigua*.

38 Mnyampala's book on the Wagogo, for example, was reissued in 1971. In the postcolonial version Mnyampala's original references to the Wagogo as a nation were changed to tribe. Mnyampala, *Historia, mila na desturi za Wagogo*. See Maddox, introduction to Mnyampala and Maddox, *The Gogo*, for this point.

39 See, for example, Muhtasari wa Halimashauri ya Utamaduni wa Wilaya, March 30, 1966, TNA/540/CD/CR/46.

40 See *Nchi Yetu* [Dar es Salaam] for January 1968 through March 1973.

41 *Nchi Yetu*, February 1968, 24; for a comphrehensive account of the Tanzanian state's relationship with *ngoma*, see Askew, *Performing the Nation*.

42 Sturmer, *A Media History of Tanzania*, 63.

43 F. J. Mchauru, Katibu Mkuu, kwa Makamishna Wote wa Wilaya et al., Aug. 31, 1966, TNA/540/CD/CR/46.

44 Ataturk has been a figure of remarkable transnational circulation, having been appropriated in widely varying geographical and temporal contexts, sometimes to buttress quite diverse political projects. For a fascinating analysis of references to Ataturk in interwar Egypt, see Jacob, *Working Out Egypt*.

45 E. R. Munseri, "Kusitawisha na Kuhifadhi Utamaduni Wetu," reprinted in TNA 540/CD/CR/46. For another discussion of Munseri's intervention, see Askew, *Performing the Nation*, 177–78.

46 Mochiwa, *Habari za Wazigua*, 39.

47 Also see Askew, *Performing the Nation*, 178–80, for an analysis of this shift.

48 Nyerere, "Ujamaa—The Basis of African Socialism," 1962, reprinted in Nyerere, *Ujamaa—Essays on Socialism*.

49 TANU, *The Arusha Declaration and TANU's Policy on Socialism and Self-Reliance*.

50 Askew, *Performing the Nation*, 178.

51 Ibid., 180.

52 TANU, *The Arusha Declaration*, 14.

53 A. F. Masao, "Kazi Zetu," in Wizara ya Utamaduni wa Taifa na Vijana, *Historia Fupi ya Utamaduni wa Mtanzania*, 5.

54 Wizara ya Utamaduni wa Taifa na Vijana, *Utamaduni: Chombo cha Maendeleo*.

55 Lucas and Masao, Ministry of National Culture and Youth, Directorate of Research on Traditions and Customs, *The Present State of Research on Cultural Development in Tanzania*, 10.

56 Lucas and Masao, *Present State of Research*, 11.

57 Ibid., 13–14.

58 See, for instance, two Culture Division academics' critique of the way *ngoma* (dances) were being promoted in schools: Mgughuni and Ruhumbika, "TANU and National Culture," in Ruhumbika, ed., *Towards Ujamaa*.

59 My perspective on Operation Dress-Up owes much to a series of conversations with Leander Schneider, who has also written insightfully on the campaign in the context of rural development in Tanzania. See Schneider, "The Maasai's New Clothes." For broader concerns with Maasai cultural practice expressed by the Handeni Cultural Committee, see Askew, *Performing the Nation*, 177.

60 "Kenya Masai MP hits at Tanzania dress curbs," *Standard*, Feb. 8, 1968; "MP may wear Masai robe in E. A. Assembly," *Standard*, Feb. 9, 1968. This exchange gives a glimpse of some of the different inflections to the varying, often opposed ways in which the Tanzanian and Kenyan governments dealt with questions of culture and ethnicity: Tanzania by playing down ethnicity and ethnic display in favor of a nationalized (quasi-socialist) modernization; Kenya by often encouraging ethnic display, not least as part of an increasingly profitable tourist industry.

61 "Nyerere condemns Masai progress plan critics," *Nationalist*, Feb. 12, 1968.

62 "Masai leaders back dress-up campaign," *Standard*, March 14, 1968.

63 Schneider, "The Maasai's New Clothes."

64 "Maendeleo ya Wamasai," *Nchi Yetu*, March 1968.

65 See, for instance, *Nchi Yetu*, February 1967; August 1968; December 1968.

66 Cf. Askew, *Performing the Nation*, 171, 178–80.

67 See, for instance, the section entitled "Utamaduni Wetu" in the primary school textbook *Elimu ya Siasa kwa Shule za Msingi: Nchi Yetu—Kitabu cha Kwanza* (Arusha: East Africa Publications, Ltd., 1984) and the voluminous account of the Ministry of National Culture and Youth's "Seminar on Culture" in Shinyanga, 1978, TNA folios.

68 Ruskin College is an adult education institute with historically close ties to the trade unions, set up with loose ties to Oxford University. Joan Wicken, President Nyerere's longtime personal secretary and trusted confidant who began working with TANU in the mid-1950s, played an instrumental part in the initiative to found Kivukoni. Wicken herself was a graduate of Ruskin College.

69 In this sense Kivukoni was more elite than Ruskin.

70 This paragraph is drawn from Kivukoni College, "People's Education Plan," a mimeographed report from 1965 written by Lionel Cliffe and accessed on the web at http://www.eric.ed.gov (accessed Sept. 25, 2008).

71 A. P. Ng'asi, "A Thought on Traditional Music in Tanzania."

72 E. M. Mwano, "Polygamy and Its Effects."

73 See E. Mhamba, "Should Bridewealth Be Retained in Our Modern Society?"; H. W. Malale, "Uganga Kama Mpango wa Unyonyaji," *Mwenge*, Toleo na. 11; H. M. J. Mwenda, "Mila na Desturi Yanavyoweza Kusaidia au Kuzorotesha Shughuli za Ujamaa," *Mwenge*, Toleo na. 12.

74 TANU, Arusha Declaration, February 5, 1967, in Nyerere, *Ujamaa: Essays on Socialism*, 28.

75 TANU, *Azimio la Arusha*, 15.

76 Burton, *African Underclass*; James R. Brennan, "Blood Enemies, Exploitation and Urban Citizenship in the Nationalist Political Thought of Tanzania, 1958–75."

77 The quotation that is the title of this section was the title of an editorial by Okwudiba Nnoli in the *Nationalist*, Oct. 21, 1968.

78 "TANU Youths Ban 'Minis': Sijaona announces 'Operation Vijana,'" *Standard*, Oct. 3, 1968. See also the front-page coverage in *Uhuru, Ngurumo*, and the *Nationalist*, Oct. 3, 1968.

79 *Ngurumo*, Sept. 23, 1968.

80 Moses Nnauye to Katibu Mkuu, Umoja wa Vijana wa TANU, "Taarifa ya Operation Vijana," Dec. 20, 1968, in TNA TYL/OV/40/C/46, 1.

81 Moses Nnauye, "Taarifa ya Operation Vijana," 1.   •

82 *Standard*, Dec. 30, 1968.

83 See, for instance, White, *The Comforts of Home*; Parpart, "'Wicked Women' and 'Respectable Ladies'"; McCurdy, "Urban Threats"; Allman, "Rounding Up Spinsters"; Lovett, "'She Thinks Like a Man'"; Silberschmidt, "Masculinities, Sexuality, and Socio-Economic Change in Rural and Urban East Africa."

84 *Standard*, Oct. 25, 1968.

85 "Taarifa ya Operation Vijana," Dec. 20, 1968, in TNA TYL/OV/40/C/46, appendix.

86 Peter Tweedy, letter to *Standard*, Oct. 17, 1968.

87 See letters by Ukaka Mpwenku (Oct. 14), Zainabu (Oct. 14), Augine Moshi (Oct. 16), "Regular Reader" (Oct. 22), J. N. Lohay (Oct. 23), "Revolutionary Youth," (Oct. 23), John C. R. Mpate (Oct. 24), M. Sheya (Oct. 10), and R. N. Okonkwu (Oct. 14)—all in *Standard*, 1968.

88 R. N. Okonkwu, letter to *Standard*, Oct. 14, 1968.

89 *Standard*, Oct. 22, 1968.

90 See, for instance, *Nationalist*, Feb. 8, Feb. 11, Feb. 17, Oct. 16, 1968; *Nchi Yetu*, Feb. 1969; *Standard*, Oct. 10, Oct. 12, 1968.

91 *Nchi Yetu*, December 1968.

92 "Sadru," letter to *Standard*, Oct. 25, 1968.

93 John Nakomo, letter to *Standard*, Oct. 22, 1968.

94 Peter Tweedy, letter to *Standard*, Oct. 17, 1968.

95 *Standard*, Oct. 10, 1968.

96 Issac T. Ngomuo, letter to *Standard*, Oct. 16, 1968.

97 Ngomuo, letter to *Standard*, Oct. 16, 1968.

98 M. S. Sulemanjee, letter to *Standard*, Oct. 12, 1968. See also the letters by Abu Abdallah (Oct. 4), M. W. Kibani (Oct. 9), M. Sheya (Oct. 10), Ernestos S. Lyimo (Oct. 11), Pakilo P. Patitu (Oct. 11), "Django" (Oct. 11), R. M. Okonkwu (Oct. 14), Ngomuo (Oct. 16), "Concerned" (Oct. 17), Sr. Mberwa Sleepwell (Oct. 22), Y. Makwillo (Oct. 23), "Unconcerned" (Oct. 24), all in *Standard*, 1968.

99 Django, letter to *Standard*, Oct. 11, 1968.

100 Andrew Shija, quoted in *Standard*, Oct. 17, 1968.

101 Okwudiba Nnoli, *Nationalist*, Oct. 21, 1968 (emphasis added).

102 Appadurai and Breckenridge, "Public Modernity in India."

103 Gaonkar, *Alternative Modernities*; Appadurai and Breckenridge, "Public Modernity in India"; Brian Larkin, "Indian Films and Nigerian Lovers"; Lau, ed., *Multiple Modernities*; Schoss, "Dressed to Shine"; Appadurai, *Modernity at Large*.

104 Ferguson, *Global Shadows*, chapters 6, 7.

105 Ngomuo, letter to *Standard*, Oct. 16, 1968.

106 Ferguson, *Global Shadows*, chapter 7.

107 The question in this subsection's head is from Bob Eubanks, letter to Standard, Nov. 20, 1969.

108 J. K. Obatala, "U.S. 'Soul' Music in Africa."

109 Ibid., 81.

110 Ibid., 81–82.

111 "Songambele bans 'soul' music," Standard, Nov. 13, 1969.

112 A. A. Riyami, "Government backs ban," letter to Standard, Nov. 20, 1969.

113 Message from the Editor, Standard, Nov. 20, 1969.

114 For an insightful portrait of the African American expatriate community in Nkrumah's Ghana, see Gaines, American Africans in Ghana.

115 For details of Pete O'Neal's biography, see "A Panther in Arusha," interview with O'Neal in the East African (Dar es Salaam), Jan. 13, 2003, and the film A Panther in Africa (dir. Aaron Matthews, 2004).

116 This paragraph is drawn from the following sources: "Two from U.S. held after police find guns and bullets," Daily News, May 28, 1974; "Police probe packages from the U.S." Daily News, May 29, 1974; "Afros ready to help probe infiltration," Daily News June 17, 1974; Mwakikagile, Relations Between Africans and African Americans, chapter 7.

117 Hadji Konde, "Air Bantou—Dar's top soul songsters," Sunday News, Sept. 21, 1969.

118 The quotation is from an article on the Rifters: "If you dig soul you won't be alone," Nov. 2, 1969.

119 Interviews with Anne Methusela Majige (Dar es Salaam, July 20, 2005), Omar Mwaulanga (Dar es Salaam, March 16, 2001), Sipora Kyara (Dar es Salaam, July 20, 2005).

120 Bob Eubanks, letter to Standard, Nov. 20, 1969.

121 According to Brian Ward, many activists on the left were, like Obatala, concerned about Brown's seemingly inconsistent political stances (veering from conservative up-by-the-bootstraps positions to his "I'm Black and I'm Proud" message). Among a broader majority of African Americans, though, Brown was lauded as an emblem of resistance and pride. See Ward, Just My Soul Responding, 389–92.

122 Standard, Nov. 14, 1969.

123 A. A. Riyami, letter to Standard, Nov. 20, 1969.

124 Abdon D. Mally, letter to Standard, Nov. 20, 1969.

125 Bob Eubanks, letter to Standard, Nov. 20, 1969.

126 Burton, "The Haven of Peace Purged," 130, 133.

127 Mike P. Francis, letter to Standard, Nov. 20, 1969.

128 "Fairness," letter to Standard, Nov. 19, 1969.

129 Ungando, A. C. L. Mynah and Pilly, letters to Standard, Nov. 20, 1969.

130 Charles M. Njau, letter to Standard, Nov. 20, 1969.

131 P.A.L., letter to Standard, Nov. 19, 1969.

132 Abdon D. Mally, letter to Standard, Nov. 20, 1969

133 Mike P. Francis, letter to Standard, Nov. 20, 1969.

134 Abdon D. Mally, letter to Standard, Nov. 20, 1969.

135 See also letters from K. M. Songwe (Nov. 13), Salum R. H. Hemedi (Nov. 19), "Soulman" (Nov. 19), Flavian C. Mwingira (Nov. 19), P.A.L. (Nov. 19), Charles M. Njau (Nov. 20), and the statement by the Editor (Nov. 14), all in Standard, Nov. 1969.

136 A. J. Kanoni, letter to *Standard*, Nov. 19, 1969.

137 Editorial statement, *Standard*, Nov. 14, 1969.

138 "Soulman," letter to *Standard*, Nov. 19, 1969.

139 P.A.L., letter to *Standard*, Nov. 19, 1969.

140 Ungando, letter to *Standard*, Nov. 20, 1969.

141 Maganja-Stone Chimlo, letter to *Standard*, Nov. 20, 1969.

142 Pilly, letter to *Standard*, Nov. 20, 1969.

143 A. J. Kanoni, letter to *Standard*, Nov. 19, 1969.

144 Charles M. Njau, letter to *Standard*, Nov. 19, 1969.

145 Thomas, "Gendering Reproduction: Placing Schoolgirl Pregnancies in African History."

146 Charles M. Njau, letter to *Standard*, Nov. 20, 1969.

147 *Nchi Yetu*, October 1973, 1.

148 Lawrence A. Mtawa, "Mavazi ya Heshima," *Nchi Yetu*, October 1973, 3.

149 A. Likoko, "Mgigania haki sawa za Binadamu," *Nchi Yetu*, October 1973, 12–13.

150 *Nchi Yetu*, November 1973, 7.

151 Jackson, introduction to Elam Jr. and Jackson, eds., *Black Cultural Traffic*; Edwards, *The Practice of Diaspora*.

152 Ebron, *Performing Africa*; Cole, "When Is African Theater 'Black'?"

153 Joseph, *Nomadic Identities*, 38.

154 Charles M. Njau, letter to *Standard*, Nov. 20, 1969.

155 A. C. L. Mynah, letter to *Standard*, Nov. 20, 1969.

Chapter 2. "The Age of Minis"

1 *Standard*, Oct. 8, 24, 1968; *Ngurumo*, Oct. 9, 1968; *Uhuru*, Oct. 9, 1968; Criminal Investigation Department, Ref. CID/229/3/235, Oct. 10, 1968, in TNA /S.H/ C.480/1.

2 Campaigns against indecent dress were also launched in the late 1960s and early 1970s in Zanzibar. For an analysis of the Zanzibari campaigns, see Burgess, "Cinema, Bell-Bottoms, and Miniskirts."

3 See, for instance, Moses Nnauye to Katibu Mkuu, Umoja wa Vijana wa TANU, "Taarifa ya Operation Vijana," Dec. 20, 1968, in TNA TYL/OV/40/C/46, 1–2.

4 See, for instance, "Mob attacks girls in mini-skirts," *Standard*, Nov. 23, 1968.

5 *Standard*, Oct. 8, 1968.

6 For the display of posters, see *Standard*, Dec. 29, Dec. 30, 1968; *Nationalist*, Dec. 30, 1968. Decent dress included modest collared shirts and slightly baggy trousers; long "maxi" dresses; socialist-style suits inspired by Mao, Chou-en-Lai, and Kaunda; and dress common in coastal Dar, such as the Islamic-inspired *kanzu* and *bui-bui* and the *khanga*. Indecent dress included, for men, tight "drain-pipe" trousers and cowboy-inspired outfits ("Texas costume"), and for women, tight "slim-line" dresses and, most notoriously, the miniskirt. For details on the enforcers and their accoutrements, see *Standard*, Jan., 1969, and *Nationalist*, Jan. 2, 1969.

7 See, for instance, "Mini ban 'surprise' to U.W.T.," *Standard*, Oct. 14, 1968.

8 Sabot, *Economic Development and Urban Migration*, 43–50.

9 Ibid., 71, 142. The number of primary school leavers entering the workforce shot up from 4,925 in 1964 to 58,252 in 1970.

10 Campbell, "The State, Urban Development and Housing."

11 The statistics for 1928, 1931, and 1940 are drawn from census data quoted in Andrew Burton, *African Underclass*, 56; the figure for 1948, also from census data, is quoted in Sabot, *Economic Development and Urban Migration*, 90.

12 Leslie, *A Survey of Dar es Salaam*, 168–69; Burton, *African Underclass*, 56; Brennan, "Nation, Race and Urbanization in Dar es Salaam, Tanzania, 1916–1976," 56; for a comparable phenomenon in Mwanza, see Iliffe, *A Modern History of Tanganyika*, 531.

13 Geiger, *TANU Women*, 31–38; Burton, *African Underclass*, 56.

14 The quote is from Leslie, *A Survey of Dar es Salaam*, 4, see also 14; Burton, *African Underclass*, 56; Swantz and Bryceson, "Women Workers in Dar es Salaam," 29; Little, *African Women in Town*, 24, 90–91, 96; White, *The Comforts of Home*.

15 Sabot, *Economic Development and Urban Migration*, 90; Campbell, "Conceptualizing Gender Relations and the Household in Urban Tanzania," 183.

16 Sabot, *Economic Development and Urban Migration*, 90; Sembajwe, "Secondary Statistics on Overall Demography and Demographic Trends (Especially Migration) in Urban Areas with Special Reference to Dar es Salaam," 144.

17 Sabot, *Economic Development and Urban Migration*, 94–95; Bryceson, "Social, Political and Economic Factors Affecting Women's Material Conditions in Tanzania," 157.

18 By 1971, for example, some 38 percent of those renting houses in Dar es Salaam were reportedly female. Bryceson, "A Review of Statistical Information on Women in the Work Force Seeking Employment in Dar es Salaam and Their Families' Economic Welfare," 188.

19 The statistic is from Sabot, *Economic Development and Urban Migration*, 92.

20 Bryceson, "A Review of Statistical Information on Women in the Work Force Seeking Employment in Dar es Salaam and Their Families' Economic Welfare," 17.

21 Swantz and Bryceson, "Women Workers in Dar es Salaam"; Bryceson, "A Review of Maternity Protection Legislation in Tanzania," 175–78.

22 Bryceson, "A Review of Statistical Information." Factory jobs, like Urafiki, would often require Std. 4 education, while secretarial jobs would often ask for Std. 7 completion or a certificate from a secretarial college.

23 Bryceson, "A Review of Statistical Information," 186–87.

24 Ibid., 195.

25 The quote is from Little, *African Women in Town*. 28. See also Leslie, *A Survey of Dar es Salaam*; Geiger, *TANU Women*, 37–38; Swantz and Bryceson, "Women Workers in Dar es Salaam," 25; Akyeampong, "'Wo pe tam won pe ba' ('You like cloth but you don't want children')"; Obbo, *African Women*; White, *The Comforts of Home*; Stambach, *Lessons from Mount Kilimanjaro*.

26 Leslie, *A Survey of Dar es Salaam*, 4.

27 For hints of gender tension arising out of the political economy of sex in late colonial Dar es Salaam, see ibid., 229; and in a broader, comparative context of East and Central Africa, see Little, *African Women in Town*, chapter 7.

28 See, for instance, Fair, "Dressing Up"; Ranger, *Dance and Society in Eastern Africa, 1890–1970*.

29 Leslie, *A Survey of Dar es Salaam*, 112–13. Also see Burton, "Urchins, Loafers, and the Cult of the Cowboy."

30 Leslie, *A Survey of Dar es Salaam*, 110.

31 Ibid., 112.

32 Allman, "Fashioning Africa," 2.

33 Comaroff and Comaroff, *Of Revelation and Revolution*, vol. 2, chapter 5; Hansen, *Salaula*; Allman, ed., *Fashioning Africa*; Hendrickson, *Clothing and Difference*.

34 See, for instance, Benstock and Ferris, eds., *On Fashion*; Warwick and Cavallaro, *Fashioning the Frame*; Benstock and Ferris, eds., *Footnotes*.

35 Hendrickson, introduction, in Hendrickson, ed., *Clothing and Difference*, 11.

36 Burton, *African Underclass*.

37 Burton, "The 'Haven of Peace' Purged," and Brennan, "Blood Enemies: Exploitation, and Urban Citizenship in the Nationalist Political Thought of Tanzania, 1958–75."

38 TANU, *The Arusha Declaration and TANU's Policy on Self-Reliance*.

39 See chapter 1 for more on this theme.

40 Konde, *Freedom of the Press in Tanzania*, 208.

41 Moses Nnauye to Katibu Mkuu, Umoja wa Vijana wa TANU, "Taarifa ya Operation Vijana," Dec. 20, 1968, in TNA TYL/OV/40/C/46, p. 2.

42 Mohamedi Jeuri, letter to *Uhuru*, Oct. 22, 1968.

43 Thomas Changa, "Sikai Tena Mjini," *Nchi Yetu*, February 1969.

44 Cartoon reprinted in G. Kamenju and F. Topan, *Mashairi ya Azimio la Arusha*, 48. Artist unknown.

45 *Ngurumo*, Jan. 2, 1969.

46 "Supporter," letter to *Standard*, Oct. 25, 1968.

47 *Standard*, March 18, 1968.

48 White, *The Comforts of Home*; Little, *African Women in Town*.

49 Mbah, "Prostitution in Tanzania (A Case Study of Dar es Salaam City)."

50 Thomas, *The Politics of the Womb*, 114; see also Thomas, "Schoolgirl Pregnancies, Letter-Writing, and 'Modern' Persons in Late Colonial East Africa," and, in the context of northern Tanzania, Stambach, *Lessons from Mount Kilimanjaro*.

51 Dinan, "Sugar Daddies and Gold Diggers"; Thomas, *The Politics of the Womb*, 165. For fictional portrayals from Tanzania, Kenya, and Malawi, see Mkufya, *The Wicked Walk*; Bukenya, *The People's Bachelor*; Owino, *Sugar Daddy's Lover*; Rubadiri, *No Bride Price*.

52 Moses Nnauye to Katibu Mkuu, Umoja wa Vijana wa TANU, "Taarifa ya Operation Vijana," Dec. 20, 1968, in TNA TYL/OV/40/C/46, 1–2.

53 *Ngurumo*, Oct. 14, 1968.

54 "Anti-mini militants meet modern misses," *Standard*, Oct. 17, 1968; "Wolfson Corner: Women in Revolt," *University Echo*, Nov. 8, 1968, 7.

55 S. S. Tofiki, "Kina Mama Nambieni," *Ngurumo*, Nov. 1, 1968.

56 "Socialist," letter to *Standard*, Oct. 23, 1968.

57 D. Chokunegela, "Nami Natoa Pongezi," *Uhuru*, Oct. 17, 1968.

58 "Supporter," letter to *Standard*, Oct. 25, 1968.

59 Kilua J., letter to *Nationalist*, Oct. 25, 1968.

60 Christopher Mwesiga, letter to *Standard*, Aug. 20, 1972.

61 I am grateful to Lynn Thomas for pointing this out.

62 S. S. M. Owino, "Current Anxieties—Exploration," *University Echo* (1972), 8.

63 TANU Publicity Section, *Arusha Declaration* (1967), 2. A cartoon from 1970 subtitled "I don't want the mini's exploitation anymore," condemned miniskirts

in these very terms; *Nchi Yetu*, Feb. 1970. For a treatment of the vocabulary around exploitation (*unyonyaji*) in Tanzania, see Brennan, "Blood Enemies." The opponent is quoted in De Leon, letter to *Ngurumo*, Oct. 24, 1968.

64 For a fictionalized portrayal of campus sexual politics, see Bukenya, *The People's Bachelor.*

65 For UWT statements on the issue of indecent dress, see *Nationalist*, Oct. 14, Oct. 15, 1968; *Uhuru*, Oct. 14, Oct. 15, Oct. 21, 1968.

66 "Bibi Mapinduzi Asema: Mabibi Viwandani," *Ngurumo*, Dec. 14, 1968.

67 See, for instance, Lucy Lameck's letter, "Minis Lower the Dignity of Women," *Nationalist*, Oct. 29, 1968, a particularly virulent attack on "derogatory" dress.

68 For an example of a male defense, see, for instance, the letter by T. K. Malendeja in *Standard*, Oct. 24, 1968.

69 "Mini ban 'surprise' to U.W.T.," *Standard*, Oct. 14, 1968.

70 "Freedom Lover (Miss)," letter to *Standard*, Oct. 18, 1968.

71 "Mrs. Freedom Lover," letter to *Standard*, Oct. 23, 1968.

72 The phrase is from Mbilinyi, "The 'New Woman' and Traditional Norms in Tanzania."

73 *Uhuru*, Aug. 2, 1969; *Standard*, Sept. 11, 1969; *Ngurumo*, Nov. 22, 1969.

74 "Aibu mpaka lini," editorial in *Uhuru*, Oct. 7, 1970.

75 The quotation is from Anselmi Nere, letter to *Uhuru*, July 23, 1970.

76 Anselmi Nere, letter to *Uhuru*, July 23, 1970. Also see Pembe A. Ng'amba, letter to *Uhuru*, July 30, 1970; J. M. Makuyu, letter to *Uhuru*, Aug. 19, 1970; Fausta A. Matemba, letter to *Uhuru*, Aug. 21, 1970.

77 "Girls in court after swoop," *Standard*, Sept. 29, 1970.

78 "Onyo kwa wenye mabaa," *Uhuru*, March 18, 1971; "Aibu mpaka lini?" editorial in *Uhuru*, Oct. 7, 1970.

79 Hatibu H. Kimbwera, letter to *Uhuru*, Aug. 31, 1970.

80 "13 Women Held in Second Police Swoop," *Standard*, Oct. 5, 1970.

81 Ibid.

82 For details of the events of October 3 as they were told to the court in testimony, see "Girl Denies 'Indecency' Charges," *Standard*, Jan. 28, 1971; "Witness sends Dar court into laughter," *Standard*, Feb. 8, 1971.

83 Of the women arrested on the same night as Joseph, most were given sentences of a 100/- fine or two months in prison. "Warning to Married Women," *Standard*, Oct. 7, 1970.

84 Public attention had been directed at the debate in 1970, in and out of the national assembly, of a controversial overhaul of Tanzania's Uniform Law of Marriage. Discussion of the bill, which was finally passed by the legislature in January 1971, raised questions about women and accumulation, while also displaying a culture of jocular masculinity that dominated the national assembly (see chapter 4).

85 The quotation is from Felician S. Makwaya, "Good Work," letter to *Standard*, Oct. 24, 1970.

86 Among the venues repeatedly targeted were the New Palace Hotel, the Airlines Hotel, and Margot's Night Club. See "Police swoop draws a blank," *Standard*, Nov. 1, 1970.

87 For an example of the insistence that police were targeting prostitutes, see Felician S. Makwaya, "Good Work," letter to *Standard*, Oct. 24, 1970. For hints of

a broader category of targets, see, for instance, "Warning to Married Women," *Standard*, Oct. 7, 1970; and "Police swoop draws a blank," *Standard*, Nov. 1, 1970.

88 Testimony by defense witness, Mr. Mwinyipembe, as described in "Witness sends Dar court into laughter," *Standard*, Feb. 6, 1971.

89 See "Girl Denies 'Indecency' Charges," *Standard*, Jan. 28, 1971, for a description of the UWT chair's testimony, and "No law on length of dress, court told," *Standard*, Feb. 13, 1971, for that of the defense counsel's statements.

90 "No law on length of dress, court told," *Standard*, Feb. 13, 1971.

91 "Mini girl cleared in test case," *Standard*, Feb. 18, 1971; "Court frees miniskirt girl," *Nationalist*, Feb. 18, 1971.

92 "'I don't think the mini is indecent,'" interview with Pauline Joseph, *Sunday News*, March 7, 1971.

93 Ibid.

94 Dixon Mubeya, letter to *Standard*, March 3, 1971.

95 "Sipendelei," letter to *Standard*, Nov. 12, 1969.

96 On the vigilante character of the TYL, see Brennan, "Youth, the TANU Youth League, and Managed Vigilantism in Dar es Salaam, Tanzania, 1925–73."

97 The quotation is from T. N. Mshuza, "Elimu na Maendeleo ya Wanawake," *Uhuru*, Nov. 7, 1970. The more conservative line promoted a hierarchy of women's worth to the nation, charging those with more advanced formal education with the duty of instructing their less fortunate sisters in the arts of modern life—even as this view went little beyond highlighting the realm of home economics. See, for instance, UWT officer Anna Mgaya's contribution to *Uhuru*'s "Women's Page": "Jinsi wanawake wanavyoweza kuhudumia Taifa," *Uhuru*, March 20, 1971.

98 T. N. Mshuza, "Elimu na Maendeleo ya Wanawake," *Uhuru*, Nov. 7, 1970.

99 T. N. Mshuza, "Wanawake wa Tanzania ya leo," *Uhuru*, Nov. 14, 1970. See also T. N. Mshuza's report on Esther Mwaikambo, Tanzania's first female medical doctor, in *Uhuru*, Feb. 13, 1971.

100 See, for instance, "Fundi wa Kwanza Mwanamke," *Uhuru*, March 13, 1971; T. N. Mshuza, "Tusidharauliwe katika kazi," *Uhuru*, Jan. 16, 1971; "Chakubanga" cartoon of *Uhuru*, March 16, 1971 (artist: C. Gregory).

101 For a characteristic comment on women and office work, see a letter to the *Standard* from "Akili-Kuambiana," July 13, 1970. Giving voice to perceptions of preferential treatment for "girls" in hiring for office jobs, this young man wrote, "Many experienced boys are visiting every office seeking for employment while you find most girls in Tanzania are enjoying life. The prohibition of employing Std. VII school leavers as clerks in government offices applies only to boys. It is surprising to note that many girls with Std. VII education are employed even in they don't have any kind of experience. You will find them roaming in groups competing in receiving telephone calls [competing for receptionist jobs?], as a result many girls do not want to get married simply because they are employed. . . . Girls will get married by boy[s] who will support them. What about boys?"

102 Theresia N. Mshuza, "Kwa nini ndoa nyingi kati ya wafanya kazi katika miji huvunjika?" *Uhuru*, Aug. 15, 1970.

103 Alli Abdallah, quoted in Mshuza, "Kwa nini?" *Uhuru*, Aug. 15, 1970.

104 Emiliana Chaulaya, quoted in Mshuza, "Kwa nini?" *Uhuru*, Aug. 15, 1970.

105 Mariamu Omari, quoted in Mshuza, "Kwa nini?" *Uhuru*, Aug. 15, 1970. Interviews with women who had worked in formal sector jobs in the 1960s and

1970s in Dar es Salaam confirmed that working gave them an autonomy vis-à-vis their husbands or boyfriends that they otherwise would have not had. Interviews with Sipora Kyara (Dar es Salaam, July 20, 2005), "Mama Kweka" (Dar es Salaam, July 25, 2005), Tukupasya Kapupa (Dar es Salaam, Aug. 3, 2005), Anne Methusela Majige (Dar es Salaam, July 20, 2005), Mwanaisha Salenge (Dar es Salaam, Aug. 12, 2005), Mwajuma Juma (Dar es Salaam, Aug. 2, 2005), Simbagile Swila (Dar es Salaam, Aug. 6, 2005), Fatuma Said (Dar es Salaam, July 23, 2005), "Lucyenga" (Dar es Salaam, Aug. 5, 2005).

106 Casian John Hale, quoted in Mshuza, "Kwa nini?" Uhuru, Aug. 15, 1970. The comments on dowries were made by Frank Mkwemba, quoted in the same article.

107 For instance, see Nchi Yetu, April and September 1970 and February 1971; Uhuru, April 26, 1970; Nationalist, May 1, 1971.

108 Reliable statistics on the number of women being hired in the formal sector are lacking, but there is some anecdotal evidence of such numbers being high, though not nearly as high as perceived in some quarters. See, for instance, T. N. Mshuza, "Tatizo la ukosefu wa kazi mijini," Uhuru, Oct. 17, 1970; exchange on "Women at Work" between Kessi Hassan Dibwa and a spokesperson for the Urafiki Textile Mill, Standard, June 29, 1970.

109 Thade S. Pella, letter to Uhuru, March 3, 1971.

110 J. T. Mnali, letter to Uhuru, Feb. 24, 1971.

111 "Mtumishi wa Serikali," letter to Uhuru, Feb. 5, 1971. One interesting feature of some of these letters on women and work was the expression by longtime, male civil servants of nostalgia for the work habits of the colonial period.

112 Buchuchu B. Kwazaho, letter to Uhuru, Feb. 15, 1971.

113 Ibid.

114 See, for instance, "Mtumishi wa Serikali," letter to Uhuru, Feb. 5, 1971; Buchuchu B. Kwazaho, letter to Uhuru, Feb. 15, 1971; "Tarishi wa Zamani," letter to Uhuru, Feb. 15, 1971.

115 Thade S. Pella, letter to Uhuru, March 3, 1971.

116 Bi. M. Mwaka, letter to Uhuru, March 19, 1971; Sarah Towela, letter to Standard, Oct. 4, 1970; "Miss E. Maria," letter to Standard, Oct. 25, 1970.

117 "Miss E. Maria," letter to Standard, Oct. 25, 1970.

118 Called the "War over Short Dresses" by the editors of Uhuru, the broader debate began with, and continued to feature, insistent critiques that the government was shirking its duty to intervene and eradicate indecent dress. See, for instance, Anselmi Nere, "'Taiti' katika Tanzania ya Ujamaa," letter to Uhuru, July 23, 1970; Pembe A. Ng'amba, "Mbona jambo hili latupya kando?" letter to Uhuru, July 30, 1970.

119 Anselmi Nere, "'Taiti' katika Tanzania ya Ujamaa," letter to Uhuru, July 23, 1970; Pembe A. Ng'amba, "Mbona jambo hili latupya kando?" letter to Uhuru, July 30, 1970. Uhuru's report on the parliamentary comments on dress, which both Nere and Pembe cited, consisted only of a couple of brief sentences buried deep in the paper's regular summary of National Assembly proceedings (the headline of which did not refer to dress). "Mambo ya Ulinzi yajadiliwe faraghani—Mbunge," Uhuru, July 17, 1970.

120 Bi. L. I. Minja, "Vazi Fupi Lidumu," letter to Uhuru, Aug. 6, 1970.

121 Pembe A. Ng'amba, letter to Uhuru, Aug. 11, 1970; Terry J. Maona, "Wazazi tunalaani vikale vazi lenu," letter to Uhuru, Aug. 15, 1970; C. A. Mnyangule,

"Mgunduzi wa Vazi Hilo Nani?" letter to *Uhuru*, Aug. 15, 1970; K. S. Litundubile Mkiu, "Sikiliza ya Wazee Wako," letter to *Uhuru*, Aug. 15, 1970; R. G. Chacha, "Kwa Nini Tuige?" letter to *Uhuru*, Aug. 15, 1970.

122 K. S. Litundubile Mkiu, letter to *Uhuru*, Aug. 15, 1970. For the animal comparisons, see Terry J. Maona, letter to *Uhuru*, Aug. 15, 1970; K. S. Litundubile Mkiu, letter to *Uhuru*, Aug. 15, 1970.

123 Bi. L. I. Minja, "Mtasema Mtachoka Hatusikii," letter to *Uhuru*, Aug. 18, 1970.

124 "Annoyed," letter to *Standard*, Sept. 17, 1970; Peter Claver F. Temba, letter to *Standard*, Oct. 6, 1970.

125 Peter Claver F. Temba, letter to *Standard*, Oct. 6, 1970.

126 This count is of interventions appearing in *Uhuru*, in which pages the debate mostly took place.

127 In additon to the many already-cited letters illustrating this, see "Aibu mpaka lini?" an editorial in *Uhuru*, Oct. 7, 1970, which, referring to miniskirts, lamented, "These days we are told that one of the characteristics desired before a girl is hired is what is called 'modern style clothes.'"

Chapter 3. Of Students, 'Nizers, and Comrades

1 Comaroff and Comaroff, "Refections on Youth."

2 For a study of some of the dynamics around youth in Tanzania and Zanzibar, see Burgess, "Youth and the Revolution," and Brennan, "Youth, the TANU Youth League and Managed Vigilantism." Some of the Tanzanian state's attempts to valorize a disciplined, youth vanguard drew inspiration from similar practices in socialist bloc states at the time. See Nothnagle, *Building the East German Myth*.

3 Although "'nizer," "naizesheni" and "'nization" were widely used terms in the 1960s and early 1970s, the only academic discussion of them that I have found is an unpublished paper from the 1970s by Micaela von Freyhold, "The Workers and the Nizers."

4 This shift can also be traced through the notable humanities and social science scholarship emerging from the University College of Dar es Salaam in the latter half of the 1960s and early 1970s. In the history department, the period of dominance for a liberal-nationalist historical approach was marked on either end by the publication of two important volumes: International Congress of African Historians, 1965 (Ranger, ed.), *Emerging Themes of African History*; and Kimambo and Temu, *A History of Tanzania*. The arrival on the scene of scholars working in Marxist and dependency school theory gradually led to the eclipsing of the liberal-nationalists and resulted in work like Rodney, *How Europe Underdeveloped Africa*, which Rodney wrote during his years in Dar es Salaam.

5 The detail of the demonstrators' choice of dress is from Coulson, *Tanzania: A Political Economy*, 225.

6 Morrison, *Education and Politics in Africa*, 244–45.

7 Examples of this dominant narrative include Coulson, *Tanzania*; Morrison, *Education and Politics in Africa*.

8 This paragraph is largely based on Morrison, *Education and Politics in Africa*, 75–87.

9 The Department of Education promoted the latter scheme in the face of a growing crisis of unemployed primary school leavers as a way to enable such

pupils to "play a more useful part in the development of the locality to which they belong." However, like similar initiatives before it, the plan drew intense criticism from Africans who saw it as a way to further deny to Tanganyika's African children the education that might ensure urban wage employment. In one case, villages near Mwanza burned down a school in protest of the policy, and African nationalists routinely voiced opposition to the plan. See Morrison, *Education and Politics in Africa*, 84–85. Ironically, perhaps, the postcolonial state's most comprehensive attempt to restructure education—the Education for Self-Reliance plan of 1967—bore striking resemblances to the colonial schemes of the 1950s. See Nyerere, *Education for Self-Reliance*.

10 Morrison, *Education and Politics in Africa*, 75.

11 Coulson, *Tanzania*, 224–25.

12 Barkan, *An African Dilemma*, 12.

13 Ibid., 35 n. 1.

14 Not until the 1970s did some of these rooms have to be shared (with bunk beds to accommodate the added students). A steady increase in student numbers and (particularly in the late 1980s and 1990s) a collapse of public funding led to the current housing conditions on campus in which students are forced to enter into informal bidding for a space sharing a bed in rooms housing at least four.

15 Morrison, *Education and Politics in Africa*, 249 n. 12.

16 Coulson, *Tanzania*, 224.

17 Nyerere, Address of the Chancellor on the 10th Anniversary of the University of Dar es Salaam, Aug. 29, 1980. Quoted in Mzirai Kangero, "The University and the State, 1964–1984," report prepared for the University of Dar es Salaam Faculty of Arts and Science, (mimeograph), 1984.

18 Nyerere, Address on the opening of the University College campus, Aug. 21, 1964, in Nyerere, *Freedom and Unity*, 306.

19 Government of Tanganyika, First Five-Year Plan (1964–69), quoted in Kangero, "The University and the State, 1964–84," 262.

20 Nyerere, *Freedom and Unity*, 309.

21 Saul, "Socialism in One Country," 261.

22 Naomi Kaihula, personal communication, Dar es Salaam, April 5, 2001.

23 "The Campus Rift Valley," *University Echo* (1972), no. 2, 7.

24 The quotation is from Mallya P. H., "Women's Attitude Questioned," *University Echo* February 1973, 6.

25 See, for instance, "Entertainment," *University Echo*, Feb. 20, 1970; "The Native Is Always There," *University Echo*, Aug. 8, 1970, 8; "Campus Whispers," *University Echo*, Oct. 16, 1972, 7; "The Campus in Brief," *University Echo*, February 1973, 4.

26 See, for instance, "Wolfson Corner," Feb. 20, 1970, 3; "Women's Attitude Questioned," *University Echo*, February 1973, 6; W. I. Msuya, "Minister Questioned (In Absentia) on Social Functions in Nkrumah Hall," October 1973, 20–21.

27 See, for instance, "Women's Attitude Questioned"; "Campus Male/Female Relations"; "Wolfson Baby House," *University Echo*, October 1973, 13.

28 A. V. Wilson, "Girls and Your Love Stars," *University Echo*, January 1975.

29 See, for instance, Mauri Yambo, "Purses Per Se," Aug. 8, 1970; "The Native Is Always There," *University Echo*, Aug. 8, 1970, 8; "Wolfson," March 1974, 31.

30 "Kaleidoscope, Campus Roundabout," *University Echo*, March 1974, 30.

31 See, for instance, "Women's Attitude Questioned," *University Echo*, October 1973, 6; "Echo Interviews a Wolfsonian," *University Echo*, January 1975, 19–21; S. J. Mwamba, "Campus Pressure Groups," *University Echo*, October 1973, 4; P. H. Mallya, "Campus Male/Female Relations," *University Echo*, October 1973, 7–8. For an alternate and more extensive reading of Punch, see Ryan Ronnenberg, "The Laughter on His Side: Mzee Punch and the Dialectic of the Foolish."

32 The quotations are from "Wolfson Corner," *University Echo*, Feb. 20, 1970, 3.

33 "Ah Me!" anonymous letter to the editor from a female student, *University Echo*, Aug. 8, 1970, 7; also see "A Freshman's Impressions," *University Echo*, Aug. 3, 1969.

34 "Echo Interviews a Wolfsonian," *University Echo*, January 1975, 19–21.

35 Miss Mary Hugo, "Counsel to Women," *University Echo*, October 1973, 9–10.

36 "Echo Interviews a Wolfsonian," *University Echo*, January 1975, 19–21.

37 The quotation is from "ECHO pays tribute to fresh women," *University Echo*, Aug. 8, 1970, 7.

38 Saul, "High-level Manpower for Socialism," 279.

39 Ibid.

40 United Republic of Tanzania, *Ten Years of National Service, 1963–1973*.

41 Morrison, *Education and Politics in Africa*, 238; Tanzania, *Ten Years of National Service*, 6. Letters from young people petitioning—often begging—for entrance into the National Service vividly illustrate the desirability of a service position for youth of a particular background (usually primary school leaver). Dozens of such handwritten letters are preserved in TNA 518 N.10/3.

42 Tanzania, *Ten Years of National Service*, 56.

43 Morrison, *Education and Politics in Africa*, 239.

44 B. M. Kimulson, letter to *Standard*, Dec. 17, 1965.

45 "Elton and Daniel," letter to *Standard*, Dec. 31, 1965.

46 "Baba Kabwella," letter to *Standard*, Jan. 6, 1966.

47 Elice Leo, letter to *Standard*, Jan. 3, 1966.

48 Juma A. Kilimo, letter to *Standard*, Dec. 24, 1966.

49 B. M. Kimulson, letter to *Standard*, Jan. 8, 1966 (emphasis added).

50 W. K. Parmena, letter to *Standard*, Jan. 19, 1966.

51 See *Standard*, Jan. 15, Jan. 22, and Feb. 2, 1966.

52 The three quotations, respectively, are from N. E. R. Mwakasungula, letter to *Standard*, Feb. 10, 1966; B. M. Kimulson, letter to *Standard*, Jan. 31, 1966; and Damien Zefrin Lubuva, letter to *Standard*, Jan. 14, 1966.

53 Damien Zefrin Lubuva, letter to *Standard*, Jan. 14, 1966.

54 Simmy M. Massawa, letter to *Standard*, Dec. 31, 1965.

55 A. B. Mkelle, letter to *Standard*, Feb. 14, 1966.

56 "Youth 'must know of country's need,'" *Standard*, Jan. 13, 1966.

57 "Students 'Could Become Outcasts,'" *Standard*, Feb. 17, 1966.

58 J. K. Nyerere, speech to the World University Service, June 27, 1966, reproduced in *Standard*, June 28, 1966.

59 "New Bill to Come on NS Says Kawawa," *Standard*, July 19, 1966.

60 "Student union votes to remove president," *Standard*, July 19, 1966; "Chagula plea for stability," *Standard*, July 25, 1966. A tradition at the University College, the "Baraza" was a semiformal gathering of students called on short notice to publicly discuss and take positions on issues of importance to students.

61 "New Bill to Come on NS Says Kawawa," Standard, July 19, 1966; "Service plan defended," Standard, Oct. 4, 1966; Morrison, Education and Politics in Africa, 239–40.

62 "Proposals on Compulsory N.S. Released," Standard, Sept. 28, 1966; Morrison, Education and Politics in Africa, 240.

63 See both the Standard and the Nationalist for the weeks of Oct. 1–21, 1966.

64 Although there was considerable debate on the issue—a debate that lasted two days—the lone MP voting against the final bill was F. K. Chogga of Iringa South, who had walked out of the debate protesting that it was being rushed. "Service plan approved," Standard, Oct. 5, 1966.

65 "White Paper Approved," Nationalist, Oct. 5, 1966.

66 "Service plan approved," Standard, Oct. 5, 1966.

67 W. Mufumya, Standard, Oct. 10, 1966. See also the letter by O. L. K. Chawe of NAUTS in Standard, Oct. 21, 1966, in which the author contends that "history has shown that young men are as wise as other people and can lead nations. In African tradition some have participated in discussions with the so-called old wise men."

68 University College TANU Club, quoted in "Tanu club students attack NS," Standard Oct. 19, 1966.

69 G. D. T. Lusinde, letter to Nationalist, Oct. 19, 1966.

70 "Socialist Student," letter to Nationalist, Oct. 15, 1966. See also Kawawa's speech to a National Service officers' seminar, in which he pointedly declared that "youths must know that life did not mean comfort but meant difficulties." Nationalist, Oct. 18, 1966.

71 National Union of Tanzania Students, official statement quoted in "Students Reject N.S. White Paper," Nationalist, Oct. 1, 1966.

72 "Tanu Club students attack NS," Standard, Oct. 19, 1966.

73 C. L. K. Chawe, National Union of Tanzania Students, letter to Standard, Oct. 21, 1966.

74 Nationalist, Nov. 13, 1965.

75 "Students trap envoy," Standard, Jan. 29, 1966.

76 "Student protests," Sunday News, Feb. 20, 1966.

77 "Indian Students Revolt," Standard, Oct. 6, 1966.

78 Morrison, Education and Politics in Africa, 244–45; "Youths back Mwalimu," Standard, Oct. 24, 1966. For reports of Indonesian student protests in the Tanzanian press, see "Troops use bayonets on students," Standard, Feb. 25, 1966, and "Sukarno Ban on Students," Standard, Feb. 27, 1966.

79 Sunday News, Oct. 23, 1966, quoted in Morrison, Education and Politics in Africa, 244.

80 For accounts of this speech, see "Rais Achukua Hatua Kali Baada ya Maandamano," Nchi Yetu, November 1966; Morrison, Education and Politics in Africa; William Edgett Smith, We Must Run While They Walk.

81 Julius Nyerere, quoted in Smith, We Must Run, 29–30.

82 "Ministers Cut Down Their Salaries," Nationalist, Oct. 25, 1966.

83 Morrison, Education and Politics in Africa, 245.

84 "Students' Protest Snubbed," Nationalist, Oct. 24, 1966; "Youths back Mwalimu," Standard, Oct. 24, 1966.

85 For example, see "Increasing Support for Mwalimu," Nationalist, Oct. 26,

1966; "Entitled to Know," editorial in *Nationalist*, Oct. 26, 1966; "Overwhelming Support: Parents Condemn Unpatriotic Sons," *Nationalist*, Oct. 27, 1966; "Regions Rally to Nyerere's Action," *Standard*, Oct. 26, 1966; "The Country Approves: Nyerere Applauded for Firm Action," Oct. 25, 1966; "Students are Condemned by TAPA and UWT," *Standard*, Oct. 27, 1966.

86 "Challenge to Youth," editorial in *Nationalist*, Nov. 3, 1966.

87 "Students' Expulsion," editorial in *Nationalist*, Oct. 24, 1966.

88 NAUTS statement, as quoted in "Students apologise," *Nationalist*, Nov. 5, 1966. The apology came over a week after an earlier NAUTS statement that, while attempting to be conciliatory without issuing an apology, had included the rather defiant line, "We [students] could be against the government, TANU . . . and the President, but never against the nation." "Statement by Students' Union," *Nationalist*, Oct. 27, 1966.

89 Nyerere, *Education for Self-Reliance*. See also Morrison, *Students and Politics in Africa*. For an incisive critique of ESR, written by one of the University College's former student leftists as the plan was being implemented, see Karim Hirji, "School, Education and Underdevelopment in Tanzania."

90 "Proposals for Discussion Tabled by a Group of Staff Members," in "Report: Conference on the Role of the University College, Dar es Salaam in a Socialist Tanzania," Dar es Salaam, March 11–13, 1967 (mimeograph).

91 Ibid., 117–19.

92 Ibid., 118–21.

93 Ibid., 122–31.

94 For instance, see "Yankee No," letter to *Nationalist*, Oct. 31, 1966; "Another Socialist," letter to *Nationalist*, Nov. 3, 1966; and a call for reforms by one of the Committee of Nine immediately following the National Service crisis: Grant Kamenju, letter to *Nationalist*, Oct. 29, 1966.

95 In addition to the conference report itself, the remainder of this paragraph is drawn from a reading of a few, mostly firsthand accounts commenting on the debate over reform at the University College: Barkan, *An African Dilemma*, 17–19; Coulson, *Tanzania*, 227–28; Kamenju, "In Defense of a Socialist Concept of Universities," 15–17; Morrison, *Education and Politics in Africa*, 268–69; Saul, "High-Level Manpower for Socialism."

96 "Final Recommendations of the Conference on the Role of the University College, Dar es Salaam in a Socialist Tanzania Held on 11th and 12th March, 1967," in "Report" (1967), 56–59; the quotation is on page 57. Also see "Recommendations of the Conference Committees" in "Report" (1967), 47–56.

97 Coulson, *Tanzania*, 228.

98 Saul, "Radicalism and the Hill"; reprinted in Lionel Cliffe and John Saul, eds., *Socialism in Tanzania*, 289.

99 Y. Museveni, "My Three Years in Tanzania (Glimpses of the Struggle Between Revolution and Reaction)."

100 Issa Shivji, "Rodney and Radicalism on the Hill, 1966–1974," speech delivered at a memorial symposium to celebrate Walter Rodney's life, held on July 22, 1980, at the University of Dar es Salaam; also published in *MajiMaji 43*, and reprinted in Shivji, *Intellectuals at the Hill: Essays and Talks, 1969–1993*, 34.

101 Museveni, "My Three Years," 13; Shivji, "Rodney and Radicalism," 34.

102 Museveni, "My Three Years," 13.

103 Shivji, *Intellectuals at the Hill.*

104 Issa Shivji, "What Is Left of the Left Intellectual at 'the Hill,'" a lecture delivered during an electricity outage at the University College on Jan. 10, 1992; reprinted in Shivji, *Intellectuals at the Hill,* 201.

105 Shivji, "Rodney and Radicalism," 37. The quotation, cited by Shivji, was part of an official USARF mission statement.

106 Shivji, "Rodney and Radicalism," 36; Saul, "Radicalism and the Hill," 290.

107 Shivji, "Rodney and Radicalism," 37.

108 Statement from the chairman, *Cheche* no. 1 (1969), quoted in Shivji, "Rodney and Radicalism," 38.

109 From the announcement for Rag Day 1968 published in the *University Echo* and quoted in Shivji, "Rodney and Radicalism," 35.

110 Ibid., 35–36.

111 The preceding description of the events of November 9, 1968, are culled from newspaper reports, letters to the editor, and Shivji, "Rodney and Radicalism," 35–36.

112 S. Amos Wako, Chairman, World University Service (Tanzania), letter to *Standard,* Nov. 13, 1968.

113 See letters by Bak Orach-Oywelowo (Nov. 18), E. R. Byarushengo (Nov. 26), "Pro-Rag Student" (Nov. 15)—all in *Standard,* 1968.

114 See, for example, letters by "Concerned" (Nov. 19), E. R. Byarushengo (Nov. 26), both in *Standard,* 1968.

115 Ajmal Andani, letter to *Standard,* Nov. 19, 1968.

116 E. R. Byarushengo, letter to *Standard,* Nov. 26, 1968.

117 The quotation is from Yoweri Museveni's letter to *Standard,* Nov. 18, 1968.

118 Museveni, USARF Chairman, letter to *Standard,* Nov. 18, 1968.

119 Andrew Lyall, letter to *Standard,* Nov. 18, 1968.

120 B. G. Choka and Wasilwa Barasa, letters to *Standard,* Nov. 19, 1968.

121 Walter Rodney, speech delivered to the East and Central African Youth Seminar, Dar es Salaam, Dec. 10, 1969; published in *Nationalist,* Dec. 11, 1969.

122 Shivji, "Rodney and Radicalism," 32; Saul "Radicalism and the Hill," 290.

123 "Revolutionary Hot Air," editorial in *Nationalist,* Dec. 13, 1969.

124 "Dr. Rodney Clarifies," letter to *Nationalist,* Dec. 15, 1969.

125 See Saul, "Radicalism and the Hill," 291.

126 Museveni, "My Three Years," 14; "Mwalimu Restores Rationality on the Hill," *University Echo,* Feb. 20, 1970, 1.

127 Saul, "Radicalism and the Hill," 291; and "Mwalimu Restores Rationality on the Hill," *University Echo,* Feb. 20, 1970, 1.

128 Museveni, "My Three Years" (1970), 14. For another memory of the above event, see Swift, *Dar Days,* 107–9.

129 On this charged mood, from the perspective of a student frustrated with USARF, see Ementono Ekarapa J., "No Longer Sensible," *University Echo,* Feb. 20, 1970.

130 See the advertisement for Up with People's performance at the Kilimanjaro Hotel, *Standard,* Oct. 31, 1970.

131 "Students snub American entertainers," *Sunday News,* Oct. 16, 1970.

132 Issa Shivji, "Tanzania: The Silent Class Struggle," *Cheche* special issue (1970); reprinted in Shivji et al., *The Silent Class Struggle,* 39.

133 "Hill Students' Front Asked to Cease," *Nationalist*, Nov. 13, 1970.

134 "Students' Front," masthead editorial in *Nationalist*, Nov. 14, 1970.

135 "Hill Students' Front Asked to Cease," *Nationalist*, Nov. 13, 1970.

136 "Students' Front," masthead editorial in the *Nationalist*, Nov. 14, 1970. Also see "Ban Claim by USARF," *Standard*, Nov. 13, 1970.

137 Issa Shivji, "What Is Left of the Left Intellectual at 'the Hill'?" Public Talk at the University College, Dar es Salaam, Jan. 10, 1992; reprinted in Shivji, *Intellectuals at the Hill*, 208.

138 In official reaction to *Cheche*'s Shivji issue, it may not have helped that Shivji was of South Asian origin, though I have not found mention of this in statements and discussions of USARF. On the relationship between Tanzania's sizeable South Asian community and nationalism, see Brennan, "Nation, Race and Urbanization in Dar es Salaam, Tanzania, 1916–1976."

139 Shivji, *Intellectuals at the Hill*, 38.

140 The tension between these constructions of youth was embodied in a statement like the following, contained in a caption in a *Nationalist* feature on the first National Youth Festival: "As communication stands now in the world, it would be very easy for the youth of this country to be involved in Beatlemania and the Hippies. But the youth has shown us that they have no time. They have time only for activities which will strengthen this nation." *Nationalist*, Jan. 31, 1968.

141 Honwana and de Boeck, eds., *Makers and Breakers*.

142 Bayart, *L'état en Afrique*, 151, as quoted in Nicholas Argenti, *The Intestines of the State*, 185 (trans. Nicholas Argenti).

143 Honwana and de Boeck, eds., *Makers and Breakers*; Argenti, *The Intestines of the State*; Richards, *Fighting for the Rain Forest*.

144 Richards, *Fighting for the Rain Forest*; Honwana, "The Pain of Agency, the Agency of Pain"; Argenti, *The Intestines of the State*.

Chapter 4. "Marriage Goes Metric"

1 "Marriage Goes Metric," *Nationalist*, March 25, 1970, 5. All quotations in the following paragraph are from this article.

2 "Marriage Discussed by N.E.C.," *Standard*, Sept. 24, 1969.

3 Lovett, "'She Thinks She's Like a Man,'" 49; Wilson, "Zig-Zag Change"; Jane Guyer, "The Value of Beti Bridewealth"; Lindsay, "Money, Marriage and Masculinity on the Colonial Nigerian Railway," 140; Peel, *Ijeshas and Nigerians*, 118–19; Chanock, *Law, Custom, and Social Order*.

4 See, for instance, Mann, *Marrying Well*; Byfield, "Women, Marriage, Divorce and the Emerging Colonial State in Abeokuta (Nigeria), 1892–1904"; Oppong, *Marriage Among a Matrilineal Elite*; Schroeder, "'Gone to Their Second Husbands'"; Wambui wa Karanja, "'Outside Wives' and 'Inside Wives' in Nigeria"; Obbo, "The Old and the New in East African Elite Marriages."

5 See Thomas, *The Politics of the Womb*, chapter 5, for an illuminating analysis of the debate over the Affiliation Act in 1960s Kenya. For an examination of the debate over the failed attempt to enact an overhaul of the Kenyan marriage law, see Thomas, *The Politics of the Womb*, 157–58, and Thomas, "Contestation, Construction, and Reconstitution."

6 See Mbembe, *On the Postcolony*, chapter 3.

7 Ghai, "The New Marriage Law in Tanzania," 101.

8 For an analysis of the Kenyan attempt, see Thomas, *Politics of the Womb*, 157–58; and Thomas, "Contestation, Construction, and Reconstitution."

9 Read, "A Milestone in the Integration of Personal Laws," 19.

10 Calaguas, Drost, and Fluet, "Legal Pluralism and Women's Rights."

11 Ghai, "The New Marriage Law in Tanzania," 101–2.

12 Government Paper No. 1 of 1969, "Uniform Law of Marriage," as published in *Standard*, Sept. 10, 1969, 4.

13 As Lynn Thomas has noted, this attempt to balance validation of religious and customary practice with a commitment to women's rights was also a prominent feature of the (ultimately failed) attempts to reform the marriage law in Kenya in the late 1960s and 1970s. Thomas, *The Politics of the Womb*, 157–58; Thomas "Contestation, Contruction, and Reconstitution."

14 Majadiliano ya Bunge (Hansard), Taarifa Rasmi, March, 17–23, 1970, 174.

15 Ibid., 177.

16 Government Paper No. 1 of 1969, as published in *Standard*, Sept. 10, 1969, 4.

17 "Marriage Bill," editorial in *Nationalist*, Jan. 19, 1971, 4.

18 Chatterjee, *The Nation and Its Fragments*.

19 See, for instance, Kawawa's statements to Parliament reported in "M.P.s give go-ahead to marriage code," *Standard*, March 22, 1970, 1: "On giving a woman the right to take action against another woman who had committed adultery with her husband, Mr. Kawawa said that there was nothing strange about this as it was common to see a woman in a village taking action against another woman who slept with her husband. He said that the law was just intended to give women the right to take action against other women who run with their husband. He said this was human rights and it had grounds."

20 "Marriage," editorial in *Standard*, Sept. 10, 1969.

21 Almost universally, the term used in the marriage debate to describe bridewealth—the transfer of payments or goods by the husband or his family to the bride's family—was "dowry." Despite the difference in meaning between the two terms, I have chosen here and in much of this chapter to use the term "dowry" rather than "bridewealth"—especially when discussing interventions in the debate—in order to hew to the term used by participants in the debate.

22 Government Paper No. 1 of 1969, as published in *Standard*, Sept. 10, 1969, 4.

23 See "Kawawa Winds Up Marriage Bill Debate," *Standard*, Jan. 27, 1971, and "Marriage Story," *Standard*, March 22, 1970.

24 For a thorough analysis of this Kenyan debate, see Thomas, "Contestation, Construction, and Reconstitution."

25 "Marriage," editorial in *Standard*, Sept. 10, 1969, 4.

26 "Marriage Discussed by N.E.C.," *Standard*, Sept. 24, 1969.

27 "Marriage," editorial in *Standard*, Oct. 9, 1969, 4.

28 *Standard*, Sept. 28, 1969, 1; *Standard*, Dec. 2, 1969, 1.

29 John Z. Nzwala, letter to *Standard*, Oct. 14, 1969, 4.

30 Simbaulanga Adolphe, letter to *Standard*, May 23, 1970, 6.

31 "Feeling Cheated," letter to *Standard*, Sept. 15, 1969, 2.

32 "A Wife," letter to *Standard*, Sept. 23, 1969, 2; J. A. Wadood, letter to *Standard*, Sept. 18, 1969, 4. See also the (different) letter by "A Wife," *Standard*, Oct. 24, 1969, 4.

33 Mrs. T. S. Karumuna, letter to *Standard*, Sept. 24, 1969, 4.

34 See, for instance, unsigned letter to *Standard*, Sept. 24, 1969, 4, and the resolutions by the UWT over the bill, discussed below.

35 "White Paper on Marriage Explained," *Nationalist*, Sept. 25, 1969, 5. A stipulation that polygamous unions must have the consent of the existing spouses was also a feature of the Kenyan draft bill on marriage. See Thomas, *The Politics of the Womb*, 158.

36 Unsigned letter to *Standard*, Sept. 24, 1969, 4.

37 Unsigned letter to *Standard*, Sept. 24, 1969, 4.

38 Alice Mkumbukwa, letter to *Standard*, Oct. 1, 1969, 4.

39 "Feeling Cheated," letter to *Standard*, Sept. 15, 1969, 2. See also the letter by "A Wife," who in arguing against polygamy, wrote, "Cocks and hens . . . cannot be taken as models for developing our society. Man has passed the developmental stage of those already millions of years ago. And, even if it is understandable that some men still enjoy the feeling of a cock among hens, women don't want to feel like hens around the cock. Not in the 20th century!" *Standard*, Oct. 24, 1969, 4.

40 "UWT Condemns Polygamy," *Nationalist*, Sept. 6, 1969, 8.

41 Ibid.; "Heated Debate at U.W.T.," *Standard*, Sept. 6, 1969, 1.

42 Mbilinyi, "The 'New Woman' and Traditional Norms in Tanzania."

43 Geiger, *TANU Women*, esp. chapter 9.

44 "One Wife Is Enough, Says U.W.T.," *Standard*, March 5, 1970, 1. Such sentiments were the source of occasional criticisms launched by young single women that the UWT catered overwhelmingly to the needs of married women and neglected the interests of young, single women. See, for instance, "Is UWT for Married Women Only?" letter to *Nationalist*, July 15, 1971, 4.

45 M. K. Kazwika, letter to *Standard*, Sept. 24, 1969, 4.

46 For instance, see also A. R. Mtui, letter to *Standard*, Oct. 2, 1969, 4.

47 "Neptus," letter to *Standard*, Oct. 7, 1969, 9.

48 Miss Hyperrhenia Rufa, letter to *Standard*, Oct. 9, 1969, 4.

49 Mrs. J. S. M., letter to *Standard*, Oct. 16, 1969, 4.

50 "Political Juggler," letter to *Standard*, Oct. 14, 1969, 4.

51 E. K. Buberwa, letter to *Standard*, Sept. 23, 1969, 2.

52 S. L. Mwinuka, letter to *Standard*, Oct. 15, 1969, 4.

53 K. K. John, letter to *Standard*, Oct. 17, 1969, 4.

54 Ibine A. J. Mwabwalwa, letter to *Nationalist*, Sept. 16, 1969, 4.

55 "Nuptus," letter to *Standard*, Oct. 7, 1969, 9.

56 Thomas, *The Politics of the Womb*, 170.

57 Ibine A. J. Mwabwalwa, letter to *Nationalist*, Sept. 16, 1969, 4.

58 O. O. Ntima, letter to *Standard*, Oct. 13, 1969, 2.

59 On the ubiquity of the widespread charge of exploitation (*unyonyaji*) in Tanzanian official discourse of the 1960s and 1970s, see Brennan, "Blood Enemies: Exploitation and Urban Citizenship in the Nationalist Political Thought of Tanzania, 1958–75."

60 S. S. Selubyogo, letter to *Standard*, Oct. 17, 1969, 4.

61 Ibid.

62 "A Husband," letter to *Standard*, Nov. 21, 1969, 6.

63 Majadiliano ya Bunge (Hansard), Taarifa Rasmi, March 17–23, 1970, 220–21. See also the statement by Bi. Machibya (207) for another expression of exasperation

with husbands' spending money on entertainment, food, drink, and women outside the home while materially neglecting the senior wife at home.

64 Majadiliano ya Bunge (Hansard), Taarifa Rasmi, March 17–23, 1970, 198.

65 Ibid., 178.

66 Ibid., 180.

67 Ibid., 191.

68 See, for instance, ibid., 298, 312–13.

69 Ibid., 190.

70 Ibid., 193; Majadiliano ya Bunge (Hansard), Taarifa Rasmi, Jan. 19–25, 1971.

71 Majadiliano ya Bunge (Hansard), Taarifa Rasmi, March 17–23, 1970, 193.

72 Ibid., 300.

73 Mbembe, "Provisional Notes on the Postcolony," 9, quoted in Thomas, *Politics of the Womb*, 170.

74 Wipper, "The Politics of Sex," 479–80.

75 Kassam, "Comments on the White Paper."

76 Ibid.

77 See, for instance, Majadiliano ya Bunge (Hansard), Taarifa Rasmi, Jan. 19–25, 1971, 80, 135–38; *Standard*, Jan. 22, 1971.

78 "Marriage Bill," *Nationalist*, Jan. 19, 1971, 4; "'Bill Does Not Interfere with Religions,'" *Nationalist*, Jan. 23, 1971, 1; "Kawawa Winds Up Marriage Bill Debate," *Nationalist*, Jan. 27, 1971; "Refer Marriages Bill to Peasants, Urge MPs," *Nationalist*, Jan. 22, 1971.

79 "Marriage Bill Goes Through," *Nationalist*, Jan. 28, 1971, 8.

80 Ibid., 8.

81 I am grateful to Lynn Thomas for pointing this out.

82 The "Bachelor" question in this section's head is from a letter to *Standard*, Oct. 22, 1969, 4.

83 Peter Mwitta, Jr., letter to *Standard*, Sept. 20, 1969, 4.

84 A. S. Magooge, letter to *Standard*, Sept. 17, 1969, 4.

85 Peter Mwitta, Jr., letter to *Standard*, Sept. 20, 1969, 4.

86 See, for instance, M. A. M. Haulle's letter to *Standard* on Oct. 1, 1969, 4, for an extended meditation on all of the possible undesirable scenarios that might emerge under an installments regime.

87 Peter Mwitta, Jr., letter to *Standard*, Sept. 20, 1969, 4; for letters supporting the abolishing of the dowry system, see Muyooki Katambi, letter to *Standard*, Oct. 8, 1969, 4; Mhoja Hamis, letter to *Standard*, Oct. 9, 1969, 4.

88 "Matongo VM," letter to *Standard*, Oct. 10, 1969, 4; "Matongo," letter to *Standard*, Oct. 22, 1969, 4; Kamugumya Lugakingira, letter to *Standard*, Oct. 7, 1969, 9; Mhoja Hamis, letter to *Standard*, Oct. 9, 1969, 4.

89 "No Dowry," letter to *Standard*, Oct. 29, 1969, 4.

90 G. J. Kinyaoiko, letter to *Standard*, Sept. 26, 1969, 4.

91 Mrs. S. Nyakire, letter to *Standard*, Sept. 25, 1969, 7. The geographic and ethnic labels being deployed here were freighted with complex meanings in relation to material inequality. Tanzanians whose family origins were in the coastal region around Dar es Salaam (as opposed to those migrating to the capital, commonly from upcountry) were often identified as of Zaramo ethnicity. In the 1960s, in terms of economic and social capital Dar es Salaam residents born on the coast were often less well off than those who had migrated to the capital from upcountry

regions (such as Musoma). What is especially curious about Mrs. Nyakire's statement, however, is the fact that her interlocutor, A. S. Magooge, identified himself in his letter as being "from Musoma" and as a migrant to the coast. Nyakire's questioning of his Musoma (and upcountry) roots, and her hinting that he may as well be Zaramo were therefore a way of mocking his limited means.

92 Quotes are from Y. M. Mdage, letter to *Standard*, Oct. 8, 1969, 4, and Mhoja Hamis, letter to *Standard*, Oct. 9, 1969, 4.

93 Sylvester M. Nyag'ana, letter to *Standard*, Oct. 11, 1969, 4.

94 A. S. Magooge, letter to *Standard*, Oct. 9, 1969, 4.

95 Peter Mwitta, Jr., letter to *Standard*, Oct. 14, 1969, 4. The precise marking by Mwitta of 1954 as the endpoint of a period when herds were plentiful is particularly intriguing as a generational marker. It was also the year in which the ruling party, TANU, was formed. It also might be expressive of the demographics of the young male anxiety being expressed in the dowry commentary.

96 A. S. Magooge, letter to *Standard*, Oct. 9, 1969, 4; "Matongo VM," letter to *Standard*, Oct. 10, 1969, 4.

97 Thomas, *The Politics of the Womb*, 151.

98 D. C. Shayo, letter to *Standard*, Oct. 18, 1969, 4; see also "No Dowry," Oct. 29, 1969, 4.

99 Sylvester M. Nyang'ana, letter to *Standard*, Oct. 11, 1969, 4.

100 A. D. S. Mwakaje, letter to *Standard*, Oct. 15, 1969, 4.

101 See, for instance, "Miss J.S.M.," letter to *Standard*, Oct. 16, 1969, 4; and "Not for Sale," letter to *Standard*, Oct. 1, 1969, 4.

102 Lovett, "'She Thinks Like a Man'"; Lovett, "On Power and Powerlessness: Marriage and Political Metaphor in Colonial Western Tanzania."

103 *1967 Population Census*, quoted in Claeson and Egero, "Migration and the Urban Population," 4.

104 "Realist," letter to *Standard*, Oct. 2, 1969, 4.

105 Ibid. See also Didier R. Bashome, letter to *Standard*, Oct. 11, 1969, 4.

106 "Bachelor," letter to *Standard*, Oct. 22, 1969, 4.

107 "MP hits at new marriage code," *Standard*, Jan. 23, 1970, 5.

108 The quotations are from "Experienced," letter to *Standard*, Oct. 2, 1969, 4, and "Kiyengo," letter to *Standard*, Sept. 26, 1969, 4, respectively.

109 Peter R. Kamugisha, letter to *Standard*, Sept. 18, 1969, 4.

110 (Rev.) C. K. Omari, letter to *Standard*, Sept. 30, 1969, 4.

111 For example, see C. R. Mulokozi, letter to *Standard*, Sept. 30, 1969, 4.

112 "A Civil Servant," letter to *Standard*, Sept. 23, 1969, 2.

113 C. J. Mtenga, letter to *Standard*, Oct. 9, 1969, 4.

114 "Bachelor," letter to *Standard*, Oct. 22, 1969, 4.

115 Ibid.

116 Bayart, *The State in Africa*.

117 See, for example, "Realist," letter to *Standard*, Oct. 30, 1969, 4.

118 For example, see "Bachelor," letter to *Standard*, Oct. 22, 1969, 4.

119 Ibid.

120 Mbembe, "Provisional Notes on the Postcolony"; the quotation is from page 2.

121 See "Janja Yake," *Ngurumo*, Sept. 15, 1966, 1; "Kamkosa naizi kwa dufamani vinono," *Ngurumo*, April 29, 1966, 4; "Wake za watu wawili wafumaniana kwa naizi," *Ngurumo*, May 5, 1966, 3; "Kaamriwa asiingie chumbani mpaka saa sita

usiku," *Ngurumo*, May 19, 1966, 3; "Janja Yake," *Ngurumo*, Oct. 12, 1966, 2; "Janja Yake," *Ngurumo*, Sept. 16, 1966, 1; "Kisura mpenda kufilisi wanaume kapindu-liwa," *Ngurumo*, Oct. 21, 1966, 4; "Janja Yake," *Ngurumo*, Oct. 13, 1966, 1.

122 See, for instance, A. Adija, letter to *Ngurumo*, Sept. 17, 1966, 2; P. R. Banzil, letter to *Ngurumo*, Sept. 24, 1966, 2; A. K. Dome, letter to *Ngurumo*, Sept. 24, 1966, 2.

123 "Kisura kacharazwa mikwaju taiti ikamvuka," *Ngurumo*, June 7, 1966, 4.

124 "Gea Yako," *Ngurumo*, Sept. 6, 1966. The phrase "master plan" (or "masta-plan") was rendered in English in the original.

125 See, for example, "Kama juso lake baya hatakiwi," *Ngurumo*, July 5, 1966, 1; "Yaya na taiti," *Ngurumo*, Aug. 16, 1966, 1; "Kisura kamsahau mtoto wa miezi 6 dansini," *Ngurumo*, Feb. 8, 1965, 4; "Watoto kapigwa," *Ngurumo*, Feb. 17, 1966, 3.

126 Examples of such endings include "Kisura kacharazwa mikwaji taiti ikam-vuka," *Ngurumo*, June 7, 1966, 4; "Kisura kakojolea chumbani," *Ngurumo*, June 8, 1966, 4; "Kisura kakojolea chumbani kasusiwa chumba," *Ngurumo*, July 28, 1966.

127 L. A. Sherehe, "Naizi Mwawaonea," *Ngurumo*, June 22, 1966, 3.

128 "Kaamriwa asiingie chumbani mpaka saa sita usiku," *Ngurumo*, May 19, 1966, 3.

129 "Magari ya Serikali Yasibebe Visura—Saileni," *Ngurumo*, June 17, 1966, 4.

130 See, for instance, "Kamwacha mkewe kwa taiti lakini matunzo yake ni ma-gumu," *Ngurumo*, May 24, 1966, 3; "Kamdhania polo kumbe anazo noti," *Ngu-rumo*, Sept. 17, 1966, 4; "Kisura mpenda kufilisi, wanaume kapinduliwa," *Ngu-rumo*, Oct. 21, 1966, 4.

Conclusion

1 Apter, *The Pan-African Nation*, 105.

2 Hansen and Stepputat, eds., *States of Imagination*, 5.

3 For a classic argument on the Tanzanian state's weakness in "capturing" its citizens, see Hyden, *Beyond Ujamaa*. Mbembe uses the term *commandement* to de-note "the authoritarian modality" in its embrace of "the images and structures of power and coercion, the instruments and agents of their enactment, and a degree of rapport between those who give orders and those who are supposed to obey them, without, of course, discussing them." Mbembe, "Provisional Notes on the Postcolony," n. 7.

4 Mbembe, "Provisional Notes on the Postcolony."

5 I thank Lynn Thomas for helping me think this point through.

6 Clifford, *Routes*, 10.

7 Ibid.

8 On "ujamaa villagization," see Schneider, "Developmentalism and Its Fail-ings: Why Rural Development Went Wrong in 1960s and 1970s Tanzania"; von Freyhold, *Ujamaa Villages in Tanzania: Analysis of a Social Experiment*.

9 Interviews with James Nindi (Dar es Salaam, Oct. 9, 2000), Mwanaisha Salenge (Dar es Salaam, Aug. 12, 2005), Miriam Zialor (Dar es Salaam, May 3, 2001).

10 Askew, *Performing the Nation*, 184–91.

11 Graebner, "The *Ngoma* Impulse: From Club to Nightclub in Dar es Salaam"; Joseph, *Nomadic Identities*, 54.

12 Author's field notes. Interview with Mathias Machimba (Dar es Salaam, Nov. 4, 2000, and Jan. 30, 2001).

13 Author's field notes, April 11, 2001.

14 Indeed, one of Dar es Salaam's early rap groups, in reference to the professions of its members' parents, named itself The Deplowmatz. On hip-hop music and culture in Dar es Salaam, see the work of Ian Alexander Perullo, especially "The Life That I Live" and "Hooligans and Heroes."

15 Burton, "Urchins, Loafers and the Cult of the Cowboy."

16 Interviews with Mathias Machimba (Dar es Salaam, Nov. 4, 2000, and Jan. 30, 2001), Limi Ally (Dar es Salaam, July 18, 2004), Majeshi Wanzagi (Dar es Salaam, Feb. 28, 2001), Sabbi Masanja (Dar es Salaam, April 27, 2001), Miriam Zialor (Dar es Salaam, May 3, 2001), Esther Ngomba (Dar es Salaam, July 20, 2004).

Bibliography

Archives

Africa Collection, Library of the School of Oriental and African Studies; London, United Kingdom
East Africana Collection, Library of the University of Dar es Salaam; Dar es Salaam, Tanzania
Melville J. Herskovits Library of African Studies, Northwestern University; Evanston, Illinois
Tanzania National Archives (TNA); Dar es Salaam, Tanzania

Newspapers and Periodicals

Cheche [Dar es Salaam]
Daily News [Dar es Salaam]
East Africa Journal [Nairobi]
Kwetu [Dar es Salaam]
MajiMaji [Dar es Salaam]
Mambo Leo [Dar es Salaam]
Mwenge [Dar es Salaam]
Nationalist [Dar es Salaam]
Nchi Yetu [Dar es Salaam]
Ngurumo [Dar es Salaam]
Standard [Dar es Salaam]
Sunday News [Dar es Salaam]
Transition [Kampala]
Uhuru [Dar es Salaam]
University Echo [Dar es Salaam]

Interviews

James Nindi (Dar es Salaam, Oct. 9, 2000)
Mathias Machimba (Dar es Salaam, Nov. 4, 2000 and Jan. 30, 2001)
Majeshi Wanzagi (Dar es Salaam, Feb. 28, 2001)
Omar Mwaulanga (Dar es Salaam, March 16, 2001)
Generali Ulimwengu (Dar es Salaam, April 20, 2001)
Sabbi Masanja (Dar es Salaam, April 27, 2001)
Miriam Zialor (Dar es Salaam, May 3, 2001)
Limi Ally (Dar es Salaam, July 18, 2004)

Esther Ngomba (Dar es Salaam, July 20, 2004)
Sipora Kyara (Dar es Salaam, July 20, 2005)
Anne Methusela Majige (Dar es Salaam, July 20, 2005)
Fatuma Said (Dar es Salaam, July 23, 2005)
"Mama Kweka" (Dar es Salaam, July 25, 2005)
Mwajuma Juma (Dar es Salaam, Aug. 2, 2005)
Tukupasya Kapupa (Dar es Salaam, Aug. 3, 2005)
"Lucyenga" (Dar es Salaam, Aug. 5, 2005)
Simbagile Swila (Dar es Salaam, Aug. 6, 2005)
Mwanaisha Salenge (Dar es Salaam, Aug. 12, 2005)

Films

A Panther in Africa (dir. Aaron Matthews, 2004)
Zonk! (dir. Hyman Kirstein, African Film Productions, 1950), available at the University of Michigan's Film and Video Library.

Books, Journals, and Dissertations

Akyeampong, Emmanuel. "Wo pe tam won pe ba (you like cloth but you don't want children): Urbanization, Individualism and Gender Relations in Colonial Ghana, c. 1900–39." Africa's Urban Past, ed. David M. Anderson and Richard Rathbone. Portsmouth, N.H.: Heinemann, 2000.

Allman, Jean. "Rounding Up Spinsters: Gender Chaos and Unmarried Women in Colonial Asante." "Wicked" Women and the Reconfiguration of Gender in Africa, ed. Dorothy Hodgson and Sheryl McCurdy. Portsmouth, N.H.: Heinemann, 2001.

———. "Fashioning Africa: Power and the Politics of Dress." Fashioning Africa: Power and the Politics of Dress, ed. Jean Allman. Bloomington: Indiana University Press, 2004.

Ambler, Charles. "Popular Films and Colonial Audiences: The Movies in Northern Rhodesia." American Historical Review 106.1 (2001), 81–105.

Amoko, Apollo O. "The Problem with English Literature: Canonicity, Citizenship, and the Idea of Africa." Research in African Literature 32.4 (2001), 19–43.

———. "The Problem with English Literature: Canonicity, Citizenship, and the Idea of Africa." PhD diss., University of Michigan, 2002.

Anderson, Benedict. Imagined Communities: Reflections on the Origin and Spread of Nationalism. London: Verso, 1983.

Anthony, David Henry. "Culture and Society in a Town in Transition: A People's History of Dar es Salaam, 1865–1939." PhD diss., University of Wisconsin, Madison, 1983.

Appadurai, Arjun, ed. The Social Life of Things: Commodities in Cultural Perspective. New York: Cambridge University Press, 1986.

———. Modernity at Large: Cultural Dimensions of Globalization. Minneapolis: University of Minnesota Press, 1996.

———, ed. Globalization. Durham, N.C.: Duke University Press, 2001.

Appadurai, Arjun, and Carol Breckenridge. "Public Modernity in India." Consuming Modernity: Public Culture in a South Asian World, ed. Carol Breckenridge. Minneapolis: University of Minnesota Press, 1995.

Apter, Andrew. "The Pan-African Nation: Oil Money and the Spectacle of Culture in Nigeria." *Public Culture* 8.3 (1996), 441–66.

———. "The Subvention of Tradition: A Genealogy of the Nigerian Durbar." *State/Culture: State Formation after the Cultural Turn*, ed. George Steinmetz. Ithaca: Cornell University Press, 1999.

———. *The Pan-African Nation: Oil and the Spectacle of Culture in Nigeria*. Chicago: University of Chicago Press, 2005.

Argenti, Nicholas. *The Intestines of the State: Youth, Violence, and Belated Histories in the Cameroon Grassfields*. Chicago: University of Chicago Press, 2007.

Armah, Ayi Kweh. *The Beautyful Ones Are Not Yet Born*. Boston: Houghton Mifflin, 1968.

Arnoldi, Mary Jo. "Youth Festivals and Museums: The Cultural Politics of Public Memory in Postcolonial Mali." *Africa Today* 52.4 (2006), 55–76.

Askew, Kelly. *Performing the Nation: Swahili Music and Cultural Politics in Tanzania*. Chicago: University of Chicago Press, 2002.

Bakhtin, Mikhail. *Rabelais and His World*. Bloomington: Indiana University Press, 1984.

Barber, Karin. "Popular Arts in Africa." *African Studies Review* 30.3 (1987), 1–78.

———, ed. *Readings in African Popular Culture*. Bloomington: Indiana University Press, 1997.

———, ed. *Africa's Hidden Histories: Everyday Literacy and Making the Self*. Bloomington: Indiana University Press, 2006.

Barkan, Joel. *An African Dilemma: University Students, Development and Politics in Ghana, Tanzania and Uganda*. Nairobi: Oxford University Press, 1975.

Bayart, Jean-François. *L'état en Afrique: La politique du ventre*. Paris: Fayard, 1989.

———. *The State in Africa: The Politics of the Belly*. London: Longman, 1993.

Benstock, Shari, and Suzanne Ferris, eds. *On Fashion*. New Brunswick, N.J.: Rutgers University Press, 1994.

———, eds. *Footnotes: On Shoes*. New Brunswick, N.J.: Rutgers University Press, 2001.

Bienen, Henry. *Tanzania: Party Transformation and Economic Development*. Princeton: Princeton University Press, 1970.

p'Bitek, Okot. *Africa's Cultural Revolution*. Nairobi: Macmillan Books for Africa, 1973.

———. *Song of Lawino and Song of Ocol*. London: Heinemann, 1984 (1966, 1967).

Bourdieu, Pierre. *Distinction: A Social Critique of the Judgment of Taste*. Cambridge, Mass.: Harvard University Press, 1984.

Bowman, James Cloyd. *Pecos Bill: The Greatest Cowboy of All Time*. Chicago: Albert Whitman, 1937.

Brennan, James R. "Nation, Race and Urbanization in Dar es Salaam, Tanzania, 1916–1976." PhD diss., Northwestern University, 2002.

———. "Blood Enemies: Exploitation and Urban Citizenship in the Nationalist Political Thought of Tanzania, 1958–75." *Journal of African History* 47.3 (2006), 389–413.

———. "Youth, the TANU Youth League and Managed Vigilantism in Dar es Salaam, Tanzania, 1925–73." *Africa* 76.2 (2006), 221–46.

Brennan, Timothy. *At Home in the World: Cosmopolitanism Now*. Cambridge, Mass.: Harvard University Press, 1997.

British Film Institute. *The Film in Colonial Development: A Report of a Conference.* London: British Film Institute, 1948.

Bryceson, Deborah Fahy. "A Review of Maternity Protection Legislation in Tanzania." *Tanzania Country Report for the IUNS Study "Rethinking Infant Nutrition Policies Under Changing Socio-Economic Conditions,"* ed. Olivia Mgaza and Han Bantje. Tanzania Food and Nutrition Centre and Bureau of Resource Assessment and Land Use Planning (BRALUP), November 1980.

———. "A Review of Statistical Information on Women in the Work Force Seeking Employment in Dar es Salaam and Their Families' Economic Welfare." *Tanzania Country Report for the IUNS Study "Rethinking Infant Nutrition Policies Under Changing Socio-Economic Conditions,"* ed. Olivia Mgaza and Han Bantje. Tanzania Food and Nutrition Centre and Bureau of Resource Assessment and Land Use Planning (BRALUP), November 1980.

———. "Social, Political and Economic Factors Affecting Women's Material Conditions in Tanzania." *Tanzania Country Report for the IUNS Study "Rethinking Infant Nutrition Policies Under Changing Socio-Economic Conditions,"* ed. Olivia Mgaza and Han Bantje. Tanzania Food and Nutrition Centre and Bureau of Resource Assessment and Land Use Planning (BRALUP), November 1980.

Bujra, Janet. *Serving Class: Masculinity and the Feminisation of Domestic Service in Tanzania.* Edinburgh: Edinburgh University Press, 2000.

Bukenya, Austin. *The People's Bachelor.* Dar es Salaam: East African Publishing House, 1972.

Burgess, Thomas. "Remembering Youth: Generation in Revolutionary Zanzibar." *Africa Today* 46.2 (1999), 29–50.

———. "Youth and the Revolution: Mobility and Discipline in Zanzibar, 1950–1980." PhD diss., Indiana University, 2001.

———. "Cinema, Bell-Bottoms, and Miniskirts: Struggles over Youth and Citizenship in Revolutionary Zanzibar." *International Journal of African Historical Studies* 35.2/3 (2002), 287–313.

———. "Introduction to Youth and Citizenship in East Africa." *Africa Today* 51.3 (2005), 1–19.

———. "The Young Pioneers and the Ritual of Citizenship in Revolutionary Zanzibar." *Africa Today* 51.3 (2005), 3–29.

Burke, Timothy. *Lifebuoy Men, Lux Women: Commodification, Consumption, and Cleanliness in Modern Zimbabwe.* Durham, N.C.: Duke University Press, 1996.

———. "'Our Mosquitoes Are Not So Big': Images and Modernity in Zimbabwe." *Images and Empires: Visuality in Colonial and Postcolonial Africa*, ed. Paul Landau and Deborah Kaspin. Berkeley: University of California Press, 2003.

Burns, J. M. *Flickering Shadows: Cinema and Identity in Colonial Zimbabwe.* Research in International Studies, Africa Series # 77. Athens: Ohio University Press, 2002.

———. "John Wayne on the Zambezi: Cinema, Empire, and the American Western in British Central Africa." *International Journal of African Historical Studies* 35.1 (2002), 103–18.

Burton, Andrew. "Wahuni (The Undesirables): African Urbanization, Crime, and Colonial Order in Dar es Salaam, 1919–1961." PhD diss., University of London, 2000.

———. "Urchins, Loafers and the Cult of the Cowboy: Urbanization and Delinquency in Dar es Salaam, 1919–61." *Journal of African History* 42:2 (2001), 199–216.

———. *African Underclass: Urbanisation, Crime, and Colonial Order in Dar es Salaam.* Oxford: James Currey, 2005.

———. "The 'Haven of Peace' Purged: Tackling the Undesirable and Unproductive Poor in Dar es Salaam, c. 1954–85." *International Journal of African Historical Studies* 40.1 (2007), 119–51.

Burton, Andrew, and Michael Jennings. "The Emperor's New Clothes? Continuity and Governance in Late Colonial and Postcolonial East Africa." *International Journal of African Historical Studies* 40.1 (2007), 1–25.

Byfield, Judith. "Women, Marriage, Divorce and the Emerging Colonial State in Abeokuta (Nigeria), 1892–1904." *"Wicked" Women and the Reconfiguration of Gender in Africa*, ed. Dorothy Hodgson and Sheryl McCurdy. Portsmouth, N.H.: Heinemann, 2001.

Cabral, Amilcar. "National Liberation and Culture." *Colonial Discourse and Post-Colonial Theory*, ed. Patrick Williams and Laura Chisman. 1970. Reprint, New York: Columbia University Press, 1994.

Calaguas, Mark J., Christina M. Drost, and Edward R. Fluet. "Legal Pluralism and Women's Rights: A Study in Postcolonial Tanzania." *Columbia Journal of Gender and Law* 16.2 (2007), 471–549.

Campbell, John. "The State, Urban Development and Housing." *Capitalism, Socialism and the Development Crisis in Tanzania*, ed. Norman O'Neill and Kemal Mustafa. Aldershot, U.K.: Avebury, 1990.

———. "Conceptualizing Gender Relations and the Household in Urban Tanzania." *Gender, Family and Household in Tanzania*, ed. Colin Creighton and C. K. Omari. Aldershot, U.K.: Avebury, 1995.

Caute, David. *The Year of the Barricades: A Journey through 1968.* New York: Paladin, 1988.

Chakrabarty, Dipesh. *Provincializing Europe: Postcolonial Thought and Historical Difference.* Princeton: Princeton University Press, 2000.

Chanock, Martin. *Law, Custom, and Social Order: The Colonial Experience in Malawi and Zambia.* Cambridge: Cambridge University Press, 1985.

Chatterjee, Partha. *The Nation and Its Fragments.* Princeton: Princeton University Press, 1993.

Chaudhury, K. N. *Asia Before Europe: Economy and Civilization of the Indian Ocean from the Rise of Islam to 1750.* Cambridge: Cambridge University Press, 1991.

Chauncey, George Jr. "The Locus of Reproduction: Women's Labour in the Zambian Copperbelt, 1927–53." *Journal of Southern African Studies* 7 (1981), 135–64.

Claeson, Claes-Fredrik, and Bertil Egero. "Migration and the Urban Population: A Demographic Analysis of Population Census Data for Tanzania." *Geografiska Annaler. Series B, Human Geography* 54.1 (1972), 1–18.

Cliffe, Lionel, and John Saul, eds. *Socialism in Tanzania: An Interdisciplinary Reader.* Vol. 2. Dar es Salaam: East African Publishing House, 1972.

Clifford, James. *Routes: Travel and Translation in the Late Twentieth Century.* Cambridge, Mass.: Harvard University Press, 1997.

Cohen, David William, and E. S. Atieno Odhiambo. *Burying SM: The Politics of Knowledge and the Sociology of Power in Africa.* Portsmouth, N.H.: Heinemann, 1992.

———. *The Risks of Knowledge: Investigations into the Death of the Hon. Minister John Robert Ouko in Kenya, 1990.* Athens: Ohio University Press, 2006.

Cohen, David William, Stephan Miescher, and Luise White, eds. *African Words, African Voices: Critical Practices in Oral History*. Bloomington: Indiana University Press, 2001.

Cohen, Stanley. *Folk Devils and Moral Panics: The Creation of the Mods and Rockers*. New York: St. Martin's Press, 1980.

Cole, Catherine. "When Is African Theater 'Black'?" *Black Cultural Traffic: Crossroads in Global Performance and Popular Culture*, ed. Harry Elam Jr. and Kennell Jackson. Ann Arbor: University of Michigan Press, 2005.

Comaroff, Jean, and John L. Comaroff. *Of Revelation and Revolution*. Vol. 2, *The Dialectics of Modernity on a South African Frontier*. Chicago: University of Chicago Press, 1997.

———. "Reflections on Youth: From the Past to the Postcolony." *Makers and Breakers: Children and Youth in Postcolonial Africa*, ed. Alcinda Honwana and Filip de Boeck. Trenton, N.J.: Africa World Press, 2005.

Cooper, Frederick, ed. *Struggle for the City: Migrant Labor, Capital and the State in Urban Africa*. Beverly Hills, Calif.: Sage Publications, 1983.

———. *On the African Waterfront: Urban Disorder and the Transformation of Work in Colonial Mombasa*, New Haven, Conn.: Yale University Press, 1987.

———. *Decolonization and African Society: The Labor Question in French and British Africa*. Cambridge: Cambridge University Press, 1996.

———. "What Is the Concept of Globalization Good For? An African Historian's Perspective." *African Affairs* 100.399 (April 2001), 189–213.

———. *Africa Since 1940: The Past in the Present*. Cambridge: Cambridge University Press, 2002.

———. *Colonialism in Question: Theory, Knowledge, History*. Berkeley: University of California Press, 2005.

Coplan, David. *In Township Tonight!: South Africa's Black City Music and Theatre*. London: Longman, 1985.

Cory, Hans. *The Ntemi: The Traditional Rites in Connection with the Burial, Election, Enthronement and Magic Powers of a Sukuma Chief*. London: Macmillan, 1951.

———. *The Indigenous Political System of the Sukuma and Proposals for Political Reform*. Dar es Salaam: Eagle Press for the East African Institute of Social Research, 1954.

Coulson, Andrew. *Tanzania: A Political Economy*. Oxford: Clarendon Press, 1982.

Craig, Timothy, and Richard King, eds. *Global Goes Local: Popular Culture in Asia*. Vancouver: University of British Columbia Press, 2002.

Daniels, Robert. *Year of the Heroic Guerilla: World Revolution and Counterrevolution in 1968*. New York: Basic Books, 1989.

Davis, J. Merle. "The Cinema and Missions in Africa." *International Review of Missions* 25.99 (1936), 378.

———. Foreword to *The African and the Cinema* by L. A. Notcutt and G. C. Latham. London: Edinburgh House Press, 1937.

Davis, Peter. *In Darkest Hollywood: Exploring the Jungles of Cinema's South Africa*. Athens: Ohio University Press, 1996.

Deutsch, Jan-Georg, Peter Probst, and Heike Schmidt, eds. *African Modernities*. Portsmouth, N.H.: Heinemann, 2002.

Diawara, Manthia. "The Sixties in Bamako: Malick Sidibé and James Brown." *Black Cultural Traffic*, ed. Harry Elam Jr., et al. Ann Arbor: University of Michigan, 2005.

Dinan, Carmel. "Sugar Daddies and Gold Diggers: The White-Collar Single Woman in Accra." *Female and Male in West Africa*, ed. Christine Oppong. Winchester, Mass.: Allen and Unwin, 1983.

Dirks, Nicholas B., Geoff Eley, and Sherry B. Ortner, eds. *Culture/Power/History: A Reader in Contemporary Social Theory*. Princeton: Princeton University Press, 1994.

East African High Commission. *East Africa Literature Bureau Annual Report, 1952*. Nairobi, 1953.

———. *East Africa Literature Bureau Annual Report, 1953*. Nairobi, 1954.

———. *East Africa Literature Bureau Annual Report, 1954*. Nairobi, 1955.

———. *East Africa Literature Bureau Annual Report, 1955–6*. Nairobi, 1956.

———. *East Africa Literature Bureau Annual Report, 1956–7*. Nairobi, 1958.

———. *East Africa Literature Bureau Annual Report, 1958–9*. Nairobi, 1960.

———. *East Africa Literature Bureau Annual Report, 1960–61*. Nairobi, 1962.

———. "Helps and Explanations for African Authors, No. 3—Notes on Recording the Social and Political Organisation of African Tribes." Nairobi: EALB, 1961 (mimeograph).

Ebron, Paulla A. *Performing Africa*. Princeton: Princeton University Press, 2002.

Edwards, Brent Hayes. *The Practice of Diaspora: Literature, Translation, and the Rise of Black Internationalism*. Cambridge, Mass.: Harvard University Press, 2003.

Elimu ya Siasa kwa Shule za Msingi: Nchi Yetu—Kitabu cha Kwanza. Arusha, Tanzania: East Africa Publications, 1984.

Ellis, Stephen. "Writing Histories of Contemporary Africa." *Journal of African History* 43 (2002), 1–26.

Englund, Harry. "Cosmopolitanism and the Devil in Malawi." *Ethnos* 69.3 (2004), 293–316.

Epstein, A. L. *Politics in an Urban African Community*. Manchester: Manchester University Press, 1958.

Erlmann, Veit. *Music, Modernity, and the Global Imagination: South Africa and the West*. Oxford: Oxford University Press, 1999.

Evans, David R. "Image and Reality: Career Goals of Educated Ugandan Women." *Canadian Journal of African Studies* 6.2 (1972), 213–32.

Fair, Laura. "Dressing Up: Clothing, Class and Gender in Post-Abolition Zanzibar." *Journal of African History* 39.1 (1998), 63–94.

Fanon, Frantz. *The Wretched of the Earth*. 1961. Reprint, New York: Grove Press, 1966.

Fenn, John, and Alex Perullo. "Language Choice and Hip-Hop in Tanzania and Malawi." *Popular Music and Society* 24.3 (fall 2000), 73–94.

Ferguson, James. "The Cultural Topography of Wealth: Commodity Paths and the Structure of Property in Rural Lesotho." *American Anthropologist* 94.1 (1995), 55–73.

———. *Expectations of Modernity: Myths and Meanings of Urban Life on the Zambian Copperbelt*. Berkeley: University of California Press, 1999.

———. *Global Shadows: Africa in the Neoliberal World Order*. Durham, N.C.: Duke University Press, 2006.

Fink, Carole, et al., eds. *1968: The World Transformed*. Cambridge: Cambridge University Press, 1998.

Finnucane, James. *Rural Development and Bureaucracy in Tanzania: The Case of Mwanza Region*. Uppsala, Sweden: Scandinavian Institute of African Studies, 1974.

Freyhold, Micaela von. "The Workers and the Nizers." Manuscript (n.d.).

———. *Ujamaa Villages in Tanzania: Analysis of a Social Experiment*. London: Heinemann, 1979.

Fugelsang, Minou. *Veils and Videos: Female Youth Culture on the Kenyan Coast*. Stockholm: Stockholm Studies in Social Anthropology, 1994.

Gaines, Kevin. *American Africans in Ghana: Black Expatriates and the Civil Rights Era*. Chapel Hill: University of North Carolina Press, 2006.

Gandalou, J. D. *Dandies à Bakongo: Le culte de l'élégance dans la société congolaise contemporaine*. Paris: L'Harmattan, 1989.

Gaonkar, Dilip Parameshwar. *Alternative Modernities*. Durham, N.C.: Duke University Press, 2001.

Geiger, Susan. *TANU Women: Gender and Culture in the Making of Tanganyikan Nationalism, 1955–1965*. Portsmouth, N.H.: Heinemann, 1997.

Geschiere, Peter. *The Modernity of Witchcraft: Politics and the Occult in Post-Colonial Africa*. Charlottesville: University of Virginia Press, 1997.

Ghai, Y. P. "The New Marriage Law in Tanzania." *Africa Quarterly* 11 (July/September 1971), 101–9.

Giblin, James. *History of the Excluded: Making Family a Refuge from State in Twentieth-Century Tanzania*. Athens: Ohio University Press, 2006.

Gikandi, Simon. "Reason, Modernity, and the African Crisis." *African Modernities*, ed. Jan-Georg Deutsch, Peter Probst, and Heike Schmidt. Portsmouth, N.H.: Heinemann, 2002.

Glassman, Jonathan. *Feasts and Riot: Revelry, Rebellion, and Popular Consciousness on the Swahili Coast, 1856–1888*. Portsmouth, N.H.: Heinemann, 1995.

———. "Sorting Out the Tribes: The Creation of Racial Identities in Colonial Zanzibar's Newspaper Wars." *Journal of African History* 41.3 (2000), 395–428.

Gondola, Ch. Didier. "Dream and Drama: The Search for Elegance among Congolese Youth." *African Studies Review* 42.1 (1999), 23–48.

Gugler, Josef. "The Second Sex in Town." *Canadian Journal of African Studies* 6.2 (1972), 289–301.

Gulliver, P. H. *Labor Migration in a Rural Economy: A Study of the Ngoni and Ndenduli of Southern Tanganyika*. Kampala, Uganda: East African Institute for Social Research, 1955.

Guyer, Jane. "The Value of Beti Bridewealth." *Money Matters: Instability, Values and Social Payments in the Modern History of West African Communities*, ed. Jane Guyer. Portsmouth, N.H.: Heinemann, 1995.

Halimoja, Yusuf. *Utamaduni wa Taifa*. Dar es Salaam: Mwangaza Publishers, 1981.

Hall, Stuart, and Tony Jefferson, eds. *Resistance Through Rituals: Youth Sub-cultures in Post-war Britain*. 1976. Reprint, London: Routledge, 1998.

Hannerz, Ulf. *Transnational Connections: Culture, People, Places*. London: Routledge, 1996.

Hansen, Karen Tranberg. *Salaula: The World of Secondhand Clothing and Zambia*. Chicago: University of Chicago Press, 2000.

Hansen, Thomas Blom, and Finn Stepputat, eds. *States of Imagination: Ethnographic Explorations of the Postcolonial State*. Durham, N.C.: Duke University Press, 2001.

Hasty, Jennifer. *The Press and Political Culture in Ghana*. Bloomington: Indiana University Press, 2005.

Hebdige, Dick. *Subculture: The Meaning of Style*. London: Methuen, 1979.

Hendrickson, Hildi, ed. *Clothing and Difference: Embodied Identities in Colonial and Post-colonial Africa*. Durham, N.C.: Duke University Press, 1998.

Higginson, John. *A Working Class in the Making: Belgian Colonial Labor Policy, Private Enterprise, and the African Mineworker, 1907–51*. Madison: University of Wisconsin Press, 1989.

Hirji, Karim. "School, Education and Underdevelopment in Tanzania." *MajiMaji* [Dar es Salaam] 12 (1973), 12–25.

Hodgson, Dorothy, and Sheryl McCurdy, eds. *"Wicked" Women and the Reconfiguration of Gender in Africa*. Portsmouth, N.H.: Heinemann, 2001.

Hofmeyr, Isabel. "'Waiting for Purity': Oral Studies in Southern African Studies." *African Studies* 54.2 (1995).

Honwana, Alcinda. "The Pain of Agency, the Agency of Pain: Child Soldiers as Interstitial and Tactical Agents." *Makers and Breakers: Children and Youth in Postcolonial Africa*, ed. Alcinda Honwana and Filip de Boeck. Trenton, N.J.: Africa World Press, 2005.

Honwana, Alcinda, and Filip de Boeck, eds. *Makers and Breakers: Children and Youth in Postcolonial Africa*. Trenton, N.J.: Africa World Press, 2005.

Hunt, Nancy Rose. "Noise over Camouflaged Polygamy, Colonial Morality Taxation, and a Woman-Naming Crisis in Belgian Africa." *Journal of African History* 32.3 (1991), 471–94.

———. *A Colonial Lexicon: Of Birth Ritual, Medicalization and Mobility in the Congo*. Durham, N.C.: Duke University Press, 1999.

Hunter, Emma. "Revisiting Ujamaa: Political Legitimacy and the Construction of Community in Post-Colonial Tanzania." *Journal of Eastern African Studies* 2.3 (2008), 471–85.

Hyden, Goran. *Beyond Ujamaa in Tanzania: Underdevelopment and an Uncaptured Peasantry*. Berkeley: University of California Press, 1980.

Iliffe, John. *A Modern History of Tanganyika*. Cambridge: Cambridge University Press, 1979.

International Congress of African Historians, 1965 (T. O. Ranger, ed.). *Emerging Themes of African History; Proceedings*. 1965. Reprint, Nairobi: East African Publishing House, 1968.

Ivaska, Andrew M. "Colonial Frames: Wholesome Cinema, Censorship, and the Urban/Rural Divide in 1930s Tanganyika." Manuscript.

———. "Custom and Tradition for the Modern African: The East African Literature Bureau." Manuscript.

Jackson, Kennell. Introduction. *Black Cultural Traffic: Crossroads in Global Performance and Popular Culture*, ed. Harry Elam Jr. and Kennell Jackson. Ann Arbor: University of Michigan Press, 2005.

Jacob, Wilson Chacko. *Working Out Egypt: Colonial Modernity and Subject Formation, 1870–1940*. Durham, N.C.: Duke University Press, forthcoming.

Joseph, May. *Nomadic Identities: The Performance of Citizenship*. Minneapolis: University of Minnesota Press, 1999.

Kaba, Lansine. "The Cultural Revolution, Artistic Creativity, and Freedom of Expression in Guinea." *Journal of Modern African Studies* 14.2 (1976), 201–18.

Kamenju, Grant. "In Defense of a Socialist Concept of Universities." *Transition*, no. 35 (February/March 1968), 15–17.

Kamenju, Grant, and F. Topan, eds. *Mashairi ya Azimio la Arusha*. Dar es Salaam: Longman Tanzania, 1971.

Kangero, Mzirai. "The University and the State, 1964–1984." Report prepared for the University of Dar es Salaam Faculty of Arts and Science, 1984 (mimeograph).

Karanja, Wambui wa. "'Outside Wives' and 'Inside Wives' in Nigeria: A Study of Changing Perceptions in Marriage." *Transformations of African Marriage*, ed. David Parkin and David Nyamwaya. Manchester: Manchester University Press, 1987.

Kassam, F. M. "Comments on the White Paper." *East African Law Review* 2.3 (1969).

Katsiaficas, George. *The Imagination of the New Left: A Global Analysis of 1968*. Boston: South End Press, 1987.

Kimambo, I. N. *Penetration and Protest in Tanzania: The Impact of the World Economy on the Pare, 1860–1960*. London: James Currey, 1991.

Kimambo, I. N., and A. J. Temu, eds. *A History of Tanzania*. Nairobi: East African Publishing House for the Historical Association of Tanzania, 1969.

Konde, Hadji. *Freedom of the Press in Tanzania*. Arusha, Tanzania: East Africa Publications, 1984.

Kopytoff, Igor. "The Cultural Biography of Things." *The Social Life of Things*, ed. Arjun Appadurai. New York: Cambridge University Press, 1986.

Larkin, Brian. "Indian Films and Nigerian Lovers: Media and the Creation of Parallel Modernities." *Africa* 67.3 (1997), 406–40.

Lau, Jenny Kwok Wah, ed. *Multiple Modernities: Cinemas and Popular Media in Transcultural East Asia*. Philadelphia: Temple University Press, 2003.

Leslie, J. A. K. *A Survey of Dar es Salaam*. London: Oxford University Press on behalf of the East African Institute for Social Research, 1963.

Lihamba, Amadina. "Politics and Theatre in Tanzania after the Arusha Declaration, 1967–1984." PhD diss., University of Leeds, 1985.

Lindsay, Lisa. "Money, Marriage and Masculinity on the Colonial Nigerian Railway." *Men and Masculinities in Modern Africa*, ed. Lisa Lindsay and Stephan Miescher. Portsmouth, N.H.: Heinemann, 2003.

———. *Working with Gender: Wage Labor and Social Change in Southwestern Nigeria*. Portsmouth, N.H.: Heinemann, 2003.

Lindsay, Lisa, and Stephan Miescher, eds. *Men and Masculinities in Modern Africa*. Portsmouth, N.H.: Heinemann, 2003.

Little, Kenneth. *African Women in Town: An Aspect of Africa's Social Revolution*. London: Cambridge University Press, 1973.

Lovett, Margot. "'She Thinks She's Like a Man': Marriage and (De)constructing Gender Identity in Colonial Buha, Western Tanzania, 1940–1960." *"Wicked" Women and the Reconfiguration of Gender in Africa*, ed. Dorothy Hodgson and Sheryl McCurdy. Portsmouth, N.H.: Heinemann, 2001.

Lucas, S. A., and A. F. Masao, Ministry of National Culture and Youth, Directorate of Research on Traditions and Customs. *The Present State of Research on Cultural Development in Tanzania*. Dar es Salaam, 1974 (mimeograph).

Maddox, Gregory. Introduction. Mathias Mnyampala, *The Gogo: History, Customs and Traditions*. Translated by Gregory H. Maddox. Armonk, N.Y.: M. E. Sharpe, 1995.

Magubane, Bernard. "A Critical Look at Indices Used in the Study of Social Change in Colonial Africa." *Current Anthropology* 12 (1971), 419–45.

Malale, H. W. "Uganga Kama Mpango wa Unyonyaji." *Mwenge*, Toleo na. 11.

Mamdani, Mahmood. *Citizen and Subject*. Princeton: Princeton University Press, 1996.

Mann, Kristin. *Marrying Well: Marriage, Status, and Social Change among the Educated Elite in Colonial Lagos.* Cambridge: Cambridge University Press, 1985.

Maro, P. S., and W. I. F. Mlay. "People, Population Distribution and Employment." *Tanzania Notes and Records* 83 (1976), 1–20.

Marotti, William. "Japan 1968: The Performance of Violence and the Theater of Protest." *American Historical Review* 114.1 (2009), 97–135.

Mazrui, Ali A. "Miniskirts and Political Puritanism." *Africa Report* (October 1968), 9–12.

———. "The Robes of Rebellion: Sex, Dress and Politics in Africa." *Encounter* 34.2 (1970), 19–30.

Mbah, F. U. "Prostitution in Tanzania (A Case Study of Dar es Salaam City)." BA thesis, University of Dar es Salaam, 1979.

Mbembe, Achille. "Provisional Notes on the Postcolony." *Africa* 62 (1992), 3–37.

———. *On the Postcolony.* Berkeley: University of California Press, 2001.

Mbilinyi, Marjorie. "The 'New Woman' and Traditional Norms in Tanzania." *Journal of Modern African Studies* 10.1 (1972), 57–72.

———. "'City' and 'Countryside' in Colonial Tanganyika." *Economic and Political Weekly* 20 (1985), 88–96.

———, ed. *Gender Profile of Tanzania.* Dar es Salaam: Tanzania Gender Networking Project, 1993.

Mbughuni, L. A. *The Cultural Policy of the United Republic of Tanzania.* Paris: UNESCO, 1974.

Mbughuni, L. A., and G. Ruhumbika. "TANU and National Culture." *Towards Ujamaa: Twenty Years of TANU Leadership,* ed. G. Ruhumbika. Dar es Salaam: East African Literature Bureau, 1974.

McCurdy, Sheryl. "Urban Threats: Manyema Women, Low Fertility, and Venereal Diseases in British Colonial Tanganyika, 1926–36." *"Wicked" Women and the Reconfiguration of Gender in Africa,* ed. Dorothy Hodgson and Sheryl McCurdy. Portsmouth, N.H.: Heinemann, 2001.

McGovern, Michael. "Unmasking the State: Developing Modern Political Subjectivities in 20th Century Guinea." PhD diss., Emory University, 2004.

McKinsey and Company. *Coordinating the Development of Culture and Youth: The Ministry of National Culture and Youth, United Republic of Tanzania.* 1975 (mimeograph).

McRobbie, Angela. *Feminism and Youth Culture: From "Jackie" to "Just Seventeen."* Houndmills, Basingstoke, Hampshire: Macmillan, 1991.

Meillassoux, Claude. "From Reproduction to Production: A Marxist Approach to Economic Anthropology." *Economy and Society* 1.1 (1972), 93–105.

Mhamba, E. "Should Bridewealth Be Retained in Our Modern Society?" *Mwenge* 6 (1966).

Miescher, Stephan F., Takwiyah Manuh, and Catherine M. Cole, eds. *Africa after Gender?* Bloomington: Indiana University Press, 2007.

Miller, Daniel, ed. *Worlds Apart: Modernity Through the Prism of the Local.* London: Routledge, 1995.

Mitchell, J. Clyde. *The Kalela Dance.* Rhodes-Livingstone Paper No. 27. Lusaka, Zambia: Rhodes-Livingstone Institute, 1957.

Mitchell, Timothy. "Society, Economy and the State Effect." *State/Culture: State Formation after the Cultural Turn,* ed. George Steinmetz. Ithaca, N.Y.: Cornell University Press, 1999.

————, ed. *Questions of Modernity*. Minneapolis: University of Minnesota Press, 2000.

Mkufya, W. E. *The Wicked Walk*. Dar es Salaam: Tanzania Publishing House, 1977.

Mnyampala, Mathias E. *Historia, mila na desturi za Wagogo*. Nairobi: East African Literature Bureau, 1954.

Mnyampala, Mathias E., and Gregory H. Maddox. *The Gogo: History, Customs, and Traditions*. Translated by Gregory Maddox. Armonk, N.Y.: M. E. Sharpe, 1995.

Mochiwa, Anthony. *Habari za Wazigua*. London: Macmillan, 1954.

Molohan, M. J. B. *Detribalization: A Study of the Areas of Tanganyika Where Detribalized Persons Are Living with Recommendations as to the Administrative and Other Measures Required to Meet the Problems Arising Therein*. Dar es Salaam: Government Printer, 1957.

Morrison, David R. *Education and Politics in Africa: The Tanzanian Case*. London: C. Hurst, 1976.

Moyer, Eileen. "Street-Corner Justice in the Name of Jah: Imperatives for Peace among Dar es Salaam Street Youth." *Africa Today* 51.3 (2005), 31–58.

Mtawa, Lawrence A. "Mavazi ya Heshima." *Nchi Yetu*, October 1973.

Mudimbe, V. Y. *The Invention of Africa: Gnosis, Philosophy, and the Order of Knowledge*. Bloomington: Indiana University Press, 1988.

Mumford, W. B. "Malangali School." *Africa* 3 (1930), 265–92.

Museveni, Y. "My Three Years in Tanzania (Glimpses of the Struggle between Revolution and Reaction)." *Cheche* [Dar es Salaam], no. 2 (July 1970), 12–13.

Mutongi, Kenda. "'Worries of the Heart': Widowed Mothers, Daughters and Masculinities in Maragoli, Western Kenya, 1940–1960." *Readings in Gender in Africa*, ed. Andrea Cornwall. Bloomington: Indiana University Press, 2005.

Mwakikagile, Godfrey. *Relations Between Africans and African Americans: Misconceptions, Myths and Realities*. New York: Continental Press, 2006.

Mwakipesile, J. S. *Mila na Desturi za Wasangu, Wasafwa na Wasagara*. Dar es Salaam: Idara ya Utafiti na Mipango, Wizara ya Utamaduni wa Taifa na Vijana, early 1970s[?].

Mwano, E. M. "Polygamy and Its Effects." *Mwenge* 4 (1964).

Mwenda, H. M. J. "Mila na Desturi Yanavyoweza Kusaidia au Kuzorotesha Shughuli za Ujamaa." *Mwenge*, Toleo na. 12 (1972).

Newell, Stephanie. *Literary Culture in Colonial Ghana: "How to Play the Game of Life."* Bloomington: Indiana University Press, 2002.

Ng'asi, A. P. "A Thought on Traditional Music in Tanzania." *Mwenge* 5 (1965).

Ngugi wa Thiong'o. Introduction. Okot p'Bitek, *Africa's Cultural Revolution*. Nairobi: Macmillan Books for Africa, 1973.

————. "On the Abolition of the English Department." *Homecoming: Essays on African and Caribbean Literature, Culture and Politics*, ed. Ngugi wa Thiong'o. London: Heinemann, 1972.

Nixon, Rob. *Homelands, Harlem and Hollywood*. New York: Routledge, 1994.

Notcutt, L. A., and G. C. Latham. *The African and the Cinema*. London: Edinburgh House Press, 1937.

Nothnagle, Alan L. *Building the East German Myth: Historical Mythology and Youth Propaganda in the German Democratic Republic, 1945–1989*. Ann Arbor: University of Michigan Press, 1999.

Ntiro, S. J. *Desturi za Wachagga*. Nairobi: Eagle Press, 1957[?].

Nyerere, Julius K. *Education for Self-Reliance*. Dar es Salaam: Government Printer, 1967.

———. *Freedom and Unity*. London: Oxford University Press, 1967.

———. *Ujamaa: Essays on Socialism*. London: Oxford University Press, 1968.

Obatala, J. K. "U.S. 'Soul' Music in Africa." *African Communist*, no. 41 (1970).

Obbo, Christine. *African Women: Their Struggle for Economic Independence*. London: Zed Press, 1980.

———. "The Old and the New in East African Elite Marriages." *Transformations of African Marriages*, ed. David Parkin and David Nyamwaya. Manchester: Manchester University Press, 1987.

Oppong, Christine. *Marriage Among a Matrilineal Elite: A Family Study of Ghanaian Senior Civil Servants*. Cambridge: Cambridge University Press, 1974.

Owino, Rosemarie. *Sugar Daddy's Lover*. Nairobi: Spear, 1975.

Parpart, Jane. "'Wicked Women' and 'Respectable Ladies': Reconfiguring Gender on the Zambian Copperbelt, 1936–64." *"Wicked" Women and the Reconfiguration of Gender in Africa*, ed. Dorothy Hodgson and Sheryl McCurdy. Portsmouth, N.H.: Heinemann, 2001.

Peel, J. D. Y. *Ijeshas and Nigerians: The Incorporation of a Yoruba Kingdom, 1890s–1970s*. Cambridge: Cambridge University Press, 1983.

Pemberton, John. *On the Subject of Java*. Ithaca, N.Y.: Cornell University Press, 1994.

Perullo, Ian Alexander. "The Life That I Live: Popular Music, Agency, and Urban Society in Dar es Salaam, Tanzania." PhD diss., Indiana University, 2003.

Perullo, Ian Alex. "Hooligans and Heroes: Youth Identity and Rap Music in Dar es Salaam, Tanzania." *Africa Today* 51.4 (2005), 75–101.

Peterson, Derek. *Creative Writing: Translation, Bookkeeping and the Work of Imagination in Colonial Kenya*. Portsmouth, N.H.: Heinemann, 2004.

Pollack, Sheldon, Homi K. Bhabha, Carol A. Brekenridge, Arjun Appadurai. "Cosmopolitanisms." *Cosmopolitanism*, ed. Sheldon Pollack, Homi K. Bhabha, Carol A. Brekenridge, Arjun Appadurai. Durham, N.C.: Duke University Press, 2002.

Powdermaker, Hortense. *Copper Town: Changing Africa; The Human Situation on the Rhodesian Copperbelt*. New York: Harper and Row, 1962.

Prestholdt, Jeremy. "East African Consumerism and the Genealogies of Globalization." PhD diss., Northwestern University, 2003.

———. *Domesticating the World: African Consumerism and the Genealogies of Globalization*. Berkeley: University of California Press, 2008.

Ranger, Terrance. *Dance and Society in Eastern Africa: The Beni Ngoma*. Berkeley: University of California Press, 1975.

———. "The Invention of Tradition in Colonial Africa." *The Invention of Tradition*, ed. Eric Hobsbawm and Terrance Ranger. Cambridge: Cambridge University Press, 1983.

Read, James S. "A Milestone in the Integration of Personal Laws: The New Law of Marriage and Divorce in Tanzania." *Journal of African Law* 16.1 (1972), 19–39.

"Report: Conference on the Role of the University College, Dar es Salaam in a Socialist Tanzania." Dar es Salaam, March 11–13, 1967 (mimeograph).

Resnick, I., ed. *Tanzania: Revolution by Education*. Dar es Salaam: Longman, 1968.

Richards, Paul. *Fighting for the Rain Forest: War, Youth and Resources in Sierra Leone*. Portsmouth, N.H.: Heinemann, 1996.

Rodney, Walter. *How Europe Underdeveloped Africa*. London: Bogle-L'Ouverture Publications, 1972.

Ronnenberg, Ryan. "The Laughter on His Side: Mzee Punch and the Dialectic of the Foolish." PhD diss., University of Wisconsin, 2007.

Ross, Kristin. *May '68 and Its Afterlives*. Chicago: University of Chicago Press, 2002.

Rostow, W. W. *The Stages of Economic Growth: A Non-Communist Manifesto*. Cambridge: Cambridge University Press, 1961.

Rowbotham, Sheila. *Promise of a Dream: Remembering the Sixties*. London: Allen Lane, 2000.

Rubadiri, David. *No Bride Price*. Nairobi: East African Publishing House, 1967.

Ruhumbika, G., ed., *Towards Ujamaa: Twenty Years of TANU Leadership*. Dar es Salaam: East African Literature Bureau, 1974.

Sabot, R. H. *Economic Development and Urban Migration: Tanzania, 1900–1971*. Oxford: Oxford University Press, 1979.

Samoff, Joel. *Tanzania: Local Politics and the Structure of Power*. Madison: University of Wisconsin Press, 1974.

Saul, John S. "Radicalism and the Hill." *Socialism in Tanzania: An Interdisciplinary Reader*. Vol. 2, ed. Lionel Cliffe and John S. Saul. Dar es Salaam: East African Publishing House, 1972.

———. "High-level Manpower for Socialism." *Socialism in Tanzania: An Interdisciplinary Reader*. Vol. 2, ed. Lionel Cliffe and John S. Saul. Dar es Salaam: East African Publishing House, 1972.

———. "Socialism in One Country: Tanzania." *Essays on the Political Economy of Africa*, ed. John Saul and Giovanni Arrighi. New York: Monthly Review Press, 1973.

Scarnecchia, Timothy. "The Politics of Gender and Class in the Creation of African Communities, Salisbury, Rhodesia, 1940–56." PhD diss., University of Michigan, 1993.

———. *The Urban Roots of Democracy and Political Violence in Zimbabwe: Harare and Highfield, 1940–1964*. Rochester: Rochester University Press, 2008.

Schneider, Leander. "Developmentalism and Its Failings: Why Rural Development Went Wrong in 1960s and 1970s Tanzania." PhD diss., Columbia University, 2003.

———. "The Maasai's New Clothes: A Developmentalist Modernity and Its Exclusions." *Africa Today* 53.1 (2006), 100–131.

Schoss, Johanna. "Dressed to 'Shine': Work, Leisure and Style in Malindi, Kenya." *Clothing and Difference: Embodied Identities in Colonial and Postcolonial Africa*, ed. Hildi Hendrickson. Durham, N.C.: Duke University Press, 1998.

Schroeder, Richard A. "'Gone to Their Second Husbands': Marital Metaphors and Conjugal Contracts in the Gambia's Female Garden Sector." *"Wicked" Women and the Reconfiguration of Gender in Africa*, ed. Dorothy Hodgson and Cheryl McCurdy. Portsmouth, N.H.: Heinemann, 2001.

Schumaker, Lynn. *Africanizing Anthropology: Fieldwork, Networks, and the Making of Cultural Knowledge in Central Africa*. Durham, N.C.: Duke University Press, 2001.

Sembajwe, Israel. "Secondary Statistics on Overall Demography and Demographic Trends (Especially Migration) in Urban Areas with Special Reference to Dar es Salaam." *Tanzania Country Report for the IUNS Study "Rethinking Infant*

Nutrition Policies Under Changing Socio-Economic Conditions," ed. Olivia Mgaza and Han Bantje. Tanzania Food and Nutrition Centre and Bureau of Resource Assessment and Land Use Planning (BRALUP), November 1980.

Shadle, Brett. "Girl Cases": Marriage and Colonialism in Gusiiland, Kenya, 1890–1970. Portsmouth, N.H.: Heinemann, 2006.

Sheriff, Abdul. Slaves, Spices, and Ivory in Zanzibar: Integration of an East African Commercial Empire into the World Economy, 1770–1873. London: James Currey, 1987.

Shivji, Issa, et al. "Tanzania: The Silent Class Struggle." Cheche special issue (1970).

———. Class Struggles in Tanzania. New York: Monthly Review Press, 1976.

———. Intellectuals at the Hill: Essays and Talks, 1969–1993. Dar es Salaam: Dar es Salaam University Press, 1996.

Silberschmidt, Margrethe. "Masculinities, Sexuality, and Socio-Economic Change in Rural and Urban East Africa." Re-Thinking Sexualities in Africa, ed. Signe Arnfred. Uppsala, Sweden: Nordic Africa Institute, 2004.

Smith, William Edgett. We Must Run While They Walk: A Portrait of Africa's Julius Nyerere. New York: Random House, 1972.

Southall, Aidan, and Peter C. W. Gutkind. Townsmen in the Making. Kampala, Uganda: East African Institute of Social Research, 1957.

Spear, Thomas. Mountain Farmers: Moral Economies of Land and Agricultural Development in Arusha and Meru. Dar es Salaam: Mkuki na Nyota with James Currey, 1997.

Stallybrass, Peter, and Allon White. The Politics and Poetics of Transgression. London: Routledge, 1986.

Stambach, Amy. Lessons from Mount Kilimanjaro: Schooling, Community and Gender in East Africa. London: Routledge, 2000.

Steinmetz, George, ed. State/Culture: State Formation after the Cultural Turn. Ithaca, N.Y.: Cornell University Press, 1999.

Sturmer, Martin. The Media History of Tanzania. Ndanda, Tanzania: Ndanda Mission Press, 1998.

Suri, Jeremi. "The Rise and Fall of an International Counterculture, 1960–1975." American Historical Review 114.1 (2009), 45–68.

Sutton, J. E. G. "Dar es Salaam: A Sketch of a Hundred Years." Tanzania Notes and Records 71 (1970), 1–19.

Swantz, Marja-Liisa, and Deborah Fahy Bryceson. "Women Workers in Dar es Salaam: 1973/74 Survey of Female Minimum Wage Earners and Self-Employed." BRALUP Research Paper no. 43, 1976.

Swift, Charles R. Dar Days: The Early Years in Tanzania. Lanham, Md.: University Press of America, 2002.

Tanganyika. Annual Report of the Social Development Department, 1951. Dar es Salaam: Government Printer, 1952.

———. Annual Report of the Social Development Department, 1952. Dar es Salaam: Government Printer, 1953.

———. Annual Report of the Social Development Department, 1953. Dar es Salaam: Government Printer, 1954.

———. Annual Report of the Social Development Department, 1954. Dar es Salaam: Government Printer, 1955.

———. Annual Report of the Social Development Department, 1955. Dar es Salaam: Government Printer, 1956.

———. *Annual Report of the Social Development Department, 1956*. Dar es Salaam: Government Printer, 1957.

———. *Annual Report of the Social Development Department, 1957*. Dar es Salaam: Government Printer, 1958.

———. *Annual Report of the Social Development Department, 1958*. Dar es Salaam: Government Printer, 1959.

———. *Annual Report of the Social Development Department, 1959*. Dar es Salaam: Government Printer, 1960.

———. *Annual Report of the Social Development Department, 1960*. Dar es Salaam: Government Printer, 1961.

———. *Annual Report of the Social Development Department, 1961*. Dar es Salaam: Government Printer, 1962.

———. *Annual Report on Social Welfare, 1948*. Dar es Salaam: Government Printer, 1950.

Tanganyika African National Union. *The Arusha Declaration and TANU's Policy on Socialism and Self-Reliance*. Dar es Salaam: Publicity Section, TANU, 1967.

———. *Azimio la Arusha na Siasa ya TANU juu ya Ujamaa na Kujitegemea*. Dar es Salaam: Idara ya Habari, TANU, 1967.

Thomas, Lynn. "Contestation, Construction, and Reconstitution: Public Debates over Marriage Law and Women's Status in Kenya, 1964–1979." BA/MA thesis, Johns Hopkins University, 1989.

———. "'The Politics of the Womb': Kenyan Debates over the Affiliation Act." *Africa Today* 48.3 (2001), 150–77.

———. *The Politics of the Womb: Women, Reproduction, and the State in Kenya*. Berkeley: University of California Press, 2003.

———. "Schoolgirl Pregnancies, Letter-Writing, and 'Modern' Persons in Late Colonial East Africa." *Africa's Hidden Histories: Everyday Literacy and Making the Self*, ed. Karin Barber. Bloomington: Indiana University Press, 2006.

Tipps, Dean. "Modernization Theory and the Comparative Study of Societies: A Critical Perspective." *Comparative Studies in Society and History* 15 (1973), 199–226.

Topan, Farouk. "Tanzania: The Development of Swahili as a National and Official Language." *Language and National Identity in Africa*, ed. Andrew Simpson. Oxford: Oxford University Press, 2008.

United Republic of Tanzania. *Government Paper No. 1 of 1969, Uniform Law of Marriage*. Dar es Salaam: Government Printer, 1969.

———. *Majadiliano ya Bunge (Hansard), Taarifa Rasmi*, March 17–23, 1970.

———. *Majadiliano ya Bunge (Hansard), Taarifa Rasmi*, January 19–25, 1971.

———. *1967 Population Census*. Dar es Salaam: Bureau of Statistics, 1971.

———. *Ten Years of National Service, 1963–1973*. Dar es Salaam: Tanzania Publishing House, 1973[?].

———. Ministry of National Culture and Youth, *Cultural Revolution in Tanzania*. Dar es Salaam: Ministry of National Culture and Youth, 1974[?].

———. Wizara ya Utamaduni wa Taifa na Vijana, *Historia Fupi ya Utamaduni wa Mtanzania*. Nairobi: Foundation Books, 1974.

———. Wizara ya Utamaduni wa Taifa na Vijana, *Utamaduni: Chombo cha Maendeleo*. Dar es Salaam: Wizara ya Utamaduni wa Taifa na Vijana, 1979[?].

———. *Analysis of African Women and Men: The Tanzanian Case*. Dar es Salaam: Bureau of Statistics and Ministry of Community Development, Women Affairs and Children, 1995.

Vaughan, Megan. *Curing Their Ills: Colonial Power and African Illness*. Stanford, Calif.: Stanford University Press, 1991.

Vellenga, Dorothy Dee. "Who Is a Wife? Legal Expressions of Heterosexual Conflicts in Ghana." *Female and Male in West Africa*, ed. Christine Oppong. London: George Allen and Unwin, 1983.

Wallerstein, Immanuel. *The Modern World-System*. Vols. 1–3. New York: Academic Press, 1974, 1980, 1989.

Ward, Brian. *Just My Soul Responding: Rhythm and Blues, Black Consciousness, and Race Relations*. Berkeley: University of California Press, 1998.

Warwick, Alexandra, and Dani Cavallaro. *Fashioning the Frame: Boundaries, Dress, and the Body*. Oxford: Berg, 1998.

Waterman, Christopher. *Juju: A Social History and Ethnography of an African Popular Music*. Chicago: University of Chicago Press, 1990.

Weinbaum, Alys Eve, Lynn Thomas, Priti Ramamurthy, Uta G. Poiger, Madeline Yue Dong, and Tani E. Barlow, eds. *The Modern Girl Around the World: Consumption, Modernity, and Globalization*. Durham, N.C.: Duke University Press, 2008.

White, Bob W. *Rumba Rules: The Politics of Dance Music in Mobutu's Zaire*. Durham, N.C.: Duke University Press, 2008.

White, Luise. *The Comforts of Home: Prostitution in Colonial Nairobi*. Chicago: University of Chicago Press, 1990.

———. *Speaking with Vampires: Rumor and History in Colonial Africa*. Berkeley: University of California Press, 2000.

Wilson, Monica. "Zig-Zag Change." *Africa* 46.4 (1976), 399–409.

Wipper, Audrey. "The Politics of Sex: Some Strategies Employed by the Kenyan Power Elite to Handle a Normative-Existential Discrepancy." *African Studies Review* 14.3 (1971), 479–80.

———. "African Women, Fashion and Scapegoating." *Canadian Journal of African Studies* 6.2 (1972), 329–49.

Yongolo, N. D. *Maisha na Desturi za Wanyamwezi*. London: Sheldon Press in association with the EALB, 1953.

Yurchak, Alexei. *Everything Was Forever Until It Was No More: The Last Soviet Generation*. Princeton: Princeton University Press, 2006.

Index

ANDREW IVASKA IS AN ASSOCIATE PROFESSOR OF HISTORY AT CONCORDIA UNIVERSITY, MONTREAL.